AQA
A-level

Business

1 **Fifth Edition**

Malcolm Surridge and
Andrew Gillespie

Approval message from AQA

This textbook has been approved by AQA for use with our qualification. This means that we have checked that it broadly covers the specification and we are satisfied with the overall quality. Full details of our approval process can be found on our website.

We approve textbooks because we know how important it is for teachers and students to have the right resources to support their teaching and learning. However, the publisher is ultimately responsible for the editorial control and quality of this book.

Please note that when teaching the **AQA A-level Business** course, you must refer to AQA's specification as your definitive source of information. While this book has been written to match the specification, it does not provide complete coverage of every aspect of the course.

A wide range of other useful resources can be found on the relevant subject pages of our website: www.aqa.org.uk.

DYNAMIC
LEARNING

HODDER
EDUCATION
AN HACHETTE UK COMPANY

Every effort has been made to trace all copyright holders, but if any have been inadvertently overlooked the Publishers will be pleased to make the necessary arrangements at the first opportunity.

Although every effort has been made to ensure that website addresses are correct at time of going to press, Hodder Education cannot be held responsible for the content of any website mentioned in this book. It is sometimes possible to find a relocated web page by typing in the address of the home page for a website in the URL window of your browser.

Hachette UK's policy is to use papers that are natural, renewable and recyclable products and made from wood grown in sustainable forests. The logging and manufacturing processes are expected to conform to the environmental regulations of the country of origin.

Orders: please contact Bookpoint Ltd, 130 Milton Park, Abingdon, Oxon OX14 4SB. Telephone: +44 (0)1235 827720. Fax: +44 (0)1235 400454. Lines are open 9.00a.m.–5.00p.m., Monday to Saturday, with a 24-hour message answering service. Visit our website at www.hoddereducation.co.uk

Cover photo © alphaspirit – Fotolia

Illustrations by Integra Software Services Pvt., Pondicherry, India.

Typeset in ITC Berkeley Oldstyle Std Book 11/14 pt by Integra Software Services Pvt., Pondicherry, India.

Printed in Dubai

A catalogue record for this title is available from the British Library

ISBN 978 1471 83613 8

Contents

Introduction   v

Unit 1 **What is business?**   1

    1 Understanding the nature and purpose
    of business   2

    2 Understanding different business forms   17

    3 Understanding that businesses operate within
    an external environment   32

    Case study: **Unit 1 What is business?**   45

Unit 2 **Managers, leadership and decision making**   47

    4 Understanding management, leadership and
    decision making   48

    5 Understanding management decision making   59

    6 Understanding the role and importance of
    stakeholders   70

    Case study: **Unit 2 Managers, leadership and
    decision making**   81

Unit 3 Decision making to improve marketing
performance   83

    7 Setting marketing objectives   84

    8 Understanding markets and customers   95

    9 Segmentation, targeting and positioning (STP) 111

    10 Using the marketing mix   120

    Case study: **Unit 3 Decision making to improve
    marketing performance**   145

Unit 4 Decision making to improve operational performance   147

11   Setting operational objectives   148
12   Analysing operational performance   162
13   Increasing efficiency and productivity   168
14   Improving quality   178
15   Managing inventory and supply chains   183
Case study: Unit 4 Decision making to improve operational performance   193

Unit 5 Decision making to improve financial performance   195

16   Setting financial objectives   196
17   Analysing financial performance   208
18   Sources of finance   233
19   Improving cash flow and profits   244
Case study: Unit 5 Decision making to improve financial performance   253

Unit 6 Decision making to improve human resource performance   255

20   Setting human resource objectives   256
21   Analysing human resource performance   268
22   Improving organisational design and human resource flow   279
23   Improving motivation and engagement   297
24   Improving employer–employee relations   313
Case study: Unit 6 Decision making to improve human resource performance   326

Acknowledgements   327

Index   329

Introduction

Welcome to your AS or A-level course in Business. This book has been written to meet the precise requirements of Year 1 of the AQA's A-level specification as well as its AS specification. The material covered by the two programmes is the same and this offers you the opportunity to switch between the two (from AS to A-level and vice versa) during your first year of studying AQA Business.

Book structure

This book is divided into chapters that match exactly the content and structure of the AQA specifications which will help you to understand where you are in terms of covering the relevant material. The AS, or Year 1 A-level course, is divided into six units of study, each comprising between three and five chapters. The book assumes that you have no prior knowledge of Business and this is reflected in the title of Unit 1: 'What is business?' At the start of each chapter we give an overview of issues that will be covered and a list of the topics that you will need to make sure that you have understood by the end.

Decision making is a key theme for the specification and therefore for this book. Unit 2 focuses on the people who have to make decisions within business and the techniques they may use to make these decisions. The remaining four units (3 to 6) reflect the importance of decision making and are structured accordingly. Each of these units covers an aspect of the operation of a business such as managing finance, marketing or human resources. The units have three distinct elements:

- identifying and explaining the objectives that may be set for this aspect or function of the business
- looking at the information that may be available to help decision makers
- considering the types of decisions that may be made in this function of the business.

As you read the book you will study a number of models and theories. Mastering these will help you to understand situations which businesses and managers encounter. They also give you a framework to analyse the issues involved in a specific situation and can guide you in making relevant judgements and in justifying them.

Book features

Within each chapter, we have included a number of features to support you in studying the material. These are:

Business in focus

This feature should help to bring each topic to life by showing it in action in a real context. We hope to show you how theories and models can be applied to real businesses, and can be used to help understand and analyse the decisions that managers, and others associated with businesses, have to make. Each Business in focus feature will have two questions at the end to encourage you to think further about the topic.

What do you think?

This feature is designed to encourage you to reflect on what you have just covered in a particular part of the book. It may ask you to relate an idea or concept to other topics in the book or to your own experience, or to consider what you might decide to do in a specific situation.

Maths moment

This feature offers you an opportunity to apply your numerical skills to a topic and to interpret the meaning of business-related data.

Study tip

This feature helps you to think about the material in relation to the examinations that you will take at the end of the course. It might, for example, advise you on how to revise a particular topic.

Weblinks

These will give you links to important sites where you can get more information on a particular story or topic and allow you to carry out further research to deepen your understanding.

ASSESSMENT ACTIVITIES

At the end of each chapter we provide a series of features which are relevant for you whether you are studying A-level or AS Business. Answering these will help you to develop the skills necessary to tackle examination questions. The features we have included are:

Knowledge check questions

These are questions intended to test your knowledge and understanding of the material set out in the chapter.

Short answer questions

These require you to develop relatively brief responses to a variety of questions, some of which will be calculations.

Data response questions

These provide a business scenario and ask you to answer three questions by using your knowledge and understanding of the material in the chapter and relating it to the scenario given.

Essay questions

These are only for A-level students because AS Business students are not required to answer essays questions in their examinations, although if you are an AS student you may want to test yourself by answering them!

Case study

In addition, at the end of each unit we have written a case study which covers all the material covered within that unit and also may draw on topics covered in earlier units. Each end-of-unit case study has two sets of questions at the end. One is designed for those of you who are taking AS-level, and the other for those who are taking A-level. The topics covered are very similar – it is just the style of the questions that differ so that they reflect the examinations that you will take at the end of your course.

AQA's AS examination in Business

If you are taking AS Business you will take two examinations at the end of the year. Both exams test all of the AS material covered in this book.

Paper One

This paper is worth 50% of the total AS marks and its duration is 1½ hours. It comprises three sections:

- Section A – 10 multiple-choice questions
- Section B – approximately four short-answer questions
- Section C – Two data-response questions.

Paper Two

This paper is also worth 50% of the total AS marks and also lasts for 1½ hours. It is based around a case study which is likely to include some numerical data. There will be approximately eight questions relating to the case study.

AQA's A-level examination in Business

If you are studying A-level Business, you *may* still take the AS examinations set out above, but these will not contribute to your A-level qualification as the two are entirely separate. (Your teachers will be able to advise you on whether you will take these AS examinations as practice.) However, as an A-level student you will take the three A-level examination papers at the end of your second year of study. The A-level examinations will cover the Year 1 material set out in this book as well as the Year 2 content of the AQA Business specification.

The three examinations include multiple-choice questions, short-answer questions, data-response questions, a case study and essay questions. More information about these examinations is given in the Year 2 companion volume to this book.

Wider study

This book will guide you through the AQA AS and Year 1 A-level Business programme of study, although you should supplement this with research and wider reading. You are fortunate in that there is an immense amount of information available about businesses, their behaviour, their decision making and the environments in which they operate. The Internet is an enormous and valuable resource and you will also find much relevant information in magazines, newspapers and on television programmes. However, business activity takes place around you all the time: when you are shopping, travelling to and from school or college, or enjoying leisure activities. There are many opportunities for you to see the operation of some of the theories and models that you will study.

Business is a subject that will have great relevance to your future life, whatever you choose to do. We hope that you enjoy studying it and wish you good fortune in your examinations.

Malcolm Surridge and *Andrew Gillespie*

Unit 1

What is business?

Chapter 1

Understanding the nature and purpose of business

Introduction

The purpose of this chapter is to introduce you to Business as a subject and to encourage you to think about the range of organisations that exist in a modern economy. The UK has businesses of all sizes, from those employing just one person to those who employ many thousands. They supply diverse products, from high technology products, such as military equipment, to relatively simple services such as painting and decorating. This chapter also invites you to consider the targets that businesses attempt to achieve and how they might measure their achievements.

What you need to know by the end of this chapter:

- why businesses exist
- the relationship between a business's mission and its objectives
- the objectives that businesses commonly set themselves
- the reasons why businesses set objectives
- how businesses measure profit and why it is important.

Why businesses exist

1. What are businesses?

The word 'business' is derived from the idea of 'busy-ness'. This notion of 'busy-ness' is a good description of many business organisations. They are busy finding and buying resources, organising and using these resources in production, selling their products and making sure they supply what their customers want. This tells us that businesses are organisations that transform inputs or resources into outputs or **products** that are purchased by their customers.

Businesses are very diverse as well as being present in many aspects of our lives. They supply an enormous range of **goods** and **services** that are demanded by individual consumers and other businesses. They

supply essential products such as electricity, health care and education as well as luxury products including jewellery, gourmet meals and designer clothes. Businesses supply goods and services. Goods have a physical existence and can be seen or held. Examples include televisions and furniture. Services are products that are intangible, such as cleaning, dental care or the provision of hotel accommodation.

Key terms

A **good** is a physical product such as a house or designer suit.

A **service** is an intangible item such as insurance or decorating.

A **product** is a more general term which includes goods and services.

Businesses are very important for the UK. They bring a number of benefits to the country, its economy and its inhabitants.

- **Businesses create employment**. In September 2014 there were 30.79 million people working in the UK. This represented a rise of 694,000 compared with March 2013. Being in employment allows people to earn incomes and to benefit from being able to purchase a range of goods and services. The UK is an attractive location for many foreign businesses (such as Nissan, HSBC and Zara) and the employment that is created attracts many migrants.
- **Businesses create wealth**. Businesses in the UK have transformed resources into goods and services that are in demand for many centuries. This process has created surpluses, which have been invested in a range of assets (such as roads, bridges and hospitals), which have brought significant benefits to the country. Over recent years, for example, businesses have built the M6 toll motorway near Birmingham, increasing the country's wealth and bringing benefits to many people and other businesses.

Figures 1.1 a and b Businesses come in many types and sizes.

Businesses in the UK pay large amounts of taxation to the Government. In 2013–2014 UK businesses paid taxes on their profits (called Corporation Tax) amounting to nearly £36 billion. The UK Government is able to use this money in a variety of ways, including building schools and power stations.

- **Businesses create new products**. Businesses can enrich the lives of people in the UK by creating new goods and services. Pharmaceutical businesses such as GlaxoSmithKline (GSK) research and develop medicines that can cure illnesses, extend life expectancy and improve the quality of people's lives. GSK created the drug *Paxil*, which has been highly successful and has generated sales of over £7.5 billion for the business.

- **Businesses can enhance a country's reputation**. Successful businesses can help to establish and maintain a country's reputation for being innovative and forward looking. The UK has a strong global reputation for producing top quality music and television programmes. The television company Wall to Wall is a relatively small business which has an international reputation for producing well-known programmes such as *The Voice* and *New Tricks*. These programmes sell in many countries and help to present the UK in a favourable light.

The size of businesses in the UK varies enormously. Figure 1.2 relates to businesses that are privately owned; that is, not owned by the Government. It shows that 99.2 per cent of the UK's businesses are small, having fewer than 50 employees. Small businesses provide a little under half the jobs in the UK but only earn 33 per cent of the revenue generated by selling goods and services. The UK has 4,682,000 small businesses.

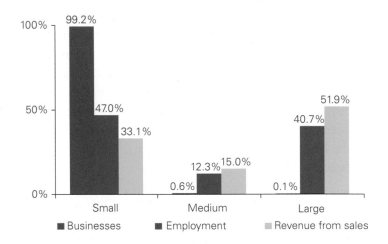

Figure 1.2 The proportions of the UK's businesses that are small, medium or large and their share of employment and sales revenue

Source: Business Population Estimates, 2013
www.gov.uk/government/uploads/system/uploads/attachment_data/file/254552/13-92-business-population-estimates-2013-stats-release-4.pdf

Permission for re-use of all © Crown copyright information is granted under the terms of the Open Government Licence (OGL).

In contrast, the UK has relatively few large businesses. Only 0.1 per cent of businesses in the UK are classified as large – that is having 250 or more employees. This means that in 2013 there were only 7,000 large businesses in the UK. However, these are the ones that are generally well-known and appear most frequently in the media.

2. What do businesses do?

Businesses exist to transform inputs or resources into goods and services that are in demand from individuals and other businesses. This transformation process is illustrated in Figure 1.3.

INPUTS
- people
- finance
- capital requirement
- land & natural resources
- materials & components

TRANSFORMATION PROCESS (adds value)

OUTPUTS
- goods
- services
- waste products

Figure 1.3 Adding value by transforming inputs or resources into goods and services

The transformation or production process undertaken by businesses adds value to the inputs that are used as illustrated in Figure 1.3. This increase in value occurs because they are demanded by certain groups of consumers who will receive benefits from having that product. Because of this the buyers are willing to pay a price that exceeds that paid for the inputs or resources used in production. For example, Apple's new versions of its iPhone sell for prices far in excess of the cost of the resources used in it. Buyers pay these prices because the phone offers a range of benefits, including the latest technology and status from owning a high-fashion product.

Businesses interact with us throughout our daily lives. It is not necessary to visit a high street or a trading estate to see a business in operation. Modern methods of communication have brought businesses into our homes, our relationships and our leisure activities. We encounter them when buying goods and services, but also when engaging in everyday activities such as using the internet to research something or communicate with friends. A business will have supplied the tablet, phone, laptop or other device you use to connect to the internet, a business will also provide the internet service and the webpages that you view. Finally, a business will have provided the energy and the telephone or satellite connection necessary to use the internet.

Businesses exist to satisfy our needs for a range of goods and services which we would be unable to provide for ourselves because we do not have the skills or time to source them, or because the costs of supplying them ourselves would be prohibitive. For example, without specialist businesses it is unlikely that we would be able to fly to other countries because we do not have the resources or skills to source this service. Privately owned businesses are an efficient means of supplying the wide variety of goods and services needed by

modern economies. Other businesses that are owned and operated by the government may supply goods and services that would not otherwise be available. For example, it is common for governments to provide services such as street lighting and national defence.

Businesses also exist to satisfy other needs. They provide a means of satisfying people's desire to be creative or to make money. Some entrepreneurs establish businesses to allow them to express their creative talents. In 1993 Cath Kidston established a business selling distinctive fabrics, wallpapers, china and clothing. Her design talents have created a successful business that operates internationally. Others have made vast fortunes from creating and expanding businesses. James Dyson, an inventor and founder of the Dyson business, has amassed net wealth estimated in 2013 to be £3 billion.

The people who are employed by businesses have to make many decisions. The people who create new businesses, called entrepreneurs, have to make vital decisions concerning how to turn their ideas into a business, such as where to locate the business, how many products should be produced and at what price should they be sold. The decision-makers in larger businesses, normally their managers, make decisions such as whether or not to produce a new product, to try and sell in a foreign market or to buy another business.

3. Types of businesses

It is possible to categorise businesses and the products they supply in different ways. Some businesses supply products directly to the final consumers and these are called business to consumers (or B2C) firms. Well-known businesses such as McDonald's and Sony are examples of B2C businesses. In contrast, some other businesses supply their products to other business organisations. For example, Tata Steel manufactures large amounts of steel in locations throughout the world. It sells its steel to other businesses, such as car manufacturers, to help them to supply their own products.

Business in focus: JCB

J.C. Bamford Excavators Limited, normally known as JCB, is a British multinational manufacturer of equipment used in the construction, agriculture, power generation, waste management and demolition industries. JCB produces a range of over 300 machines and maintains a reputation for excellent customer service. JCB is one of the world's top three manufacturers of equipment such as excavators, forklift trucks, power generators, dump trucks and lighting equipment. It employs around 11,000 people on four continents and sells products in 150 countries.

Figure 1.4 JCB's products are bought principally by businesses for use in their own production processes. Some of JCB's customers are large businesses themselves and can place substantial orders with the company.

Questions

1. Why is one of JCB's machines of more value than the inputs used by the business to create it?
2. JCB is a B2B firm and sells its products to a relatively small number of businesses. Do you think that it is easier for a B2B business to sell its products?

A business can also be categorised according to the sector of the economy in which it is based. Businesses are classified into one of three sectors according to the types of goods and services they supply. The three sectors are:

- **Primary** – agriculture, forestry, fishing, mining and quarrying, oil and gas extraction
- **Secondary** – manufacturing, construction and the supply of electricity, gas and water

- **Tertiary** – the supply of services, for example hotels, catering, transport, education and health.

Some businesses may operate in more than one sector. For example, BP is one of the world's largest oil businesses. Its gas extraction activities place it in the primary sector and processing the mineral oil into petrol and other products is a manufacturing process (secondary sector). Finally, the business sells its products via retail outlets, which are part of the tertiary sector.

Over time the tertiary sector has supplied an increasing proportion of production (measured by **gross domestic product** or GDP) in the UK while manufacturing businesses have become relatively less important. One reason for this trend is that businesses overseas are able to supply manufactured products more cheaply. However, rising incomes in the UK have led to increased demand for services such as hotels, travel and catering. Figure 1.5 illustrates the changing importance of the three sectors in the UK since 1964.

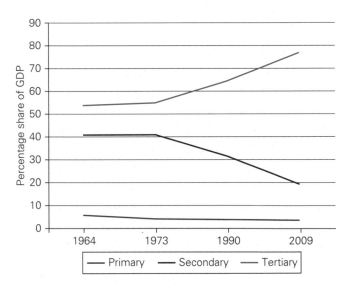

Figure 1.5 Percentage shares of GDP for primary, secondary and tertiary sectors in the UK, selected years

Source: Office for National Statistics (2010e), United Kingdom National Accounts and previous issues

Permission for re-use of all © Crown copyright information is granted under the terms of the Open Government Licence (OGL).

Key term

Gross domestic product (GDP) measures the total value of the production of an economy (that is all a country's businesses) over a period of time, normally one year.

The relationship between mission and objectives

Mission statements

A **mission statement** sets out what a firm is trying to achieve, that is, the reason it exists. For example, a business may set out to be 'the lowest-cost producer in the industry' or to 'maximise the returns for our owners'. The mission may include a statement of what the firm believes it is, what it values, which markets it wants to compete in and how it intends to compete. Mission statements commonly focus on:

- the organisation's values
- non-financial goals it may pursue
- the benefits of the business to the community
- how consumers are to be satisfied.

By setting out a mission, everyone within the business knows what they should ultimately be trying to do. All of their actions should be directed towards the same thing. This should make decision making easier: when faced with a series of options managers can compare them in relation to the overall objective of the business. Mission statements can also motivate people – they know exactly why they are there and what the business is trying to achieve, and this can give them a sense of belonging and direction.

However, some mission statements are so unrealistic, or clearly just public relations exercises, and so employees pay little attention to them. A mission statement will only have value, therefore, if the behaviour of everyone within the firm supports it. In these circumstances it can be a powerful way of uniting people and developing a corporate spirit.

The list below sets out some mission statements used by well-known organisations:

- '… to provide the finest, most technologically advanced power systems. Whether our products are for use on land, at sea or in the air …' (Rolls Royce)
- to bring inspiration and innovation to every athlete in the world (Nike)
- to ensure the ability of Earth to nurture life in all its diversity (Greenpeace)
- '… to give people the power to share and make the world more open and connected. (Facebook)

Aims and objectives

1. Aims

Aims are long-term plans from which a business's objectives are derived; these are often referred to as corporate aims, meaning that they relate to the whole business. Businesses do not normally state aims as numerical targets, but rather in qualitative terms. For example, the house-builder Taylor Woodrow states that its corporate aim is 'to make our homes environmentally sustainable to build and to live in.' Tesco's aim is to broaden the scope of the business to enable it to deliver strong, sustainable long-term growth. Although these are quite different aims, sustainability is becoming a major and growing influence on business thinking.

Corporate aims (and mission statements) are set by the senior employees within the business and are intended to provide guidance for setting other objectives and also to guide and assist more junior managers in their decision making. So for example, managers throughout Tesco's stores will take decisions intended to achieve the organisation's aims of broadening the business's scope and delivering strong, sustainable growth. In this context, opting to open supermarkets in China and to sell electrical products and clothing are all important long-term decisions that the business has taken with the intention of meeting its corporate aims.

From its corporate aims (and from its mission statement) a business can set quantifiable objectives, such as gaining a 35 per cent share of a particular market in Europe within three years.

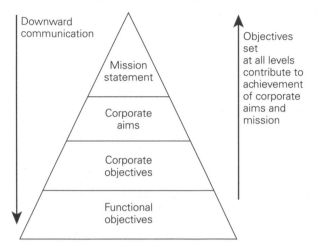

Figure 1.6 The hierarchy of objectives

2. Objectives

Once a firm has established its mission it can set its objectives. The objectives turn the mission statement into something that is more quantifiable. Rather than simply being a statement of intent, an objective sets out clearly what has to be achieved.

Objectives are medium- to long-term goals established to coordinate the business. Objectives should be quantified and have a stated timescale, such as 'to earn a 20 per cent return on capital next year'.

To be effective objectives should be SMART. SMART objectives must be:

- **Specific** – they must define exactly what the firm is measuring, such as sales or profits.
- **Measurable** – they must include a quantifiable target, for example a 10 per cent increase.
- **Agreed** – if targets are simply imposed on people they are likely to resent them; if, however, the targets are discussed and mutually agreed, people are more likely to be committed to them.
- **Realistic** – if the objectives are unrealistic (for example, they are too ambitious) people may not even bother to try and achieve them. To motivate people the targets must be seen as attainable.
- **Time specific** – Employees need to know how long they have to achieve the target – is it two or three years?

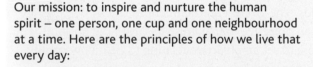

Business in focus: Starbuck's mission statement

Our mission: to inspire and nurture the human spirit – one person, one cup and one neighbourhood at a time. Here are the principles of how we live that every day:

Our Coffee

It has always been, and will always be, about quality. We're passionate about ethically sourcing the finest coffee beans, roasting them with great care, and improving the lives of people who grow them.

Our Partners

We're called partners, because it's not just a job, it's our passion. Together, we embrace diversity to create a place where each of us can be ourselves. We always treat each other with respect and dignity. And we hold each other to that standard.

Our Customers

When we are fully engaged, we connect with, laugh with, and uplift the lives of our customers – even if just for a few moments. Of course, it starts with the promise of a perfectly made beverage, but our work goes far beyond that.

Our Stores

When our customers feel this sense of belonging, our stores become a haven, a break from the worries outside, a place where you can meet friends. It's about enjoyment at the speed of life – sometimes slow and savoured, sometimes faster.

Our Neighbourhood

Every store is part of a community, and we take our responsibility to be good neighbours seriously. We want to be invited in wherever we do business. We can be a force for positive action – bringing together our partners, customers, and the community to contribute every day.

Source: Starbucks' website
www.starbucks.co.uk/about-us/business-information/mission-statement

Questions

1. Explain how senior managers at Starbucks could use this information to set objectives for the business.

2. Why do many well-known businesses publicise their mission statements on their websites?

An example of a good objective might be: 'to increase profits by 25 per cent over the next four years'. By comparison, a bad objective would be 'to do much better' – it is not clear what 'doing better' actually means, how it will be measured or how long you have to achieve it.

Common business objectives

Businesses may set themselves a number of objectives, including those below.

1. Profits and profit maximisation

Profits are maximised when the difference between sales revenue and total costs is at its greatest. Some firms set objectives that involve achieving a minimum level of profit, allowing the business and its managers to focus on other objectives. This approach, known as satisficing, may be pursued by smaller family-owned organisations. This allows the owners of these businesses to achieve other targets such as entering new markets or increasing the size of the business.

Other businesses may seek to earn the greatest possible profits to satisfy their shareholders' desire for high dividends. This might be a shorter-term objective. Others may pursue the longer-term objective of providing acceptable levels of dividends, but also growth in the value of the business and therefore in the share price. This can provide shareholders with long-term financial benefits.

2. Growth

Many businesses pursue growth because their managers believe that the organisation will not survive otherwise. If a firm grows, it should be able to exploit its market position and earn higher profits. This benefits shareholders (in the long term) by providing greater dividends as well as offering better salaries and more job security to the employees and managers of the business. We saw earlier that Tesco has set itself the aim of strong, sustainable growth and this will have been transferred into quantified objectives, possibly relating to sales figures or grocery market share in other countries.

3. Survival

This objective is for the business to continue to trade over a defined period of time, rather than to submit to some form of commercial pressure and be forced to cease trading. This is an important objective, even for the largest of businesses at certain times. Times when survival can become a key objective include:

- periods of recession or intense competition
- times of crisis, such as during a hostile takeover bid.

4. Cash flow

For most businesses, **cash flow** is a vital element of success as it is essential to be able to pay debts on time. This is especially true of businesses that have long cash cycles. A cash cycle is the time that elapses between the outflow of cash to pay for the resources needed to produce a product and the receipt of cash following the sale of the product. Businesses in industries such as pharmaceuticals and construction may face long cash cycles. The global entertainment business Walt Disney has an objective to maximise its cash flow position. The failure to set an objective relating to cash flow could have dire consequences for a business if it is unable to pay its debts as they fall due. In the worst case a shortage of cash could result in a business having to cease trading.

5. Social and ethical objectives

Social objectives include targets that relate to matters such as providing employment for people or improving facilities for local people (for example building a play park for local children). Ethical objectives are those that are based on moral principles. Examples of ethical objectives include protecting the environment through the use of sustainable production techniques and ensuring that suppliers receive fair and prompt payment. Such objectives have received much attention over recent years. In part this is the result of increasing awareness on the part of many individuals and groups who have an interest in a business. Some investors

Business in focus: Marks & Spencer and its Plan A

Plan A is all about doing the right thing.

Plan A has 180 commitments with the aim of making the business the most sustainable major retailer by 2015. We launched Plan A in January 2007, setting out 100 commitments to achieve in 5 years. We have extended Plan A to 180 commitments to achieve by 2015.

Through Plan A we are working with our customers and our suppliers to combat climate change, reduce waste, use sustainable raw materials, trade ethically and help our customers to lead healthier lifestyles.

We are doing this because it's what you want us to do. It's also the right thing to do. We're calling it Plan A because we believe it's now the only way to do business.

There is no Plan B.'

Source: Adapted from Marks & Spencer's website http://plana.marksandspencer.com/about

Questions

1. Analyse the benefits that Marks & Spencer would expect to receive from having social and ethical objectives set out in its Plan A.

2. Do you think that any retailer can expect to succeed in the future without setting and publicising social and ethical objectives?

Figure 1.7 These campaigns emphasise M&S's ethical behaviour.

will only invest in businesses that trade with ethical or social objectives. Importantly, a significant proportion of customers seek to purchase products from businesses with social and ethical objectives. Pursuing such objectives, and publicising the fact, can offer a business a distinctive and attractive image.

6. Diversification

Diversification is an objective where a firm produces an increased range of unrelated goods and services. Adopting this objective allows a business to spread its risk by selling a range of products (rather than one) or through trading in different markets. Thus, if one product becomes obsolete or a market becomes significantly more competitive, then the alternative products or markets will provide a secure source of revenue for the business while it seeks

new projects. Diversification avoids a business having 'all its eggs in one basket' and has been the principle behind the creation of conglomerate businesses. Pepsico Inc, the multinational soft drink and snack producer, pursued the objective of diversification to extend its product range beyond soft drinks to help it to compete with its powerful rival Coca-Cola.

Short-run and long-run objectives

When deciding what they want to achieve, businesses can set both short-run and long-run objectives. If a business has a long-run growth objective it may want to invest in training employees to improve skills and performance, expanding into new markets and investing in developing new products. All these activities may help to achieve the long-run growth objective. However, they will prove expensive and short-run profits may fall.

By comparison, a business that wanted to maximise its profits in the short run and was not concerned about the long term might cut back on all these activities. It would reduce expenditure on training and developing new products. In the short run, profits may jump up but in the long run this business may be in a much weaker position.

UK firms are often criticised for setting objectives that are too short-term and do not involve long-term planning. Critics say that UK businesses fail to invest enough in ensuring they are strong enough over the long term and that investment by UK businesses is very low. Instead, they often go for short-term rewards. In their defence, UK managers often blame their investors for insisting on short-term rewards. Many shareholders in the UK are businesses such as pension funds and banks. These businesses need to make money for their own investors and often want these earnings quickly; if a business cannot deliver, pension funds and banks will simply move their investment elsewhere.

Why businesses set objectives

By setting objectives a business and the people who have an interest in it (known as its **stakeholders**) can gain a number of benefits.

By agreeing on objectives with other people within the business, managers can ensure that everyone is working towards the same overall goal. Without any clear objectives people are much more likely to do their own thing. Coordinating the efforts of all employees can improve organisational performance, especially in large businesses that may have people employed in different locations. For example, one of Tesco's objectives is to expand its retail services in all areas. This helps to encourage all the retailer's employees to seek ways to increase the business's sales and can be supplemented with individual sales targets for specific stores.

Objectives can also be very motivating for employees because they set out exactly what the firm wants them to achieve. If an employee is set a target they know precisely what they have to do. Without a target they may not be sure whether or not they are doing the right thing. Having a target also enables employees to measure progress: they can see how they are doing and whether or not they (or the relevant part of the business) are going to reach its target.

Objectives are also used to review the success of a business's plans. Managers can measure how much has been achieved compared to the target that was set. For example, the management team at Tesco can see if it has achieved the sales or growth targets that it set for various parts of the business. If the objective has not been hit managers and employees can discuss why this has happened and what they can do differently to achieve the target next time. Tesco announced in April 2014 that its overall sales had fallen by 1.5 per cent. These kind of results mean that a business does not achieve its sales objective. The business's managers and employees can learn from this and look to improve future performance.

The measurement and importance of profit

Costs and revenues

The relationship between profit, cost and revenue

Profit is a very important objective for many, but not all businesses. Making a certain level of profit, or the maximum possible, will be an important objective for many of the UK's largest and best-known businesses such as Vodafone or Centrica, but not for others such as charities, which pursue other objectives.

One of the most important relationships for a business is:

profit = total revenue – total costs

This formula allows businesses to calculate whether they might make a profit and, if so, how much it might be.

> ### Key terms
>
> **Stakeholders** are individuals or groups (such as employees, customers and local residents) who have an interest in a business.
> **Revenues** are the earnings or income generated by a firm as a result of its trading activities.
> **Profit** is the surplus of total revenue over total costs for a business over a trading period.

Business costs

What is a cost? It is simply the expenditure a firm makes as part of its trading. Some of the expenses or costs firms face include payments for raw materials, fuel and components, as well as for labour (paid as wages and salaries).

These costs can be classified in a number of ways, though the most common is to divide them into fixed and variable costs.

Fixed costs

Fixed costs do not change when a business alters its level of output. As an example, a business's rent will not vary if there is an increase or decrease in the level of production. Other examples of fixed costs include management salaries and maintenance costs paid by the business.

Figure 1.8 relates to NTV plc, a business that researches, designs and manufactures televisions for sale throughout Europe. You can see that whether the business produces 1 million or 7 million televisions annually, the fixed costs faced by the business will remain the same – £250 million.

The reason that fixed costs do not alter is that NTV plc simply uses its existing facilities more intensively at times when it is receiving larger orders – this may be in the autumn months as Christmas approaches. As a further example, in the summer months an ice cream manufacturer may increase its output, thereby using existing production facilities more intensively. However, the manufacturer's rent, rates and other fixed costs will be unchanged.

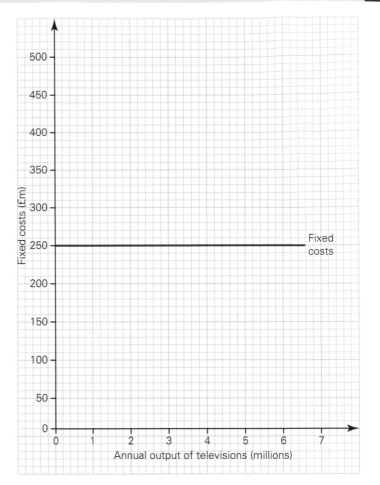

Figure 1.8 Fixed costs for NTV plc

Variable costs

In contrast to fixed costs, **variable costs** alter directly with the level of a firm's output. This means that, a business that is increasing its output is likely to have to pay higher variable costs, whereas one that is reducing output could expect variable costs to fall. Expenditure on fuel, raw materials and components are all examples of variable costs.

NTV faces variable costs of £350 for each television it manufactures (see Figure 1.8); this is necessary to pay for the components, fuel, packaging and labour. So, to produce 2 million televisions, the business faces variable costs of £700 million (2,000,000 x £350); to manufacture 5 million televisions results in variable costs of £1,750 million (5,000,000 x £350). This level of production is illustrated on Figure 1.9.

Variable costs are usually shown as a straight line.

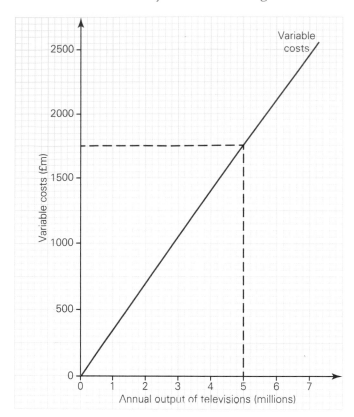

Figure 1.9 Variable costs for NTV plc

Figure 1.9 shows that expenditure on items such as fuel, labour, raw materials and other materials rises directly along with output. Variable costs are drawn as a straight line for simplicity. However, in the real world, the line may gradually flatten out as businesses frequently negotiate lower prices when placing large orders. For example, NTV is obviously a large business and would have a lot of power when negotiating with its suppliers. NTV plc may be able to purchase materials more cheaply per unit if it places exceptionally large orders. This would reduce the variable costs for each unit of production (or average variable costs) as output increased, causing the variable cost line to flatten slightly at higher levels of output. The variable costs associated with the production of 5 million televisions might, for example, be £1,600 million. If so, this would mean that the variable cost of one television is actually £320, not £350.

Semi-variable costs

Some firms face costs that should be classified as semi-variable: they have fixed and variable elements.

Transport costs can be an example of a semi-variable cost. Most businesses pay a fixed, annual charge for renting vehicles and for insurance. However, they also have to pay costs such as fuel and drivers' wages, which are likely to increase if output rises and more products are transported. The rental and insurance costs are fixed, as they do not change as the firm increases or lowers its output levels. However, fuel and wage costs are likely to be variable and increase along with output as more products are transported. So, taken together these elements mean transport costs can be semi-variable.

Total costs

The calculation of **total costs** assumes that all the costs faced by a business are either fixed or variable. This means total costs can be calculated simply using the following formula:

total costs = fixed costs + variable costs

Level of production (televisions, millions)	Fixed costs (£ million)	Variable costs (£ million)	Total costs (£ million)
0	250	0	250
1	250	350	600
2	250	700	950
3	250	1,050	1,300
4	250	1,400	1,650
5	250	1,750	2,000
6	250	2,100	2,350
7	250	2,450	2,700

Table 1.1 Cost information for NTV plc

Total costs can be used to calculate the average cost of producing a single unit of production. In Table 1.1 we can see that the average cost of production is £600 per television if NTV plc manufactures 1 million televisions. However, this falls to £400 per television if it increases its production to 5 million televisions per year. This reduction takes place because the business's fixed costs are being spread over a higher level of production or output and therefore have a diminishing impact on average costs of production.

What do you think?

Why are televisions normally manufactured by large businesses, rather than small ones?

Costs and decision-making

Total costs of production are an important piece of information for a business. Managers of a business can use this information when taking decisions on levels of output and prices to be charged. For example, firms that have very high levels of fixed costs, perhaps due to expensive equipment, will seek to produce large quantities of output. This reduces the effect of fixed costs on selling price by spreading them over a large quantity of sales.

Study tip

Always seek to identify and explore the many links that exist within the subjects that make up Business. We look more closely at the relationship between the scale of a business and its costs in Chapter 2.

Information relating to costs can be extremely helpful to managers when deciding on prices. It is unlikely that a business will want to set prices below the costs of production for any length of time. If a business knows the average cost of producing a product, then it can set a price that is higher, which will ensure it makes a profit, so long as it is able to sell all that it produces. This is known as 'cost-plus pricing'.

Sometimes businesses are not able to control the price at which they sell their products – they might be a small firm in a very competitive market. In these circumstances it is important to know costs of production to decide whether it is possible to sell products at a profit. This will help the business's managers to make a decision on whether to enter, or to remain in, a market.

In reality it can be difficult for many businesses to calculate the average costs of production. Many businesses produce a range of products using the same production facilities. This means that the business's fixed costs may relate to a number of different products and it can be difficult to divide these fixed costs accurately between different products.

Business revenues

A business's **revenue** is its income over a period of time. You may also encounter the terms sales revenue, sales income or turnover, which have the same meaning. Businesses calculate the revenue from the sale of a single product as well as from their entire product range. In either case the calculation is the same:

revenue = quantity sold x average selling price

In most circumstances, a firm can exercise some control over the quantity it sells and hence over the revenue it receives.

If a business reduces its selling price, it can normally expect to sell more. Whether or not this increases its revenue depends on the number of additional sales it makes as a result of reducing its price. If competitors also reduce their prices, then few extra sales will result and revenue is likely to be relatively unchanged or may even fall. However, if the price reduction makes the product cheap compared to those of competitors, and it offers similar benefits, then a price reduction might increase sales significantly increasing the revenue received by the business.

Similarly, a rise in price can be expected to reduce sales. The size of the fall in sales will depend on many factors, including the loyalty of customers and the relative quality of the products. The amount by which sales fall

Business in focus: EasyJet

The airline EasyJet is one of the UK's more successful businesses. The company was founded as recently as 1995, yet had over 60 million passengers flying with it in 2013. One of the key reasons for the business's success is that its prices are attractive to customers. A survey by *Which?* found that its average fare was £76.05. However, during the same period rival airline Ryanair was reported to have an average fare of £70.53.

One key element in offering low prices is that the business strictly controls its costs. Its website states: 'By cutting out unnecessary frills and carefully controlling the cost of doing business, we are able to offer fares that represent great value for money – often at a fraction of the prices offered by other airlines.

Sources: Adapted from *The Daily Telegraph*, 21 October 2013 and EasyJet's website
www.telegraph.co.uk/travel/travelnews/10393475/Ryanair-not-the-cheapest-airline.html
www.easyjet.com/en/aboutourfares

Questions

1. Explain why it is important for EasyJet to control its costs.
2. Do businesses always benefit from controlling costs as tightly as possible?

will determine whether the firm receives more or less revenue following its price rise. Some businesses sell products that are unique or regarded as highly desirable, perhaps because they are fashionable. For example, some producers of fashion clothing, such as Gucci, can charge high prices and still enjoy relatively high sales.

Weblink   www

To find out more about Gucci and its prices visit www.gucci.com/uk/home

What do you think?

Why is Gucci able to set high prices for its products and not suffer a large fall in sales and in sales revenue?

The relationship between price and sales revenue is explained by the concept of the price elasticity of demand (see pages 102–03).

Profits

A business makes a profit when, over a period of time, its revenue exceeds its total costs of production. The formula necessary to calculate profit is:

profit = total revenue – total costs

A business's profits depend upon two main factors: profit margins and the quantity (or volume) of sales.

- A profit margin is the amount or percentage of the final selling price that is profit. If a business sells products where a large percentage (or margin) of the price is profit, then it is likely to make large profits.
- However, the quantity a firm sells will also affect the amount of profits it earns. In general, if a business sells a greater quantity of its products it will make more profit, so long as it does not have to reduce price (and therefore its profit margin) to achieve higher sales.

If a business's costs are greater than its revenues over an accounting period the enterprise will make a loss rather than a profit.

Why are profits important?

For many businesses, profits are very important and are often used as a measure of success. Many people

who invest in enterprises do so in the hope and expectation of making a handsome return on their money. For such investors it is not simply profits that are important, but rather the size of the profit. A larger profit means a greater return for the investor.

Making a profit brings a range of benefits to a business and its owners and can influence a number of decisions.

- A profitable business may be attractive to customers. The financial performance of many of the UK's better-known businesses is reported in the media. Customers may believe that profitable businesses are selling desirable products and may be willing to make long-term arrangements with a business that they consider to be financially secure.
- A business that makes a profit, especially one which exceeds expectations, is likely to be able to persuade individuals and institutions such as banks to invest in it. This can make it cheaper to raise finance and may encourage and support expansion decisions.
- A profitable business may be bought by a larger rival. A profitable business is attractive in itself and may own valuable brands or be popular in a market which the larger business would like to enter. This can earn the original owners large sums of money. In 2014 Equifax, a multinational American finance business, bought TDX, a profitable Nottingham-based business offering similar services in a £200 million deal. This purchase offered Equifax a stronger foothold in the UK market.
- A profitable business is more likely to have the confidence of its suppliers and they may be more willing to allow the business time between the delivery of suppliers and payment. This is effectively an interest-free loan.

Study tip

Profit can often be judged better when it is compared to something else. We compare profits to the business's revenue from sales in Chapter 17.

For some businesses, earning a profit may not be at all important. A number of businesses are not established and operated with the aim of making profits. Charities, for example, do not seek to make profits. This type of business seeks to raise the maximum amount of income possible, or to provide a high-class product, while earning enough to cover costs. In 2013, the RSPB, the UK's largest wildlife charity, announced it had generated a surplus of £90.1 million. This figure was recorded in the charity's accounts as 'net income available for charitable purposes' and will be reinvested in a range of ways, including buying new wildlife sites.

Business in focus: Prezzo's expansion plans

Restaurant chain Prezzo announced pre-tax profits of £20.4 million in the year to December 2013, up 11 per cent on the previous year. They had opened 28 new restaurants in 2013 and planned another 25–30 for 2014. The group consists of Prezzo, which sells Italian food, Chimichanga, which is Tex-Mex, and in 2013 it opened its first Cleaver restaurants, which serve burgers, chicken and ribs.

The group has grown rapidly in recent years and now has 194 Prezzo restaurants as well as 37 Chimichanga and 4 Cleaver restaurants.

Source: adapted from various news sources

Questions

1. Prezzo is expanding very quickly. Why might this make it more challenging for the business to increase its profits rapidly?

2. Do you think that all of a business's owners would be in favour of a decision to use increased profits to finance expansion?

ASSESSMENT ACTIVITIES

Sections (a), (b) and (c) of these assessment activities are relevant for students taking AS and A-level examinations. The questions in section (d) are for A-level students only.

(a) Knowledge check questions

1 What is the difference between a service and a product?

2 State two reasons why businesses exist.

3 List two inputs used by a business to make goods or services.

4 State two features of a business's operations that may be reflected in its mission statement.

5 Is the following statement true or false: 'When drawn on a graph, variable costs always start at the origin (where the two axes intersect)'.

6 State two features of a good objective.

7 Complete the following formula: revenue = ... x average selling price

8 A business has total costs of £12.5 million for producing 500,000 items. The variable cost per unit of producing an item is constant at £20. What are the business's fixed costs?

   i)   £12 million   iii) £1.5 million
   ii) £2.5 million   iv) £3.5 million

9 A business sold 37,000 garden sheds last year at an average price of £250. This year it plans to reduce its price to £225 and expects its sales to rise by 15 per cent. How much revenue can it expect to receive this year?

   i)   £9,573,750   iii) £10,637,500
   ii) £8,325,000   iv) £9,775,750

10 A business has gathered the following information in relation to its most recent year of trading:
   ● It produced and sold 75,000 items.
   ● The average selling price was £150.
   ● Its fixed costs were £4.5 million.
   ● Its average cost per unit of production was £85.

   How much profit or loss did the business make during the year?

   i)   £375,000 profit
   ii) £6,750,000 profit
   iii) £375,000 loss
   iv) £4,875,000 loss

(b) Short answer questions

1 Explain one benefit to a rapidly expanding business of setting clear business objectives.   (4 marks)

2 The following data applies to a recently established business:
   - selling price = £500
   - fixed costs = £255,000
   - variable costs per unit of output = £120
   - sales = 1,000 units.

   Calculate the business's profits. Show your workings.   (5 marks)

3 Merlin plc constructs bridges and tunnels throughout the EU. Explain why the business might consider setting cash flow objectives to be important.   (5 marks)

4 Explain **one** reason why it is important for a business that is expanding into new markets to record a profit.   (6 marks)

(c) Data response questions

Levi Strauss & Company

Levi Strauss & Co has been voted one of the world's most ethical businesses and has many social and ethical objectives. It's a private company, with $4.6bn in revenue in 2012 and is known for selling high-quality clothing.

The business is developing a new product: a Dockers line of clothes called Wellthread. The aim of this line is to deliver the high-quality products Levis is known for, while ensuring best practice is followed in all parts of the supply chain and production process. This includes making sure that factory workers in Bangladesh are properly paid and provided with appropriate benefits.

Strauss faces a big challenge in finding ways to sell Wellthread to consumers, as operating in this way means that the cost to consumers is high: roughly £30 for T-shirts, £90 for khakis and £165 for jackets.

It will be key for Strauss to make these products attractive in the mainstream, so that the principles can be deployed throughout the business. The company needs to balance its desire to produce high-quality products in a socially and environmentally sustainable way with its need to sell more products.

Source: adapted from various news sources

1 Explain why Levi Strauss & Co might face a big challenge in selling its Wellthread range to mainstream consumers.   (6 marks)

2 Analyse the reasons why Levi Strauss & Co sells its products at high prices.   (9 marks)

3 To what extent do the benefits of operating with ethical objectives outweigh the drawbacks for Levi Strauss & Co.   (15 marks)

(d) Essays

1 To what extent is maximising profit always the most important objective for large well-known businesses whose activities are reported regularly in the media?   (25 marks)

2 To what extent are mission statements only of value to large businesses?   (25 marks)

Chapter 2

Understanding different business forms

Introduction

This chapter builds on Chapter 1: Understanding the nature and purpose of business. It considers the forms that may be adopted by the UK's diverse businesses and the issues that relate to these. It will explore the implications of different forms of ownership for important aspects of a business's operations, such as its decisions and performance. It will examine the role of shareholders as owners of companies and why company share prices alter and what this means for the organisation and its stakeholders.

What you need to know by the end of this chapter:

- why businesses choose to operate in a particular form or to change the form that they use
- the issues that businesses face arising from decisions about which business forms to use
- the role played by shareholders and the reasons they decide to invest in companies
- the factors that influence share prices and the significance of changes in the prices of companies' shares
- the effects of different types of ownership on a business's mission, its objectives, decisions and ownership.

Private sector businesses

If a business operates in the private sector of the economy it is owned by shareholders (in the case of companies) or by private individuals. Large businesses such as GlaxoSmithKline and small ones such as a local corner shop are part of the private sector. Private sector businesses are not owned by government, local authorities or other state organisations. Most businesses in the UK are part of the private sector and this is the case in most developed economies.

1. Sole traders

When individuals establish and operate a business on their own they are known as '**sole traders**', or sometimes as 'sole proprietors'. This is a very popular form of business. In 2013 there were 3.1 million sole trader businesses in the UK – 62.6 per cent of all businesses in the private sector.

Sole traders are normally relatively small businesses such as plumbers, decorators, window cleaners and hairdressers. The people running these sole trader businesses work for themselves. It is not uncommon for sole traders to hire other people to help them out, but they remain responsible for the overall business and are actively involved in the running of it on a daily business. In 2013 only 9 per cent of sole trader businesses hired any employees.

Sole traders may work on their own, and must have the confidence to take decisions and the range of skills necessary to run the business, including managerial skills. Sole traders may have to serve customers, decide what equipment to buy, deal with suppliers and keep accurate and up-to-date business records. This can require a wide range of skills and an enormous degree of flexibility.

Operating as a sole trader requires a high level of self-discipline because there is no one checking up or offering guidance. This can be exciting. It does, however, place a considerable emphasis on self-motivation. Sole traders have to make things happen and ensure they manage their time effectively.

The advantages of operating as a sole trader

One of the main advantages of being a sole trader is that it is so easy to start up and manage this form of business. Unlike starting other types of organisation, such as companies, it is not necessary to register the business with a government agency or fill in any forms. Sole traders can simply start trading, provided any profits are declared to HMRC (Her Majesty's Revenue and Customs), which is responsible for collecting taxes

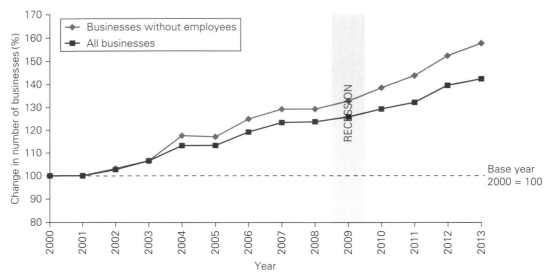

Figure 2.1 The rising popularity of businesses without employees

Source: Business population estimates, 2013 (Department for Business, Skills & Innovation)

Permission for re-use of all © Crown copyright information is granted under the terms of the Open Government Licence (OGL).

on profits in the UK. Thus it is possible for someone to start up and operate as a web designer, an artist, an interior decorator or cleaner at short notice and with little administration required.

Many sole traders also enjoy not having to take orders from others. They like the freedom to make their own decisions, to decide when and where to work, what to do and how to do it. Working as a sole trader allows people to make decisions quickly as they do not have to consult or request permission from their boss. It can be incredibly motivating to be your own boss.

Another important advantage of being a sole trader is that any profits made by the business do not have to be shared. Many entrepreneurs begin and continue to trade as sole traders for these reasons.

The benefits of operating as a sole trader are reflected in the increasing number of this form of business in the UK. Figure 2.1 shows the increase in the number of businesses in the UK that do not have any employees over the period 2000 to 2013, compared with all businesses.

Not all businesses without employees will be sole traders, but most will.

What do you think?

Why do you think that the number of businesses without employees grew while the UK was suffering a deep recession (when employment, incomes and spending fall) between 2008 and 2010?

The number of sole traders in the UK has been boosted by the increasing popularity of becoming self-employed, that is working for yourself. The number of people registered as self-employed in the UK has risen from 3.8 million in 2008 to 4.4 million in 2014. The prospects of high financial rewards do not appear to be driving this trend as the average income of self-employed people in the UK was £13,500 per year in 2014, not much more than 50 per cent of the average annual income in the UK.

The challenges of being a sole trader

While working as a sole trader can be very fulfilling, it also brings with it many challenges. Making all the decisions can be exciting, but there is the pressure of holding all the responsibility if anything goes wrong. When working with, or for someone else and there is a real problem, there is someone else to work with to solve it. Being a sole trader can be quite lonely – some people find it difficult to cope with this aspect of the pressure. The hours may be quite demanding, too. This is particularly likely to be an issue in the early years when an entrepreneur is trying hard to build up the business. Also, sole traders may not be able to take much time off for holidays because they may not be able to afford to close the business and risk losing customers.

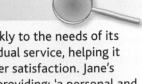

Business in focus: Jane's social media

Jane Binnion is a sole trader in Lancashire. Her business provides training to local businesses and other organisations on the use of social media such as Facebook and Twitter. Jane spent 25 years employed in a range of businesses. However, an injury led to her becoming unemployed and she retrained for her new role. In her own words: 'I'm a great networker so I trained in social media, got a business adviser, a website, joined a start-up course and on March 10th 2011, aged 48 1/3, I launched Jane's Social Media!'

Jane believes that the freedom to make decisions about working life, particularly working patterns, brings benefits to sole traders and their families. One of her reasons for starting Jane's Social Media was that she needed more flexible working hours. 'I work from home and ensure that 90 per cent of the time I am here when my daughter gets home from school. I have never been happier.' Operating as a sole trader means such decisions will not be challenged.

Jane's business can respond quickly to the needs of its customers and provide an individual service, helping it to achieve high levels of customer satisfaction. Jane's Social Media promotes itself as providing: 'a personal and very individual service that helps your company grow by getting you better connected via the appropriate social media platforms.'

Source: Adapted from various sources including:
www.janebinnion.com
www.theguardian.com/small-business-network/2012/nov/28/starting-up-jane-s-social-media

Questions

1. Was being able to be her own boss the most important reason behind Jane becoming a sole trader?

2. Do you think that operating as a sole trader means that a business will always be able to make quick, effective decisions?

Sole traders often face difficulties in raising finance to set up and expand their businesses. Major sources of finance are their own money (perhaps from savings or redundancy pay) or money from friends and family. Using these sources of finance means that the amount that can be raised is often quite limited. Of course, it is possible to borrow from a bank or other financial institution but they often charge smaller businesses quite high interest rates because they are worried about the risk of failure and want to cover their losses. And since the financial crash of 2008 and the recession that followed it, banks in the UK have been much more cautious in lending money to businesses, especially those that they judge to be risky.

Being a sole trader is also quite risky if anything goes wrong. This is because sole traders have **unlimited liability**. The sole trader keeps any rewards the business makes, but is also personally responsible for any losses. If their businesses have problems, sole traders can lose their personal possessions such as houses and savings.

Advantages	Disadvantages
Making key decisions can be motivating.	Sources of finance are limited.
Decisions can be made quickly and sole traders can respond rapidly to changes in the market.	Sole traders rely heavily on their own ability to make decisions.
Sole traders often have direct contact with the market.	It can entail working long hours, with limited holidays, leading to stress.
Setting up is straightforward.	The personal possessions of sole traders are vulnerable due to unlimited liability.

Table 2.1 The advantages and disadvantages of being a sole trader

2. Companies

Operating a business as a **company** can overcome many of the difficulties associated with being a sole trader. To set up a company, the owners have to complete various documents, including a Memorandum of Association and Articles of Association and register the business at Companies House. This process is known as **incorporation**.

A company is owned by **shareholders**. Each share represents a part of the company. The more shares someone owns, the more of the company that belongs to them.

A company has its own legal identity, separate from that of its owners. The company can own property, equipment and other goods in its own right and is responsible for its own debts. If the company fails, the

Key terms

A **sole trader** is a business that is owned and managed by one person, but it may employ other people.

Unlimited liability occurs when an individual or group of individuals is personally responsible for all the actions of their business. With sole traders, there is no distinction in law between the individual and the business so they could lose their personal assets if the business has financial problems.

shareholders can lose the money that they invested in the business when they bought shares, but they cannot lose more than this. This is because a company has **limited liability**. This means that a company is responsible for the money it owes but that the personal possessions of its owners (shareholders) are safe. This is different from a sole trader, who has unlimited liability and could lose everything if the business had severe financial problems.

Having limited liability is essential for companies to be able to raise money by selling shares. Without it, investors would be far less likely to buy shares because of the risk to their personal possessions. If a shareholder invested in a business with unlimited liability it would mean giving money to others and risking everything. With limited liability, the maximum amount that could be lost is fixed.

The shareholders can potentially benefit in two ways from owning shares.

- The value of the company and hence the value of the shareholder's part ownership of the company may increase. In effect this increases the price at which the shares may be sold at a later date. However, company values and share prices can also fall. For example, following an announcement of lower than expected profits, the share price of Mothercare, one of the UK's well-known retailers fell by 31 per cent from 425 pence per share to 293 pence per share. At the time of writing it is 188 pence per share.
- Shareholders may receive a share of the company's profits, if they are sufficiently large. Profitable companies will distribute some of their profits to shareholders in proportion to the number of shares they hold. Profits paid to shareholders in this way are called **dividends**. Some types of shares, for example preference shares, receive fixed amounts of dividends, irrespective of the level of profits earned by the company.

Trading as a company means that the business must pay to have its accounts checked annually by independent accountants (called auditors). Furthermore the company accounts must be made public, so that outsiders can see the revenue and profits of the business, as well as what it owes. This means that a company's affairs are less private than for a sole trader.

Key terms

A **company** is a business organisation that has its own legal identity and that has limited liability.

Incorporation is the process of establishing a business as a separate legal identity that allows it to benefit from limited liability.

A **shareholder** is an investor in and one of the owners of a company.

Limited liability means that in the event of financial difficulties, the personal belongings of shareholders are safe.

Dividends are a share in the profits of a company that are distributed to the holders of certain types of company shares.

Every year in the UK new companies are created (or registered) and existing ones fail and are dissolved. As shown in Table 2.2 this involves a large number of companies. In 2012 the number of companies created in the UK increased by 13.7 per cent compared with 2011, while the number dissolved fell by 17.4 per cent. This suggests that companies in the UK were operating in an increasingly favourable environment.

	2011	2012	Percentage change
Companies registered	400,600	455,600	13.7
Companies dissolved	348,400	287,800	−17.4

Table 2.2 Births and deaths of companies in the UK, 2011 and 2012

Source: Companies House

Permission for re-use of all © Crown copyright information is granted under the terms of the Open Government Licence (OGL).

Companies in the UK are divided into two legal categories: private limited and public limited companies.

(a) Private limited companies

Private limited companies have 'Ltd' after their names. They are generally smaller than public limited companies, and are relatively cheap to set up. It can cost as little as £15 to register a private limited company with the Registrar of Companies in the UK.

Private limited companies also benefit from limited liability. Normally this means that the liability of the shareholders is limited to the amount they invested in buying shares. However, for some private limited companies, limited liability takes the form of a guarantee that the owners of the company agree to pay if it fails. They cannot be required to pay more than they have guaranteed thereby limiting their liability.

As with all companies, they are owned by shareholders and the owners can place restrictions on who the shares are sold to in the future. For example, many (but not all) private limited companies are owned by families who limit the sale of shares to other members of the family – this makes sure that 'outsiders' do not become involved. Owners of shares in private limited companies cannot advertise their shares for sale – they have to sell them privately.

Business in focus: Cargill

Cargill is an American-owned multinational that describes itself as providing: 'food, agriculture, financial and industrial products and services to the world.' This statement reflects the diversity of Cargill's business interests. It is heavily involved in global agriculture. It purchases and trades agricultural commodities, such as palm oil; the company breeds livestock and produces food ingredients such as starch and glucose syrup, vegetable oils and fats for processed foods and industrial use. It is also involved in the energy, steel and transport industries. Cargill also has significant interests in financial services industry.

Cargill was founded in 1865 and by 2014 it had 145,000 employees working in 67 countries. The company's accounts for 2013 show that it achieved annual sales of $136,000 million and profits of $2,310 million. It is larger than the Ford Motor Company.

Cargill is a family-owned private company. The descendants of the founders own approximately 85 per cent of the company. Most of the company's spectacular growth has been due to reinvestment of the company's own profits. By refusing to become a public limited company, Cargill's owners have denied themselves the opportunity to sell shares to the general public through markets such as the London Stock Exchange.

Source: Adapted from Cargill's website
www.cargill.co.uk/en/about-cargill-uk/cargill-overview/index.jsp

Questions

1. What are the benefits to Cargill resulting from trading as a private limited company?
2. Would it be possible for a business in any industry to become a major multinational organisation while remaining a private limited company?

Weblink

You can find out more about Cargill's global activities by exploring its website at www.cargill.com/worldwide/index.jsp

There is a range of reasons why the owners of private limited companies might decide to retain this legal status, rather than becoming a public limited company.

- **The desire to retain control over the company**. Becoming a public company is likely to be accompanied by the sale of large volumes of shares through stock exchanges. If a sufficient number are sold, it may be that the original owners only hold a minority of the company's shares and that control of the business has passed to those who own the majority of the shares. It is possible for companies to raise capital by issuing shares which do not give their owners' voting rights. However, companies and other organisations who purchase large quantities of the shares issued by public companies are likely to want to have a say in decision-making.
- **Taking decisions in the company's long-term interests**. If a private company converts to become a public company (through a process known as "going public") many of the people and organisations who buy its shares will be seeking short-term profits in the form of dividends. This may put the senior managers of the company under pressure to make decisions which might generate attractive levels of profits over the next year or two, but may not be in the company's best long-term interests. For example, pressure to improve profits may lead the senior managers of a company to use less environmentally-friendly production methods which could damage the company's reputation in the long-term.
- **Enjoying the profits generated by the company**. Going public and selling more shares means that there are more shareholders between whom dividends have to be shared. This results in a dilution of profits and potentially lower returns for the original owners of the business.

(b) Public limited companies

Public limited companies have the term 'plc' after their names and include many well-known businesses. Marks & Spencer, BSkyB and Vodafone are all examples of public companies based in the UK. Public companies tend to be much larger than private companies. One way to measure the size of a public limited company is through its **market capitalisation**. Market capitalisation is the total value of the issued shares of a public limited company. The value of a company's market capitalisation is calculated by multiplying the company's current share price by the number of shares outstanding (that is, the number of shares issued and held by shareholders).

Key term

Market capitalisation is the total value of the issued shares of a public limited company.

The table below shows the UK's largest five companies as measured by market capitalisation in May 2014.

Maths moment

Calculate the number of shares HSBC and GlaxoSmithKline had issued by 16 May 2014.

As with private companies, public companies are owned by shareholders, but restrictions cannot be placed on the sale of these shares. Shareholders in public companies can sell their shares to whoever they like. This can cause problems if another firm starts to buy up shares in the business in an attempt to gain control of it. Some of the shareholders may want to resist this **takeover**, but they cannot stop fellow shareholders from selling their shares.

Another difference between private and public limited companies is that shares in public companies can be advertised in the media. This is why the share prices of public companies are listed in the newspapers, but not

those of private companies. Most companies become public because they want to advertise their shares to the general public and raise relatively large sums of money.

If the owners of a private company do not need to raise large sums via the sale of shares and want to maintain control over their company then they probably would not want to make it a public company.

There are benefits to businesses from trading as a public limited company.

- **Access to capital**. Public limited companies are able to sell shares freely using stock exchanges, which are efficient markets for buying and selling shares. This enables them to raise large sums of capital to fund a range of activities without having to take out expensive loans. Raising capital through share issues means that public companies are not committed to fixed interest payments as is the case when taking out a loan. The amount public companies pay shareholders in the form of dividends will reflect the profitability of the business and will not be more than it can afford.
- **Publicity**. Public limited companies are often in the media because of their size and importance. This has the possibility of generating a lot of free, or at least low-cost publicity, which can enhance the company's public image. BT, the UK's largest telecommunications company, received much positive publicity for its plans to improve its standards of customer service and speed of repairs to

Business in focus: Market capitalisation and the UK's largest companies

Rank	Company name	Sector	Share price* (pence)	Market capitalisation (£ million)	Number of employees
1	Royal Dutch Shell	Oil & gas	2,572.0	154,153	90,000
2	HSBC	Banking	632.5	119,097	267,000
3	BP	Oil & gas	507.1	96,648	97,700
4	GlaxoSmithKline	Pharmaceuticals	1,643.5	79,806	97,389
5	British American Tobacco	Tobacco products	3,513.0	66,288	87,813

*As at close of trading on 16 May 2014

Table 2.3 The UK's largest five public companies by market capitalisation, May 2014

Source: Adapted from the Stockchallenge website

www.stockchallenge.co.uk/ftse.php

Questions

1. Why would a company's market capitalisation change regularly?
2. Is market capitalisation of any value in measuring the size of a public company?

broadband services by creating an additional 1,600 jobs in 2014. This story was newsworthy because of the company's importance within the UK.

- **The ability to take over other companies**. Public limited companies are more able to buy other companies as they have access to capital through selling shares. They can also purchase other companies by offering the target company's shareholders their own shares in part or full payment. This can make it easier for public companies to grow relatively quickly.

Key terms

A **takeover** occurs when one company acquires control of another by buying more than 50 per cent of its share capital.

Privatisation is the process under which the state sells businesses that it has previously owned and managed to private individuals and businesses.

Reasons for changing business forms

Growth is a key factor encouraging businesses to change their forms. As a sole trader business becomes larger, the owner may decide that it requires more access to capital and that the protection of limited liability is vital and the business's potential to incur debts increases. This may result in a business becoming a private limited company. The desire to access more capital and attain a higher profile may result in companies opting to 'go public' and convert from private limited to public limited status. SAGA, a company that supplies holiday, financial and other services to people aged 50 and over, announced in April 2014 that it was to convert to public limited company status to assist it in its aim of continued growth.

The UK has seen numerous businesses transfer from the public sector to the private sector in a process known as **privatisation.** The popularity of privatisation in the UK and elsewhere can be explained by its ability to raise large sums of capital for governments and by the belief among many decision-makers that businesses tend to be more efficient when run privately rather than by the state. In October 2013 the Royal Mail was privatised and raised £3.3 billion for the UK Government.

Public sector businesses

The public sector comprises the organisations that are owned by (and sometimes funded by) national or local government. There are three major elements of the public sector:

- **Public corporations.** These are enterprises owned by the state but offering products for sale to the public and private sector businesses. These may be managed by central government (such as Channel 4 television) or by local governments, for example Manchester Airport.
- **Public services**. This category of the public sector includes organisations that provide services to the whole nation. The National Health Service (NHS) is an example.
- **Municipal services**. These are services offered by local governments and councils. Examples include libraries and leisure centres.

The size of the public sector in the UK has declined due to a series of privatisations in the 1980s and 1990s. This resulted in the sale of a large number of government-owned industries to the private sector. British Rail, the water and electricity supply industries were privatised along with British Telecommunications (BT). The aim was to increase the efficiency of these industries and to reduce the need for government subsidies. This resulted in many job losses, for example in the coal industry, as the new owners sought to create competitive businesses.

Figure 2.2 shows the declining importance of the public sector to the UK economy. Employment in the public sector has fallen steadily since 2009, while employment generally in the UK has risen with many new jobs being created by the private sector.

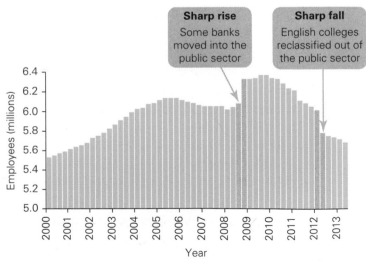

Figure 2.2 Employment in the UK's public sector

Source: Office for National Statistics

www.ons.gov.uk/ons/rel/pse/public-sector-employment/q2-2013/sty-public-section-employment.html

Permission for re-use of all © Crown copyright information is granted under the terms of the Open Government Licence (OGL).

Not-for-profit businesses

Not all enterprises are set up to make a profit. For example, local sports clubs, government organisations and charities do not have profit as their main objective. They are set up for some other purpose and can be part of the public sector or part of the private sector.

Business in focus: Wikipedia

Wikipedia was created in 2001. It is a multilingual, web-based, free-content encyclopedia project. It is written by volunteers all over the world and contains more than 4.5 million articles in English. Its articles can be edited by anyone with internet access and currently has approximately 77,000 editors.

It is now one of the largest online encyclopedias in the world, attracting 470 million visitors each month. Articles are continually updated and improved by online contributors. The website was created by the not-for-profit Wikipedia Foundation, which is a charitable organisation based in San Francisco in California. The Wikipedia foundation was set up by Jimmy Wales and employs 142 people.

Questions

1. Explain why 77,000 people work for Wikipedia without pay.
2. Is it only not-for-profit businesses that are good for society?

Weblink

To find out more, visit www.wikipedia.com

Social enterprises, for example, are businesses that have social aims and trade in order to benefit the community or society in general. Examples of social aims are job creation and training, providing community services and 'fair trade' with developing countries. Well-known social enterprises include Cafédirect, The Big Issue, The Co-operative Group, the Eden Project and Jamie Oliver's apprentice programme Fifteen. Many others (over 55,000) exist, operating in a wide range of industries from farmers' markets and recycling companies to transport providers and childcare.

Weblink

For more information on social enterprises, visit www.socialenterprise.org.uk

The owners of not-for-profit businesses operate them for a variety of reasons. They may have a strong belief in a particular issue, such as protecting the environment or caring for animals and therefore establish a charitable business to raise funds for their particular cause.

Others may be established to provide a hobby or to replace employment. Jamie Oliver has invested heavily in his restaurant chain Fifteen in part because he believes in offering a chance to unemployed young people to acquire cooking skills. His website summarises the reasons he established the chain to offer young, unemployed people the chance to gain employment skills in a restaurant.

'Fifteen represents the way I would have loved to have been taught myself; it embraces many of the things I love and feel passionate about, not only in the catering industry but also in friendship and family life.' Jamie Oliver (www.jamieoliver.com)

Study tip

When studying this chapter you need to think about the advantages and disadvantages of the different forms of business. What determines the right structure for a business? What issues are involved in choosing a business format? This involves issues such as: How much does someone need to work with others? Is outside investment required? How critical is limited liability?

Mutual businesses

Mutual businesses are relatively common in the UK, especially in certain industries such as building societies. The Co-operative Group operates a range of businesses, including retailing, agriculture, travel services, banking and funeral services.

The term 'mutual' covers several different ownership models. Mutuals are characterised by the fact that mutual businesses are run for the benefit of their members, whether they are employees, customers, suppliers or the local community. In contrast most public companies are owned and controlled by outside investors.

Mutuals can be based on a variety of different legal structures. However, there is a legal structure developed solely for mutual businesses that offers the benefit of limited liability. This is the Industrial and Provident Society (IPS). Some mutual businesses use this legal structure whereas others, including many co-operatives, are limited companies.

Co-operatives are a well-known example of mutual businesses and are run by groups of people (called members) each of whom has a say in the management of the business. Co-operatives must reflect four ethical values: honesty, openness, social responsibility and caring for others. They should also operate according to the following principles: voluntary and open membership, democratic member control, provision of education, provision of training and information and concern for the community.

Different types of co-operatives exist:

- consumer co-operatives, in which customers are the members of the business
- worker co-operatives, owned and operated by employees
- producer co-operatives, where a group of businesses work together to benefit from factors such as increased bargaining power.

Co-operatives can be popular but have faced criticism for not employing sufficient or suitably skilled professional managers, instead relying on elected members who may be well intentioned, but not suited to their roles.

Shareholders and share prices

We saw earlier that companies sell shares to raise capital for a variety of reasons and that public companies can sell shares freely.

Who buys shares?

In the UK, financial institutions such as banks, pension funds and insurance companies own most company shares. These organisations buy shares to make a profit through the dividends they receive and by selling the shares at a higher price later on. They can then pass their profits on to their own investors.

As you can see in Figure 2.3, individuals own less than 15 per cent of shares in the UK. Foreign investors own more than 50 per cent of shares in the UK.

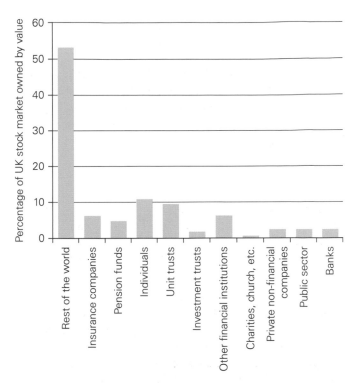

Figure 2.3 Share ownership in the UK

Source: Office for National Statistics

Permission for re-use of all © Crown copyright information is granted under the terms of the Open Government Licence (OGL).

The reasons for and risks of buying shares

Shareholders invest in business primarily for financial reasons. They may benefit (hopefully) from an increase in the share price and from receiving a share of the profits in the form of dividends. The more profit a firm makes, the bigger the dividends are likely to be. Some shareholders invest to make a quick return and may seek out risky companies that may offer high returns. Other groups of investors, such as pension funds and insurance companies, who have large sums of other people's money to invest, may seek longer-term, more secure returns.

However, there is a substantial risk in buying shares in most circumstances. The price of shares can easily fall and this can be true of a well-managed and profitable business if the economy is not performing well. Figure 2.4 illustrates the performance of share prices for the UK's 100 largest companies (by market capitalisation) from 2008 to 2014. There was a very sharp fall in share prices during 2008 and early 2009. During this time the share prices of many well-managed, profitable companies fell sharply as their sales dipped and nervous shareholders sold their shares, depressing share prices further.

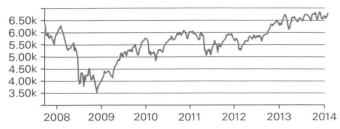

Figure 2.4 The UK's FTSE, 2008–2014

Source: Yahoo

https://uk.finance.yahoo.com/q?s=%5EFTSE

Companies can also make lower profits than expected which means dividend payments for all types of shareholder may be lower than expected and also can have the side-effect of reducing share prices, at least in the short-term.

What do you think?

You are thinking of buying shares in a company. What would you want to know before deciding which ones to buy?

The degree of risk involved in buying shares also depends on the type of shares that are purchased. Many shareholders purchase ordinary shares. These are the most risky type of share because the holders only receive a dividend after many other stakeholders in the company have received payments. Ordinary shareholders will only be paid after those who have lent the company money in the form of long-term loans or debentures. They also receive payment after those who have bought preference shares who receive a fixed payment. So, in a poor trading year, such as 2008, shareholders may receive little or no dividend. However, in a good year they may be well rewarded, as their payments are not fixed. The situation of ordinary shareholders illustrates how risk and reward go hand-in-hand.

Business in focus: Serco profits warning leads to share price slump

Serco plc is a company that carries out many contracts on behalf of national and local governments in many countries. The services supplied by Serco include transport, health care, rehabilitating offenders and protecting national borders.

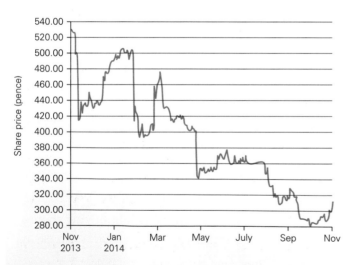

Figure 2.5 Serco's share price

Source: Money AM

www.moneyam.com

At the end of April 2014 the company's shares fell 18% to 340.1 pence each after the firm faced a series of crises. It announced that it was looking to raise funds to bolster its finances. In a statement that amounted to a third profits warning in less than a year, the company, which has been struggling following a criminal tagging

scandal, said its 'performance this year … has been more challenging than expected'. As a result, this could 'require a material downward revision to expectations, and for us to review the appropriateness of our financing position'. Serco added that it was considering the sale of shares to raise further capital.

'We will, therefore, be consulting with shareholders regarding the possibility of strengthening the balance sheet through an equity placing', Serco added.

The announcement raised concerns that the problems facing incoming chief executive Rupert Soames are much bigger than originally indicated.

'This suggests Serco's problems are more deeply rooted than previously thought,' said Caroline de la Soujeole, an analyst at Cantor Fitzgerald. 'The shares will come under pressure. Rupert Soames has a hard task ahead of him; he will have his work cut out.' Some shareholders were concerned that the fall in share prices might not just be in the short-term.

Source: Adapted from The Daily Telegraph, 29 April 2014

www.telegraph.co.uk/finance/newsbysector/supportservices/10794197/Serco-considers-fundraising-after-profits-warning.html

Questions

1. Why might this profit warning make it more difficult for Serco plc to sell new shares in the future?

2. Will a short-term fall in Serco plc's share price matter to its shareholders?

The role of shareholders

Shareholders can influence the decision-making of companies. Most types of shares grant their owners voting rights. Each share is worth one vote. So, by buying more shares, people can get more votes and have a greater influence over what the company actually does. If someone, or more likely an organisation, owns more than 51 per cent of the shares in a company, they control the business and, therefore, can decide company policy.

All companies must have an Annual General Meeting (AGM) to which the shareholders are invited and every shareholder must receive a copy of the company's Annual Report. The Annual Report reviews the performance of the business over the last year. At the AGM, the directors and managers give an overview of the company's position and respond to any questions that shareholders might have.

In practice it is relatively rare for shareholders in UK companies to have a strong influence on the policies and decisions of public companies. However, over recent years, shareholders have become increasingly critical about what they regard as unacceptably high levels of pay for senior managers and have on occasions voted against it at AGMs.

Influences on share prices

Share prices can be affected by a wide variety of issues but the two major factors are the company's performance and the business environment in which it trades.

Public limited companies publish their financial results and provide trading updates twice a year. These communications provide the company's stakeholders with a lot of information about the company's performance. Companies are also obliged to give information about any event that could influence their share prices, such as a takeover bid. These are known as regulatory announcements.

If a company is performing well, and is expected to continue to do well, its share price should benefit. Share prices tend to anticipate the future, so they can rise if a company has good prospects and fall if the outlook is not promising.

Share prices are also affected by the business environment. If economic conditions are good and expected to continue that way, investors tend to feel confident. So good news about a country's employment levels or positive data on manufacturing production, for example, will encourage investors and may help to push share prices up. Companies are more likely to perform well and deliver strong profits when the business environment is favourable as sales and product prices are likely to rise. As a consequence they are likely to generate higher profits and pay rising dividends. Under such circumstances, demand for shares tends to rise and prices increase.

If the economic climate is troubled, as happens regularly in the UK and elsewhere, investors may feel nervous. They may worry that a company's profitability will suffer if economic conditions are difficult. Fears about future profits tend to reduce demand for shares so prices may fall. This means that, in a challenging business environment, companies can see their share price fall, even if they are performing well. Equally, companies can benefit from a positive business environment and their share price may go up, even if the business is not performing well.

The significance of share prices

The effects of changes in the share price of an individual company

If a company's share price alters it does not have a direct impact on the company's immediate financial position. Remember the company that sold these shares at the time they were first made available to the public and received the capital inflow in return. Most, if not all, of this capital will have been invested into the company to provide assets such as property, vehicles and machinery as well as to finance the purchase of raw materials and to provide cash. Thus, if the share price rises or falls, it does not affect the amount of finance that the business has available at that time.

However, changes in share prices can have significant effects on a business over a slightly longer timescale.

- **Rising share prices.** A rising share price tends to reflect well on the company's management team - they are more likely to be considered to be doing a good job and may receive bonuses as a result. In many circumstances a business may find it easier to raise capital when share prices are rising. Potential shareholders will be more willing to buy an asset that is rising in price; similarly banks may be more willing to offer loans to such companies, especially if they believe that the rising share price is the result of the business performing well. These arguments are particularly relevant if a company's share price is performing better than share prices generally.

- **Falling share prices.** This may be judged to be the result of a poor performance by the management team and may make it difficult for it to raise capital. It may also make the company vulnerable to a takeover as the cost of buying a controlling interest in the company is reduced. This is more likely to be the case if the company's share price is considered to be too low, making it undervalued. However, this might be a response to a short-term factor, such as profits being below expectations and not be an indication of the company's likely long-term performance.

Obviously the longer the trend in share prices lasts, the greater the impact. Thus a prolonged decline in share prices might affect a company's ability to recruit top-quality employees or to raise finance for major investments.

The effects of a general change in share prices

If there is a substantial fall in share prices for most companies the effects on businesses generally can be significant. Figure 2.4 shows that share prices in the UK fell very heavily in 2008 and again in 2011. This can pose difficulties for many businesses and especially those that sell non-essential products or luxury products. At a time of falling share prices, many consumers and organisations may feel that their wealth is declining and cut their spending accordingly. This reduces the sales made by a wide range of businesses, which in turn reduce their own spending, 'multiplying' the negative effect. This can provoke an economic recession, where the level of national production declines over a period of at least six months.

A period of rising share prices can have the opposite effect, causing a positive wealth effect and making it easier for companies to raise capital by issuing new shares.

The effects of ownership on businesses

1. The effects on mission

We saw in Chapter 1 that a business's mission sets out what it is trying to achieve, that is, the reason it exists. The type of ownership may have a considerable impact on the organisation's overall direction. Thus, for example, a public limited company is likely to have a mission that will allow it to provide sufficient financial rewards to its shareholders. Nike's mission is 'to bring inspiration and innovation to every athlete in the world'. Succeeding in this mission will allow the American sportswear company to produce popular and valued products that will generate high profits with which to reward its shareholders. In contrast, the Midcounties Co-operative, based in the English Midlands, strives to 'be a successful consumer co-operative working towards creating a better, fairer world and to enhance the lives of our colleagues, members, customers, and the communities we serve'. This mission is unlikely to result in the business seeking to maximise its profits but in operating in a way that benefits communities and many of its stakeholders.

2. The effects on objectives

A business's mission naturally gives rise to the objectives that it follows. Thus Nike may seek to achieve its mission by setting objectives relating to achieving a certain level of sales, producing innovative products regularly or being the leading company in its market. The Midcounties Co-operative may operate with objectives relating to the impact its business has on its stakeholders and the communities it serves.

Type of business	The effects on:			
	Mission	**Objectives**	**Decisions**	**Performance**
Sole trader	May be unlikely to have a mission, but sole owner provides sense of direction.	May centre around meeting personal goals such as generating sufficient income.	Potentially rapid and responsive, but lacking support and possibly information.	Ownership allows business to be responsive to customers' needs, but may not be too price competitive.
Private limited company	Mission may centre on maintaining family-run business or on reputation.	Could relate to a satisfactory level of profits or financial stability to ensure continued survival.	More complex as more people likely to be involved. May have more information available and some specialist input.	Scale of this type of business varies hugely. Performance could be based meeting personal needs or on benefits of being large scale.

Type of business	The effects on:			
	Mission	Objectives	Decisions	Performance
Public limited Company	Mission can play an important role to project the company's image and to provide a focus for consistent decision-making.	Likely to relate to costs, prices, business image and market share and link to financial performance in the longer term.	Can be very complex and have long-term implications. Some decisions require specialist input and need to be based on extensive information. Many routine decisions also need to be made.	Access to capital and pressure from shareholders likely to place emphasis on being competitive in terms of price, customer service or desirable products.
Not-for-profit	Mission can be important in establishing the ethos of the business and underpinning all decision-making.	Likely to be non-financial and can be less easy to measure such as benefiting the community or protecting the environment.	May lack specialists. Desire to meet social or other objectives may cloud judgements.	Probably measured in non-financial terms, but need to perform well enough financially to meet other goals.

Table 2.4 The effects of ownership

Business in focus: The Co-operative Group

The Co-operative Group started life as a small shop in Lancashire. It has since become Britain's largest mutually owned company and one of the longest-standing names on British High Streets. It employs over 100,000 people and has a diverse range of businesses, including grocers, financial products, funeral parlours and farming.

However, in 2013 a £1.5 billion hole was discovered in the finances of the Co-op bank and it declared a loss of £2.5 billion in 2014. In response to this the Co-op sold off various parts of its business. Its farms were sold to the charity The Wellcome Group for £249 million and its chain of pharmacies went to the Bestway Group for £620 million.

Big job cuts were also threatened in order to try and plug the hole in the group's finances – there were rumours that 4,000–5,000 jobs would be lost.

The cost-cutting measures caused much tension within the group as many members objected to the threat of job losses and of losing the parts of the business that they considered the 'crown jewels' of its portfolio. There was particular tension between the elected board members and the professional management of the group.

Source: adapted from various news sources

Questions

1. How should the Co-operative Group measure its performance?
2. Is a co-operative model suitable for managing a large organisation such as the Co-operative Group?

3. The effects on decisions

The type of business is likely to have an impact on the complexity of the decisions that have to be made as well as the speed of decision making. At times, public companies have to make major decisions with enormous implications for the business. In 2014, EE, the mobile telephone company which owns T-Mobile and Orange, announced that it was moving its call centre operations back to the UK from Asia. This will create 1,000 jobs in the UK but may increase the company's costs. Such a major decision would have been researched thoroughly beforehand to determine the effect of the decision on key stakeholders such as

customers, employees and shareholders and may have taken time to complete because of this and the extent of communication involved. To an extent it is the scale of the business and its operations that determine the complexity and need for information and expertise in taking this type of decision, but most larger businesses are public companies.

At the other end of the scale, decision making can be a strength for small, sole trader businesses. Decisions are likely to be less complex and involve fewer participants, speeding and simplifying the process. This enables sole traders to be responsive to changes in their markets.

4. The effects on performance

The performance of a business can be measured in many ways, not just on its profits. It is influenced by a wide range of factors such as the state of the economy and technological changes, as well as the form of business that is adopted.

However, it is true to say that larger organisations, which are mainly public companies, may be able to produce at lower costs due to the use of specialist employees and up-to-date technology. This offers the potential to increase profits. Similarly, public companies may be more innovative (as they can spend large sums on researching new products) and this may enhance their performance, as in the case of Apple. Not-for-profit businesses may judge their performance in other ways, and not simply financially. Thus they may measure performance in terms of raising public awareness for an issue or on alleviating poverty.

ASSESSMENT ACTIVITIES

Sections (a), (b) and (c) of these assessment activities are relevant for students taking AS and A-level examinations. The questions in section (d) are for A-level students only.

(a) Knowledge check questions

1   State two reasons why an entrepreneur may choose to operate a business as a sole trader.

2   What is meant by the term 'unlimited liability'?

3   Is the following statement true or false? 'A company is owned by its stakeholders.'

4   State two differences between a private limited company and a public limited company.

5   What is meant by the term privatisation?

6   Finn plc has a current share price of 75 pence and has issued 725 million shares. It currently has £275 million in outstanding bank loans. What is its market capitalisation?

    i) £543,750,000   iii) £286,750,000

    ii) £54,375,000,000   iv) £54,100,000,000

7   What is the difference between a public company and a public corporation?

8   What are mutual businesses?

9   State two factors that might influence the share price of a public company.

10 Is the following statement true or false? 'If a public company's share price falls this immediately reduces the amount of capital available to the business.'

(b) Short answer questions

1   Explain one effect of a significant fall in a share price on the company concerned.   (4 marks)

2   Explain why the owners of a private limited company might want to convert it to a public limited company.   (5 marks)

3   Explain why sole traders are the most popular form of business in the UK.   (5 marks)

4   Benacre plc manufactures a range of components for high technology products such as mobile phones. It is very profitable and has a rising share price. Explain two risks in buying shares in Benacre plc.   (6 marks)

(c) Data response questions

Wrentham plc

Wrentham plc recently converted from a private limited to a public limited company. The company designs and manufactures a range of stylish furniture for homes. Initially the company was family owned and sold its products just in the UK, but in 2013 it expanded successfully into Europe. Its profits have been rising at an average rate of 19 per cent each year since 2010 and dividends have been high since it went public. The company's share price has fallen slightly since it became a public company.

The company's charismatic chief executive, Fran D'Alcorn, set out a clear vision for the company at the time it went public, based around consolidating its position as a major competitor in the European furniture market. She is aiming for rapid growth and expects to gain 12 per cent of the European market within three years and to strengthen the company's reputation for modern design and quality manufacturing.

The European furniture market is highly competitive with many large companies that sell their products throughout the world. Sales in the market have not been rising recently as many European workers have lost their jobs or have suffered flat or declining incomes and some analysts think that this trend will continue for the next few years. One large American company has started to buy large numbers of Wrentham plc's shares.

1   Explain why shareholders may have been attracted to buy shares in Wrentham plc once it had 'gone public'. (6 marks)

2   Analyse the possible effects of the decision to 'go public' on the company's objectives. (9 marks)

3   To what extent do you think that converting from a private to a public limited company was the correct decision for Wrentham plc? (15 marks)

(d) Essays

1   Is it inevitable that a mutual business will perform less well than a public limited company when trading in a competitive market? Justify your view. (25 marks)

2   Thousands of UK businesses fail every year. To what extent does this make it essential for all entrepreneurs to establish their businesses as private limited companies and not sole traders? (25 marks)

Chapter 3

Understanding that businesses operate within an external environment

Introduction

This chapter takes you outside the business itself to consider the external forces that can impact upon businesses large and small. The scope of this chapter is very precise as the external environment is an extensive topic and one that could not be covered effectively in a single, relatively short chapter. Thus we will consider a limited range of external factors and we will further limit the scope of this chapter by examining how these chosen external factors impact upon a business's costs and the level of demand (or sales) it experiences for its products. We will look at other elements of the external environment and consider how businesses respond to change in this environment in this book's accompanying volume *AQA Business for A-level 2*.

What you need to know by the end of this chapter:

● The ways in which the following elements of a business's external environment may affect its costs and demand:
  ● market conditions and competition
  ● incomes
  ● interest rates
  ● demographic factors
  ● environmental issues and fair trade.

What is the external environment?

All businesses, whether large or small or whether supplying services or goods, operate within an external environment. The external environment comprises those external forces that can influence a business's activities. These forces might arise from a number of possible sources, as summarised in Figure 3.1. We will look at each of them in detail in the following section.

(There are other factors that determine a business's external environment and these are covered in the strategy section of AQA's Year 2 Business specification.)

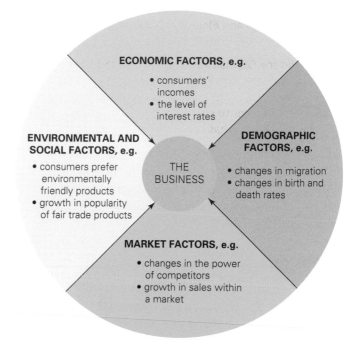

Figure 3.1 Some factors that shape the external environment for businesses

These forces are unpredictable and can change suddenly without warning, as illustrated by the case study on Tesco on page 33. We saw in the UK in 2008–09 that, as a result of the financial crisis, incomes and spending by UK consumers fell significantly and unexpectedly, resulting in many businesses suffering large falls in demand for their products. Similarly, an unexpectedly large number of people have moved to live and work in the UK in recent years, boosting demand for many goods and services.

These factors also combine and interact to shape the external environment in which businesses trade. They should not be viewed as individual factors. So in the Tesco case study, the fact that consumers' incomes in the UK have either fallen or risen very slowly since 2008 has assisted and encouraged the expansion of price competitive rivals such as Aldi and Lidl into the market for selling groceries. A further example of the

Business in focus: Tesco suffers heavy fall in sales

Tesco's like-for-like sales declined by 3.7 per cent in the first quarter of 2014, and Chief Executive Philip Clarke told investors that he'd 'never seen sales fall like this before'. Tesco is still Britain's largest supermarket after rapid expansion and a diversification in the products it offers, to include clothing and household items, electrical items (including its own tablet – the Hudl) and even financial services. It still has over 28 per cent of market share, but, along with the other 'Big Four' supermarkets (Asda, Sainsburys and Morrisons), it's being squeezed on both sides.

At one end the German 'discounters' Aldi and Lidl have gained popularity, attracting cash-strapped customers in increasing numbers. The leading supermarkets have had to slash prices in order to compete and Clarke acknowledges that Tesco's revenue has been affected by this. At the other end Tesco is under pressure from more upmarket grocers: Waitrose and Marks & Spencer.

As well as industry price cuts forced by the discounters, Clarke also quotes the cost of refurbishing existing stores and 'subdued' customer spending as reasons for their poor financial performance. He has warned that he doesn't expect an immediate improvement in sales and expects the current trend to continue into 2015.

Source: adapted from various news sources

Questions

1. Explain why cutting prices might lead to a fall in the revenue Tesco receives from its sales.

2. Is competition the only part of Tesco's external environment that might affect the company? Justify your view.

---

effects of a change in the external environment is the relationship between interest rates and incomes. A rise in interest rates may mean that consumers have to pay more on any loans they have arranged (and especially on mortgages) leaving less income available to spend on other goods and services.

The effects of changes in the external environment

External forces have the power to affect a business's activities in a number of ways. In this chapter we will focus on the effects of changes in the external environment on the level of demand for a business's goods and services and on the costs that it incurs in producing those goods and services.

It is important to understand that these external forces can have both positive and negative effects on a business's costs and its sales. For example, an increase in competition might result in a fall in sales for a company, as in the case of Tesco. In contrast, an increase in competition in a market from which a business buys raw materials or components might result in prices falling, thereby reducing the business's costs of production. Increased levels of competition in the food manufacturing industry may result in lower prices for tinned or frozen foods. This may result in

lower prices for grocery retailers such as Tesco. This would enable the company to reduce its prices or to maintain them and enjoy higher profits on the sale of each product.

Positive factors	Negative factors
• A product becomes popular or fashionable, raising demand • A major competitor leaves a market • The number of consumers in a country increases • Interest rates fall, making it cheaper to borrow money to buy products • Consumers enjoy steadily rising incomes, increasing demand for products	• Consumers demand environmentally friendly products, increasing businesses' costs • New businesses enter a market, increasing the degree of competition • A market is over-supplied with products, depressing prices • More people become unemployed, reducing consumers' incomes and spending

Table 3.1 A selection of positive and negative factors arising from changes in the external environment

The components of the external environment

The factors considered below represent some of the elements that make up the external environment for all types of business.

1. Market conditions and competition

This part of the external environment contains two interrelated elements.

- **Market conditions** is a broad term that encompasses a number of factors which can affect a market. Good market conditions would include rising sales figures and possibly rising prices. This would be particularly attractive if sales were rising at a similar rate. Further elements of good market conditions would include competition that is not too threatening and perhaps a shortage of supply of products, which would encourage prices to continue to rise.

- Competition is a part of the conditions of a market but is worthy of a separate mention. The competitive element of a business's external environment includes the number, size and power of rivals and potential rivals that a business faces in its battle to win customers. In the case study we saw that Tesco is facing an increasingly competitive external environment as Aldi and Lidl win customers by being highly price competitive.

Changes in the conditions of a market and/or the degree of competition can impact negatively on both the level of **demand** or sales achieved by a business and also the costs that it incurs. For example, the entry of a rival into a market can have a series of consequences for the businesses already operating in that market, especially if the entrant is a large and competitive business. In 2014 the American technology company Microsoft announced that it was to enter the market for manufacturing smartphones using its Windows technology. The company will offer phones at competitive prices with the objective of winning a significant share. This will have substantial implications for existing manufacturers of smartphones. It is likely that the level of demand for their products will decline (or perhaps not rise

as quickly) as some new consumers opt to purchase the new entrant's products rather than those of existing suppliers. Thus businesses such as Apple and Samsung may suffer a decline in demand following the entry of Microsoft into the market. The entry of a new competitor such as Microsoft may also result in existing producers facing higher costs. Microsoft is likely to promote its products strongly to ensure that consumers are aware that it is operating in this new market. This is likely to provoke existing suppliers to increase expenditure on their own promotional activities as a defensive response.

Figure 3.2 The entry of Microsoft into the smartphone market is bad news for existing suppliers such as Apple and may affect demand for their products as well as possibly increasing marketing costs.

A range of other factors can have adverse effects on the conditions faced by businesses in a specific market.

- Some markets are vulnerable to large and dramatic changes in demand – this is more common in markets such as those for fashion or technological products where new products are launched more frequently.
- Existing suppliers may join together to form larger and more competitive businesses.
- Consumers may become more price-conscious, putting suppliers under pressure to match these expectations.
- One business may launch a new, innovative product that makes existing products appear relatively obsolete. This is likely to result in other businesses losing sales and having to invest in developing their own updated products in response.

Of course market conditions can move in favour of businesses as well. For example, demand for a particular product may increase in popularity, which may also result in higher prices being received by producers in that market. A major business may leave a specific market, leaving its customers available to those businesses that remain. In 2014, Cheque Centre, one of the UK's largest payday lenders, left the short-term loan market after criticism of its business practices to concentrate on its other financial activities such as pawn-broking.

2. Incomes

A major influence on the demand for a business's products is the level of income earned by its customers. In many cases rises in the level of income earned will result in increased sales. Consumers' incomes are determined by the level of a nation's **gross domestic product** (GDP) in that a rise in GDP will increase the incomes received by many consumers. A rise in GDP is likely to result in a rise in demand for many products as consumers and businesses increase spending on a range of goods and services.

Key term

Gross domestic product (GDP) measures the value of a country's total output of goods and services over a period of time, normally one year.

Real incomes are incomes that are adjusted for the rate of inflation (or increase in prices) to show changes in purchasing power.

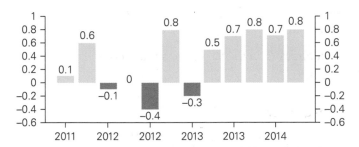

Figure 3.3 The percentage change in the UK's quarterly GDP 2011–2014

Source: Trading Economics (ONS figures)

www.tradingeconomics.com/united-kingdom/gdp-growth

Permission for re-use of all © Crown copyright information is granted under the terms of the Open Government Licence (OGL).

Incomes and the level of demand for goods and services

It can be seen in Figure 3.3 that the rate of change of GDP in the UK, measured quarterly or over a period of three months, has varied significantly even over a relatively short three-year period. In 2012 and early 2013 there were quarters in which the UK's growth in GDP was negative. This means that the value of production in the UK fell during these quarters and, since production fell in value, the incomes paid to people and business organisations to produce these goods and services would also have declined. Fewer people would have been employed, resulting in increasing numbers receiving benefits rather than wages. The incomes of those remaining in employment would fall, for example, as opportunities to work extra hours became less common. As a consequence it is likely that many businesses experienced a fall in demand for their products during these times in which consumers' incomes declined.

In contrast, since late 2013 the UK has enjoyed a period of steady increases in GDP equating to an increase over a year of about 3 per cent. This means that on average consumers and businesses in the UK have seen their **real incomes** rise by 3 per cent which, assuming they choose not to increase their savings, could lead to a similar increase in demand for goods and services.

There is a positive relationship between incomes and the level of demand for products that are considered luxury items rather than necessities. Thus companies selling holidays in exotic destinations may experience a substantial rise in demand if the level of earnings in a country generally rises. This positive relationship may be less evident for products considered to be essential such as basic foodstuffs. Table 3.2 illustrates the businesses that might see a rise in demand following an increase in incomes and those that may be expected to benefit little, if at all, from rising incomes. Even within these two categories the sensitivity of demand or sales to income can vary. For example, jewellery sales may be highly sensitive to income levels as they are considered to be a luxury good, while consumers may be less willing to reduce demand for restaurant meals even when their incomes are falling.

We explore the relationship between the income received by consumers and organisations and their levels of demand for goods and services as part of a theory called income elasticity of demand. This is covered on pages 105–07.

Products for which demand is strongly influenced by income levels	Products for which income has little influence on demand
• jewellery • luxury electrical items (e.g. widescreen HD televisions) • restaurant meals • long-haul holidays • household furniture	• bread, milk and other basic foods • cigarettes and tobacco • petrol • water • lottery tickets

Table 3.2 Products for which demand is dependent upon incomes and those with little or no relationship

Incomes and the costs of production

Changes in the level of income do not only affect the level of demand for a business's products, it can also impact on costs of production. If income levels are rising rapidly in an economy, as has been the case in China where GDP has increased at an annual rate of around 10 per cent, then wages will be rising too. This can result in businesses facing sharp increases in costs, especially if they rely heavily on labour in their production processes. This may result in difficulties in maintaining competitiveness in terms of prices.

The opposite can apply during periods in which GDP is falling, especially if this occurs for a prolonged period. The case study about UK workers explores the circumstances in which GDP and real wages are falling.

3. Interest rates

Interest rates are normally expressed as a percentage. A bank may allow a business to borrow money at an interest rate of 10 per cent. This means the business will have to pay a charge of 10 per cent of the amount borrowed for each year that the loan lasts. Most textbooks and media refer to the interest rate as if there is only a single

rate. In fact, a range of interest rates operates in the UK at any time. Interest rates operating in the UK economy depend on the length of the loan and the amount of risk associated with it. However, the authorities in the UK set the base rate and all other interest rates relate to this.

In May 1997 the government gave the Bank of England responsibility for setting interest rates. The Bank of England's Monetary Policy Committee (MPC) meets each month and takes decisions on whether to alter the base rate of interest.

Changes in interest rates have significant effects on businesses and the environment in which they operate. Recent UK governments have relied heavily upon interest rates to control the level of economic activity in the economy and to avoid the worst effects of the fluctuations in the level of business activity. Since 2009 interest rates in the UK have been maintained at very low levels to encourage borrowing and discourage saving. This helps to increase demand for many products and so can boost production and employment levels.

Key term

Interest rates are the price of borrowed money.

Interest rates and the level of demand

Interest rates affect the level of spending by UK citizens and thus the level of demand for businesses' products. The level of their spending is dependent upon interest rates for a number of reasons.

● Consumers are more likely to take a decision to save during a period in which interest rates are rising. The return on their saving is greater and will persuade

Business in focus: UK employees suffer falls in real wages

UK workers suffered a 7.6 per cent fall in real wages between 2008 and the end of 2013, with those in the construction industry hit by the sharpest drop. Construction workers have been subjected to real hourly wage cuts – those adjusted for inflation – of 13.4 per cent between the first quarter of 2008 and the fourth quarter of 2013, according to the Office for National Statistics.

Workers in other sectors of the economy have been less severely hit by the drop, with wages in the financial services industry, for example, just 4.2 per cent lower.

The general secretary of the Trades Union Congress (TUC), which represents many workers in the UK, Frances O'Grady, said the latest analysis by the ONS was evidence that living standards are not rising despite the recent

increases in the level of GDP in the UK. She said: 'Workers across the economy have experienced a deep squeeze in their pay packets since 2008. Construction workers have been hit the hardest and are currently receiving just 86p for every pound they earned before the crash.'

Source: From ONS and Trades Union Congress, 2 April 2014
www.tuc.org.uk/economic-issues/economic-analysis/laabour-market/official-figures-show-living-standards-falling

Questions

1. Explain the likely effects of falling real wages for businesses that sell essential products and those that sell luxuries.
2. To what extent do you think that the managers of all businesses will be pleased that real wages have fallen?

some consumers to postpone spending decisions, reducing demand. Conversely when rates are falling consumers might save less and spend more

- Changes in interest rates alter the cost of borrowing. Many goods are purchased on credit, for example cars and satellite TV systems. If rates fall then the cost of purchasing these goods on credit will decline, persuading more people to buy the product. Demand for consumer durables is sensitive to interest rate rises and sales of these products decline significantly following an upward movement in the base rate.

- An increasing number of UK consumers have mortgages. A rise in interest rates will increase the amount paid each month by householders. This reduces the income available for expenditure on other products. Demand for a range of products will fall in these circumstances. A fall in rates will have the opposite effect.

- Britain's population is steadily ageing, meaning that more people are dependent upon pensions and savings. This means that their income (which is often based on earnings from savings and investments) is highly dependent upon the rate of interest and this makes consumer expenditure highly sensitive to rate changes.

Businesses, interest rates and costs

Interest rates affect businesses in a number of ways. It is not simply a case of whether they rise or fall: businesses also take into account the overall level of rates. A small increase in interest rates may have little impact if rates are low. This is unlikely to be the case when rates are high before the change is introduced.

A rise in interest rates will increase the costs of production for many businesses. This occurs because most businesses borrow money and are therefore subject to interest charges. A rise in interest rates will therefore increase their costs. Businesses may borrow in the short term to fund their day-to-day operations or long-term for investment purposes. In 2014 Ineos, the company that owns the Grangemouth oil refinery in Scotland, announced that it had arranged to borrow £230 million to build a new important terminal and ethane store. An increase in interest rates of just half of one per cent on this loan could result in Ineos's annual costs rising by £1.15 million.

There is also a relationship between interest rates and the exchange rate of a currency. Thus if the Bank of England increases the base rate of interest in the UK, it is likely that the exchange rate of the pound will rise. This will result in imports of goods and services from overseas becoming cheaper, which may benefit businesses that import raw materials, components or services from other countries. However, this will also make UK exporters' products more expensive overseas.

Not all businesses will be affected equally by changes in interest rates. Those that have high levels of borrowing could benefit from a fall or be penalised

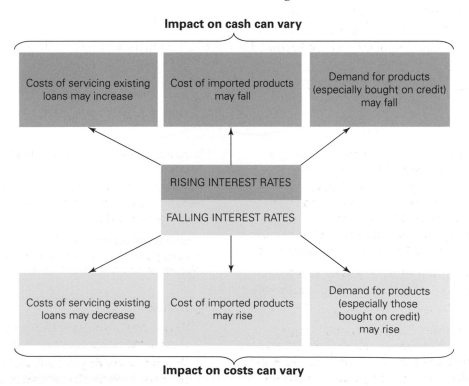

Figure 3.4 The effects on businesses of changes in interest rates

by an increase in interest rates if the rates charged on their loans are variable. Some businesses can protect themselves by arranging fixed-rate loans, meaning that the interest charged will remain constant throughout the duration of the loan.

4. Demographic factors

Demography is the study of human populations. The size and make-up of a population in terms of age can have important implications for businesses. The human population of a country represents two stakeholder groups for businesses: it provides the workforce and represents consumers. Thus, changes in population can impact upon a business's costs of production as well as the level of demand for its products.

The population of the UK has changed relatively rapidly in recent years. It has shown several notable trends, including the following:

- The UK's population is growing quickly and more rapidly than that of any other European country except Sweden. In 2013 it grew by 400,000 (or 0.63 per cent) to reach 64 million.
- Immigration has made a major contribution to the growth of the UK's population, especially since the turn of the century. Net migration into the UK (that is numbers entering the UK [immigrants] minus those leaving the country [emigrants]) reached

183,400 in 2013. During the same year there was an excess of births over deaths of 212,000 – this is known as the natural increase.

- The UK's population is ageing. At the time of writing (2014) there are 7.85 million people aged 70 and over in the UK. The equivalent figure for 2025 is forecast to be 10.44 million.

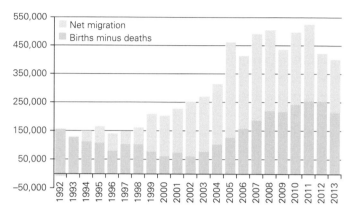

Figure 3.5 The main drivers of the UK's population, 1992–2013

Source: The Daily Mail, 26 June 2014

www.dailymail.co.uk/news/article-2670751/Number-people-UK-smashes-64million-one-biggest-population-increases-Europe.html

The implications of the UK's changing population

These changes in the UK's population size and structure will have considerable implications for businesses. At the most simple level the increase in the size of the population can be expected to increase

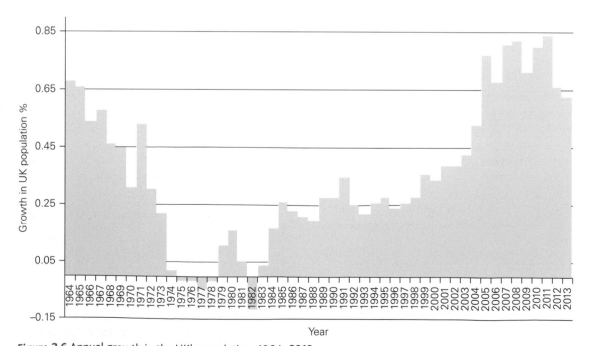

Figure 3.6 Annual growth in the UK's population, 1964–2013

Source: *The Daily Mail,* 26 June 2014

www.dailymail.co.uk/news/article-2670751/Number-people-UK-smashes-64million-one-biggest-population-increases-Europe.html

demand for most goods and services. The increase of 400,000 people in 2013 would have led to higher demand for housing, clothing, food and drink, transport and leisure services as well as all other products. Many migrants have relatively low incomes so the increase in demand may be more pronounced in businesses operating in certain markets, for example those supplying public transport, rather than in markets for luxury products. The effect of migration has been regional within the UK. London and other cities as well as rural areas such as parts of East Anglia have received large numbers of migrants, prompting substantial rises in demand for local services such as health care.

The pattern of demand for goods and services will also be affected by the ageing of the UK's population. Businesses supplying products associated with older age groups may experience a rise in demand simply because there are more people in these age groups. The projected 33 per cent rise in people aged over 70 in the UK between 2014 and 2025 will represent a substantial increase in the customer base for businesses selling to this market.

Changes in population size and structure also affect the workforce that is available to businesses. The UK has received large numbers of migrants from Eastern Europe since 2005. Many of these migrants are of working age and entered the UK to join the labour force. The high recent level of migration has increased the size of the UK's workforce and will have helped to control wage costs as shortages of labour are less likely to occur. A study conducted over the period 2000 to 2007 by Howard Reed and Maria Latorre found that a 1 per cent increase in the share of migrants in the UK's working-age population lowers the average wage by 0.3 per cent.

What do you think?

Would all businesses in the UK benefit if migration to the UK was not controlled in any way?

5. Environmental issues and fair trade

How the environment affects businesses

The media take a great interest in business activities in relation to the environment. When firms are found to be guilty of an act of pollution, adverse publicity is likely to follow. Society increasingly expects higher standards of environmental performance from businesses than in the past. Being seen to be environmentally friendly can represent an opportunity for businesses to differentiate themselves from competitors.

Business in focus: Migrants boost labour force in the East of England

The migrant population in Suffolk has risen significantly in the last ten years, with Ipswich experiencing a 120 per cent increase in numbers, according to recent research.

Jobs in agriculture and the hospitality industry are frequently filled by migrants, with business leaders saying migrant workers play an important role in offering employers seasonal flexibility as well as taking jobs that otherwise might be difficult to fill. The research shows that Ipswich saw its non-UK born population grow 121 per cent to 15,783 in the ten years between 2001 and 2011, while St Edmundsbury experienced a 70 per cent increase to 9,461 people over the same period.

Overall, the East of England region now has the third-largest migrant population of the ten regions of England and Wales – after London and South East England – with more than 640,000 people, around 11 per cent of the population, having been born outside of the UK.

Business leaders say agriculture, especially in areas like Cambridgeshire, as well as hotels and restaurants throughout the region are two sectors which employ a high number of migrant workers and are 'key drivers' for the upward trend in numbers.

Brian Finnerty, regional spokesman for the National Farmers Union, said migrant workers can offer employers crucial flexibility when they need it. He added: 'The picking and harvesting of fruit and vegetables is very seasonal and weather dependent, so a farmer needs a workforce that can be flexible and be there to do the work when there is the opportunity.'

Source: Adapted from *East Anglian Daily Times*, 29 November 2013

www.eadt.co.uk/news/east_anglia_unsustainable_immigration_rises_to_nearly_300_000_over_last_two_decades_1_3054727

Questions

1. Explain why migrant labour is important to the agriculture industry in the East of England.
2. Will immigration inevitably lead to businesses enjoying increased demand for their products? Justify your views.

There are many potential causes of damage to the environment. A major environmental concern identified by the government is global warming. This is caused by the release of a mix of industrial gases (principally carbon dioxide) that has formed a layer around the earth. This layer allows the sun's rays in but prevents heat escaping causing the so-called 'greenhouse effect'. Other environmental problems include the pollution of rivers and land and the dumping of waste, some of which is toxic and harmful to wildlife and humans alike.

Businesses contribute in many ways to the creation of environmental damage.

- The emission of gas through production processes.
- Pollution caused by transporting raw materials and products, particularly using road vehicles that emit noxious gases and create congestion and noise. A report by the EU suggested that pollution from vehicles in the UK could be responsible for up to 40,000 deaths among elderly people each year.
- The pollution of the sea by businesses using it as a 'free' dumping ground. The North Sea is one of the most polluted stretches of water in the world.
- Destruction of natural environments as a result of activities such as logging (for example, cutting down trees for commercial purposes as in the Amazon rainforest) and the building of homes on greenfield sites.

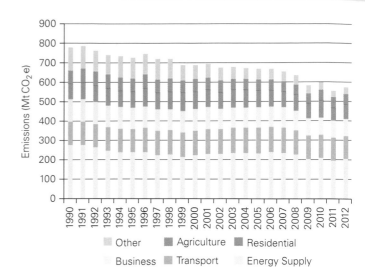

Figure 3.7 UK greenhouse gas emissions by source, 1990–2012

Source: *2012 UK Greenhouse Gas Emissions, Final Figures*, Department of Energy & Climate Change

www.gov.uk/government/uploads/system/uploads/attachment_data/file/295968/20140327_2013_UK_Greenhouse_Gas_Emissions_Provisional_Figures.pdf

Permission for re-use of all © Crown copyright information is granted under the terms of the Open Government Licence (OGL).

Despite engaging in activities that damage the environment there is evidence that businesses are improving some aspects of their environmental performance. The contribution to greenhouse gas emissions by the non-household sector (UK companies

Business in focus: Companies responsible for global warming emissions

Two-thirds of global industrial greenhouse gas emissions between 1751 and 2010 can be attributed to just 90 companies according to a report by the Climate Mitigation Services in 2014. Half of the emissions of these gases (carbon dioxide and methane) happened in the last 25 years.

Of the 90 companies, 83 were energy companies, producing oil, gas and coal, and seven were cement companies. Between them emissions from the 90 companies amounted to 914 gigatonnes of CO_2 emissions over the period. It is also likely that these companies currently have huge reserves of fossil fuels, which could contribute even further to global climate change.

The companies include Exxon Mobil, BP, Gazprom and ChevronTexaco. ChevronTexaco alone was responsible for 3.5 per cent of global emissions in the period, closely followed by Exxon with 3.2 per cent.

Richard Heede, the author of the report, says this: 'There are thousands of oil, gas and coal producers in the world. But the decision makers, the CEOs, or the ministers of coal and oil if you narrow it down to just one person, they could all fit on a bus or two.'

Source: adapted from various news sources and Carbon Majors: Accounting for carbon and methane emissions 1854-2010 Methods & Results Report, Climate Mitigation Services, April 2014

Questions

1. Explain possible reasons why demand for the products produced by these 90 companies is not falling in response to their apparent damage to the environment.

2. Do you think that it is decisions by consumers or decisions by the managers of the 90 companies that is resulting in damage to the environment?

and the public sector) fell between 1990 and 2012. However, average temperatures in the UK, and across the globe, continue to rise, with a rapid increase since 1990.

Costs of polluting the environment

Businesses are acutely aware of their private costs, that is the costs of production they have to pay themselves, such as wages and expenses for raw materials. These are easy to calculate and form part of the assessment of profitability. However, environmental pressure groups and others have pressed for businesses to acknowledge the costs they create for other groups in society – the external costs of production.

Noise, congestion, air and water pollution all impose costs on other individuals and groups in society. A firm extracting gravel from a quarry may create a number of external costs. These could include congestion on local roads caused by their lorries. This would impose costs in terms of delay and noise pollution on local residents. The destruction of land caused by the quarrying could create an eyesore for people living nearby and may reduce the value of their properties. Dust may be discharged into the atmosphere. The quarrying firm will not automatically pay for these costs. It requires government action to ensure that they pay these external costs as well as their internal ones.

Thus, the total (or social) costs of production equal internal or private costs plus external costs borne by third parties. By ensuring that firms pay all the costs associated with the production of a product, governments can avoid what is termed market failure. Oversupply is one consequence of market failure because producers are not paying the full social costs of production and making the activity profitable and attractive to businesses.

Government legislation and the environment

The government has passed a series of Acts of Parliament designed to protect the environment. Two acts are of particular importance.

1. The Environmental Protection Act, 1991 introduced the notion of integrated pollution control, recognising that to control only a single source of pollution is worthless as damage to one part of the environment means damage to it all. This Act requires businesses to minimise pollution as a whole.

2. The Environment Act, 1995 established the Environment Agency with a brief of co-ordinating and overseeing environmental protection. The Act also covered the control of pollution, the conservation of the environment and made provision for restoring contaminated land and abandoned mines.

The UK Government imposes fines on firms who breach legislation relating to the protection of the environment. These are intended to force firms to bear the full social costs of their production (including external costs) although environmental pressure groups and other critics believe that the sums are not sufficient to deter major businesses with budgets of billions of pounds annually. The Government also attempts to encourage 'greener' methods of production through the provision of grants. It has also created the Carbon Trust, which gives capital grants to firms who invest in energy-saving technologies.

The EU has also passed hundreds of directives relating to environmental protection. The UK is also a signatory to a number of international agreements intended to provide environmental protection on a global scale. For example, the UK Government has attended a number of Earth Summits at which targets for reducing the production of carbon dioxide have been agreed.

Study tip

You should not always think that laws relating to the environment constrain business activity. The passing of various laws to limit damage to the environment have created opportunities for many businesses, including those that manufacture equipment to reduce harmful emissions or those that provide advice on how to adjust operations to meet newly created laws.

The environment, costs and demand

Being environmentally friendly (or at least being believed to be so) by consumers offers businesses a number of advantages. It can form the basis for highly effective and distinctive promotion and can lead to increased recognition of the brand and possibly the opportunity to charge higher prices. This can enable relatively small businesses to compete with larger ones. Many large businesses have recognised the benefits of projecting an environmentally friendly image. Unilever, the Anglo-Dutch multinational consumer products company, which is responsible for well-known brands such as Ben & Jerry's, Knorr and Dove, has publicised its environmentally friendly approach widely. It intends to reduce the effects of its operations on the environment by 50 per cent by 2020. Such an approach may be particularly productive when rival products are not differentiated in other ways.

Webink

You can find out more about Unilever's plans to reduce it environmental impact by following the link below and looking for a further link to pages on sustainable living: www.unilever.com/

Opting to become more environmentally friendly can increase costs for many businesses. It may involve investing in new production processes that produce fewer emissions or waste and therefore lower pollution. Alternatively it may entail using resources from sustainable sources, which are frequently more expensive. Both factors may push up the costs of production, making it more difficult for the businesses concerned to compete with rivals. However, this is not inevitably the case. Many businesses have sought to cut energy usage to reduce their adverse impact on the environment. Du Pont, the American chemical company, committed itself to a 65 per cent reduction in greenhouse gas emissions in the 10 years prior to 2010. By 2007, DuPont was saving £1.3 billion annually as a result of reduced energy use, equal to its total profits that year.

What do you think?

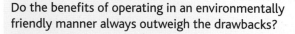

Do the benefits of operating in an environmentally friendly manner always outweigh the drawbacks?

Fair trade

Fair trade is a social movement that operates with the goal of assisting businesses in less-developed countries to achieve improved trading terms. The movement hopes to improve living standards in the less-developed countries and to promote **sustainable** methods of **production**. This movement supports the paying of higher prices to producers, who are often exporters to consumers in developed countries. There is a wide range of fair trade products available to consumers in the UK and other developed countries, most notably coffee, sugar, tea, bananas, wine and cotton.

The impacts of fair trade for businesses are similar to those of environmentally friendly production. Selling fair trade products has the potential to allow businesses to charge higher prices without an unacceptable loss of sales. It may however, limit businesses to selling to a smaller group of consumers for whom supporting producers in less developed countries through free trade is an important issue. It is also likely to increase costs as paying a 'fair' price is a cornerstone of the movement.

Key terms

Fair trade is a social movement that exists to promote improved trading terms and living conditions for producers of products in less-developed countries.

Sustainable production occurs when the supply of a product does not impose costs on future generations by, for example, depleting non-renewable resources.

Webink

You can find out more about fair trade by following the link below:

www.fairtrade.org.uk

ASSESSMENT ACTIVITIES

Sections (a), (b) and (c) of these assessment activities are relevant for students taking AS and A-level examinations. The questions in section (d) are for A-level students only.

(a) Knowledge check questions

1 Identify two factors that make up the external environment for a business.

2 What is meant by the term market conditions?

3 Is the following statement true or false? 'Real wages are an employee's wages adjusted to allow for the rate of price increase or inflation.'

4 State two products for which income has little influence on the level of demand.

5 What is meant by the term interest rates?

6 Is the following statement true or false? 'The level of savings tends to rise when interest rates fall.'

7 State two factors that may lead to a change in the size of a country's population.

8 Is the following statement true or false? 'Changes in the size of a country's population will only affect local businesses by altering the level of demand for the products they produce.'

9 State one benefit to a business arising from it adopting policies to become environmentally friendly.

10 What is meant by the term fair trade?

(b) Short answer questions

1 Explain the difference between incomes and real incomes. (4 marks)

2 Explain why a decision by a manufacturer to produce environmentally friendly products might increase its production costs. (5 marks)

3 Give one reason why a grocery retailer might decide to sell fair trade products. (5 marks)

4 Explain why a fall in interest rates might have a significant impact on demand for new houses. (6 marks)

(c) Data response questions

Handel Ltd is based in Lincolnshire and produces frozen foods from products supplied mainly by local farmers. It has a strong reputation for supplying basic foodstuffs at very competitive prices. The company is long established, has good facilities and very low levels of borrowing. The company employs large numbers of unskilled workers in its factories as it aims to keep its costs as low as possible. Its business is seasonal and it requires larger numbers of employees during peak seasons.

The company's external environment is undergoing a period of rapid change. The Bank of England has just announced that interest rates are to rise by 0.75 per cent and the level of immigration into the UK has continued to rise with a net migration figure of 450,000 for the last 12 months. Approximately 12,500 migrants entered Lincolnshire in the last twelve months.

Most notably a new German food-processing company has recently established a new high-technology factory in Lincolnshire, investing £35 million, and is targeting the UK food market. It sells a range of foods, mainly focusing on the higher price end of the market, although its efficient use of technology allows it to be very price competitive.

1 Explain why the rise in interest rates will only have a limited effect on Handel Ltd. (6 marks)

2 Analyse how the increase in net migration to the UK might affect Handel Ltd's costs (9 marks)

3 Do you think that the entry of the new German company to the market is certain to reduce demand substantially for Handel Ltd's products? Justify your decision. (15 marks)

d) Essays

1 To what extent is competition always the most important element of the external environment for fast-food chains? (25 marks)

2 'Consumers becoming more aware of environmental issues inevitably has a negative impact on businesses' costs and revenues.' Do you agree with this statement? Justify your viewpoint. (25 marks)

Case study: Unit 1 What is business?

Poundland Group plc goes public

The Poundland Group plc is a UK retailer with 528 stores in the UK and Europe. It sells most items in its stores for £1. It was established in 1990 by Stephen Smith and Dave Dodd. The retailer's stores stock approximately 3,000 items comprising mainly home and kitchen ware, healthcare products and gifts. The company changes its product lines constantly and attracts an average of 30,000 customers each week.

Item	2014	2013
Sales revenue, including VAT (£m)		1,015.87
Profits after tax (£m)	27.3	21.8
Number of new stores	70	69
Average number of transactions per week (m)	4.9	4.4
Average value of customer transaction (£)	4.55	4.44

Table 1 Key data for Poundland, 2013 and 2014

Source: Poundland website
http://otp.investis.com/clients/uk/poundland/rns/regulatory-story.
aspx?newsid=431382&cid=791

Poundland faces a lot of competition as value and discount retailers have been very successful in the UK since the recession of 2008–2009 – its sales revenue has risen quickly in percentage terms. It faces direct competition from Poundworld and 99p Stores as well as less direct competition from discount grocers such as Aldi, Lidl and Netto (now owned by Asda). Despite this tough competitive environment Poundland's chief executive, Jim McCarthy, is confident that the company's objective of rapid growth will allow it to eventually operate more than 1,000 stores in the UK alone, while also expanding into Europe. He is also unconcerned about the company's future performance as the UK's economy recovers and consumers' incomes continue to rise. He believes that the company will benefit as consumer confidence recovers, though he admits that this is 'counter-intuitive'.

Year	Median income	Increase from previous year	Inflation rate %
2013	27,000	1.9%	2.7
2012	26,500	1.5%	2.8
2011	26,100	0.8%	4.4
2010	25,900	0.4%	3.3
2009	25,800	2.6%	2.1

Table 2 UK median income and inflation rate, 2009–2013

Source: Office for National Statistics
Permission for re-use of all © Crown copyright information is granted under the terms of the Open Government Licence (OGL).

Going public

Poundland took the decision to convert from a private limited company to a public limited company with effect from March 2014. The decision followed a very successful trading period for the company during which its revenues have risen steadily. One reason why Poundland has performed well in recent years is that consumers have sought to make savings at a time when incomes have been rising less quickly than prices as shown in Table 2.

The company has received favourable publicity in the media recently due to its strong financial performance and Jim McCarthy was interviewed on BBC Radio 4. The company's share price was 300 pence at the time of its flotation and has fluctuated between about 360 pence and 288 pence since that time. Poundland's shares are recorded on the UK's FTSE 250. In 2014 Poundland opened its first Spanish store and has plans to open 10 more by 2016.

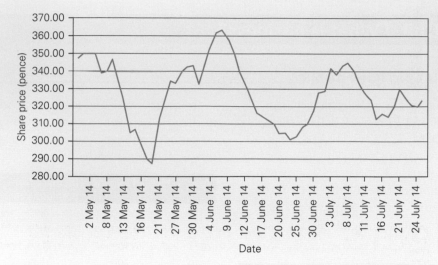

Figure 1 Poundland's share price, May–July 2014

Source: London South East Limited website

www.lse.co.uk/ShareChart.asp?sharechart=PLND

AS questions

(50 marks)

1 Use the information in Table 1 to calculate the increase in Poundland's sales revenue for 2014 compared to 2013.   (5 marks)

2 Analyse why it is important for Poundland to increase its profits over time.   (10 marks)

3 Incomes in the UK have been rising less quickly than inflation for several years. To what extent has this change in its external environment benefited Poundland?   (15 marks)

4 To what extent will a company with an objective of growth always benefit from 'going public'?   (20 marks)

A-level questions

(70 marks)

1 Analyse the ways in which Poundland may have been affected by fluctuations in its share price.   (10 marks)

2 Assess the possible impact of the changes in Poundland's external environment on the company since 2008.   (15 marks)

3 Do you think that profit is an important objective for Poundland? Justify your view.   (20 marks)

4 Will converting from a private to a public limited company improve a retailer's ability to meet its objectives? Justify your view.   (25 marks)

Unit 2

Managers, leadership and decision making

Chapter 4

Understanding management, leadership and decision making

Introduction

This chapter introduces you to some important ideas. Decision making is an important theme for the entire AS and A-level specification and this chapter will consider what managers and leaders do within businesses, including the crucial task of taking decisions. The chapter will also look at two theories of **management** and **leadership** and use these to help you to analyse the effectiveness of different approaches to management and leadership. (There may be a distinction between a leader and a manager in large businesses. The leader may provide vision and overall direction, while the manager(s) focus on 'getting things done'. This is not the case in many smaller organisations where the leaders are also likely to be managers. We will not focus on this distinction in this chapter.)

What you need to know by the end of this chapter:

● what managers do
● the types of management and leadership styles
● the influences on the choice of management and leadership styles
● the effectiveness of different styles of management and leadership.

What managers do

Over a hundred years ago, the management theorist Mary Parker Follet wrote that management was 'the art of getting things done through other people'. Since then, various writers over the years have argued that

this involves different functions. However, those set out in Figure 4.1 would be considered the key functions that are carried out by most managers.

Figure 4.1 The functions of management

The functions of management

Businesses operate in different ways and may require managers to undertake varying tasks and duties. However, these various management duties and tasks can be categorised into four basic functions – the functions of management. The four principal functions are:

● planning
● organising
● directing
● controlling.

Each of these functions involves managers in making decisions, which is a constant and central element of any manager's work.

(a) Planning

Planning is the first of the functions of management and involves looking to the future. It is the foundation upon which the other three functions of management should be based. Planning requires management to evaluate where the company is currently, and where it would like to be in the future. This allows managers to take decisions so that the company moves forward in an organised and coherent manner. It gives managers something against which to judge their decisions.

Planning may involve a variety of tasks, including the following:

- setting objectives or targets for the business or for the area of the business for which the manager is responsible
- conducting analysis to gather together forecasts of key data such as the business's costs and revenues, consumers' incomes, competitors' prices and products
- drawing up plans for functional areas within the business such as finance, human resources or marketing – these plans should fit together to help the business achieve its agreed objectives
- estimating the likely resource needs for any proposed plans.

The planning process is continual, as external factors (such as the amount and cost of available labour, for example) change all the time. These changes may cause a company to adjust its course of action to ensure that it achieves its objectives.

Planning helps managers to reduce the chance of projects failing in the future. A plan can highlight problems and encourage managers to develop solutions. It helps to make sure that managers have the resources they need. A plan can also be extended to help managers to overcome emergencies or crises – these are called contingency plans.

(b) Organising

Management must assemble the resources that they need to carry out the actions set out as part of the planning process. Through the process of getting organised, management will determine the internal organisational structure and establish and maintain relationships, as well as allocating necessary resources.

The engineering company, Cosworth, has announced it is to build a new factory in Northamptonshire. The new factory will be opened in 2015 and will manufacture components for use in some of world's most sophisticated and advanced er order to organise this expansion into a new factory the company's managers will need to assemble the following resources:

- land on which the new factory will be built
- 70 suitably skilled employees to staff the factory
- approximately £19 million to fund the building of the new factory.

Acquiring resources is an essential element of the effective management of establishing the new factory. A well-managed business will plan carefully and may seek to use a minimum of resources to achieve its objectives.

What do you think?

Should managers always seek to minimise the amount of resources that a business uses to produce its goods and services?

(c) Directing

The third function of management is directing. Through directing, management is able to influence and oversee the behaviour of the staff in achieving the company's goals, as well as assisting them by providing the necessary resources. Directing employees entails leading employees through motivation and communication.

- **Motivation** is the willingness to achieve a target or goal. Employees that are highly motivated generally perform better. This assists businesses in achieving objectives. For this reason, managers tend to put a lot of focus on motivating their employees. For example, they provide financial incentives programmes to encourage employees and also may grant them authority to take decisions to help improve motivation and performance.
- **Communication** is the exchange of information between one or more people. Effective communication can take a number of forms. It may simply be praise, or clear guidance. Whatever form it takes it can help to achieve high levels of productivity and encourages employees to use their initiative as well as to solve problems.

(d) Controlling

Controlling involves setting standards using the company's objectives, and reviewing and reporting performance. Once management has done both of these things, it should compare the objectives and performance to determine any necessary corrective or preventive action. Reviewing is a very important part of a manager's role as it allows reflection and judgement on what has been achieved and encourages further decisions to ensure the business meets its objectives.

Managers can report on business performance in a number of ways.

- **Financial reports**. Many companies publish details of their financial performance each year. This gives interested parties information on their sales, revenues and profits. In many countries there is a legal requirement for companies to report on profits or losses to assist governments in assessing that the correct amount of tax has been paid.
- **Employee performance**. Such reports may provide information on productivity (the quantity produced per employee per week for example), absenteeism or training costs. For many businesses supplying services these can be vital measures of performance.
- **Social performance**. Managers can measure a business's performance in terms of behaving ethically, minimising pollution and creating jobs.

When Cosworth Engineering opens its new factory in Northamptonshire it may need information on each of the above areas to assess whether its factory is progressing according to its plans. The control process is a constant task for managers. Through the process of control a manager is able to identify potential problems and take the necessary decisions to overcome them.

Managers and decision making

Each of the functions that managers have to undertake entails decision making.

- **Planning**. In this stage managers will need to decide what objectives should be set for the organisation, or their element of it. These objectives may relate to profits or, for some businesses, they could be about achieving social or ethical targets. They may be influenced by analysis of competitors or of consumers' expectations. The analysis may reveal a gap in the market (for, say, ethical products) that are not being met by competitors' products. This analysis will inform decision making.
- **Organising**. Managers have to decide what resources will be needed to allow the business to fulfil its objectives as efficiently as possible. This could entail making decisions about where to locate, whether to use technology or labour as the cornerstone of production and whether or not to use sustainable resources.

Business in focus: Cuadrilla explores for shale gas in Lancashire

Cuadrilla Resources Ltd is an oil and gas exploration and production company. It recently announced plans to frack for shale gas at two sites in Lancashire between Blackpool and Preston. Initially the company had intended to operate on seven sites in Lancashire but reduced this to limit any potential impact on the environment. Fracking, or hydraulic fracturing, is a controversial technique used to exploit reserves of gas held in shale rock layers deep within the earth. The process requires the injection of highly pressurised fluids into the layers of rock.

The company has to apply for planning permission but hopes to commence drilling in 2015. It expects to face opposition from groups seeking to protect the environment, such as Friends of the Earth, as well as from local residents. Cuadrilla has promised that communities near the sites will receive financial benefits to help to allay fears about possible pollution. They will

receive £100,000 for every shale well that is opened as well as 1 per cent of any revenues received by the company from selling the gas.

Cuadrilla argues that commercial extraction of natural gas from shale would see it along with its suppliers become one of the biggest employers in Lancashire, with specialist companies also moving to the region. Cuadrilla has already invested £1.5 million into its activities in Lancashire to pay for geological surveys. It expects that the new sites could create several hundred jobs directly and be operational for up to 10 years.

Questions

1. Explain why decision making will be an important part of managing this project if it goes ahead.
2. Do you think that planning will be the most important function for the managers at Cuadrilla's proposed sites in Lancashire?

- **Directing**. A central task for managers here is leading. This will require managers to decide the best way to motivate the employees that they are managing. They may decide to use money as the main method of encouraging their employees to work effectively or opt to design interesting jobs that will stimulate their colleagues.
- **Controlling**. This final function entails further decision making. The process of reviewing will compare actual performance against objectives and create two types of decision. What aspects of the business's performance require corrective action and what action should be taken?

What do you think?

Advances in information technology mean that much more information is available to managers to help them to take decisions. Do you think that this makes their roles easier?

Mintzberg's roles of management

In 1990 Henry Mintzberg set out the ten roles performed by managers within businesses. He argued that management is not about functions but about what managers do.

Mintzberg proposed that managers performed ten roles and that these fall into three categories as shown in Table 4.1.

Role	Category
1. Figurehead 2. Leader 3. Liaison	Interpersonal management
4. Monitor 5. Disseminator 6. Spokesperson	Informational management
7. Entrepreneur 8. Disturbance handler 9. Resource allocator 10. Negotiator	Decisional management. (This category of management uses information to take decisions.)

Table 4.1 Henry Mintzberg's management roles and categories

(a) Interpersonal category

The roles in this category involve managing through other people.

- **Figurehead**. Figureheads represent their colleagues. They carry out social, ceremonial and legal responsibilities and are expected to be a source of inspiration. Figureheads are considered to have authority.
- **Leader**. A leader creates and maintains an effective working environment and motivates and develops more junior employees. In this role employees manage the performance and responsibilities of everyone in their team.
- **Liaison**. In this role managers must communicate with internal and external contacts. They need to network effectively to gather information.

(b) Informational category

The roles in this category involve **processing** information.

- **Monitor**. In this role, managers search for internal and external information that are relevant to the business, looking for changes in the business environment. Monitors also look after their teams in terms of performance and welfare.
- **Disseminator**. This is a central communication role. This type of manager passes on valuable information to others in the organisation.
- **Spokesperson**. Managers represent and speak for their organisation. In this role the manager is responsible for transmitting information about the organisation and its goals to the people outside it.

(c) Decisional category

This category of management role uses information to take decisions.

- **Entrepreneur**. As a manager, the entrepreneur plans and initiates change within a business organisation.
- **Disturbance handler**. In this role managers deal with the unexpected and with crises. In the case of disputes, these managers take control and attempt to solve them.
- **Resource allocator**. This manager takes decisions on the most effective use of an organisation's resources including finance, staff and capital equipment.
- **Negotiator**. In this role managers engage in important negotiations within and outside the business.

Mintzberg reached a number of conclusions from his studies.

- Managers work is fragmented as they move from one task to another. They need to focus on what really matters and what really makes a difference (80 per cent of results usually come from 20 per cent of the effort, so try and work out what that 20 per cent is).

- Managers focus on short-term immediate problems. They are often firefighting, dealing with the problem in front of them; this pushes them away from long-term planning and thinking.
- Managers actually control little of what they do from day to day – things happen *to* them!

Mintzberg's work on management roles was based on observing senior managers, which is both a weakness and a strength of his work. He did analyse what managers really do, but did not consider the working lives of middle or junior managers, so in this respect, his analysis may be considered incomplete.

Types of management and leadership styles

Over the years many theories have been presented concerning management and leadership. Views have altered with time, and this has been reflected in the changing approaches adopted by businesses.

Trait theory

Many writers have argued that all leaders or managers should have a set of traits or characteristics, though there is some disagreement as to the precise nature of these traits. However, the consensus is that certain personality traits differentiate a good leader or manager from other people. Trait theories have developed from the concept of the charismatic individual – Nelson Mandela or Barack Obama, for example. Examples such as these have led to trait theory being termed 'great person theory'. Supporters of the idea of the charismatic leader or manager contend that such individuals have identifiable characteristics that set them apart from ordinary mortals.

One of the reasons for the decline in popularity of trait theories is that successful leaders have been found to exhibit different characteristics from each other.

Behavioural theories

These theories focus on how an individual behaves in a management or leadership role. The theories try to identify the right way of leading or managing rather than the characteristics of the person. There have been many studies looking at styles of leadership and management and considering which are successful.

Researchers at Ohio State University used questionnaires to ask employees to describe the behaviour of their managers. They identified two dimensions: 'consideration' and 'initiating structure'.

- A **considerate style** focuses on the wellbeing of subordinates. Are they comfortable at work? Do they feel at ease and well treated? Managers with this style focus on listening to employees and encouraging them. This type of manager is approachable and rewards good performance. Staff may feel looked after. However, they may not necessarily complete the task effectively.
- An **initiating structure** focuses on defining and planning work. The leader concentrates on getting the work done. They allocate tasks, inform subordinates of their tasks and monitor progress. The work gets done, but staff may feel that they are being treated unfairly.

Another study by researchers at Michigan University called the relevant dimensions 'task orientation' and 'relationship orientation'. These different styles can be analysed using the Blake Mouton grid, as shown in Figure 4.2. The vertical scale on this grid reflects a leader's concern for people. The horizontal scale reflects concern for task or production done.

If a leader or manager focuses on getting the job no matter what, they are 'task focused'. The risk here is that the goodwill and support of the team will be lost which may cause problems over time. However, a leader who is concerned about keeping people happy may create a pleasant working environment in which tasks are not always completed efficiently. This is called 'country club management'.

Another classification of styles is to consider the extent to which managers or leaders 'tell' or 'listen to' their staff. Using this approach, individuals have been classified as being autocratic, democratic or *laissez-faire* (literally 'leave alone'). However, there are many more different styles of managing and leading that can be identified using this approach. The Tannenbaum and Schmidt continuum shown in Figure 4.3 emphasises that there is a range of leadership behaviour depending upon the extent to which managers take decisions or whether subordinates contribute significantly to decision making.

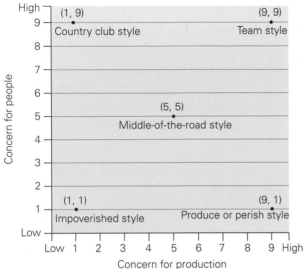

The Blake Mouton grid examines management styles in terms of their concern for production and their concern for people. You can plot a manager's style on the grid. Different styles of management include:

Country club leadership – this places a lot of focus on people and very little on the task itself. This type of leader is most concerned about the needs and feelings of members of the team. The work environment is likely to be relaxed and fun but the work may suffer due to lack of control and supervision.

Produce or perish leadership – this places a great deal of emphasis on the task and little on the people. It is likely to be very authoritarian. Employees are a means to an end; getting the job done is the key, regardless of the implications for the people.

Impoverished leadership – this has a low concern for the task and the people. The type of leader is ineffective. He or she does not focus on getting the job done or creating an environment where people want to work. The result is both work and people are neglected.

Middle-of-the-road leadership – this has some focus on the task and on people but not a great deal. It is a compromise between meeting people's needs and getting the job done but neither is fully met. The result is an average performance.

Team leadership – this approach has a high focus on the task and people. Employees are involved in the task and want to get it done. They are involved in the process and their needs are met by doing a good job.

Figure 4.2 The Blake Mouton grid

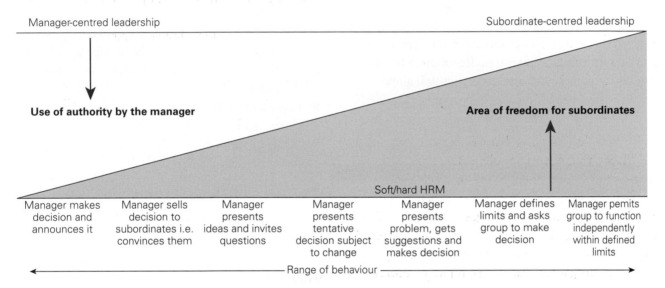

Figure 4.3 The Tannenbaum–Schmidt continuum

A key factor in differentiating between leadership styles is communication. At the autocratic end of the spectrum communication is likely to be downward only as the leader or manager 'instructs' his or her subordinates as to their duties. Democratic leadership is more likely to result in two-way communication as consultation and 'selling' of the final idea take place. *Laissez-faire* leadership may result in relatively little communication as the problem or task may be outlined, with subordinates then having considerable freedom to work as they see fit.

Who takes the decisions also has a very important effect. Autocratic managers are likely to retain control of decision making, while democratic managers will seek to involve a wider group in contributing to joint decisions. *Laissez-faire* managers tend to leave decision making to subordinates.

(a) Autocratic leadership

This is also sometimes termed authoritarian leadership. It refers to a leadership or management style that assumes that information and decision making are best kept at the top of the organisation. It is also characterised by:

● primarily one-way communication (downward)
● minimal **delegation** or **decentralisation** (one person with **authority**)
● close supervision of employees.

Martha Stewart, an American entrepreneur, built up a vast global business venture, including publishing, television broadcasting and online commerce despite, or perhaps because of, her reputation as an autocratic leader. With this style, the leader determines objectives, allocates tasks and expects obedience from subordinates. In these circumstances employees become very dependent upon their leaders, as they do not have the necessary information (or confidence) to act on their own initiative.

Organisations managed in an authoritarian style can face difficulties. People avoid making decisions so that matters to be decided are either passed up for the decisions to be made at a higher level, or decisions are made by committees, as it is more difficult to dismiss all the members of a committee for jointly making a wrong decision. Senior management tends to be overworked and large numbers of staff may leave. This style of leadership becomes more difficult to operate successfully as an organisation grows.

As with all the behavioural leadership classifications, the term autocratic manager covers a spectrum of actual styles. Extreme autocratic management will result in subordinates having no freedom of action. More benevolent autocratic leadership will allow for the possibility of some discussion or persuasion. This implies that limited two-way communication may occur.

Appropriate	Inappropriate
When a rapid decision is needed – perhaps in an emergency.	When taking highly complex decisions requiring diverse knowledge and skills.
When it is important that the same message is given out by everyone in the organisation – maybe as part of crisis management.	When leading a talented, self-motivated and creative group of employees.
When managers are responsible for a large number of (possibly unskilled) subordinates.	In circumstances in which junior managers are expected to develop a full range of managerial skills.

Table 4.2 Autocratic management: circumstances in which it may or not be applicable

Key terms

Authority is the power or ability to carry through an action.

Delegation means passing authority down the organisational hierarchy. This is only genuine if the manager relinquishes some control to the subordinate.

Empowerment provides subordinates with the means to exercise power or control over their working lives.

Decentralisation entails passing authority from the centre of an organisation to those working elsewhere in the business.

(b) Democratic leadership

Democratic leadership (sometimes called participative leadership) entails operating a business according to decisions agreed by the majority. Decisions may be agreed formally through a voting system, but it is more likely to be the result of informal discussions. Typically, democratic leadership encourages some or all of the following:

- the leader delegates a great deal and encourages decentralisation
- the leader and subordinates discuss issues and employee participation is actively encouraged
- the leader acts upon advice, and explains the reasons for decisions
- subordinates are empowered and have greater control over their working lives.

The successful operation of this style requires excellent communication skills on the part of the leader and the ability to generate effective two-way communications. A considerable amount of management time may be spent on communicating in one form or another. This approach helps to develop the skills of subordinates and generally results in a more satisfied workforce.

Democratically led groups usually have low dependency on their leader, offer constructive ideas and suggestions and derive great satisfaction from their employment. As a consequence, such groups have high levels of self-motivation and may require relatively little supervision.

There is evidence of a trend towards more democratic styles of leadership, though this depends on many factors including the size of a business and its culture. The trend towards democratic leadership has a number of possible causes.

- Management theory has developed and provided substantial evidence that people are more likely to be motivated (and productive) through the use of a democratic leadership style.
- Leadership has become more complex. Globalisation means that businesses are larger and more complicated and the environment in which they operate is dynamic and subject to rapid change. Individuals are more likely to need the support that democratic leadership provides to succeed in these circumstances.

Business in focus: Richard Branson assesses Steve Jobs' leadership style

Figure 4.4 Richard Branson

Figure 4.5 Steve Jobs

Richard Branson assesses the leadership style of Apple Inc.'s co-founder, chairman and CEO, Steve Jobs, in the following way:

Leadership doesn't have a secret formula; all true leaders go about things in their own way. It's this ability to think differently that sets them apart – and that enabled the late Steve Jobs to create perhaps the most respected brand in the world.

Steve Jobs' leadership style was autocratic; he had a meticulous eye for detail, and surrounded himself with like-minded people to follow his lead. While he was incredibly demanding of his people, he wasn't the best delegator – he wanted to involve himself in every detail, which is the opposite of my own approach. Personally, I have always believed in the art of delegation – finding the best possible people for Virgin and giving them the freedom and encouragement to flourish.

Steve Jobs was always at the centre of everything Apple did. Over his extraordinary career, he learnt that it is vital that you don't solely lead your company from a distance. Walk the floor, get to know your people. Even though I don't run Virgin's companies on a day-to-day basis any more, I still find it crucial to get out and about among our staff. No one has a monopoly on good ideas or good advice, so as a leader you should always be listening.

Of course, there will be times when strong and decisive leadership is necessary; to make sure the right moves are made. If you place the emphasis on getting the little things right, and address the everyday problems that come up, you can encourage a culture of attention to detail. Jobs may not always have been the best leader of people – which may, in part, have been due to his health problems – but he was innovative, determined and, above all, passionate. Finding gaps in the market, and creating products that make a real difference to people's lives, can only be accomplished if you have passion for what you are doing. If you make something you are proud of, that filters down to your staff, as well as your customers. Today, more than ever, you've got to do something radically different to make a mark.

Source: Adapted from *The Daily Telegraph*, 6 October 2011
www.telegraph.co.uk/technology/steve-jobs/8811232/Virgins-Richard-Branson-Apple-boss-Steve-Jobs-was-the-entrepreneur-I-most-admired.html

Questions

1. Explain the key features of an autocratic leader, such as Steve Jobs.
2. To what extent is being a good communicator, or being decisive, more important than the leadership style adopted by a leader?

(c) *Laissez-faire* leadership

This approach is sometimes described as mild anarchy. Under this approach the leader has a minimal input into the operation of the business. Employees are **empowered** to take the majority of the decisions with little reference to the leader. As a consequence the organisation can lack a sense of direction as well as coordination and planning.

The *laissez-faire* style of leadership may occur because of the shortcomings of the leader, who may lack the essential skills needed to carry out the role successfully. Alternatively, it may be a conscious and brave policy decision to give staff the maximum scope for showing their capabilities. It may be an appropriate style to adopt in certain circumstances. For example, the leader

of a highly creative team may deliberately adopt this style in the expectation of bringing out the best in his or her subordinates.

Laissez-faire leadership may be successful in the following circumstances:

- The manager or leader is one among a number of equals in terms of experience and qualifications.
- The workforce is self-motivated and understands the role of managers.
- The workforce understands and agrees with the organisation's objectives.

Laissez-faire leadership tends to result in highly independent employees who are willing to voice their opinions. Staff may be satisfied or dissatisfied with this

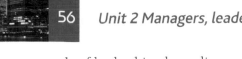

style of leadership, depending on their skills and the complexity of the tasks to be completed.

Style versatility

Building on the contention that there is not a single perfect style of leadership, it is possible to argue that the best managers are those who adopt a style suitable to the circumstances. The most talented managers might be the most versatile, able to call on one or more of the styles we have discussed having assessed the demands of the situation. A versatile manager might adopt a democratic approach when reaching a decision on a proposed marketing campaign with a small group of writers and artists but demonstrate a more autocratic style when dealing with a crisis.

Study tip

Investigate the styles of leadership and management used by senior figures in businesses and consider why they might have adopted their particular styles.

Influences on the styles of management and leadership

A number of factors may influence the style adopted by managers and leaders. Some of these are considered below.

- **The tradition and history of the business**. Some businesses have a history of particular management styles. For example, the John Lewis Partnership has a tradition of involving staff in decisions and a 'considerate approach'.

- **The type of labour force**. Highly trained, skilled and confident employees may be more suited to democratic leadership as they have the ability to contribute to decision making and can bring perspectives of which managers may be unaware.

- **The nature of the task and the timescale**. A manager does not always have to deploy the same leadership style – good managers can use style versatility. An urgent short-term task may require a more task-focused, autocratic approach. In contrast, a scenario that calls for a highly creative, longer-term approach may be better managed by a *laissez-faire* style.

- **The personality of the manager or leader**. Confident individuals who are good communicators may be suited to a democratic style of leadership. Decisive individuals with a strong vision of where the business should be going may be more task-focused or autocratic. Mark Zuckerberg, the CEO of Facebook, has been criticised for establishing a corporate model in which autocratic management is encouraged.

Weblink

Find out more about how the John Lewis Partnership operates at: www.johnlewispartnership.co.uk

Business in focus: The John Lewis Partnership

The John Lewis Partnership (JLP) has 35 department stores and 321 Waitrose supermarkets located across the UK. Annual sales revenue exceeds £10 billion. The business operates in a very different way to public limited companies. The company's employees own the business and profits are not paid to shareholders in the form of dividends; instead they are distributed to the business's employees as an annual bonus. The company's ownership structure was established by the company's founder, John Spedan Lewis, in 1864.

JLP has over 91,000 well-trained permanent staff and all of them are partners. The company's organisational structure allows managers the freedom to be entrepreneurial and competitive in the way they run the business for long-term success. It also allows the company's owners, the partners, to share in the benefits and profits of a business that puts them first. JLP's structure is democratic. The Partnership Board, the divisional Management boards and the Chairman's Committee form the management of the company.

Partners have an official voice and can hold management to account as well as make suggestions. Five partners are elected as directors to the Partnership Board.

JLP is proud of its structure. Its website states: '... as a Partnership we are a democracy – open, fair and transparent. Our profits are shared, our Partners have a voice and there is a true sense of pride in belonging to something so unique and highly regarded.'

Source: John Lewis Partnership website

www.johnlewispartnership.co.uk/about.html

Questions

1. Explain the benefits that the John Lewis Partnership may receive from operating a democratic management style.

2. Do you think that the ownership structure at John Lewis is the major influence on its management style? Justify your view.

The effectiveness of different leadership and management styles

What is effective management or leadership? At its simplest it is that which allows an organisation to meet its objectives within the agreed timescale. It may also result in a workforce performing more efficiently than those of similar competitors, perhaps measured by products being produced at a lower cost per unit, though this is only a partial measure. Low-cost production may be achieved at the expense of dissatisfied employees and large numbers of employees leaving each year. Efficient employees who are satisfied by their work may provide a good measure of managerial effectiveness.

Businesses operate with a wide range of approaches to management and leadership. This suggests that different leadership styles are effective in different situations. We saw in the previous section that there are a number of reasons why this takes place and effective managers will take these factors into account. However, decisions about leadership and management styles should not be taken in isolation.

For a subordinate-centred leadership style to be effective, a business will need to ensure that it provides sufficient resources. It may need to spend heavily on training its employees to ensure they have the necessary skills to carry out the roles that are expected. Equally, a business may need to recruit its employees carefully to ensure that it has workers of sufficient calibre to carry out the desired roles effectively. This may require the payment of wages that might be higher than those paid by competitors.

Managers should recognise that they are unlikely to be effective in isolation. For any style to be effective it requires support from others in the organisation. This support should come from those higher in the organisation as well as from those below. Any style of leadership will require support for its objectives and approach from more senior employees. They may provide the necessary resources but also backing when difficult decisions have to be made. Similarly, those lower in the organisation may obstruct a manager's decisions, especially if they result in unpopular changes. This can prevent decisions being taken which are necessary to reach the organisation's objectives.

Effective management may entail making a judgement about the skills and abilities of subordinates. If they have relevant skills and abilities then it would be effective to involve them in decision making to make use of these talents. To retain control and to operate in an autocratic style in these circumstances would be to avoid making full use of the resources that are available.

ASSESSMENT ACTIVITIES

Sections (a), (b) and (c) of these assessment activities are relevant for students taking AS and A-level examinations. The questions in section (d) are for A-level students only.

(a) Knowledge check questions

1 What is meant by the term 'management'?

2 State two tasks that a manager may undertake while carrying out the role of planning.

3 Is the following statement true or false? 'Directing is a management function which includes leading employees by communicating with and motivating them.'

4 State two areas of business performance on which managers may report as part of the reviewing process.

5 State two examples of decisions that managers may have to take when carrying out the role of organising.

6 According to the Blake Mouton grid, which style of leadership combines a high concern for people with a low concern for production?

7 What are the key characteristics of Blake Mouton's 'impoverished style of leadership'?

8 State two circumstances in which autocratic leadership may be needed.

9 Is the following statement true or false? 'Under the democratic style of leadership a leader has a minimal input into the operation of the business.'

10 List two factors that might influence the leadership or management style that is adopted.

(b) Short answer questions

1   Explain why controlling is an important role for managers.   (4 marks)

2   Explain why processing information is a vital task for managers.   (5 marks)

3   Explain why a democratic manager is likely to make use of delegation.   (5 marks)

4   Explain why style versatility might be considered the most effective management style.   (6 marks)

(c) Data response questions

Patti and Ravi Shastri own and manage P&R Components Ltd, a small manufacturing business in Birmingham. The business's workforce of 125 people is diverse: it includes a large number of unskilled workers as well as creative designers and professional managers including accountants and engineers. The company experiences a high proportion of its employees leaving each year – last year 25 left and had to be replaced.

Patti is responsible for managing one of the company's divisions with 45 unskilled production line workers and uses an autocratic style of management allowing employees little freedom in making decisions. This division has to respond quickly to changes in orders from some major customers.

Ravi's approach to leadership has changed over time. He has always been very concerned about people. He has received criticism from Patti for his division being late in supplying orders to some important customers. In response he has shown an increased concern for production and has sent a number of employees on training courses.

1   Explain why Patti chose to use an autocratic style of management.   (6 marks)

2   Analyse why managing P&R Components Ltd's workforce may be challenging.   (9 marks)

3   Evaluate the possible implications of Ravi's change in leadership style using the Blake Mouton grid.   (15 marks)

(d) Essays

1   Decision making is always the most important element of a manager's job in a large public limited company. To what extent do you agree with this statement?   (25 marks)

2   To what extent do you think that an autocratic leadership style is most suitable for a newly established business?   (25 marks)

Chapter 5

Understanding management decision making

Introduction

Chapter 4 looked at management and leadership styles and emphasised the central part decision making plays in these roles. This chapter will consider the process of decision making in more detail, including decision trees. It will also cover the factors that influence managers' decision making.

What you need to know by the end of this chapter:

- the value of decision making based on data and on intuition
- the use and value of decision trees in decision making
- the influences on decision making.

Management and decision making

Making a decision entails selecting a logical choice from the options that are available. A central part of a manager's role is making decisions. Managers are in charge of various resources (such as people, money, machines and materials) and must decide how to use them most effectively to achieve the business's objectives. This involves hundreds of decisions every week. Other decisions may relate to whether or not to launch new products or to buy another business.

The decision-making process

It is possible to identify a number of stages in the decision-making process, as illustrated in Figure 5.1.

- **Setting objectives**. This is an essential starting point because the success of a decision can only be judged against the objectives or targets that were set. For example, a manager may be considering how to increase a business's weekly sales to 10,000 units. The effectiveness of the resulting decision can be measured against this objective.
- **Gathering and interpreting information**. Before making a decision a manager may decide to gather information on the options that are available,

including the costs and benefits. Advances in information technology have made this stage easier for managers to complete and more cost effective.

- **Selecting the chosen option**. Having weighed up the options available managers have to make a choice based on the data and also on their experience.
- **Implementing the decision**. The manager will take actions such as using resources in the chosen way and communicating their intentions to interested parties.
- **Reviewing**. This is an essential stage to judge whether the decision is having the desired effect and meeting the objectives that were set. This offers an opportunity to consider whether or not the objectives are still relevant and to assess whether or not the actions arising from the decision need to be amended.

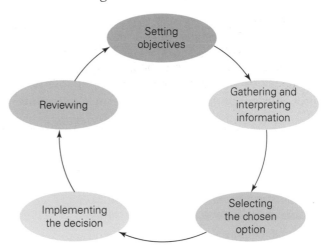

Figure 5.1 The process of decision making. Decision making is a dynamic and on-going process in which managers are continually engaged.

Types of decisions

1. Programmed and non-programmed decisions

Different types of decision have to be made. In 1960 Herbert Simon analysed types of decision in terms of programmed and non-programmed elements. **Programmed decisions** deal with problems that are familiar and where the information required to make them is easy to define and obtain. The situation is well structured and there are often established procedures, rules and policies. For example, reordering components is often a programmed decision. Employees know what has to be ordered, who to order from and how to order it. They simply decide on matters such as when and how much to order.

In contrast, **non-programmed decisions** deal with situations that are unstructured and require a unique solution. These are unusual decisions that may be risky, such as a major investment or entering a new market.

2. Tactical and strategic decisions

Some decisions are strategic, meaning that they are long term, involve a major commitment of resources and are difficult to reverse. We will consider strategy in detail in the accompanying volume, *AQA Business for A-level 2*.

Other decisions are tactical, which is the focus of this chapter. Tactical decisions are short term, taken more regularly and involve fewer resources. For example, the reordering of stock is a tactical decision. The investment in new premises is a strategic decision.

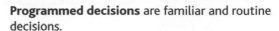

Key terms

Programmed decisions are familiar and routine decisions.

Non-programmed decisions are less structured and require unique solutions.

Strategic decisions	Tactical decisions
long term	short term
involves large commitment of resources	fewer resources involved ,
difficult to reverse	easier to reverse
usually taken by senior management	usually taken by more junior management

Table 5.1 One way of looking at types of decisions

Decision making, risks, rewards and uncertainty

Most decisions taken by managers involve some degree of **risk**. There is a chance, for example, that a decision to reduce the price of a product will not result in a significant increase in sales. There is a risk that customers will not respond to the stimulus of lower prices and that the business will suffer a fall in revenue. Risk is normally measurable. When considering a price cut, it may be possible to research the buying habits of the targeted consumer group to assess the possibility of this happening. This situation illustrates how gathering more data relating to a decision can help to reduce the risk. In this case, if the data collected suggested that consumers would not respond in sufficient numbers, then the manager would not take the decision.

Business in focus: A big decision

Maersk Oil is a Danish oil and gas exploration and production company. It is working in consortium with JX Nippon Ltd and Britoil (UK) plc on a plan to extract gas from the Culzean field in the North Sea. All three companies have extensive experience in this industry. Maersk is investing 49 per cent of the total sum. Culzean is a gas field, originally discovered in 2008 which, if exploited successfully, could provide up to 5 per cent of the UK's gas needs by 2021. However, extracting the gas will be difficult. The water depth is approximately 88 metres and the reservoir of gas is 4,300 metres below sea level.

The three companies have plans to invest over £3 billion in equipment to recover the gas and if the project goes ahead the first gas could reach customers in the UK

by 2019. A final decision on this major investment will be taken in 2015. Gas prices on world markets have fluctuated significantly over recent years, making an assessment of the expected benefits more difficult to conduct. However, the companies expect to receive some financial support from the UK government.

Questions

1. Explain why it would be important for the three companies concerned to collect and interpret information before reaching a final decision on this project.

2. Do you think that this will be a risky decision? Justify your view.

Key terms

Risk is the chance of incurring misfortune or loss.

Uncertainty is a situation in which there is a lack of knowledge and events, outcomes or consequences are unpredictable.

Opportunity cost is the next best alternative foregone.

Rewards result if managers take good decisions. If the manager considering the price cut had decided to reduce the price of the products and sales had risen substantially as a result, then the reward could have been in the form of increasing revenues and possibly profits. It is often the case that the riskier a decision, the greater the potential rewards. In 1995, Bill Gates, Founder and former CEO of Microsoft, took the decision to focus his business on the internet and received spectacular rewards. This would have been risky as there was little data available at the time on projected internet use. Since then Bill Gates has become one of the wealthiest people in the world, with his wealth estimated at $79.1 billion in 2014. In 2013 Microsoft's profits were just under $22 billion.

However, risky decisions can go badly wrong. In 1985, Coca-Cola had a 100-year history and sold the world's most popular soft drink. To celebrate its centenary, the company decided to introduce the 'New Coke', a reformulation of the original soft drink. The decision led to sales slumping by 20 per cent and Pepsi-Cola became more popular. The decision was reversed but the costs to the company were considerable.

Some types of decisions are unique and involve situations that managers have not experienced before. Accordingly, it's difficult to identify every possible outcome and even harder to establish the probability of each of these outcomes. This makes it very difficult to assess the degree of risk and the likelihood of incurring some loss or misfortune. This creates **uncertainty**. In 2013 the German energy company RWE pulled out of a project to build the UK's largest offshore wind farm. Business analysts believe that the decision was the result of uncertainty about the extent of future financial support from the UK Government for the project.

If a business takes a decision it normally involves a cost. In 2013 Jaguar Land Rover (JLR) announced that it was to invest £1.5 billion developing and building a new range of aluminium cars at Solihull in the West Midlands. Decisions also have an opportunity cost. By deciding to invest £1.5 billion in this way, JLR would

have been unable to choose a second best option, for example to develop a new range of fuel-efficient engines. **Opportunity cost** is the best option that a manager gives up in making a decision. Considering and evaluating different options is an important element of decision making. Managers at JLR would have carefully evaluated their options before deciding on the Solihull investment.

Weblink

Find out more about investments and developments at Jaguar Land Rover (JLR) at: www.jaguarlandrover.com/gl/en/

Decision making based on data and on intuition

There are many different ways of making a decision. In some cases managers will research the decision thoroughly; this means that they will gather data and analyse it before deciding what to do. In other cases they may rely on their own experience from the past or on their instinct or intuition. As we shall see, the approach taken will depend on a range of factors.

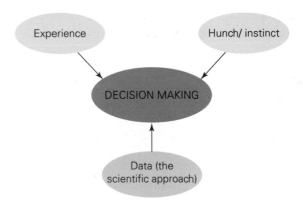

Figure 5.2 Factors that can shape decision making

1. Decision making based on data

When a manager gathers data and analyses it before making a decision this is known as a scientific approach to decision making. It is scientific because it is rational, logical and based on data. Many of the mathematical topics you will study as part of this AS or A-level course are used to help managers analyse the data as part of **scientific decision making**. In later chapters you will read about break-even analysis, ratio analysis, investment appraisal and correlation analysis. All of these management tools, and others, help managers to analyse relevant data to try and make the right decisions.

Key term

Scientific decision making is based on data and uses a logical, rational approach to decision making.

The scientific decision-making process involves:

- recognising that there is a problem or opportunity, that is, recognising that a decision has to be made
- setting objectives for what you want to achieve
- setting decision criteria and deciding how important each one is
- developing and identifying alternatives
- comparing the alternatives by analysing the available data
- choosing and implementing a course of action
- reviewing the effectiveness of the decision.

A scientific approach to decision making is rational and logical. Decisions are made based on information, not intuition. This approach is likely if there is high degree of risk that managers are seeking to reduce or if a major decision is to be taken.

If a scientific approach is adopted then managers need to understand the environment in which they operate. This means they need to consider the external environment in which the business operates and which factors within this environment are most significant for the decision they plan to make. These will vary according to the type of business and the industry of which it is a part. In the computer software industry, competition is a major influence and businesses must be aware of possible actions and reactions by rivals to any decisions taken. In the healthcare market, demographic changes may be a key factor. Managers must identify which factors are most significant for them.

Managers have a range of ways of collecting data to shape their decision making. Data for scientific decision making may be gathered, for example, through the internet, customer surveys or the business's records. Technology has made it simpler to collect and analyse data, as illustrated in the example of Tesco plc and its Clubcard on page 63. The use of technology means that businesses are frequently handling enormous amounts of data to arrive at conclusions that are likely to be more reliable. Technology makes it easier and more cost effective to collect and analyse data. Despite these advances, scientific decision making is not foolproof.

The limitations of scientific decision making

We have seen that scientific decision making is logical and rational. If the data is available and is not too expensive to collect and analyse then its use in decision making makes sense. Managers have to judge the benefits of a scientific approach to decision making against its expected costs. For some decisions, such as a small business expanding into a new geographical markets, data may simply be too expensive to collect.

The data that is available to support decision making may not always be reliable. When considering launching innovative products it may be difficult to discover customers' views on a product that is unfamiliar to them. Steve Jobs, who founded Apple, said that customers did not always know what they wanted and this could invalidate data gathered from them!

2. Decision making based on intuition, or 'hunch'

An alternative approach to making decisions is to rely on intuition or 'hunch'. This means that managers have to rely on their instinct as to whether to make a particular decision. Intuition or hunch may be appropriate when data is less likely to be available or managers fear that it may not be reliable. Other circumstances in which this may be appropriate may include:

- when an important part of a decision is making an assessment of a potential business partner's personality or character
- assessing whether an advertising campaign for a new product may catch the attention of consumers
- where sufficient quantitative data is not available or when the data that is available tells a contradictory story
- when a quick decision is necessary, leaving insufficient time to gather and analyse the data.

Some very successful entrepreneurs and managers use intuition and hunches to make decisions. Richard Branson is one manager who believes in the use of intuition. One of his frequently quoted maxims is *'I never get the accountants in before I start up a business. It's done on gut feeling.'*

What do you think?

Should all entrepreneurs rely on intuition rather than advice from professionals when deciding whether or not to start a business?

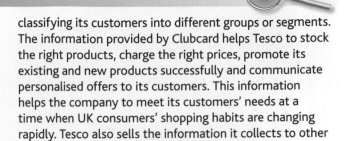

Business in focus: Tesco Clubcard

Tesco plc is the UK's largest retailer and operates in an increasingly competitive market. In 2014 it reported sales revenue amounting to £70.9 billion and profits of £2.3 billion despite the failure of its planned expansion into the USA. Over 16.5 million people in the UK have a Tesco Clubcard – the company's loyalty card. A further 27 million Clubcards are held by the company's customers overseas. Clubcard holders provide Tesco with details of age, gender and address and may also give information about their families. Details of the store shopped in, products purchased and price paid are stored against the holder's Clubcard account for every transaction. Clubcard provides Tesco with around 260 billion items of data each year to help its managers to make scientific decisions.

Clubcard costs Tesco a reported £500 million each year to operate. In return the data generated assists Tesco in classifying its customers into different groups or segments. The information provided by Clubcard helps Tesco to stock the right products, charge the right prices, promote its existing and new products successfully and communicate personalised offers to its customers. This information helps the company to meet its customers' needs at a time when UK consumers' shopping habits are changing rapidly. Tesco also sells the information it collects to other businesses for more than £50 million a year.

Questions

1. Explain why Tesco operates its Clubcard despite incurring costs each year of £500 million to do so.
2. Do you think that managers at Tesco no longer need to make any decisions using intuition or hunches? Justify your view.

Decision trees

A **decision tree** is a mathematical model which can be used by managers to help them make the right decision. Imagine that a manager is trying to decide whether to cut the price of a product or increase the amount of money spent on advertising or to do nothing. These options are illustrated in Figure 5.3.

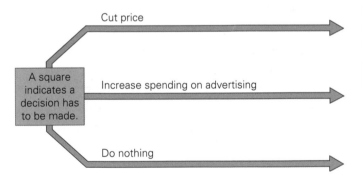

Figure 5.3 The first stage of constructing a decision tree

The square shows that a decision has to be made and the lines coming from it show the possible choices facing the manager. Note that there is a third line saying 'do nothing'. This is because managers always have the option of doing nothing at all so you should always include this as an option when drawing a decision tree.

Key term

A **decision tree** is a model that represents the likely outcomes for a business of a number of courses of action on a diagram showing the financial consequences of each.

Whenever managers choose a particular course of action such as advertising or cutting the price there will be a range of possible outcomes. For example, if the firm advertises its products there may be a big increase in sales or a small increase in sales; similarly if the price is cut this may have a big or a small impact on sales. These possible outcomes are illustrated on the decision tree as using circles to denote the existence of chance outcomes, as shown in Figure 5.4. Circles show that different outcomes are possible; these are then illustrated by the lines coming out of the circle. These circles are often numbered for ease of identification.

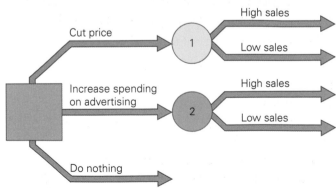

Figure 5.4 Adding possible outcomes to the decision tree

At this stage (Figure 5.4) the decision tree simply illustrates the options and the possible outcomes. To make it more useful and to help managers make the decision, some numerical data is needed.

First, in this case, managers need to know how likely it is that the predicted increase in sales will be 'high' or 'low' for each option. This is known as the **probability** of a particular outcome. The value of the probability can range from 0 to 1. The bigger the number the more likely it is that an event will happen. If the number is 1 this means the event if certain to happen.

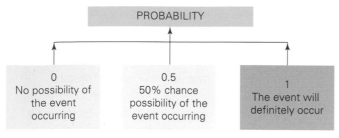

Figure 5.5 Probability

If all the outcomes of an event are considered their probabilities must add up to 1. If the probability of it raining tomorrow is estimated to be 0.4 then the probability of it not raining must be 0.6. Combined, the probabilities will equal 1 because it must either rain or not rain.

Key terms

Probability is the chance of a particular event occurring.

Expected values are the financial outcomes from a specific course of action adjusted to allow for the probability of it occurring.

Net gains are the expected values of a course of action minus the costs associated with it.

Maths moment

An event is said to have a 0.65 chance of occurring. What is the probability of this event not occurring expressed as a percentage?

In Figure 5.6 we have now added the probabilities of each outcome (shown by the number after the letter 'P' in each case). For example, the manager has estimated that if the firm increases spending on advertising there is a 0.5 chance of a high increase in sales and a 0.5 chance of a low increase in sales. In other words there is a 50 per cent chance of a high increase in sales and 50 per cent chance of a low increase. However, in the case of a price cut the manager estimates that there is 0.8 chance of a high increase in sales (that is an 80 per cent chance) and a 0.2 (or 20 per cent chance) of a low increase.

We have also added in the estimated benefits of each outcome. For example, if the firm advertises and there is a high increase in sales the benefit will be an increase in revenue of £10 million. A low increase in sales would increase revenue by £2 million.

The diagram now shows:

- the three possible decisions the firm could take (cutting price, increasing advertising or doing nothing)
- the outcomes of each one (high sales or low sales)
- the probability of each outcome (for example, 0.8 or 0.2)
- the financial benefits of each outcome – in this case the effect in terms of extra revenue.

Doing nothing would, of course result in no additional revenue and incur no additional costs.

Calculating expected values for decision tress

The next step is to work out 'the **expected value**' of each decision. This is basically a weighted average of the outcomes, taking account of the probability of each one occurring. Although the firm may gain additional revenues of £10 million by advertising, this is only 50 per cent likely, there is also a 50 per cent chance that it will gain only £2 million extra revenue.

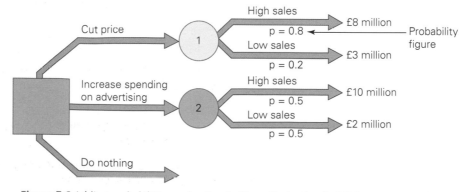

Figure 5.6 Adding probabilities and estimated benefits to the decision tree

So what, on average will it gain? Imagine if this decision was made over and over again. In this case 50 per cent of the time the firm would gain £10 million and 50 per cent of the time it would gain £2 million. This means on average it would gain £6 million.

This can be calculated using the equation:

Expected value = (probability 1 × outcome 1) + (probability 2 × outcome 2) + ...

(where '1' represents the first outcome and '2' represents the second outcome and so on.)

To calculate the expected value we multiply the probability of each outcome with the financial consequences of the outcome and add them all up. This shows how much the firm would earn on average if the decision was taken repeatedly.

For the option of cutting price we can see there is an 80 per cent chance of increased revenue of £8 million and a 20 per cent chance of £3 million rise in revenue. This means on most occasions the firm would earn £8 million additional revenue but there is a 20 per cent probability of earning £3 million. Once again we calculate the expected value using the equation:

Expected value of a price cut = (0.8 × £8m) + (0.2 × £3m) = £6.4m + £0.6m = £7m

Expected value of advertising = (0.5 × £10m) + (0.5 × £2m) = £5m + £1m = £6m

This has a higher expected value than advertising, so on this basis the manager would choose this option. The expected values are shown on the decision tree diagram above the outcome circles; the options that are not chosen are shown using a double crossed line.

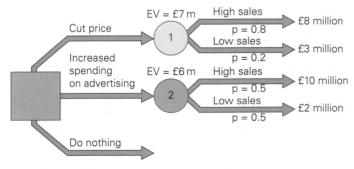

Figure 5.7 The decision tree with expected values added

However, this is not necessarily the final element of calculating and interpreting a decision tree. It is common for the various options of decision trees to have costs associated with them. Figure 5.8 has added the costs associated with cutting price (changing packaging and price lists, for example) and for advertising (paying websites and radio stations for their services could be examples). Figure 5.8 confirms that cutting prices is the preferred decision as it offers a higher net gain. Net gains are calculated by subtracting any costs associated with a decision from its expected value.

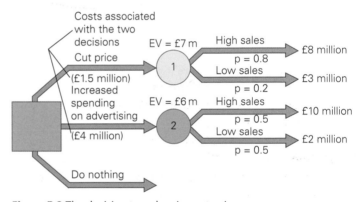

Figure 5.8 The decision tree showing net gains

Once the costs of the two options are included in the calculation the net gain from the two project is as follows:

Decision	Expected value	Associated costs	Net gains
Cut prices	£7 million	£1.5 million	£5.5 million
Increased advertising	£6 million	£4 million	£2 million

Table 5.2 The financial outcomes of the two options

Maths moment

Imagine that the probabilities for two options were different. Suppose that these were as follows:

- Cut prices: high sales P = 0.6, low sales P = 0.4
- Increased spending on advertising: high sales P = 0.7, low sales P = 0.3.

Recalculate expected values and net gains for the two options using these probabilities.

Business in focus: Calum's decision

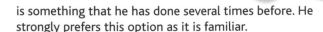

Lothian Watches Ltd is based in Edinburgh. It was founded by Calum McPhail, who still owns a majority of the company's shares. The company manufactures luxury watches which sell throughout the world at prices in excess of £3,000.

Over the last 18 months there has been a sustained rise in demand for the company's watches. This has led to a situation in which the company is unable to meet demand for its products. Calum has to decide whether to increase production or increase prices to limit demand to a level that can be fulfilled – he thinks a 20 per cent price rise will be necessary. Calum could increase production by asking his existing workers to work longer hours. Many have indicated that they are willing to do so and this

is something that he has done several times before. He strongly prefers this option as it is familiar.

However, he has conducted research among his customers in the past and thinks he knows the effect on sales of increasing prices by 20 per cent. Calum's assistant has suggested that he uses a decision tree to help him to reach a decision, but Calum can see problems with this.

Questions

1. Explain whether Calum's decision is programmable or non-programmable.
2. To what extent do you think that the use of decision trees will help Calum to make the correct decision?

Assessing the value of decision trees

Using decision trees can be very useful for managers when taking decisions for a number of reasons.

- It makes managers think about the different options they have and consider the possible consequences of each one. This process may uncover other possibilities that had not been considered before.
- Using decision trees may result in a more logical, less rushed process based on evidence rather than gut feeling.
- It forces managers to quantify the impact of each decision considering the forecast costs, benefits and probabilities of events happening.
- Decision trees provide a logical comparison of the options available to managers at a given time.

However, decision trees do have various limitations and drawbacks.

- Decision trees only include financial and quantifiable data; they do not include qualitative issues such as the workforce's reaction to different options or the impact on the firm's image.
- Decision trees use estimates of the probability of different outcomes and the financial consequences of each outcome. The value of decision tree analysis depends heavily on how accurate these estimates are. Probabilities are often estimates and this makes decision trees open to manipulation by managers determined to achieve a desired outcome.
- It is difficult to use decision trees effectively when the range of possible outcomes is not clear and those that can be anticipated can't easily be quantified. Thus

they would be less valuable in making what Herbert Simon called 'unprogrammed' decisions. Equally, they are not well suited to strategic decisions.
- Some managers may use decision trees, not because they believe in their value, but because they can be used to justify a decision. In the event of a decision proving incorrect, the managers may argue that the decision tree supported their judgement.

Influences in decision making

Decisions are not made in isolation. They are subject to a range of influences from outside and inside the business. Tactical or programmed decisions may be subject to fewer decisions but all will be influenced by the following factors to some extent.

1. The business's mission and objectives

Whether a particular decision is right will depend on whether it helps a business to do what it is there to do. A business's mission sets out its broad purpose and it may be appropriate to consider major, possibly non-programmable, decisions against this. Thus buying a rival business may make sense if the business is aiming to be the dominant business in a market.

Objectives are quantifiable and time-related targets and may be an important influence on different types of business decisions. For example, it may be appropriate to invest in training the workforce if a hotel chain has an objective to improve its ratings for customer service

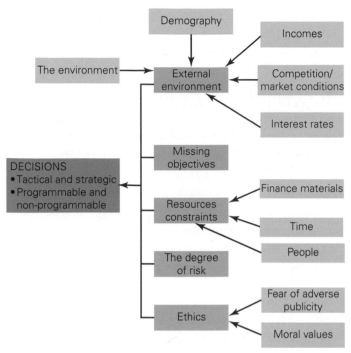

Figure 5.9 Influences on decision making

by 50 per cent over the next three years. What is the 'right' decision for one business may be the wrong decision for another because their circumstances and mission and objectives are different.

2. Ethics

Ethics can provide moral guidelines for decision making by managers. An ethical decision means doing what is morally right; it is not merely a matter of calculating the financial costs and benefits associated with a decision. Some businesses are noted for their ethical behaviour.

However, a number of businesses have been accused of taking unethical decisions. These decisions are not illegal but some would consider them to be morally wrong. For example, several businesses including Amazon and Starbucks have been criticised for taking decisions that allow the company to avoid paying some taxes in the UK. In many people's view, such decisions are immoral or unethical and this has resulted in some consumers boycotting these businesses.

Ethical factors can therefore have a strong influence on businesses' decisions especially when a business's misdemeanours, whether real or imagined, feature on social media. Information spreads quickly, having the potential to damage sales and profits. Many businesses

consider the ethical dimension of decisions carefully because they have a genuine desire to operate ethically and this may form part of their mission. Other companies seek to be seen to be taking ethical decisions because they wish to avoid the possibility of any adverse publicity.

Marks & Spencer is a company that is noted for its ethical behaviour and in 2014 it was voted one of the world's most ethical companies. This is an important accolade and helps the company to differentiate itself from its rivals. Its status as an ethical company means that ethics will be a significant influence on decisions at all levels within the company. Being judged to be ethical can also enable relatively small businesses to compete against more powerful rivals.

Weblink

Find out more about Marks & Spencer plc's ethical behaviour at the website:

http://corporate.marksandspencer.com

3. The risk involved

If a manager is taking a high-risk decision (possibly a non-programmable one), they may want to take steps to reduce the risk by gathering data on which they can base their decisions. A high level of risk will make managers more cautious and they are likely to gather more data and to seek advice as necessary.

In contrast, a low-risk programmable decision is more likely to be made relatively swiftly using intuition or hunch. Such decisions are likely to be more familiar and more able to be quantified and therefore techniques such as decision trees may be employed.

What do you think?

Should managers try to avoid taking high risk decisions whenever possible?

Key terms

Ethics are moral principles, which should underpin business decisions and actions.

The external environment comprises those external forces (such as changes in competition or consumers' incomes) that can influence a business's activities.

4. The external environment

We saw in Chapter 3 that a business's **external environment** comprises a number of forces including competition, consumers' incomes, interest rates, demographic factors and environmental issues. Changes in any of these forces can have considerable impacts on businesses, depending on their circumstances.

If a business's external environment is undergoing substantial change it may lead businesses to delay or cancel decisions. This may take place because businesses are less able to forecast future events and the degree of uncertainty surrounding a decision will increase. The response by businesses to delay or abandon decisions is more likely if the external environment is changing in unpredictable ways, increasing the degree of uncertainty. Following the financial crisis in the UK in 2008–09 many house builders delayed decisions to build new homes on land they owned as consumers' incomes were falling and demand for houses was falling as a consequence.

In contrast the sales of fair trade products in the UK rose by 14 per cent in 2013–14. These are products for which suppliers are paid a price that enables them to have a reasonable standard of living, even if it results in higher prices for consumers. This aspect of a changing external environment may have led the South African wine producer Namaqua to convert some of its best-known wine brands to become fair trade products.

5. Resource constraints

All managers want to make the best decisions. To do so, managers need the necessary resources to be available: information, time, labour and materials. However, most managers do not have all these resources available all the time. For example, they may have insufficient finance or time, or may not have the most accurate information. As a result they have to satisfice. This means to make the best decision possible with the available resources.

The amount of resources to be invested in the decision will also have an effect on its outcome. If, for example, the decision concerns the purchase of new production equipment and involves hundreds and thousands of pounds, a manager will probably research the decision very carefully. With an unfamiliar decision involving high levels of resources, managers would not want to risk getting it wrong. If, however, the decision simply involves ordering some supplies for the business the manager might be more inclined to rely on their experience and to order quickly.

ASSESSMENT ACTIVITIES

Sections (a), (b) and (c) of these assessment activities are relevant for students taking AS and A-level examinations. The questions in section (d) are for A-level students only.

(a) Knowledge check questions

1   Which stage is missing from the decision-making process shown here: setting objectives, selecting the chosen option, implementing the decision, reviewing.

2   What is meant by the reviewing stage of the decision-making process?

3   What is the difference between risk and uncertainty?

4   What is meant by the term opportunity cost?

5   What is meant by the term scientific decision making?

6   State one circumstance in which making a decision based on intuition or hunch might be appropriate.

7   What is meant by the term decision tree?

8   What is the expected value from the following situation?

   A decision has two outcomes:
   - Outcome 1 has a probability of 0.35 and an estimated benefit of £100,000.
   - Outcome 2 has a probability of 0.65 and an estimated benefit of £70,000.
   - The costs associated with the decision are £25,000.

9   Is the following true or false:
   estimated benefit × probability = net gain?

10 State one factor that might influence a manager when taking a decision.

(b) Short answer questions

1 Explain why unique decisions may be risky. (4 marks)

2 Explain two limitations of scientific decision making. (5 marks)

3 Explain why a manager might decide to use a decision tree to assist in making a decision. (5 marks)

4 Explain why managers taking decisions might be influenced by ethical factors. (6 marks)

(c) Data response questions

Helen Earthy owns and manages an art gallery, which she operates in the hope of encouraging and supporting local artists. She opened this business after many years in management roles with public limited companies where she acquired a reputation as a calm, logical and rational manager. She sells works of art that she has produced as well as those of other local artists. Recently her sales and profits have declined and continue to do so. She is considering how to improve the financial performance of her business – this is essential to maintain her living standards.

After much thought and research into the costs and benefits of various actions, Helen has been able to collect a lot of quantitative information. Based on this she has narrowed her possible options down to two: to open her gallery for longer hours, or to sell in shops locally as well as the gallery. Both will incur extra costs – but selling elsewhere will be expensive.

Helen believes that this is a suitable situation in which to use a decision tree and has constructed the one shown in Figure 5.10.

Helen has taken her time over this decision but knows she has to decide what to do soon; her accountant is pressing her to make a decision. Her decision is affected by the resource constraints she faces but also by other factors such as the rapid growth in population and income levels in nearby towns.

1 Calculate the net gains for the two options Helen is considering. (6 marks)

2 Analyse the possible reasons why Helen chose to use decision trees to assist with this decision. (9 marks)

3 To what extent would resource constraints be the major influence on this decision? (15 marks)

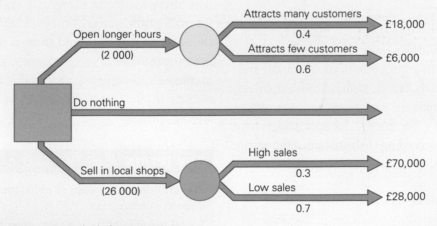

Figure 5.10 Helen's decision tree

(d) Essays

1 Do developments in information technology mean that scientific approaches to decision making will become increasingly important in the future? Justify your view. (25 marks)

2 Do you think that the external environment will always be the most important influence on decision making in businesses where the main objective is growth? Justify your opinion. (25 marks)

Understanding the role and importance of stakeholders

Introduction

This chapter builds upon the theme of decision making covered in Chapters 4 and 5. Stakeholders are an increasingly influential element in decision making at all levels within businesses. This chapter identifies the stakeholder groups that commonly exist, their power and interests, their needs and objectives and how businesses manage their relationships with stakeholders.

What you need to know by the end of this chapter:

● why businesses consider stakeholders' needs when making decisions
● stakeholder objectives and possible overlap and conflict of these objectives
● influences on the relationship with stakeholders
● how to manage the relationship with different stakeholders.

Figure 6.1 Examples of a business's stakeholders

Stakeholders

Stakeholders are individuals or groups within society who have an interest in an organisation's operation and performance. Stakeholders include shareholders, employees, customers, suppliers, creditors, the government, competitors and the local community. The interest that stakeholders have in a business will vary according to the nature of the group.

Stakeholders can be classified as shown below.

● **Primary stakeholders**. These are individuals or groups that are affected by a particular business activity, such as a decision to increase production. This category of stakeholders includes customers, employees, creditors or anyone else with a functional or financial interest in the business.
● **Secondary stakeholders**. These groups and individuals do not have direct functional or financial relationships with the business although they are affected by, or can influence, its actions. Examples are the general public, local communities, activist groups and the media.

It is also possible to categorise stakeholders as internal and external. Internal stakeholders are those that are considered to be a part of the organisation, such as employees, shareholders and managers. In contrast, external stakeholders exist outside the business. Examples are governments and suppliers.

Key terms

Stakeholders are groups or individuals who have an interest in a business.

Social responsibility is a term describing the duties a business has towards stakeholder groups such as employees, customers and the government.

Stakeholders needs

Any business has a number of stakeholder groups with interest in its affairs. Table 6.1 identifies some of the major groups and some of the needs that they might be expected to have.

Stakeholder group	Possible nature of stakeholders' needs
1. Shareholders	• Steady return on investment in form of dividends • Investment that does not lose value • Preferential treatment as customers – for example lower prices
2. Employees	• Steady and regular income • Safe working conditions • Job security
3. Customers	• Reliable supply of goods • Clear pricing policies • Safe products • After-sales service and technical support
4. Suppliers	• Frequent and regular orders • A sole-supplier agreement • Fair prices
5. Creditors	• Repayment of money owed at agreed date • Profitable returns on investments • Minimal risk of failure to repay money owed
6. The local community	• Steady employment • Avoidance of pollution and noise • Provision of facilities (e.g. parks or arts centres) for local community

Table 6.1 Stakeholders and some of their needs

Over recent years businesses have become much more aware of the differing expectations and objectives of their stakeholder groups. Previously, managers operated businesses largely in the interests of the shareholders. A growing awareness of business activities among the general public has complicated the task of the management team of a business. Today's managers must attempt to meet the conflicting demands of a number of stakeholder groups.

What do you think?

Some managers in companies consider shareholders to be the most important stakeholder group. Do you think that they are right to believe this?

The terms **stakeholders** and **social responsibility** are interrelated. Social responsibility is a business philosophy proposing that firms should behave as good citizens. Socially responsible businesses should not only operate within the law, but should avoid pollution, the reckless use of limited resources or the mistreatment of employees or consumers. Some businesses willingly accept these responsibilities, partly because their managers want to do so and partly because they fear a negative public image. We consider social responsibility more fully in Chapter 6.

Study tip

When writing on stakeholders it is important to focus on the most important groups and not to write about too many different stakeholders. You can use the concept of stakeholder mapping to identify the most important and influential stakeholders and use this information as a basis for your responses.

Stakeholder mapping

Managing stakeholders effectively is an important part of taking successful decisions. Analysing the position of stakeholders as part of the decision-making process is important and mapping on the basis of stakeholders' power and interest can help managers to consider decisions in relation to stakeholders' needs and their ability to influence it.

Analysing stakeholders in this way enables managers to consider important questions such as whether they should involve the stakeholder group in a decision, consult on their views or simply advise them of what is to happen?

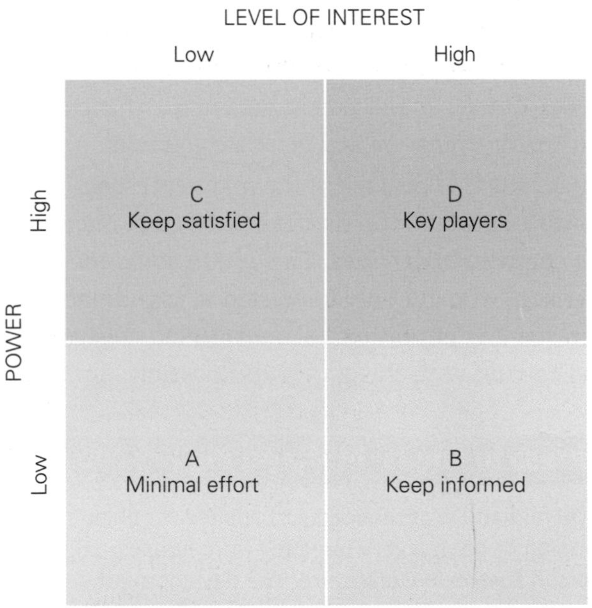

Figure 6.2 A stakeholder map

When taking decisions managers need to think about the relative power of stakeholder groups that may be affected by the outcomes. A well-organised, highly unionised workforce operating on a single site may, for example, be able to negotiate for more participation and influence on decision making than could individual employees working alone in scattered locations. Similarly, managers in a business may listen carefully to a shareholder that owns 60 per cent of the company's shares and is keen to see a good return on this investment.

Figure 6.2 shows how categorising stakeholders on a power-interest grid can guide managers on how to treat different groups. We will consider each quadrant of Figure 6.2 in turn.

1. **Quadrant A.** This is not a powerful group of stakeholders. They could be businesses that supply small quantities of low-value materials or a customer group that purchases small and declining amounts of the business's products. Managers do not need to worry too much about this group and may only update them using general communications such as newsletters and the business's website. Minimal effort is required.

2. **Quadrant B.** This group of stakeholders do not have a huge amount of power either but are interested in the business's activities. They could be a group of residents close to a manufacturing business, who are concerned about the impact of the business's operations on their lives. Managers should keep this group informed on its interest area and may choose to consult on specific low-risk matters with this group. Careful management here may enhance the business's reputation and generate goodwill.

3. **Quadrant C.** This area of the map represents powerful groups who do not have a great interest in the company's activities. This group could include investors who are only interested in high financial returns. It is important for managers to engage and consult with this group and possibly aim to increase their level of interest. Businesses that involve stakeholder groups in their activities can benefit from different perspectives and expertise as well as receiving favourable publicity for encouraging their involvement.

4. **Quadrant D.** These are the most powerful and interested stakeholder groups and are likely to have a major influence on management decisions. This group could include a customer who purchases a high proportion of the business's products and only wants to deal with reliable and ethical suppliers. Managers need to keep this group happy, possibly by involving this group in decision-making processes.

Stakeholder maps do not illustrate a static situation. Levels of interest and degrees of power may change over time. For example, the power of a strongly unionised workforce could be reduced by laws that limit the activities of trade unions. Equally, a relatively uninterested local residents' group may become very interested if a local business opts to install a large number of wind turbines nearby to generate electricity. Alternatively, rapid increases in demand for products may increase the power of suppliers if their materials and components are judged to be increasingly scarce and difficult to acquire.

Overlapping and conflicting stakeholder needs

Stakeholder groups have different objectives, which will at times conflict. Equally, on other occasions the objectives of stakeholders may coincide. Table 6.2 summarises the possible effects on a selection of

---

Business in focus: Midland Pig Producers Ltd

In 2009 Midland Pig Producers Ltd applied for planning permission to open a very large pig farm housing 26,000 animals in Foston in Derbyshire. The development was estimated at a cost of £15–20 million and forecast to create 18 jobs. The plans were rejected and the company lodged a new application with Derbyshire County Council, which in 2014 had still not received approval.

The company's plans have attracted a lot of opposition. More than 25,000 people have objected to the scheme. Local residents have expressed fears about smell and increased traffic movements on relatively small roads. Animal rights groups and staff from LUSH (Cruelty-Free

Cosmetics) have campaigned against the planned farm. They believe that it would not provide a decent level of welfare for the pigs or safe products for consumers.

Questions

1. Identify one stakeholder group in this scenario that has a high level of interest and a high level of power and one which has a high level of interest and a low level of power. Explain your reasons for your choices.

2. Do you think that the use of stakeholder mapping would have enabled Midland Pig Producers Ltd to obtain planning permission for the farm in Foston? Justify your decision.

Business in focus: Hearst Magazines UK

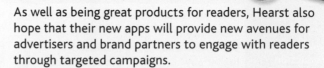

In response to unprecedented growth in mobile readership, some UK magazines are responding by creating innovative new services that enhance the experience of reading their content through mobile devices. Hearst Magazines UK has developed new mobile products for its magazines *Elle* and *Company*. It's also hoped that the publisher will be able to capitalise on this area of growth, following a 70 per cent increase in online traffic seen across Hearst Magazines UK's portfolio of titles.

Consumers are increasingly choosing to access magazine content digitally, with 30 per cent of *Elle*'s readership and 45 per cent of *Company*'s now reading on a mobile or tablet. In-house teams at Hearst developed the new products. For *Elle* they produced the Elle Fashion Cupboard, which is designed to be played with and the content is updated every 45 minutes. The Company Weekly Edit app delivers the content readers want directly to their phones.

As well as being great products for readers, Hearst also hope that their new apps will provide new avenues for advertisers and brand partners to engage with readers through targeted campaigns.

Chief operating officer at Hearst Magazines UK, Anna Jones, said: 'We are dedicated to pursuing all of the amazing opportunities presented by mobile. Hearst's work with brand partners and advertisers in this area is already achieving impressive results, and we anticipate strong revenue growth in this area throughout 2014 and beyond.'

Source: adapted from various news sources

Questions

1. Explain why the interests of customers and employees may overlap in these circumstances.
2. Was the decision to launch new mobile products taken mainly in the interest of the company's shareholders? Justify your view.

---

stakeholders arising from decisions commonly made by managers. You can see that some of these decisions generally favour certain stakeholder groups and create disadvantages for others. For example, a decision to raise prices is unlikely to offer many benefits to customers, although the rise could be necessary in the light of improvements to the good or service. However, a price rise does offer shareholders the very appealing possibility of rising profits, dividends and share prices.

On the other hand, shareholders may be concerned about the launch of new products, especially if the decision is risky as it may damage the business's financial performance. Customers will generally approve, however, as they receive a greater choice of products and the new launch may be very innovative and appealing. This decision may also have positive effects for employees if it increases the security of their jobs, or offers increased working hours or the prospects of promotion and/or higher pay rates.

In Table 6.2, the green text shows broadly favourable impacts while the red text illustrates when stakeholders may be disadvantaged. This figure illustrates that some decisions can benefit more than one stakeholder group, while disadvantaging others. However, the precise impact will depend upon the circumstances.

It is important to note however, that these effects depend on circumstances and the actions and reaction of certain stakeholders. For example, a small increase in price may have relatively little impact on a business's stakeholders, especially if competitors are also increasing prices. The impact of a price increase on stakeholders may be reduced to some extent if the product is a necessity and competitors are taking similar actions. The well-publicised decisions of many energy companies in the UK to raise prices substantially for gas and electricity have created an outcry. However, due to the nature of the products, the impact on the employees, shareholders, suppliers and creditors has been limited as demand has remained fairly constant, despite customers' attempts to reduce usage. In these circumstances, the conflict in stakeholder objectives is between those of customers and many other stakeholder groups. Energy customers want lower prices, whereas other stakeholders benefit from higher prices.

Similarly, the launch of some new products in industries such as computer games or software may have a limited impact on stakeholders as this occurs regularly in such industries and can be essential as existing products become obsolete. This may result in the objectives of stakeholders overlapping as the decision fulfils those of a number of groups.

Area of decision	Employees	Customers	Shareholders	Suppliers	Creditors
Expand production	More jobs available. Possibility of promotion and higher pay.	New products available. Increased production may reduce prices.	Investment needed may cut short-term profits. Share price and long-term profits could increase.	Possibility of larger or more regular orders. Expectation of reduced prices.	Borrowing increases, making repayment more difficult. Increased profitability.
Cut costs	Pressure to reduce wages. Longer working hours and less favourable conditions. Jobs may become less secure. More jobs may result if successful.	Lower prices possible. Quality of goods or services may be reduced.	May increase profits, dividends and share price. Customers may dislike job losses and reduced quality, reducing sales, revenue & profits.	Expectation of reduced prices. May seek alternative low cost supplier.	Reduced need for borrowing from creditors. Need to borrow short term to finance cost-cutting programme.
Raise prices	Possibility of increased wages or improved working conditions. Sales decline, resulting in job losses.	Less value received. Products no longer affordable. Competitors raise prices too.	Profits, dividends and share prices may increase. Sales may decline. Adverse publicity if this is an essential product, reducing share price.	Possibility of receiving higher prices. Orders may fall if price rises reduce demand significantly.	Increased profits may support prompt repayment of debts. Falling sales may threaten repayments.
Launch new products	More jobs may result. Higher pay and better working conditions, if launch successful.	Greater choice of products. Improved products bringing greater benefits. Prices may increase to cover development costs.	Initial costs of launch may reduce profits. Risk of unsuccessful product may damage profits and share price. Increased sales, prices and profits could boost medium-term profits and dividends.	Increased orders if product successful. New product may require different supplies resulting in loss of contract.	Increased need to borrow funds to finance launch. Rising long-term profits enhances ability to repay loans. May lead to further product launches, creating further need for borrowing.
Use more technology in production	Jobs lost as technology plays larger role. New higher-paid jobs created to manage technology.	Lower prices as technology more efficient. Services available for longer hours. Standardised products may be less likely to meet individual needs.	Initial investment may reduce profits and dividends. May lead to higher long-term profits and rising share prices. Business's image may suffer due to job losses damaging share price.	Orders received for new supplies or for the technology. Increased sales may result in larger orders. Lower production costs may reduce pressure to find cheaper supplies.	Increased need for borrowing to finance purchase of technology. If successful, enhanced ability to repay borrowing.

Table 6.2 Some possible positive and negative impacts of a range of decisions on selected stakeholders

In contrast, the decision of some other consumer product businesses to launch a new product could have a notable impact on many of the company's stakeholders and may have the potential for conflict. A new product may offer consumers increased benefits but the associated price rise could be prohibitive for many. Shareholders may be content at the rise in share price and profits that may accompany a successful launch, while competitors may bemoan a large decline in sales.

Employees and suppliers could benefit from increased workloads but large rises in sales and revenue may reduce the company's need for creditors. For example, Apple has been subject to complaints by consumers that its computers, tablets and other products are overpriced.

Table 6.2 shows that certain decisions appear to benefit particular stakeholder groups and not others. However, this may depend on the objective on which the managers' decision was based. For many years, the so-called budget airlines such as EasyJet have cut their operating costs whenever possible with the objective of increasing sales and revenue. This has been enormously successful. When the airline was launched in 1995 it carried 30,000 passengers during the year; the equivalent figure for 2013 was over 60 million. The objective of the decision to operate with low costs per passenger or flight, and to subsequently reduce them, was to achieve a growth in sales rather than simply higher profits for the business. With this objective many of the company's stakeholders have benefited from more jobs, cheaper flights, increased orders for supplies, higher levels of tax paid on profits and rising share prices. A decision to simply cut costs to increase profits might be expected to create conflict in terms of stakeholders' objectives. If successful, it could be expected to benefit shareholders, while other stakeholders such as customers and employees could be disadvantaged. This is less pronounced when cost reduction is associated with a policy of growth.

Influences in the relationships with stakeholders

Businesses take a variety of different approaches to their relationships with stakeholders. Some give meeting the needs of all stakeholders as fully as possible priority, while others focus on meeting the objectives of key stakeholder groups such as shareholders.

Key terms

Market conditions refers to number of features of a market, such as the level of sales, the rate at which they are changing and the number and strength of competitors.

What do you think?

Is it *always* easier for managers to handle relationships with stakeholders if the business is profitable?

A number of internal and external factors that influence these relationships.

1. Internal factors

(a) Business objectives

A business's objectives may, arguably, have the strongest influence on its relationship with its stakeholders. A business committed to pursuing ethical or social objectives would naturally give a high priority to meeting the objectives of as many stakeholders as possible. This would have significant implications for its decision making. The Co-operative Group is one of the UK's largest retailers and operates other businesses, including funeral services and an insurance company, with strongly ethical principles. The Co-operative Group gives its customers and employees a say in how the business is managed, seeks to protect suppliers by selling a wide

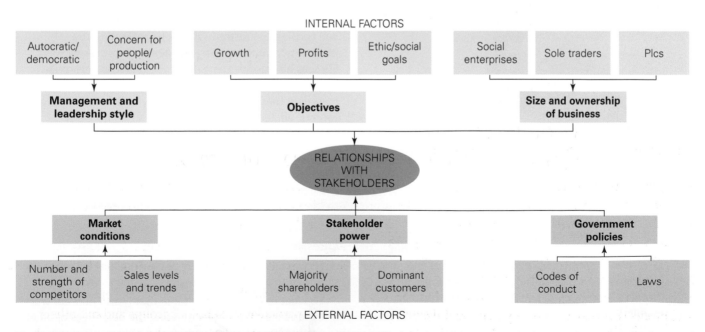

Figure 6.3 Factors influencing a business's relationships with its stakeholders

range of fair trade products and funds projects in many of the communities in which it operates.

In contrast, a business that is focused on maximising its profits or achieving rapid rates of growth may have a very different relationship with its stakeholders. Such businesses may seek to minimise costs to enable it to make the maximum profit or to allow it to offer lower prices to facilitate higher sales. This may entail making decisions that do not meet the objectives of many stakeholders. These could include paying minimal wages, ignoring the needs of local communities whenever possible and charging prices that some consumers might consider excessive. Trading with objectives to maximise short-term profits may also limit the willingness of the business to engage in communication and consultation with certain stakeholder groups. However, communication could be an uncomfortable activity if stakeholders feel their needs are not even being considered, let alone met.

(b) Management and leadership styles

In Chapter 4 we looked at the range of different management and leadership styles that may be used within a business. Managers who take an autocratic approach are likely to focus less on the objectives and needs of employees, especially in terms of non-pay issues such as the amount of delegation they allow or the extent to which employees are permitted to play a part in making decisions. Other stakeholders, including shareholders and local residents, may find that they have little or no opportunities to shape management decisions and may feel that their interests are not considered or met by the business's management team. This lack of involvement or communication can result in resentment and unnecessary opposition to decisions.

Business in focus: The Freedom Bakery

The Freedom Bakery opens in the heart of Glasgow in the autumn of 2014 with the objective of selling luxury bread and cakes in what is a very competitive market. The business plans, in the words of its founder, Matt Fountain, to 'offer a range of fully organic artisan 'real' bread, plus a few delicious surprises... to take the artisan bakery distinctly into the hearts and mouths of Scotland.'

Figure 6.4 The Freedom Bakery products

The business will be distinctive for a number of reasons. Firstly, it is a social enterprise. The bakery is to be established with an objective of providing jobs and training to those who were recently in prison. However, unlike many social enterprises, the bakery plans to put 65 per cent of its profits back into the business and its social aim is to assist offenders. The remainder of the company's profits will be paid to its investors and shareholders who will inevitably view it as a commercial enterprise rather than a social activity. The Freedom Bakery will also be a distinctive social enterprise in another way. Instead of using its social mission as a basis for promoting the business, it will emphasise the quality of its product range. This is a strategy rarely followed in social enterprise and responds to the growing consciousness of retail businesses for personal and social agendas in marketing objectives.

Despite this, Matt Fountain is determined that the bakery will pay its employees a living wage and will consider its responsibilities to protecting the environment and meeting the needs of its stakeholders. He sees his business as a new type of social enterprise that focuses on its products and the profits it can make by selling these to protect its ability to achieve social targets, while the third sector has come into great financial trouble as a result of the recession.

Source: Adapted from the *Guardian*, 12 February 2014 and The Freedom Bakery website

www.theguardian.com/social-enterprise-network/2014/feb/12/freedom-bakery-new-social-enterprise

www.freedombakery.org

Questions

1. How might the objectives of the Freedom Bakery affect its planned relationships with its stakeholders?

2. To what extent is it inevitable that Matt Fountain will experience difficulty in meeting the objectives of all of the bakery's stakeholders?

In contrast, other management styles may be based on greater democracy or involvement and a concern for the wellbeing of employees. This is likely to foster a better long-term relationship with employees but the openness and belief in two-way communication may also have significant implications for other stakeholder groups. Most stakeholders would benefit from efficient communication and consultation as well as opportunities to play a part in decision making. Many businesses profess to engage stakeholders in this way, though a smaller number do so effectively.

Satya Nadella succeeded Steve Ballmer as chief executive officer (CEO) at Microsoft in 2014 and has brought a very different style to the leadership role. Nadella is recognised for being a good listener and one who welcomes input from interested and informed stakeholders. His leadership style, as well as his calm personality and excellent communication skills are expected to have a profound effect on the company's relationship with its stakeholders.

(c) The size and ownership of the business

For some small businesses it can be simpler to communicate with and involve stakeholders in decision making simply because there are fewer of them. A sole trader may have a harmonious relationship with its stakeholders because the owner knows many of them personally and communicates with them regularly. They are able to shape this relationship as they wish without being influenced by other owners in the business.

At the other extreme, a large public limited company may develop different relationships with its stakeholders because of its legal structure. Some boards of directors may be under intense pressure from powerful shareholder groups to maximise short-term profits. This could result in a series of decisions that alienate stakeholders. For example, the company may press suppliers to reduce prices by threatening to move to competitors, refuse to negotiate with trade unions to avoid paying higher wages and acquire a poor reputation for customer service by failing to employ and train sufficient numbers of staff.

2. External factors

(a) Market conditions

A number of factors determine the market conditions faced by a business. These factors include the level of sales, the rate at which they are changing and the number and strength of competitors. In turn, the conditions a business encounters in the markets in which it trades may influence its relations with stakeholder groups. A business facing particularly intense competition from rivals may deliberately opt to engage more closely with stakeholders such as customers, employees and suppliers to establish a distinctive reputation for meeting the needs of stakeholders as fully as possible. This may help it to compete with other businesses that may be more established or financially stronger, or simply to be distinctive.

Ernst & Young (known as EY) is a large global company supplying professional services such as accountancy, auditing and advice on taxation issues. It promotes itself as focusing strongly on the needs of its stakeholders by supporting the communities in which it works as well as protecting the environment. This helps it to differentiate itself from powerful rivals such as Deloitte and KPMG.

Weblink

Find out more about Ernst & Young (EY) at www.ey.com/UK/en/Home, by clicking on the 'about us' link.

In some markets one or two businesses may be dominant, which can have implications for stakeholder groups such as suppliers. In the UK a number of large supermarkets have received criticism for imposing tough conditions on suppliers under the threat of withdrawing their custom if these are not complied with. This can lead to suppliers receiving low prices or facing overly stringent quality checks. A business that dominates a market may also be able to exploit consumers by failing to offer value for money if realistic competition does not exist. This can also occur if a few large firms dominate a market and appear to collude on pricing, for example. The six major suppliers of gas and electricity in the UK have faced claims of charging excessive prices recently.

(b) The power of stakeholder groups

Some stakeholder groups have considerable power to impact on the activities and success of a business. For example, large pension funds and insurance companies invest people's savings in a range of ways, including buying shares in public limited companies. Because of the size of their shareholding they can become very influential and managers are conscious of their likely reactions when making decisions. A majority of shareholders, including influential pension funds, voted against a pay deal for the chief executive at Burberry, the UK fashion company, in 2014. They considered the proposed pay settlement excessive and this vote may impact significantly on future decisions on management pay.

Similarly, businesses have to manage relationships with major suppliers and customers effectively. Some management teams may seek to avoid becoming too reliant on a single supplier for fear of the business gaining too much influence over decisions. In this circumstance a threat to delay supplies or to stop supplying could be worrying, especially if the supplier deals with many other businesses. Equally, a major customer could have considerable influence over a business's decisions on pricing and product range and may wish to be the sole seller of some products.

(c) Government policies

The UK Government has a substantial influence on the way in which a range of businesses manage relationships with their stakeholders. It uses laws and less formal codes of conduct to guide businesses in their relationships with suppliers, customers, employees and local communities. For businesses operating in industries that were previously owned and operated by the Government, such as rail services, energy supply and water services, these controls can be extensive, including restricting their ability to raise prices.

We will consider the impact of the law and government policy in later chapters.

Managing relationships with stakeholders

Managers can reduce the likelihood of opposition by stakeholders to a business's actions and decisions through **communication** and by involving them in the decision-making process to some extent. This approach to managing interested parties is called **stakeholder engagement**.

Stakeholder mapping and stakeholder management

Managers can use a variety of techniques to engage stakeholders in the activities land decisions of the business. These can range from communicating about

the business and its activities with stakeholders to forming a partnership to share decision making and responsibility for a particular project. Deciding the appropriate level of engagement will depend on an assessment of the power of the stakeholder group, its level of interest in the decision or project and the resources available.

Although the various methods of engaging stakeholders set out below are all valid, engaging stakeholders will be more efficient and cost effective if it is used alongside stakeholder mapping, which was discussed earlier in this chapter. Mapping allows managers to select and use means of engagement that are appropriate for the degree of power and level of interest held by the relevant stakeholder. The greater the power and level of interest a stakeholder exhibits, the more closely managers may choose to engage them in the decision-making process. Figure 6.5 summarises the approaches that are possible and relates them to stakeholder power and interest.

Key terms

Communication is the exchange of information or ideas between two or more parties.

Stakeholder engagement is a process by which managers involve individuals and groups who may be affected by their decisions in those decisions.

Consultation is a process by which one groups discovers the views of another one.

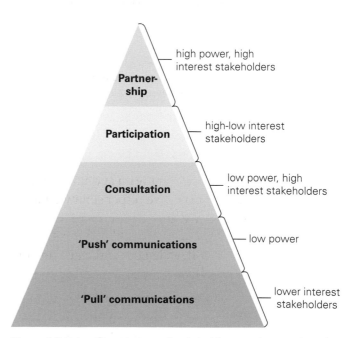

Figure 6.5 Using the outcome of stakeholder mapping to select the stakeholder engagement approach

Source: www.stakeholdermap.com/stakeholder-engagement.html

Possible approaches to stakeholder management

1. Partnership

This is the method that will involve the stakeholder group most closely in the decision or project. A partnership may mean that decisions are taken jointly by the management team and the relevant stakeholders and that the subsequent actions will also be implemented together. Responsibility will be shared and this approach will inevitably involve a great deal of two-way communication.

It is therefore most suitable for stakeholders that have considerable power and interest in the project or decision in hand. It may be worth the business concerned investing substantial resources in the partnership. A business that is undertaking a major construction project might involve its main suppliers in a joint planning and construction process to utilise their expertise and to share responsibility for the project.

Figure 6.6 The Crossrail project in London will provide a new East-West railway line across the capital at a forecast cost of £15.9 billion. Many of the large construction companies responsible for the project are working in partnership with smaller specialist suppliers.

2. Participation

This is really a lesser form of partnership. Stakeholders will still be a part of the relevant team and involved in decision making. They may have responsibility for a part of the activity and may implement that part of the decision. They are likely to be engaged in extensive two-way communication for that element of the decision or activity for which they have some responsibility.

This is possibly more suited to stakeholder groups that have high power but a relatively low level of interest. It may be used with powerful stakeholders who have a higher level of interest. For example, major customers might be invited to carry out roles in the design stage of the development of a new product. This might

be a relevant engagement approach for an aircraft manufacturer redesigning the interior of its aircraft.

3. Consultation

Consultation in this context means finding out the views of the relevant stakeholder groups. It is not unusual for such consultation to be carried out within guidelines set by the business, and with the business shaping the consultation process. Stakeholders will be expected to respond to questions and, although there will be two-way communication, stakeholders will have limited power to influence decisions and subsequent actions.

Consultation might be used when stakeholders have high interest but relatively low power. A house construction company might consult with local residents on certain aspects of a plan to build new homes in a locality, but only permit this to take place in relation to certain (perhaps less controversial) elements of the proposal.

4. 'Push' communications

This form of engagement entails one-way communication from the business to relevant stakeholder groups. Communication methods such as emails, podcasts, mailshots or letters may be used. This approach is suited to stakeholders with low levels of power and mainly low levels of interest in the project or decision in question. A business, possibly a licensed restaurant, may opt to use this approach to inform local residents of its intention to open for longer hours each evening.

5. 'Pull' communications

The final category of engagement communicates with stakeholder groups but only if they choose to engage with the business and access the communication. This would be most appropriate for stakeholder groups with little power or interest in a decision. Managers might choose this approach to advise a minor supplier of its intention to adopt a new brand image for some of its products. This is unlikely to have much impact on this particular stakeholder, provoking little interest on their part.

Summary

A business's relationship with its stakeholders can be handled efficiently and cost-effectively using an approach that starts with stakeholder mapping to analyse the stakeholders' degree of power and level of interest. The results of this analysis can then be used to determine the most suitable and cost-effective approach to stakeholder engagement.

ASSESSMENT ACTIVITIES

Sections (a), (b) and (c) of these assessment activities are relevant for students taking AS and A-level examinations. The questions in section (d) are for A-level students only.

(a) Knowledge check questions

1   What is meant by the term stakeholders?
2   State two examples of primary stakeholders and two examples of secondary stakeholders.
3   State two needs that customers may have as stakeholders.
4   Is the following statement true or false? 'In the past, managers in companies tended to operate largely in the interests of their stakeholders.'
5   State the two factors relating to stakeholders that are commonly measured on a stakeholder map.
6   Using the stakeholder map on page 71, indicate into which quadrant of the grid would the following stakeholder be classified; a shareholder of a company with only a few shares but who monitors the company's activities closely.
7   State two objectives that suppliers may have in their relationship with a business.
8   State two possible positive impacts on stakeholders following a decision by a business to reduce its costs.
9   State two internal factors that might influence a business's relationships with its stakeholders.
10 Is the following statement true or false? 'Consultation is the most appropriate way to engage high power, high interest stakeholders.'

(b) Short answer questions

1   Explain why the objectives of employees and customers might overlap if a business decides to expand production.   (4 marks)
2   Explain one reason why the situation revealed by a stakeholder map may change over time.   (5 marks)
3   Explain one way in which a business's management or leadership style might influence its relationship with its stakeholders.   (5 marks)
4   Explain why managers may want to involve stakeholders who are key players in making a particular decision.   (6 marks)

(c) Data response questions

Sinai Ltd is a construction company that has been awarded a contract to repair, renew and extend the sewer system in a large town in Lincolnshire over a two-year period. This is a large contract, worth £21.2 million, and will require the company to raise £2 million initially to fund it. Sinai Ltd will need to use the specialist services of other companies, for example, for tunnelling and for managing health and safety risks. These are likely to be very costly, though some suppliers provide important and scarce services that are essential to the project.

The company has to decide how much of the work it should undertake itself and the extent to which it should employ other businesses to carry out some activities. Making good quality decisions is important because there is the possibility of winning further contracts for similar projects.

The management team is uncertain of the extent to which it should involve the company's stakeholders in this decision and, if so, which ones. The chief executive favours inviting employees, suppliers and the customer to participate in the decision-making process, while others believe that all stakeholders are not the same and they should form a partnership with suppliers for this project.

1   Explain why Sinai Ltd should consider the needs of its employees when making this decision.   (6 marks)
2   Analyse the possible benefits and drawbacks to Sinai Ltd of inviting its stakeholders to participate in decision making in these circumstances.   (9 marks)
3   Do you think that the company should form a partnership with all of its suppliers for this project? Justify your decision.   (15 marks)

(d) Essays

1   To what extent is it more difficult for managers in a public limited company to meet the needs of stakeholders than managers in a sole trader business?   (25 marks)
2   The business's objectives are the most important influence on the relationship between a multinational company and its stakeholders. Do you agree? Justify your decision.   (25 marks)

Case study: Unit 2 Managers, leadership and decision making

Hitachi takes decision to move rail business to Europe

Hitachi is a Japanese multinational engineering and electronics company whose headquarters is in Tokyo. Hitachi is a highly diversified company that manufactures a wide range of products from nuclear power plants to construction equipment and sells them throughout the world. It is a public company, listed on the Tokyo Stock Exchange and owned by its shareholders. It faces intense competition, often from companies that specialise in particular markets such as the manufacture of trains. Hitachi operates eleven business divisions, including Digital Media and Consumer Products, Railway Systems, Information and Telecommunication Systems and Electronic Systems & Equipment. The company spends heavily on researching and developing new products and employs 4,900 people in its research activities. Some key data for the company is shown in Table 1.

Number of employees (2013)	326,000
Revenue	2013: £53,182 million*
	2014: £56,566 million
Profit for the year	2013: £1,398 million
	2014: £2,141 million
Hitachi's profits as a percentage of revenue, 2014	3.78%
Total value of company's assets, March 2014	£64,805 million
Investment in researching & developing new products	2013: £2,008 million
	2014: £2,067 million

* ¥ yen converted to £ sterling using exchange rate during September 2014.

Table 1 Selected key data for Hitachi

Source: Hitachi website
www.hitachi.com

Hitachi Rail Europe

In 2014 Hitachi took the decision to move its profitable rail subsidiary Hitachi Rail Europe to the UK. This company manufactures high technology trains, which are sold in the UK and across Europe as well as Japan. Its website proudly states that it makes use of 'the most up-to-date, modern and energy efficient engineering technology'. The headquarters of the business will move from Tokyo to London and a UK citizen, Alistair Dormer, has been appointed as CEO of HRE with control over its global operations. Relocating to the UK will bring the business's

senior managers closer to its factory, which is being constructed at Newton Aycliffe in the North East of England. This required an £82 million investment and is expected to have a very positive effect on the local economy. Plans are in hand to open a University Technical College to help to provide local people with the necessary skills to work for HRE and its suppliers.

One business analyst commented that it was an unprecedented move for a Japanese company to relocate to the UK and it must reflect a high level of faith by Hitachi's senior managers in Japan in the skills and commitment of its UK workforce. However, the decision affects relatively few jobs in Japan.

In 2012 HRE won a £1.2 billion order from the UK's Department for Transport to build intercity trains for the UK rail network on top of an order for £5.8 billion of trains that it had already agreed. This resulted in much criticism in the media and among the general public that a company that was not British was allowed to win such a large contract from the UK Government. HRE faced tough competition for this contract and others from Bombardier, a Canadian company that operates a factory in Derby and from the German firm Siemens. A spokesperson for Hitachi said that this relocation of the company would end any criticism that HRE is not sufficiently British.

HRE employs 2,500 people at the time of writing and forecasts this will increase to 4,000 by 2017. Its revenue was £1,670 million in 2014 and is forecast to rise to £2,500 million within a few years. HRE has set itself an objective of growth and its relocation to the UK is a key part of this. It is expected to bid for the £7 billion contract to build trains for the proposed High Speed 2 (HS2) line from London to Manchester and the North. However, the building of HS2 has not yet been confirmed through the approval of Parliament and a satisfactory environmental assessment.

This decision to relocate HRE to the UK is a major long-term one and some may consider it to be highly risky. The company will have carefully researched the possible outcomes of this decision and judged risks against likely benefits. Hitachi has not said whether any decision-making techniques were used as part of the decision-making process.

AS questions

(50 marks)

1   Explain why Hitachi's managers may have taken a scientific approach to making the decision to relocate its rail division to the UK.   (5 marks)

2   Analyse the possible reasons why HRE may have set itself an objective of increasing revenue from £1,670 million to £2,500 million over the next few years.   (10 marks)

3   Hitachi should use a democratic style of leadership throughout its entire business. Do you agree with this statement? Justify your view.   (15 marks)

4   To what extent were HRE's customers the most important stakeholder group influencing the company's decision to relocate to the UK? (20 marks)

A-level questions

(70 marks)

1   Analyse the possible reasons why profit is important to Hitachi.   (10 marks)

2   Discuss the extent to which Hitachi's decision to move its rail division to the UK can be considered to be highly risky.   (15 marks)

3   Assess the value to Hitachi's managers of the use of decision trees in making the decision to relocate HRE to the UK.   (20 marks)

4   Is it impossible for a business to satisfy all of its stakeholders when making a major decision? Justify your view.   (25 marks)

Unit 3

Decision making to improve marketing performance

Chapter 7

Setting marketing objectives

Introduction

In this chapter we will consider what is meant by the marketing function and what activities are involved in marketing. We will consider typical marketing objectives and the factors that might influence what objectives are set.

What you need to know by the end of this chapter:

- what is meant by marketing and marketing decision making
- typical marketing objectives such as sales volume, sales value, sales growth, market share and brand loyalty
- how to analyse internal and external influences on marketing objectives and decisions.

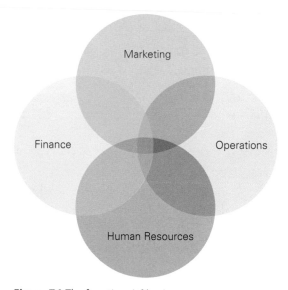

Figure 7.1 The functions of business

Marketing

The marketing function of a business provides the link between the customer and the business. This means that marketing managers need to understand the nature of the market they are operating in and feed back this information to the other functions of the business such as operations.

Figure 7.2 Marketing: the link between the business and the consumer

Marketing involves a mutually beneficial exchange process. The business provides a good or service in exchange for something else – usually money. Note that the process should be beneficial for both sides. The business itself gains from the transaction – for example, it may gain profit – and the customer gains satisfaction, for example, from buying something that they regard as good value for money. Ideally the marketing exchange is a win-win situation, where both sides gain and therefore want to trade again.

Figure 7.3 A mutually beneficial exchange process

What do you think?

'Make something people want. When you look at why companies fail it's normally because they don't have enough customers.' Drew Houston, founder of Dropbox. Do you think having 'enough customers' will guarantee that a business succeeds?

Marketing aims to satisfy or ideally delight customers so they want to come back for more. Marketing is not about one off transactions but about building a relationship with customers so they are loyal to your organisation, will return for more and will be more willing to try other products you offer. A bank, for example, wants to build a relationship with you so it helps finance the various stages of your life such as university study, getting married and buying a home.

A bank will want you to buy a range of financial products from it over time, such as:

- savings account
- borrowing
- insuring your house and possessions
- buying shares
- changing currency.

Relationship marketing attempts to build long-term partnerships with customers; it aims to retain customers and build the connections with the business – for example, getting the customer to use the business for a wider range of services.

Key term

Relationship marketing is an approach to marketing in which a company seeks to build long-term relationships with its customers by providing consistent satisfaction. It focuses on customer retention rather than one off sales.

What do you think?

Why do you think marketing managers are more focused on relationship marketing these days than they were in the past?

One of the great writers about marketing is Philip Kotler. Kotler defines marketing as 'the art and science of choosing target markets and getting, keeping and growing customers through creating, delivering and communicating superior customer value.'

- It is a science because it is data driven; marketing managers will try and make decisions based on evidence.
- It is an art because it has a creative element to it, for example, in determining how to communicate the benefits of the product.
- It involves choosing the right target markets.
- It is about building relationships so that customers are retained and end up buying more over time.
- It involves developing a product offering that is better value for money than rivals and being able to communicate and deliver this.

What do you think?

Do you think marketing should be more of a science than an art? Why do you think marketing is different from just 'selling' a product?

What is a market?

A market occurs when there are buyers and sellers. At any moment in the UK there are people who want to sell their houses and there are people who want to buy them – this creates the housing market. Similarly, there is a market for currency, shares, clothes, holidays, in fact for almost anything you can imagine. The nature of these markets inevitably varies. A taxi company provides a service for local customers, a coach company may operate nationally whereas oil is traded globally. Some businesses sell via intermediaries – for example, newspapers are sold via retail outlets whereas other business, such as restaurants, sell direct to customers. Many products are sold online but you cannot buy a haircut online. It is important therefore for managers to understand the nature of their market. Examining the particular characteristics of the market is known as 'market analysis'.

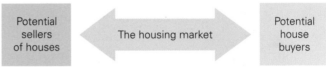

Figure 7.4 The housing market

Decision making to improve performance in marketing

The process of marketing decision making involves:

- setting marketing objectives
- understanding what customers want and can afford
- understanding the conditions in the market
- understanding what the capabilities and strengths of the business are relative to competitors
- understanding how best to deliver the benefits that customers are willing to pay for and in ways where the business earns suitable returns
- implementing marketing decisions
- reviewing.

This process is iterative, meaning that managers will regularly be going backwards and forwards from one stage to another. For example, the market analysis may provide information that leads managers to change their objectives. As marketing decisions are made more information may be required leading to more marketing analysis. The process is also ongoing. The review stage means that having seen what happened after certain decisions were made, managers may take different actions next time.

Figure 7.5 The marketing process

This model suggests that marketing decisions are driven by data. Marketing managers collect and analyse the data to make decisions. It is certainly true that if marketing managers are asking for funds to invest in promoting products or to develop new products the senior managers are very likely to want data to justify the investment. However, it is possible that hunch sometimes influences decisions. As we saw earlier, Steve Jobs, the founder of Apple, is said to have been sceptical of data gathered from customers, believing that his designers had a better idea of what people would want in the future than the customers would!

Marketing decisions will help improve performance by ensuring that the business continues to meet customer needs and wants and therefore the benefits it offers remains competitive. Marketing will help identify the opportunities, develop the right offering, ensure the benefits are communicated and that customers can access it. It should ensure the 'right product, at the right place, at the right price and the right time'.

What do you think?

Do you think there is any point in Apple asking customers what they want?

Some people wrongly say that marketing is just advertising. Explain why this is wrong.

Ethics and marketing

Like all decisions, making marketing decisions will involve ethical issues. For example:

● Should a business promote its products at children to get them to pester their parents to buy them toys?
● Should a business produce and promote a harmful product such as alcohol or cigarettes?
● Should a business that produces a new drug for a serious illness charge high prices because it can, or should it make it more widely available at a lower price?
● Should a business distribute chocolate near schools, given the levels of obesity in the UK?

What do you think?

Can you think of three other examples of ethical issues that might arise in marketing?

Key term

Business ethics refer to whether a business decision is perceived as morally right or wrong.

Business in focus: The Earth's most customer-centric company

'When Amazon.com launched in 1995, it was with the objective 'to be Earth's most customer-centric company, where customers can find and discover anything they might want to buy online, and endeavours to offer its customers the lowest possible prices.'

This objective continues today, but Amazon's customers are worldwide now, and have grown to include millions of Consumers, Sellers, Content Creators, and Developers & Enterprises. Each of these groups has different needs, and we always work to meet those needs, innovating new solutions to make things easier, faster, better, and more cost-effective.'

Source: Amazon Jobs website
www.amazon.jobs/working

Questions

1. Explain what you think is meant by a 'customer-centric company'.

2. Analyse the ways in which Amazon might attempt to meet the needs of its customers effectively.

Marketing objectives

Figure 7.6 Possible marketing objectives

Marketing objectives are the targets set for the marketing activities of a business. Like any objective, these should be specific in terms of what the objective relates to, measurable in terms of there being a numerical target and time specific in terms of there being a date by which the target needs to be achieved. For example, these might include:

1. Sales volume and sales value targets

Sales can be measured in terms of:

- **Sales value** – the value of sales is measured in terms of how much is spent on a product, for example sales of £30,000.
- **Sales volume** – the volume of sales is measured in terms of the number of units sold, for example sales of 200,000 kg or 5 million cans.

What do you think?

How could the value of sales of a product rise but the volume of sales fall?

2. Sales growth targets

Managers will not just set targets for a given level of sales volume or value, they will also want to measure how much they are increasing. For example, a target may be to increase sales volume by 5 per cent over the next three years. The rate of growth expected will depend on many factors including the growth rate of overall sales in the market. If the market is growing fast, at 10 per cent for example, it is more likely that a manager will set a relatively high sales target for her business. If the market is growing slowly it may be more difficult for a manager to increase the growth of her own sales. Of course, the growth rate will depend on the actual level of sales. When a business starts out it can be relatively easy to grow quickly because the numbers involved are so small. If sales are £10,000 it is possible to achieve 50 per cent growth by increasing sales to £15,000. However, if sales are high to start with it is more difficult to grow quickly. If sales are £20 million then to achieve 50 per cent growth requires another £10 million sales.

Maths moment $\frac{1+b}{c}=3$

(a) To calculate the percentage growth in sales, use the following formula:

change in sales over a given period / existing sales × 100

For example if sales increase from £40,000 to £50,000 this is a growth rate of

(£50,000 – £40,000) / £40,000 × 100

= (£10,000 / £40,000) × 100 = 25%

Note: if the growth rate is negative this means that sales are falling.

(b) If you are given the percentage **market growth** and the original market size it is possible to calculate the new market size.

To calculate what x per cent of a number is, use the following formula:

(x / 100) × the number

For example, if a market is worth £40,000 but is expected to grow at 5% then we need to calculate 5 per cent of £40,000 and add it on to find the new market size.

So 5% of £40,000 is:

(5 / 100) × £40,000 = £2000

The new market size is therefore £40,000 + £2000 = £42,000.

(a) If the market size increases from £50,000 to £60,000 what is the growth rate?
(b) If a market is worth £400,000 and grows by 5 per cent, what is the new market size?

Key terms

A **marketing objective** is a target set for the marketing function, for example to increase sales by 10 per cent within 3 years.

Sales value measures the level of sales in a given period in pounds sterling (in the UK).

Sales volume measures the level of sales in a given period in terms of units sold.

Market share measures the sales of one brand or business as a percentage of total market sales in a given period.

Sales growth is the percentage change in sales volume or value over a given period.

Market growth is the percentage change in the total sales in the market over a given period.

3. Market share

The **market share** of a product measures the amount it sells as a percentage of the total sales of the market. It is given by the equation:

(sales of this product / total market sales) × 100

For example, if your product has sales of £400,000 and the total market sales are £4,000,000 then the market share is

(£400,000 / £4,000,000) × 100 = 10%

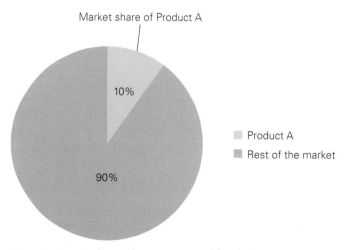

Figure 7.7 Market share

What do you think?

Sales growth
Three years ago = 3%
Two years ago = 10%
Last year = 0%
This year = −4%
With reference to the data above, explain what is happening to the absolute level of sales over the 4 years.

Market share is often given as a target rather than the absolute level of sales because it reflects what is happening in the market overall. For example, increasing your sales by 5 per cent might initially seem good. However, if sales for the market as a whole increase by 30 per cent, your business is actually losing market share because your sales are not growing as fast as others. If an objective had been set in terms of maintaining market share this would mean the marketing manager needs to increase sales at the same rate as competitors.

Managers might want a high market share because this suggests:

- relatively high sales and therefore possibly profit (depending on costs)
- relatively high outputs; this may give the business power over suppliers and other partners – this may enable it to negotiate better deals in terms of lower prices or better quality
- relatively high prominence in the market; this may raise the profile of the business, strengthen the brand and make launching new products easier.

Maths moment

If the market share of a product is given it is possible to calculate the size of the whole market. For example:

Brand A has sales of £120,000, which represents a 20 per cent market share.

To calculate the size of the whole market we can:

- calculate 1 per cent of the market
- multiply by 100 to calculate 100 per cent (that is the whole market).

So if 20 per cent of the market is £120,000 we divide by 20 to calculate 1 per cent:

1 per cent = £120,000/20 = £6000

Then we calculate 100 per cent by multiplying by 100:

100 per cent = £6000 × 100 = £600,000

(a) If the sales of brand X are £40,000 and this represents a market share of 8 per cent, what is the size of the market as a whole?

(b) If a business sells £80,000 and has 2 per cent of the market, what is the size of the market as a whole?

4. Brand loyalty

Retaining customers is often an important aspect of marketing. Managers will want to measure how many customers return to use the business again, that is how brand loyal customers are. Keeping customers is easier and cheaper than having to attract new ones and so brand loyalty is an important measure for managers especially if they are trying to build a relationship with customers. Brands are also valuable and may be sold later – the stronger the loyalty the more it may be possible to gain from the sale.

What do you think?

Can you think of the marketing objectives that the marketing manager of a hotel chain might set?

How might the marketing objectives affect the other functions of the business?

Study tip

Make sure when calculating market share or market growth that you show your calculation as a percentage.

The value of setting marketing objectives

The value of setting marketing objectives is that it helps to coordinate activities within the business. In a large organisation, for example, the marketing divisions may have many employees working in different areas, such as researching the market for new product ideas, promoting products, managing communications about the product and selling the product to intermediaries such as retailers. If the objectives are clear it helps to clarify what the priorities are (where time and money should be spent) and how everyone is contributing to the overall target. Marketing objectives will also be valuable to the other functions, as they will determine other decisions such as staffing levels, production capacity and levels of investment.

Influences on marketing objectives

Marketing objectives will be influenced by both internal and external factors.

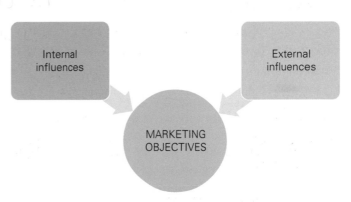

Figure 7.8 Internal and external influences on marketing objectives

Business in focus: The UK soft drinks market

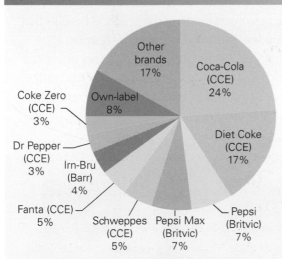

Figure 7.9 Market share of leading brands in the UK retail carbonated drinks market by value, 2013–14
Source: Mintel, Carbonated Soft Drinks, June 2014

The UK carbonated drinks market refers to fizzy soft drinks such as Coca-Cola and Pepsi. The data in Figure 7.9 shows the market share of different brands in the UK carbonated (fizzy) soft drinks market.

Questions

1. Calculate the overall market share of Coca-Cola Enterprises (CCE).
2. Explain what you think is meant by 'own label' products.
3. If you were a new business launching a brand in this market, what do you think would be a realistic objective for market share by the end of the first five years? Explain your reasoning.

Maths moment

$$\frac{1+b}{c}=3$$

Index numbers

Data, such as marketing research information, is often provided in the form of index numbers. Index numbers show relative changes – they show the percentage changes in data and this saves the reader having to work this out for herself.

Index numbers have a base point and then shows how data has changed relative to this point.

For example, in the table below the index data shows the sales of a product:

Year	Sales
2012 (base year)	100
2013	105
2014	120
2015	90

Table 7.1

We can see that relative to 2012 (which is our base i.e. our starting level of sales):

- sales have increased by 5% in 2013. There is an increase of 5 out of 100, i.e. 5%
- sales have increased by 20% in 2014. There is an increase of 20 out of 100, i.e. 20%
- sales have decreased by 10% in 2015. There is a fall of 10 out of 100, i.e. 10%.

Notice that we do not know what the value of the sales is, what we do know is the percentage change.

Look at the data below which relates to the UK breakfast cereal market:

	Total volume (m kg)	Index	Total value at current prices (£m)	Index
2011	453	109	1,530	95
2012	452	109	1,591	99
2013	436	105	1,633	101
2014	416	100	1,614	100
2015 (forecast)	409	98	1,649	102
2016 (forecast)	400	96	1,644	102
2017 (forecast)	392	94	1,669	103

Table 7.2 UK value and volume sales of the total breakfast cereals market, 2011–17

Source: Mintel, Breakfast Cereal, August 2014

The base year is 2014.

This data shows:

- The volume of sales was 9% higher in 2011 than in 2014.
- The volume of sales is forecast to be 6% lower in 2017 than in 2014.
- The value of sales was 5% lower in 2011 than in 2014. It is predicted to be 3% higher in 2017 than in 2014.

This data suggests a fall in the volume of sales but an increase in the value of sales of breakfast cereals. This is because of rising prices.

Index numbers therefore save the reader time because the percentage change in the data, relative to the base (starting) point, is shown.

Internal influences

The **internal influences** on the marketing objectives and decisions set by managers include:

- the overall strategy of the business. If this is focused on growth, for example, the target level of sales might be higher than if the strategy was to maintain the size of the business.
- the ambitions of managers. Ambitious and optimistic managers may set high and demanding marketing objectives because they want to push the business forward.
- the existing position of the business. For example, if sales are £2 million then an increase to £2.2 million within a year may be a more realistic objective than if sales at the moment are £2,000. If the brand reputation is strong then a customer satisfaction target of 97 per cent may be realistic but if the brand reputation is weak then it may be unrealistic. The objectives may be less demanding.
- the amount the business can produce. If the capacity of a business is 200,000 units a year it cannot set a sales target of more then this unless it outsources some of its production.
- finance. For example, the amount of promotional activity to make customers aware of the product's benefits that can be undertaken may be limited by finance.
- the employees of the business. This may affect the quality of design or customer service or the range of services that can be provided and therefore the target level of sales.

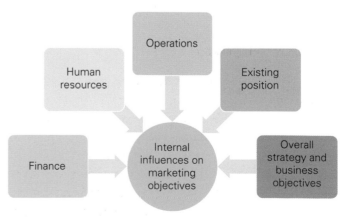

Figure 7.10 Internal influences

Key terms

Internal influences on marketing objectives and decisions refer to factors within the business such as employees and operational resources.

External influences on marketing objectives and decisions refer to factors outside of the business such as the state of the economy.

External influences

The **external influences** on marketing objectives and decisions include changes in the world in which marketing operates will affect all of its activities, from who to target and how to communicate with them to what it actually offers. For example, a business such as eBay was only founded in 1995 and could not have existed much earlier than that because the technology did not exist. It now has 149 million active buyers globally and more than 700 million items listed for sale on it. Skype, iTunes and Blinkbox are only possible due to technological change; the same is true of Google Adwords and online payments.

As technology has spread, with more online buyers, this has enabled these businesses to set ever higher sales targets.

Changes in the external business environment can be analysed using the PEST-C framework. These letters refer to Political (including legal), Economic, Social, Technological and Competitive factors.

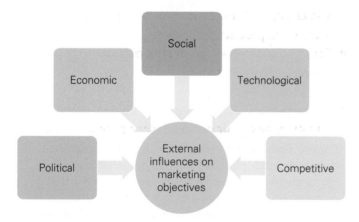

Figure 7.11 External influences

- **The political and legal environment** determines what is allowed by law. For example, in recent years there have been increasing restrictions on the packaging, promotion and distribution of cigarettes. At the same time, political decisions have led to an increase in the size of the European Union, which results in more countries where trade can occur easily, opening up new markets. This can affect marketing targets that relate to what is sold where.

Figure 7.12 Cigarettes with plain packaging

- **Economic change**. For example, changes in the economy affect how much customers can afford to pay for items. In 2008 the UK economy went into a recession, which meant that incomes fell; many customers switched to lower priced supermarkets such as Aldi and Lidl and away from Waitrose and Tesco. **Globalisation** and the growth of emerging economies such as Indonesia, Nigeria, Turkey and Vietnam create new growth markets to target. Again this will influence marketing objectives such as the expected sales in different markets.
- **Social change** is affecting customers' views of what is acceptable and what they expect from product and a producer. For example, there has been growing interest in the ethics of businesses; there is greater concern over issues such as how employees are treated in the business, suppliers and how the product is produced – for example, is it produced in an environmentally friendly manner? There has also been population growth, resulting in more movement to the cities in many countries and an ageing population in some regions, all of which lead to changes in demand patterns. All of these affect the likely targets set by marketing managers for different products in different markets.

What do you think?

What changes do you think there might be in demand patterns if there is an ageing population in a country?

- **Technological change** is affecting how businesses communicate with customers and track their behaviour, what they are offering them, how customers order products, how products are reviewed and even where ideas for new products come from as customers are invited to submit their own designs and ideas.

- **The competitive environment.** The degree of competition in a market affects the range of options open to customers and what a business might have to offer to match its rivals. For example, the internet is making it easier for customers to find alternatives which might force some businesses to be more price competitive and improve the benefits they offer. The travel and insurance industries have been transformed by the competition created by the internet. Going online reduces costs for many businesses and enables them to reach wider audiences globally.

Key term

Globalisation refers to the increasing trade between countries and the growing internationalisation of businesses.

The PEST-C framework is useful when analysing an industry and will highlight the specific issues within that industry. If we take the housing market, which we introduced earlier, factors in the external environment that might affect marketing objectives and decision making include:

- **Political/legal**:
  - laws on how contracts are enforced
  - regulations on the information sellers must provide to potential buyers
  - regulations on where houses can be built and how they can be designed.

- **Economic**:
  - the cost of borrowing money for a mortgage (which is a loan to buy a house); this will affect the number of people able to buy a house
  - incomes in the economy and the number of people in work; this will affect demand.
- **Social patterns.** These changes affect the typical size of house required (for example, a family house or a retirement home) and the number of people looking for houses. Urbanisation occurs when people move to the cities from the countryside, which affects the demand for housing in different areas.
- **Technological.** Technological change will make it easier to promote your house for sale online and for buyers to find information on the houses that are available and on what the area is like.

- **Competitive.** If more building businesses enter this market this will put pressure on existing firms to offer better value housing.

What do you think?

Can you think of any more external factors that might influence the marketing activities of businesses in the housing market? Which of the PEST-C headings do they fit under?

What do you think?

Choose a product you know such as cars, football teams or mobile phones. What do you think are the key factors in the external business environment that might affect the marketing of this product? What factors might change for a business to set an objective of increasing sales by 30 per cent in the next year? What factors might make a business set an objective of reducing sales?

Business in focus: Changes in the US retail industry

US revenues, $ billion

■ New to top 10 in 2012
■ Dropped out of top 10 by 2012

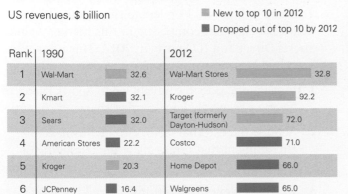

Rank	1990		2012	
1	Wal-Mart	32.6	Wal-Mart Stores	32.8
2	Kmart	32.1	Kroger	92.2
3	Sears	32.0	Target (formerly Dayton-Hudson)	72.0
4	American Stores	22.2	Costco	71.0
5	Kroger	20.3	Home Depot	66.0
6	JCPenney	16.4	Walgreens	65.0
7	Safeway	14.9	CVS Caremark	63.7
8	Dayton-Hudson	14.7	Lowe's	49.4
9	A&P	11.4	Safeway	37.5
10	May Department Stores	10.1	Amazon.com	34.4

Figure 7.13 shows how some retailers maintain their position in markets, while others gain market share and some lose.

Questions

1. Think of the UK market – can you identify similar firms in the UK?

2. What do you think might have determined the winners and losers between 1990 and 2012?

Figure 7.13 The top 10 US retailers in 1990 and 2012

Source: Stores US Securities and Exchange Commission filings; McKinsey analysis

www.mckinsey.com/insights/consumer_and_retail/how_retailers_can_keep_up_with_consumers

ASSESSMENT ACTIVITIES

Sections (a), (b) and (c) of these assessment activities are relevant for students taking AS and A-level examinations. The questions in section (d) are for A-level students only.

(a) Knowledge check questions

1 Explain two ways of measuring the size of a market.

2 State two possible marketing objectives.

3 State two external factors that might influence the marketing activities of a business.

4 State two internal factors that might influence the marketing activities of a business.

5 Sales last year were £60,000; sales this year are £80,000. Calculate the sales growth.

6 Give the equation to calculate market share.

7 If the growth rate of a market is –2 per cent what would this mean?

8 If sales rise from £250,000 to £300,000 what is the sales growth rate?

9 Sales growth last year was 3 per cent. This year it is 1 per cent. Sales have fallen. True or false? Explain your answer

10 If the market share of a business increases, its sales must be increasing. True or false? Explain your answer.

(b) Short answer questions

1 Explain one way in which brand loyalty might benefit a clothes retailer. (5 marks)

2 Explain one external factor that might influence the marketing objectives set by a tobacco business. (5 marks)

3 Explain one internal factor that might influence the target number of visitors at an entertainment park. (5 marks)

4 Explain one factor that might affect the target market share of a business entering the car insurance market in the UK. (5 marks)

5 Explain how effective relationship marketing might benefit a bank. (5 marks)

(c) Data response questions

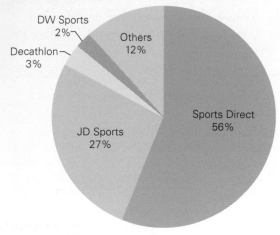

Figure 7.14 Consumer expenditure through sports goods retailers, by retailer share, 2013

Source: Mintel, Sports Goods Retailing, July 2014

The data in Figure 7.14 refers to the sports goods market. Businesses competing in this market include Sports Direct and JD Sports in 2013. This market has been highly competitive in recent years.

1   Explain one possible advantage to Sports Direct of having a relatively large market share.   (6 marks)

2   Analyse the external factors in the business environment that might affect the marketing of sports good retailers   (9 marks)

3   To what extent do you think it would be easy to enter this market and gain a 5 per cent market share within three years? Justify your answer.   (15 marks)

(d) Essays

1   To what extent do you think the main influence on the marketing objective of a business such as Coca-Cola is likely to be competitors' actions? Justify your answer.   (25 marks)

2   To what extent do you think that marketing managers should worry about the ethics of their decisions?   (25 marks)

Chapter 8

Understanding markets and customers

Introduction

In this chapter we will consider how businesses gather information to inform their marketing decision making. Making better decisions enables a business to be more competitive. We will examine the difference between primary and secondary marketing research and the use of techniques such as correlation and extrapolation.

What you need to know by the end of the chapter:

- what is meant by marketing research
- how to compare and contrast the value of primary and secondary marketing research
- the difference between qualitative and quantitative data
- the meaning of market mapping
- how to evaluate the value of sampling
- how to analyse the significance of positive and negative correlation
- the significance of confidence intervals and extrapolation
- how to analyse the value of technology in gathering and analysing data for marketing decision making
- how to interpret price and income elasticity data and assess the value of these concepts
- how data is used in decision making and planning.

Marketing research

To decide what are realistic marketing objectives and how best to achieve them a business needs to understand its market. Managers will want information to reduce the risk of making decisions. To gather this information they will use marketing research. Marketing research involves gathering and analysing data relevant to the marketing process.

Marketing research may be used to:

- analyse the existing position of the business; for example the size of the market, trends in the market and the sales and strengths of competitors

- decide on possible marketing objectives
- identify possible actions that could be taken
- decide on the actions to take and how best to implement them
- assess how effective marketing decisions have been.

Marketing research and decision making

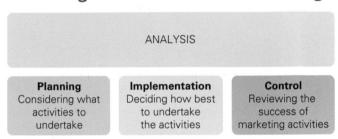

Figure 8.1 The uses of market research in decision making

The marketing research process

The process of **marketing research** is to:

- identify and define what it is the business wants to find out
- decide on how to gather the data (this might depend on factors such as the amount of money the business is willing to spend on gathering data, how long it has to gather the information and how accurate the findings have to be)
- gather the data
- analyse the data
- interpret the findings and present them to inform decision making.

Key term

Marketing research involves gathering and analysing data relevant to the marketing process. According to the American Marketing Association 'Marketing research specifies the information required to address marketing issues, designs the method for collecting information, manages and implements the data collection process, analyses the results, and communicates the findings and their implications.'

Business in focus: The UK food retail market

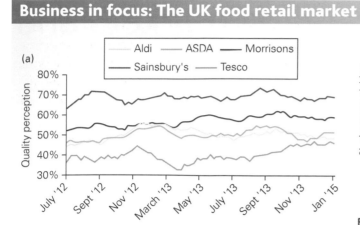

(a)

Figure 8.2a Quality perception of major discounters and traditional supermarkets

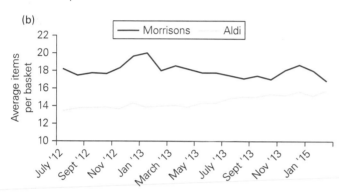

(b)

Figure 8.2b Average number of items in basket, discounters vs. traditional supermarkets

Source: Morrisons Interim Report
www.morrisons-corporate.com/Documents/Corporate%20documents/
MorrisonsPrelims2013-14_web_v2.pdf

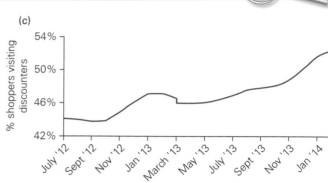

(c)

Figure 8.2c Percentage of consumers visiting discount supermarkets in 2012–14

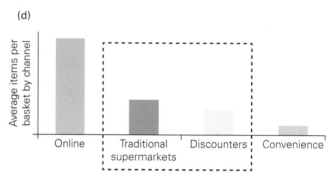

(d)

Figure 8.2d Average number of items in basket, by channel

The data in Figures 8.2a–d was produced by the food retailer, Morrisons, and published on its website.

Questions

1. Summarise the changes that have occurred in food retail market over this period.
2. How do you think these changes might affect the marketing decisions of Morrisons?

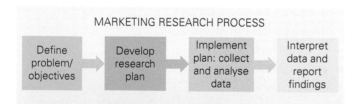

MARKETING RESEARCH PROCESS

Define problem/objectives → Develop research plan → Implement plan: collect and analyse data → Interpret data and report findings

Figure 8.3 The marketing research process

Marketing research and the customer

One of the purposes of marketing research is to understand customers in detail.

Marketing research should provide an insight on the following:

- Who buys? The person who buys the product may not be the same as the person who consumes. For example, parents may buy food, clothes, shoes and toys for their children. Marketing managers need to understand who is involved in the buying process.
- What they are buying? Sometimes this may not be as obvious as it may seem at first. Bicycles and perfume may be bought mainly as presents, newspapers to find out about sport, chewing gum to help give up smoking.
- When are they buying? For example, some products may be seasonal and bought at certain times of year (such as suncream and turkeys); some products may be bought on specific occasions (such as flowers on Mother's Day and Valentine's Day and laptops before the university year starts). Market researchers will also be interested in when you first start thinking about a purchase – for example, you may look at universities in the first year of sixth form – as this means they know when to target you in terms of communications.

Figure 8.4 Understanding the consumer

- Why are they buying? There are many reasons why people buy products. Some people buy chocolate to reward themselves; others buy chocolates because they are feeling unhappy and want to cheer themselves up.
- Who do they ask for information before buying? If you were buying a holiday, for example, who would you ask for information? Where would you search for reviews? When choosing a university, where would you look for information and whose opinion would you value?
- Where are they buying? This relates to how to distribute products. Do customers prefer to buy online or in store – are there some things you prefer to by in an outlet? Where do they expect to find the products? How far would they travel to buy them?
- What factors influence the decision to buy? The buying process for some products can be quite complex and many different factors are involved. Think about buying a new car. You might consider

Business in focus: When do people consume bottled water in the UK?

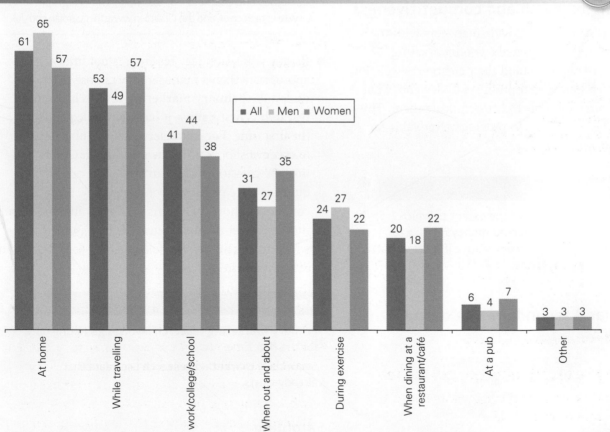

Figure 8.5 When people consume bottled water

Source: Mintel, Bottled Water, March 2014

Questions

1. What factors do you think are likely to affect sales of bottled water?

2. Analyse how the information above might be of value to the managers of a business producing bottled water when making marketing decisions.

the price, the fuel consumption, the way it looks, the brand reputation, the colour, the boot space, the number of people it fits in and many other factors. As shown in Table 8.1, some of the different factors are organised under different categories:

- Personal: Is it a brand you want to be associated with?
- Economical: What will it cost to buy and run? What can it be sold for later (residual value)?
- Social: How will the car be viewed by others? Is it fashionable? Is it a well-known brand?
- Technical: What are the features and specifications of the car? Will it last?

Personal	Economic	Social	Technical
Self image	Price	Status	Reliability
Ethics	Value for money	Social norms	How long it lasts
Emotional links	Running costs	Fashion	Features and specifications
			How it performs

Table 8.1 Factors that influence customer decisions on whether to buy

Marketing research and competitiveness

Marketing research can provide managers with the information they need to make good marketing decisions. If they understand their customers well, for example, they know what products to develop, what benefits to offer and how to communicate them. This should enable a business to provide better value for money than competitors.

Key term

Competitiveness measures the extent to which a business offers good value for money relative to competitors. A business is competitive if it offers better value for money than rivals.

Primary and secondary marketing research

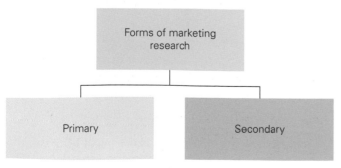

Figure 8.6 Forms of marketing research

To gather data, marketing research may be:

- **Secondary.** This type of research uses existing data. For example, managers may learn about a market by reading newspapers, looking at the annual reports produced by companies or studying information produced by the government. **Secondary marketing research**, is a good place to start because it is already available and therefore usually cheap. However, it may not be in the exact format you require – it may be out of date or in a different format from the one you want, for example you are interested in the sales of houses in Oxford but can only find secondary data for the South East as a whole.

Weblinks

An excellent website for information about the UK is the Office for National Statistics – it has a wealth of information about UK households and businesses: www.ons.gov.uk/ons/index.html

National newspapers can provide useful information on businesses and markets. For example, *The Telegraph* www.telegraph.co.uk and the *Guardian* www.theguardian.com/uk

- **Primary.** If secondary research is not fully appropriate then a manager may choose to undertake **primary marketing research**. Primary research is first hand – it has been collected for the first time. For example, managers may decide to observe shoppers' behaviour though CCTV, interview customers face to face, send out a questionnaire or have an online survey. Many film companies show their films to sample audiences and this can affect the final cut of the film; sometimes whole scenes are re-shot following the feedback from this primary research.

Key terms

Primary marketing research involves gathering data for the first time.

Secondary marketing research uses data that already exists.

Sampling

All of the people that a manager might want to interview are known collectively as the **'target population'**. However, in most cases it will not be possible to interview or survey all of the target population. This is because it is likely to take too long and be too expensive. As a result managers may choose a **sample**; this involves selecting a representative group of people or items from the target population.

The value of the sampling

Sampling provides an insight into a market. It saves money because the whole of the target population does not have to be considered. It is also quicker than trying to test or talk to all the target population. You will often see on the news on Election Day that a sample of people have been interviewed about their voting intentions and based on this sample forecasts are made about all the voting population.

However there is a risk because you are relying on a sample and if this research is undertaken badly the sample may not in fact be representative. In some cases political forecasters have made incorrect predictions about who was going to win an election because of who they surveyed or the way the research was carried out.

The value of sampling therefore depends on how it is conducted. For example it will depend on:

- how the people or items are selected. For example, if you only ask your friends what they think of your new business idea you may get biased answers; if you only ask men when most of your customers are women this might also be misleading. The sample must be chosen carefully to represent the target population
- how the sampling is conducted. For example, questions may be asked in a way which encourages people to give a certain type of answer ('Do you think this product is a) great? b) fantastic? will lead to unreliable results).
- the sample size: the smaller the sample size the less you will be able to be sure that the results reflect the target population as a whole. If you only asked three men in the UK what British males in general thought about something, your findings are unlikely to be representative. The bigger the sample size the more reliable the findings might be.

Key terms

Target population is all the items or people that are relevant to the market research being undertaken. For example, a business might be interested in all 16-to-18-year-olds in the UK.

A **sample** is a group of people or items selected to represent the target population.

Types of data: quantitative and qualitative data

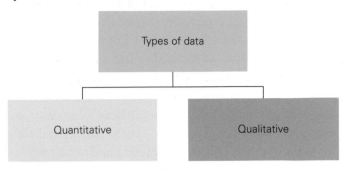

Figure 8.7 Market research can produce quantitative and qualitative data.

- **Quantitative data**. This provides data in a numerical form, for example '70 per cent of people would recommend this product', or '96 per cent of people use this product at least once a year'. It is often gathered through surveys and its value is that it can show what is happening in a market in a measurable format, for example 'sales have increased 30 per cent this year'. However, it may not necessarily explain why changes have happened.
- **Qualitative data**. This is data that is not in a numerical form and is often descriptive – it can describe why things have happened. This type of data is often used to provide information on peoples' emotions and feelings. It is data that provides an insight into why people do things or what they think about a product. However, it is usually gathered through open questions in in-depth interviews with a few people; it is therefore is often not statistically reliable. The findings are often rather open ended and not easily measurable – for example, you might have a whole series of different views about a brand. Qualitative data is often a good starting point with primary research because it shows what people are thinking and why they do things; the key issues raised by in-depth interviews can then be examined in more detail with quantitative analysis.

Market mapping

Part of marketing research should involve understanding how a product or brand is perceived relative to a competitors' brand – is it seen as more of a youth brand? More upmarket? More ethical? More reliable? Understanding these perceptions is important, either to reinforce them or to challenge them. People may perceive your products to be expensive and you want to challenge this and communicate that they are not. People may see you as the 'original' and managers want to reinforce this to highlight the differences between their products and others. One technique to identify what customers think of a brand is known as **market mapping**. Customers are asked to rate a group of products in a market in terms of different characteristics. Typically these are rated on the basis of two scales, such as low price to high price and traditional to modern, as shown in Figure 8.8. The criteria used will depend on the particular market being examined and the issues that matter to customers in these markets.

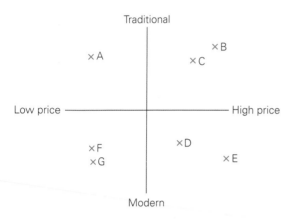

Figure 8.8 Market mapping

Market mapping may also be used by businesses thinking of setting up in a market as it might help them decide where they want to fit in the market relative to existing producers.

Key term

Market mapping analyses market conditions to identify the position of one product or brand relative to others in the market in terms of given criteria.

Interpreting marketing data

To interpret marketing data managers will use various tools such as:

● correlation
● extrapolation
● confidence intervals.

Correlation

Marketing data may help identify the correlation between different factors and the demand for a product. Correlation occurs when there is an apparent

relationship between one factor and another. For example, it may be that marketing research suggests that increases in the price leads to fewer sales; this would suggest there is a negative correlation between price and demand. It is negative because when one factor goes up the other goes down; higher prices reduce demand.

Figure 8.9 A negative correlation

By comparison, the correlation between income and demand may be positive. A positive correlation occurs when an upward change in one variable increases the value of another (and vice versa). For example, an increase in customer income may be associated with an increase in demand.

Figure 8.10 A positive correlation

If the correlation is zero then there is no apparent relationship between a factor and demand. For example, a change in the weather may have no apparent effect on the sales of mobile phones.

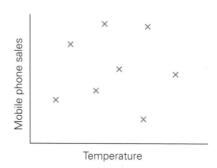

Figure 8.11 No correlation

If a manager can identify the key influences on demand then this could help forecast sales in the future. For example, if the population size seems to be a big influence on the demand for shoes, and if the population size is expected to grow, this suggests that sales of shoes should increase. If the age profile of the population affects the demand for medicines, then forecasts of an ageing population can help estimate medical sales.

Correlation is given as a value between −1 and +1, as shown in Figure 8.12:

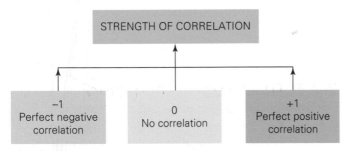

Figure 8.12 Strength of correlation

The higher figure (regardless of the sign) the stronger the correlation. For example,

- −0.8 is a strong negative correlation; +0.8 is a strong positive correlation.
- −0.2 is a weak negative correlation and +0.2 is a weak positive correlation.

It is important when analysing correlation to be aware that it simply shows an apparent relationship between two factors – it does not prove that one leads to the other or indeed show the direction of the relationship. For example, whenever ice cream sales increase so do shark attacks – they are positively correlated. However, this does not mean ice cream sales lead to shark attacks – the cause is obviously likely to be the hot weather leading to more ice cream being sold and more people going swimming which then is likely to lead to more shark attacks.

What do you think?

What do you think is the likely sign and size of the correlation between:

- income and tobacco
- consumer age and sales of suncream
- sunshine and sales of precooked meals
- sales of wine and sales of cheese
- consumer income and vegetable sales?

Extrapolation

Market research will enable a business to track what has happened to sales in the past and to estimate what sales might be in the future. One method of forecasting sales is to look at what has been happening in the past and to continue this trend into the future. This is called 'extrapolation'. If, on average, sales have grown by about 2 per cent a year for the past five years, a business may work on the assumption this will continue and project sales forward on this basis.

Extrapolation may be a valid way of forecasting sales, assuming that conditions do not change. If the government is predicting demand for healthcare and education in the future it can extrapolate from the numbers of people in different age groups at the moment. For example, the numbers starting secondary school aged 11 in five years' time can be extrapolated from the number of children aged 6 now. However, in many markets there is sometimes disruptive change that alters market conditions significantly and makes extrapolation of limited value.

What do you think?

How useful do you think extrapolation might be in:

(a) the construction industry
(b) healthcare
(c) the computing industry
(d) education
(e) the music industry?

Confidence levels and intervals

Sampling can help provide an insight into the target population as a whole but if you have not asked the whole of the target population it will not be 100 per cent accurate. Market research findings therefore have a **confidence level** that gives an indication of how certain they are of the results. For example, a 95 per cent confidence level means that the researchers are 95 per cent certain that their results are reliable and represent the population as a whole. A 68 per cent confidence level means that researchers are 68 per cent sure that their findings represent the population as a whole.

The degree of confidence will depend on factors such as:

- the size of the sample; the bigger the sample the more likely it is that the findings will reflect the population
- how the sample was constructed; for example, were the people involved selected randomly?

The degree of confidence in the findings will also depend on the margin of error that the researchers provide (known as the confidence interval). For example, the researchers may be 95 per cent confident that sales will be somewhere between £200,000 and £300,000 as this is quite a big margin of error. If you asked them to be more specific they may only be 68 per cent confident that sales would be between say £250,000 and £280,000 because there is a much smaller range (or confidence interval). The more precise you want the prediction to be, the less certain researchers can be. Equally, the bigger the margin of error you are happy to accept the more confident researchers can be. For example, they can be 100 per cent confident that sales will be somewhere between zero and infinity! This means that for any given research conducted, the higher the confidence level required the wider the confidence interval (or margin of error) they will give.

This can be shown in Figure 8.13 which shows sales forecasts for the UK soft drinks market. Looking ahead to 2019, the Mintel research company thinks that sales of soft drinks will be £8,404 million; however it cannot be 100 per cent certain so it provides a degree of confidence and the relevant margins of error. The company is 95 per cent confident that sales will be between £8,576 million and £7,232 million; this is quite a wide interval and so the researchers are very confident sales will lie somewhere in this range. If you ask them for a narrower interval, i.e. to be more specific about what sales will be, their confidence falls. This is shown by the shading – the heaviest shading is a relatively narrow range of possible outcomes and so their confidence level drops to only 50 per cent.

Key terms

A **confidence level** is the probability that the research findings are correct.

A **confidence interval** is the possible range of outcomes for a given confidence level. For example, you might have a 95 per cent confidence level that sales will be between £500,000 and £700,000 (interval).

Interpreting the price elasticity of demand

The correlation between price and the quantity demanded is measured by the price elasticity of demand. The price elasticity of demand examines the effect of a price change on the quantity demanded, all other factors unchanged.

It is measured by the equation:

Price elasticity of demand = Percentage change in quantity demanded / Percentage change in price

Business in focus: Sales of carbonated drinks in the UK

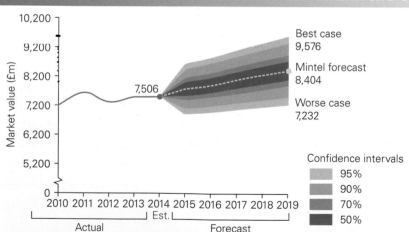

Best case
9,576

Mintel forecast
8,404

Worse case
7,232

Confidence intervals
- 95%
- 90%
- 70%
- 50%

Figure 8.13 Forecast of total value of UK sales of carbonated soft drinks, 2009–19

Source: Based on IR/Mintel

Questions

1. Using Figure 8.13:
   (i) Identify the confidence interval for carbonated soft drinks sales in 2019 when the confidence level is 50 per cent.
   (ii) What is confidence interval when the confidence level is 95 per cent?
   (iii) Why is the interval bigger the higher the confidence level?

2. Why do you think the confidence interval gets bigger the further into the future sales are being predicted?

Business in focus: Airport research

Many of the world's famous brands now believe that airports are an important part of their distribution and for the airports themselves the brands are an important source of revenue. In Qatar's new airport travellers have 25,000 square metres of shops and restaurants. Pernod Ricard, the French drinks company, and L'Oréal, the French maker of cosmetics and perfume, call airports their 'sixth continent'. Once passengers have passed through the security checks they have what is known as the 'golden hour' when they are wandering around with little to do but go shopping. Most are relatively prosperous, given that they are travelling by air. Airport retailers know the shopping habits of passengers because they can track data from their boarding cards. They also know the schedules of flights and when customer land and take off. They can change their products according to who is landing.

The World Duty Free Group (WDFG), one of the main retailers at Heathrow, tracks arrivals into its database so that it has speakers of the right languages and who are aware of cultural differences ready to serve customers.

Brazilian women are happy to allow a sales assistant to spray a perfume on them, whereas Chinese customers tend to use a tester. Shop displays are also changed to meet national tastes. For morning flights to Barbados, the cognac stand has expensive bottles of Courvoisier and Hennessy, whereas for flights to America they put cheaper brands on display.

Airports are also used for marketing research laboratories. Sales of Cath Kidston's products at airports are an early indicator of where the company might want to open stores overseas. Luxottica opened three Sunglass Hut boutiques in Italian airports to see how they might do in the country as a whole.

Questions

1. Analyse the ways in which data helps marketing decision makers at airports.

2. To what extent is it useful for businesses to use airports to test new markets and new products?

Managers will be able to examine the changes they have made in the past to the prices of products and can examine sales data to estimate the effect changes in price have on sales.

The answer to the price elasticity of demand equation is usually negative because a price increase (+) leads to fall in quantity demanded (–) and vice versa; this gives a negative answer overall.

The size of the price elasticity (i.e. the size of the number ignoring whether it is negative or positive) shows how responsive demand is to price changes; it shows how much the quantity demanded changes in response to a 1 per cent change in price. The bigger the number the more quantity demanded changes following a price change. If the size of the answer (regardless of whether it is positive or negative) is 2, for example, this means that

a 1 per cent change in price leads to a change of 2×1 per cent = 2 per cent in quantity demanded.

If the answer is 0.5 it means a 1 per cent change in price leads to a change of 0.5×1 per cent= 0.5 per cent change in quantity demanded.

If the value of the price elasticity of demand (that is, the size of the number ignoring the sign) is less than one this is described as price inelastic. This means that a given percentage change in price leads to a smaller change in the quantity demanded. Note that this does not mean that the change in quantity demanded is small, just that it is smaller than the change in price. A 50 per cent change in quantity demanded is quite big but if the price change is 75 per cent then demand is price inelastic because demand changed less than price. Price elasticity therefore measures how much demand changes relative to price.

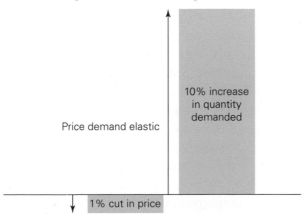

Figure 8.14 Price elasticity

If the value of the price elasticity of demand (that is, the size of the number ignoring the sign) is greater than one this is described as price elastic. This is because the change in quantity demanded is bigger than the change in price.

Maths moment

$$\frac{1+b}{c}=3$$

You can multiply the percentage change in price by the price elasticity of demand to calculate the percentage change in quantity demanded.

If the price elasticity is –3, a 5 per cent increase in price leads to a –3 x 5 = -15 per cent change in demand.

If the price elasticity is –0.1, a 5 per cent increase in price leads to a –0.1 x 5 = -0.5 per cent change in demand.

(a) If the price elasticity is –4, is this price elastic or price inelastic? Explain.

(b) If demand increases 4 per cent when price falls by 2 per cent what is the price elasticity of demand?

(c) If demand falls 6 per cent when price increases 12 per cent, what is the price elasticity of demand?

(d) How much will the quantity demand change if the price elasticity is –1.5 and price increases 20 per cent? What if the price elasticity is –0.8?

Why does the price elasticity of demand matter?

If demand is price inelastic this means that a change in price leads to a smaller change in the quantity demanded. The effect of this is to lead to an increase in revenue if prices are raised.

Imagine you are charging £10 and sell 5,000 units. The revenue from sales will be £10 x 5000 = £50,000.

If you increase the price to £15 and sales are now 4500 units this is price inelastic. The quantity demanded has changed –10 per cent following a +50 per cent increase in price; this means the price elasticity of demand is –10/+50 = –0.2, that is price inelastic.

Revenue is now £15 x 4,500 = £67,500. Revenue has increased because price has increased and there has been a relatively smaller percentage fall in demand.

By comparison if demand is price elastic then a price increase leads to a bigger percentage fall in the quantity demanded and a fall in revenue.

Now imagine you are charging £10 and sell 5,000 units. The revenue from sales is £10 x 5,000 = £50,000.

If you increase the price to £15 and sales are now 1,000 units this is price elastic.

The quantity demanded has changed -80 per cent following a +50 per cent increase in price; this means the price elasticity of demand is -80/+50 = –1.6, that is price elastic.

Revenue is now £15 x 1,000 = £1,500. The price has risen and the revenue has fallen because sales have fallen by a relatively greater percentage.

Clearly understanding the price elasticity of demand is important when setting the price because managers will want to estimate the impact on sales and revenue of any potential price change.

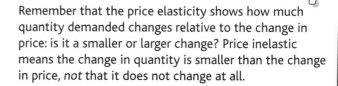

Study tip

Remember that the price elasticity shows how much quantity demanded changes relative to the change in price: is it a smaller or larger change? Price inelastic means the change in quantity is smaller than the change in price, *not* that it does not change at all.

Price elasticity is summarised in Table 8.2.

	Price elastic	Price inelastic
Price increase	The increase in price leads to a bigger percentage decrease in the quantity demanded. Revenue falls.	The increase in price leads to a smaller percentage decrease in the quantity demanded. Revenue rises.
Price decrease	The decrease in price leads to a bigger percentage increase in the quantity demanded. Revenue rises.	The decrease in price leads to a smaller percentage increase in the quantity demanded. Revenue falls.

Table 8.2 Price elasticity

What influences the price elasticity of demand for a product?

A major influence on the **price elasticity of demand** of a product is how easy it is for customers to change to an alternative product if the price of this one increases. If it is easy to switch away to something similar then demand will be price elastic – with a price increase there will be a relatively large fall in demand as customers choose cheaper alternatives. So if there are many similar products on the market, and switching to them is easy, demand will be price elastic. By comparison, if a product has a unique brand, has some special features or is protected in some way – perhaps through a **patent** or **trademark** – demand will not be sensitive to price; demand will be price inelastic.

Other influences on the price elasticity of demand include:

- the time period. Over time customers will be able to search for more alternatives and so demand becomes more price elastic.
- how expensive the product is. If it is cheap to begin with then customers may not be very sensitive to price as customers will still be able to afford the product
- who is paying for the product. For example, if your flights are paid for by your company, your demand for flights may be less sensitive to price than if you had to pay for it yourself.

Figure 8.15 How sensitive do you think flights are to price?

Factor	Effect on the price elasticity of demand
Heavily branded product	More price inelastic
Unique Selling Proposition (a quality that differentiates the product from others)	More price inelastic
Patent (legal protection of an invention) Or Trademark (legal protection of a sign)	More price inelastic
Expensive or difficult to switch to another supplier	More price inelastic
More substitutes available	More price elastic
Over time	More price elastic

Table 8.3 Factors affecting price elasticity of demand

Key terms

A **brand** is a 'promise of an experience' and conveys to consumers a certain assurance as to the nature of the product or service they will receive.

A **patent** protects new inventions and covers how things work, what they do, how they do it, what they are made of and how they are made.

A **trade mark** is a sign which can distinguish the goods and services of a business from those of its competitors (a business may refer to its trade mark as its 'brand').

What do you think?

Do you think the price elasticity of demand for coffee and food at motorway service stations is likely to be price elastic or inelastic? Justify your view.

On a Greek beach there is often a long row of beach bars selling drinks. Do you think demand for drinks in one of these bars is price elastic or inelastic? Justify your answer.

Key terms

The **price elasticity of demand** measures how responsive demand is to changes in the price, all other factors constant.

The **income elasticity of demand** measures how responsive demand is to changes in the income, all other factors constant.

Interpreting the income elasticity of demand

The **income elasticity of demand** shows the correlation between quantity demanded and customers' incomes.

It is measured by the equation:

income elasticity of demand =

$$\frac{\%\ change\ in\ quantity\ demanded}{\%\ change\ in\ consumer\ income}$$

If the answer is positive this means an increase in income increases demand. Equally, a fall in income reduces the quantity demanded. This is what happens for most 'normal' products.

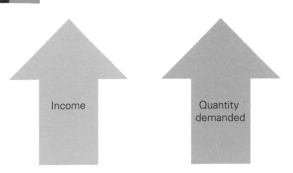

Figure 8.16 Normal product

If the answer is negative this means that as income increases the quantity demanded falls; if income falls quantity demanded increases. These products are known as 'inferior' because as incomes rise customers switch to other products (for example switching from bicycles to cars); if income falls customers switch back to these products as they are on a lower budget.

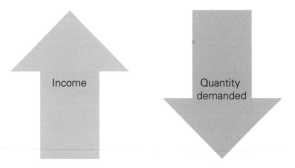

Figure 8.17 Inferior product

The size of the income elasticity (regardless of the sign) shows how sensitive demand is to income changes; it measures how much quantity demanded changes in relation to a 1 per cent change in income. The bigger the answer the more responsive demand is.

For example:

- If the income elasticity is 2, this means that the change in quantity demanded is 2 times the change in income. A 1 per cent change in income leads to a 2 per cent (2 × 1) change in quantity demanded
- If the income elasticity is 0.5 this means that the change in quantity demanded is 0.5 times the change in income. A 1 per cent change in income leads to a 0.5 per cent (0.5 × 1) change in quantity demanded.

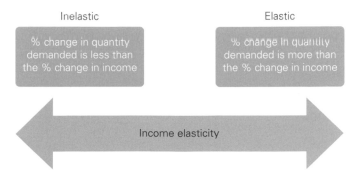

Figure 8.18 Income elasticity = 2

Study tip

Remember the income elasticity of demand shows how much quantity changes relative to the change in income – is it smaller or bigger? If demand in income is inelastic this means the change in demand is less than the change in income; it does not mean that quantity does not change at all.

What do you think?

Do you think the demand for following products is likely to income elastic or inelastic? Explain your answer.

(a) Cruise ship holidays
(b) Newspapers
(c) Luxury cars
(d) Milk
(e) Paint

Why does income elasticity matter?

An understanding of income elasticity is useful to managers because it helps them plan for changes in the incomes of their customers. For example, if the economy is doing well and incomes are rising, this will lead to relatively fast growth in the demand for products that have a high, positive income elastic demand. By comparison, in a boom, demand for inferior goods would fall.

An understanding of an impact of income on demand will affect planning for production, staffing and finance.

Income elasticity	Result
Positive	'Normal' products; an increase in income increases the quantity demanded.
Negative	'Inferior' products; an increase in income decreases the quantity demanded.
Less than one	Inelastic; the percentage change in quantity demanded is less than the percentage change in income.
More than one	Elastic; the percentage change in quantity demanded is less than the percentage change in income.

Table 8.4 Summary of income elasticity

The value of technology in gathering and analysing data for marketing decision making

Developments in technology are enabling businesses to gather more data on customers and to analyse this data more effectively and more quickly. For example, if you use a supermarket reward card the company can track what you are buying and link this to your address and all the other information they hold about you. This can help the business to understand more about the type of person buying products and what might influence their spending patterns. The increasing ability to combine data from a variety of sources is known as 'big data'. Think of when you visit an online business such as Amazon – it will track your viewing and buying habits and get to understand you so well that it can even recommend what else you might want to buy. It can link what you are doing with what others are doing, and what else is happening in the world – the weather, any major events and the major stories in the news. Its data can provide a very detailed insight into buying patterns and how they are affected by changes to (say) the product and price. It can enable businesses to link data far more effectively than in the past – for example, to find correlations it had not appreciated existed. This can help the business forecast sales more effectively and to build a relationship with you by being able to anticipate what you want.

Simply having more data does not guarantee success, however. The right data still has to be collected, the right questions have to be asked and the right decisions made and implemented. However, technology is providing better, faster and cheaper information that should improve decision making. Just think about how valuable spreadsheets are to you if you are ever doing mathematical work. Technology has given you a tool to speed up calculations, to enable you to manipulate data faster and more effectively and to present your findings in useful and visually attractive way. Technological change is enabling you to manipulate data in a way that your grandparents could not have imagined. Does that mean you inevitably get everything right? Not necessarily – it depends on whether you have the right numbers in the first place and set up the system correctly.

Key term

Big data refers to large and complex data sets. These have been difficult to analyse in the past but improvements in technology is making the use of big data more feasible.

The use of data in marketing decision making and planning

Marketing research provides the information to help make decisions regarding marketing issues such as what to produce, the price to charge and where to distribute. This is essential for planning marketing effectively and for keeping up with changes in market conditions.

However, marketing research also provides information that will feed into the plans and decisions throughout the business, as shown in Figure 18.19.

Figure 8.19 How market research affects other areas of the business

One common use of marketing research is to forecast the sales of the business. A sales forecast is essential to planning throughout the business. It is required by all of the other business functions. For example:

- Human resources need to know what staffing requirements are likely to be.
- The finance function needs to be able to estimate future cash inflows and profits.
- Operations need to know the expected level of sales to ensure this can be produced.

The sales forecast therefore influences many other plans within the organisation. Marketing research provides the information needed on what is happening outside of the business and this is essential to decide and plan what to do within the business.

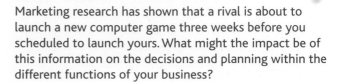

What do you think?

Marketing research has shown that a rival is about to launch a new computer game three weeks before you scheduled to launch yours. What might the impact be of this information on the decisions and planning within the different functions of your business?

Why can marketing research go wrong?

Marketing research can provide invaluable information to help marketing managers make decisions. However, this does not guarantee success. Research may help reduce the risk of a decision but does not remove it completely. This is because of:

- changes in markets. This means that the information that managers have gathered in a particular situation may be out of date or even irrelevant fairly soon if

Business in focus: The launch of New Coke

Figures 8.20a and b New Coke and Classic Coke

In 1985 Coca-Cola launched a new version of the cola product and called it 'New Coke'. Marketing research suggested it would do very well but there was a huge public outcry about taking 'Classic' Coke off the shelves. Eventually the company had to bring Classic Coke back. This is the company's version of events:

In 1985, The Coca-Cola Company's share lead over its chief competitor, in its flagship market, with its flagship product, had been slowly slipping for 15 consecutive years. The cola category in general was lethargic. Consumer preference for Coca-Cola was dipping, as was consumer awareness. That changed, of course, in the summer of 1985 as the consumer outcry over 'New Coke' was replaced by consumer affection for Coca-Cola classic. The fabled secret formula for Coca-Cola was changed, adopting a formula preferred in taste tests of nearly 200,000 consumers. What these tests didn't show, of course, was the bond consumers felt with their Coca-Cola — something they didn't want anyone, including The Coca-Cola Company, tampering with.

Many of the employees there that day had worked for the company in 1985 and remembered the thousands of calls and consumer complaints. By June 1985, The Coca-Cola Company was getting 1,500 calls a day on its consumer hotline, compared with 400 a day before the taste change. Protest groups — such as the Society for the Preservation of the Real Thing and Old Cola Drinkers of America (which claimed to have recruited 100,000 in a drive to bring back 'old' Coke) — popped up around the country. Songs were written to honor the old taste. Protesters at a Coca-Cola event in downtown Atlanta in May carried signs with 'We want the real thing' and 'Our children will never know refreshment.

In response to this Coca-Cola brought back the 'classic' and this was sold alongside Coca-Cola ('new Coke'). The two brands had distinct advertising campaigns, with the youthful, leading edge 'Catch the Wave' campaign for the new taste of Coke and the emotional 'Red, White and You' for Coca-Cola classic. Later, the name of the new taste of Coca-Cola was changed to Coke II; this product is no longer available in the United States.

Source: www.coca-cola-company.com/history/the-real-story-of-new-coke#TCCC

Questions

1. Analyse the possible reasons why the marketing research for Coca-Cola did not predict the outcry over the removal of the old product.

2. To what extent do you think the success of Coca-Cola is likely to be due the strength of its brand?

conditions are changing very rapidly – for example, with new technology and new business entering the market.

- the way the information is gathered. The business may use secondary data which may not be in the format required or may use samples that do not necessarily reflect the target population accurately.
- lack of information. In some cases, managers will be keen to make the decision and not want to spend money on undertaking research. Perhaps they assume they understand the market, assume they are right or simply lack enough finance for detailed research.

Marketing research and ethics

When gathering data, managers may need to consider the ethical implications of their marketing research. For example, to what extent should they be asking consumers' permission before collecting information on their purchasing habits? Is it acceptable, for example, to film consumers shopping without their permission? Is it acceptable to track their purchases online in order to recommend other products they may like without asking for permission?

ASSESSMENT ACTIVITIES

Sections (a), (b) and (c) of these assessment activities are relevant for students taking AS and A-level examinations. The questions in section (d) are for A-level students only.

(a) Knowledge check questions

1 Explain what is meant by marketing research.

2 State two possible uses of marketing research in decision making.

3 Distinguish between primary and secondary marketing decision making.

4 State two ways in which a business might gather primary data.

5 State two possible sources of secondary data.

6 Distinguish between quantitative and qualitative data.

7 State two ways in which a sales forecast can affect the decisions of other functions within the business.

8 If sales rise as promotional expenditure rises this is a positive correlation. True or false? Explain your answer.

9 If future sales are predicted on the basis of past sales this is known as ....

10 If the price elasticity of demand is – 2.6, demand is price elastic. True or false? Explain your answer.

(b) Short answer questions

1 Explain one possible benefit of marketing research to a business about to launch a new social networking app.   (5 marks)

2 Explain the advantages of primary market research compared to secondary research when a business is considering launching a new product. (5 marks)

3 Explain how a mobile phone business might make demand for its business more price inelastic.   (5 marks)

4 Explain how a chain of leisure clubs might forecast sales.   (5 marks)

5 Explain how an understanding of elasticity of demand might help the marketing manager of a hotel chain make decisions.   (5 marks)

(c) Data response questions

Technology and marketing decision making

Big data enables a business to bring together huge quantities of information from a variety of sources; it can then process this to find links that will aid its marketing efforts. Big data is used by the police, for example, to identify links between crime patterns and factors such as the weather, special events that are happening nearby, income levels, the time of day and year, and so on. If links can be found the police can anticipate possible problems that might occur and allocate resources accordingly. In business big data can be used to identify customer spending patterns and to develop products to more closely match customer requirements. Close interrogation of data regarding shoppers' spending linked to other pieces of information, such as who is shopping, when and where, and what else is happening in the environment, can allow a business to adjust its future marketing activities to promote more sales.

Companies can use big data to draw on several sources to understand our lives – by looking at data on our searches, our purchases, our social media purchases and our location, companies can gain a very good insight into what we do and what we are thinking about. Imagine then if in the future this was linked to in-store technology so that businesses could identify you as you walk into each shop – the sales assistants might well be able to predict what you are looking for or what you need to buy before you know yourself and direct you to the products of interest to you in the store! Specific adverts and promotions that are directly relevant to you may appear on your smartphone as you walk into a particular outlet.

One of the most famous users of big data is Amazon, the online retailer. Amazon has well over 200 million

customers and a revenue of around $75 billion. A great deal of its success is due to its ability to collect, analyse and use data on its customers. By tracking your buying patterns it is able to personalise your experience of its website, for example, making recommendations of other products you might enjoy and showing adverts of products linked to other things you have bought. Other companies such as M&S, Next, Boots and Dixons are also investing heavily in their information technology systems in order to do similar things. The ability to analyse ever bigger amounts of data from more sources means that, for example, when the weather turns colder a fashion retailer could recommend winter clothes by the same designer you have already bought from via an advert sent to your smartphone or when you log on to their website to browse the rails. All of this enables retailers to provide very personalised, tailor-made and focused communications to existing customers. However, some people worry that their lives are too open to outsiders and feel that this data analysis is an unwelcome loss of privacy.

1   With reference to the text above, explain possible ethical issues that might arise in using technology to gather data. (5 marks)

2   With reference to the text above, analyse the ways in which technology is enabling more effective marketing decision making. (9 marks)

3   To what extent do you think the success of more personalised marketing by companies such as Amazon depends on the other business functions? (15 marks)

(d) Essays

1   To what extent is marketing research an essential investment when developing and launching a new product? (25 marks)

2   To what extent do you think that primary marketing research is a better way than secondary for the marketing manager of a cosmetics business such as L'Oreal to gather information? (25 marks)

Chapter 9

Segmentation, targeting and positioning (STP)

Introduction

In the last chapter we examined the value of marketing research in gathering and analysing marketing information. This will help managers to make decisions. In this chapter we will consider how businesses use marketing research information to identify segments in a market and decide which segments to target. We will analyse how a business positions itself within a market and then how this influences its marketing activities.

What you need to know by the end of this chapter:

- the process and value of market segmentation, targeting and positioning (STP)
- the different methods of segmentation
- the influences on choosing a target market and positioning
- the value of niche and mass marketing.

The process of segmentation

By undertaking marketing research, managers aim to identify groups of similar needs and wants within a market. The process of identifying different groups of similar needs is called **segmentation**. The different groups of needs and wants are known as **market segments**. For example, in the market for toys there may be a difference between the type of toys demanded by different age groups or by boys and girls. In the hotel market there may be a difference between the requirements of businesspeople and families on holiday.

There are many different ways to group needs and wants. Common ways of categorising by segmentation include:

Demographic segmentation

The term demographics refers to characteristics of the people in the target population. For example, there may be similar needs and wants based on aspects such as age or gender: the clothes women want to buy are different from those men want to buy, the clothes 18-year-olds want to wear are different from those that their parents wear. Demographic factors may also include what stage in their lives people are at (for example, are they in full-time study, have they just got a job, are they looking after children, have their children left home). All of these things affect buying behaviour.

What do you think?

Think ahead to the next 60 years of your life and what will happen to you in terms of your lifestyle. What will change in terms of the types of products you buy or interests you have, for example? At what stage of your life might you start thinking about renting or buying a flat or house? Going on family holidays? Joining a gym?

Geographic segmentation

This method of segmentation groups needs and wants based on the geographical area in which customers are based. The types of houses required in Iceland and in Nigeria may be very different to each other due to climate conditions, for example. The types of food and drink sold in McDonald's outlets around the world may need to vary to meet the tastes of different customers.

Income segmentation

High-income users of a bank, a holiday company or a hotel may have different demands than low-income users. High-income earners are more likely to be interested in products to do with saving and investing; lower-income groups are more likely to be interested in borrowing. High-income earners generally may be more interested in overseas holidays, business-class airline seats, private healthcare insurance and advice on buying shares and new cars.

A common way of segmenting people based on income and their professions is known as socioeconomic grouping. The most common categories of socioeconomic groupings are:

A: Higher managerial, administrative or professionals

B: Intermediate managerial, administrative or professional

C1:   Supervisors, clerical and junior managerial, administrative or professional

C2:   Skilled manual workers

D: Semi and unskilled manual workers

E: Casual labour.

It is very common for the media to categorise their audiences on this basis. For example, ABs are more likely to read *The Financial Times* and *The Economist*.

Behavioural segmentation

Demographic and income segmentation methods concentrate on the characteristics of consumers, for example how old they are. Behavioural segmentation focuses on what customers actually do. For example, it analyses customers in terms of:

- when they buy (the purchase occasion). For example, many people start dieting or buy products to give up smoking in January as they start a New Year and want to change themselves
- how much they buy. For example, are they heavy users or light users of the product? Do they buy just for themselves or for family members? This could obviously affect issues such as the sizes in which products are offered.
- brand loyalty? Do they stay with the same brand or switch? If they are switchers you might be able to attract them with special offers. If they are brand loyal you might want to reward them to encourage others to become loyal.
- the benefit they want from the product. Are they buying a Harley Davidson as a means of transport or to reward themselves for their achievement in life? Or because they are getting worried about getting older and want to relive their youth? Or because it reminds them of the freedom they once had when they were young? Understanding this will influence decisions such as the way a product is promoted. When Kaluha looked at who bought their alcohol it was found it was mainly bought by mothers who at the end of a tiring stressful day looking after the children, wanted some 'me time'. Pouring a glass of Kaluha was when the mothers said to themselves: 'I am a person not just someone who has to take the children to school and tidy up after them.' This led to a highly successful promotional campaign for Kaluha entitled 'release the tiger within'.

Having identified the segments in a market managers are able to identify groups of similar needs and wants. They must then decide which of these segments they want to focus on and how best to approach them. Trying to sell more Barbie dolls to customers who already love the brand is clearly different from trying to sell them to people who prefer Bratz, or to people who don't like dolls at all. It is important therefore to understand the needs, wants and features of the different behavioural segments because this will affect the marketing decisions that are taken.

The value of segmentation

By segmenting a market, managers can understand what different groups want rather than treat all customers as the same. When we want to buy a car, is it to use in the city, or to use to transport the family around? Do we want a sports car, or an all-terrain vehicle? Different groups have different requirements and priorities and marketing managers strive to understand them to decide if they can meet them, and if so, how best to satisfy these needs.

Identifying a segment therefore enables more focused and efficient marketing – you do not waste money promoting a product in the wrong place or investing in features that are not needed. However, the more segments a business decides to focus on the more complex an operation can be and the more expensive it can be to meet all the different needs. For example, it may be relatively easy to produce one cleaning product to be used around the house. This type of product can be produced on a large scale, which may be relatively efficient. However, customers may want different products: oven-cleaners, glass cleaners, bathroom cleaners, floor cleaners and so on. Adapting the product to these different needs may mean that customers are more satisfied. However, every time the market is segmented again (for example into shower cleaners, tile cleaners, leather cleaners, computer screen cleaners) the potential market may be getting smaller and the production runs may be reducing; this may make the segment unprofitable.

Managers will want to balance a desire to meet customer needs with what is practical, efficient and profitable. For example, sixth forms want to offer a wide range of subjects to give students choice but the more subjects that are offered the more complex it becomes to timetable, with smaller class sizes, making delivery more expensive because there are more teachers with fewer students in a class. Most schools therefore have some forms of option blocks, which provides some choice but limits it.

What do you think?

How would you segment the housing market? What about the market for sportswear?

Key terms

Segmentation occurs when similar customer needs and wants are grouped within a market.

Market segments are the groups of similar needs and wants within a market.

Targeting occurs when a business decides which segments it wants to operate in.

Targeting

Segmentation uses market research to identify which segments exist in a market. However a business may not want to focus on all of them. Choosing which segments to focus on is known as **targeting**.

Influences on choosing the target market

A business will target segments where it thinks:

- there is sufficient demand and potential profit to justify the investment. Some segments may be too small to make sufficient profits (for example many universities have dropped languages as a degree course because the segment is too small).
- it has the ability to be competitive and gain sales. For example, do the requirements of the target segment match the skills and competences of the business? Does the brand of the business fit with the target segment? Can the business develop a competitive advantage in this segment? Rather than trying to offer all courses to all students, for example, a university may target certain courses (and therefore certain students) where it feels it has expertise and can excel.

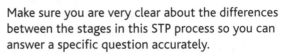

Figure 9.1 The STP process

By selecting target segments the business will be able to focus on the needs and wants of the customers in these segments and hopefully meet their needs more precisely and effectively. This should increase competitiveness and – provided the revenue is sufficient and the costs not too high – profits.

Study tip

Make sure you are very clear about the differences between the stages in this STP process so you can answer a specific question accurately.

Weblink

Acorn is a powerful consumer classification that segments the UK population. By analysing demographic data, social factors, population and consumer behaviour, it provides precise information and an understanding of different types of people. Acorn provides valuable consumer insight helping you target, acquire and develop profitable customer relationships and improve service delivery.

Have a look at this segmentation system at http://acorn.caci.co.uk

Business in focus: Acorn

Figure 9.2 Acorn's consumer classifications

Source: http://acorn.caci.co.uk/downloads/Acorn-Infographic.pdf

Questions

1. In what ways could segmenting the market in the ways described above be useful for businesses?
2. Can you think of particular products that would be aimed at each of the different groups? How might the way you communicate with these groups differ?

What do you think?

The 99p shop and Poundland have a clear target market. How do you think this affects their marketing decisions? How might it affect their decisions in other functional areas, such as operations and human resources?

In Figure 9.3, for example, the different groups being targeted by clothes retailers are shown. John Lewis targets buyers aged around 40 who are in a relatively high socioeconomic group. Asda is targeting a slightly older group in a lower socioeconomic group. Understanding their target markets will affect the marketing decision of the business such as what to sell, how to promote it and what price to charge.

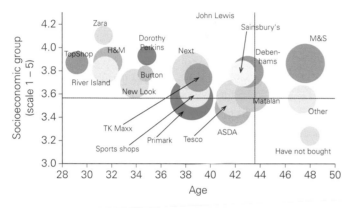

Figure 9.3 Profile of in-store clothing shoppers, by age and affluence, July 2013

Source: GMI/Mintel

A clear understanding on who is being targeted should enable more effective marketing decision making.

What do you think?

Topshop seems to be targeting the younger buyer relative to, say Marks & Spencer. How do think this affects the marketing decisions it makes?

Niche marketing and mass marketing

If a business decides to focus on a specific segment of the market this is known as **niche marketing**. For example, a clothes retailer may focus on tall people, or on Goths. These groups of customers are smaller than the market as a whole but have clearly identifiable needs and wants. Saga Holidays, for example, targets the older holidaymaker and Classic G radio targets lovers of classical music. This allows the business to focus its marketing activities more precisely.

The value of niche marketing is that by focusing on a niche it may be possible to compete within a bigger market such as fashion or the media, without directly challenging the bigger businesses and therefore not being seen as a threat by them. The danger of challenging bigger, more established players directly is that they may respond aggressively. For example, if a new manufacturer of bicycles threatened the established brands they might cut prices or put pressure on stores not to stock the new product. It might be better therefore to focus on a niche, such as bicycles that fold up for those who commute on the train and want a bike to get to and from the station, as this may not be perceived as a great threat to the big, powerful brands.

Figure 9.4 A folding bike: a product for a niche market

A retailer focusing only on pink products may not take many sales from stores such as Next or Marks & Spencer, a publisher that only produces books in Latin will not worry the big publishers too much and an Algerian fast-food takeaway may not challenge McDonald's head on. By concentrating on a niche a business is identifying a clear segment that is usually relatively small and where they are not likely to be challenged by the bigger businesses that could undercut them.

On the other hand:

- A niche market may not be particularly big and therefore a business may be vulnerable to losing a few customers. Total profits may be relatively low although this will vary from niche to niche.
- If the niche does grow and become more popular (such as organic food) then this will actually attract the bigger businesses in because they can see the profits are becoming worthwhile. Over time the niche may want to move more into the mainstream.

An alternative approach to niche marketing may be to ignore some of the differences between the segments and aim at the market as a whole. A **mass market** approach does not try to match the needs of a specific segment precisely. Instead it aims to provide products that will meet some of the needs of most of the people. A mass market newspaper such as *The Daily Mirror*, for example, appeals to many people; however some people will focus on the sport and be less interested in the politics; some will be interested in the politics and less interested in the gossip. Mass marketing aims for volume by trying to develop products that will meet some of the needs of large numbers in the market. This will involve more customers and therefore potentially more revenue and returns. However to be successful in the mass market requires:

- larger volumes (and therefore the investment and capacity) to fulfil orders
- promotional techniques to reach more customers
- potentially more competition as businesses fight in the relatively large market. Businesses will therefore want to consider where they position themselves within the mass market.

The risks of targeting mass markets are the levels of investment required and the potential difficulties competing against other businesses already in this market. Setting up to compete against established high street banks, petrol stations or soft drinks producers could be difficult as they will fight hard to retain their existing customers, with potentially high levels of resources to fight with. Also the danger is that increasing numbers of niche providers gradually reduce the demand as customers look for something that meets their needs more precisely.

In the 1970s many British families went abroad for the first time as it was the first time it was affordable thanks to cheaper transport and higher incomes. This was a mass market with large numbers of people going to resorts in Spain. These holidays were not necessarily exactly what customers wanted but it provided a holiday overseas and sun and so was attractive. Nowadays customers in the holiday market are increasingly demanding personalised holidays. They do not want a standard mass-market holiday but one that meets their own needs, which are different from those of their neighbours. This creates opportunities for niche providers, for example offering tailor-made holidays or holidays to unusual destinations.

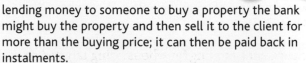

Business in focus: Islamic banking

Banks act as an intermediary between people who want to save money and people who want to borrow money. A bank typically attracts money into it from savers by offering an attractive interest rate and makes a profit by charging lenders a higher interest rate to borrow money. However, whilst this is the model of banking in the West, this type of business activity is not regarded as acceptable in all societies or religions. For example, under sharia law Islamic banks are not allowed to make profits by charging interest to lenders. Even so, a recent report by Ernst and Young has shown that the assets of Islamic banks have been growing extremely fast, at around 17 per cent a year, for the last few years; this is much faster than the growth rate of more mainstream banks.

Obviously Islamic banks need to make a profit to finance their growth, so how do they do this given the religious principles under which they operate? The answer is to find other ways of making profits apart from charging interest. For example, when an Islamic bank lends to a business the deal might involve the company paying a proportion of its profits to the bank in return. When

lending money to someone to buy a property the bank might buy the property and then sell it to the client for more than the buying price; it can then be paid back in instalments.

The growth in Islamic banking is partly due to the growth of emerging economies, such as Indonesia and Malaysian, where there are large Muslim populations. Even where Islamic banking is already quite strong, such as the Gulf States, these banks have a relatively small market share and so there are plenty of growth opportunities. However, the returns made by Islamic banks are typically much lower than mainstream banks and the industry is quite complex because there are different ways in which the banks organise their lending and repayments due to different interpretations of what is acceptable under sharia law.

Questions

1. Explain the growth in Islamic banking.
2. To what extent do you think Islamic banking is a good niche to target?

What do you think?

What are the possible implications for the different functional areas of a business of moving from a niche to a mass market? For example, having set up a small organic takeaway shop with recipes from Asia and having been successful, you decide to now expand your business across the UK and make this a mass market offering. What are the possible implications for marketing, finance, operations, human resources and management?

Key terms

Niche marketing focuses on a particular segment of the market.

A **mass market** approach aims to provide products that meet some of the needs of a large proportion of the market.

Positioning identifies the benefit and price combination of a product relative to competitors.

Positioning

Having targeted a segment, for example buyers over the age of 50 or families, managers must now consider the **positioning** of their business in the market. This means how their products are perceived relative to their competitors. *The Daily Mail* and *The Daily Telegraph* are both newspapers but are perceived very differently by readers in terms of what they offer. What about Xbox, PlayStation and Wii? All are computer consoles but users think there are significant differences between them.

The positioning of a business can be shown using the market mapping technique outlined in the last chapter. Managers identify two key aspects of the product that customers use to judge the offerings of different businesses. For example, you might describe a clothing business as modern or classic, or as expensive or great value for money. Managers can then plot where their business or product sits relative to others in the market.

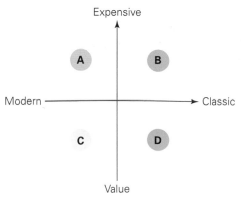

Figure 9.5 Positioning a clothing business

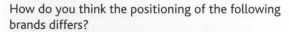

What do you think?

How do you think the positioning of the following brands differs?

- H&M and Next
- Puma and Nike
- Coca-Cola and Pepsi
- Barclays and Santander
- Facebook and Instagram
- Chelsea FC and Liverpool FC
- Samsung and Huawei

The positioning of a product relative to competitors depends on the following factors (as compared to that of its rivals):

- its price
- the benefits it offers
- its brand image
- the level of service it provides.

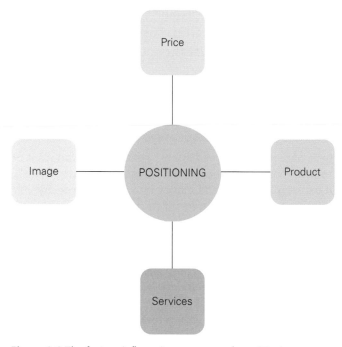

Figure 9.6 The factors influencing a company's positioning

Positioning and competitiveness

As we have seen, the **positioning** of a business can be described in terms of the benefits it provides (in terms of the product, the level of service and its image) relative to competitors, and the price charged relative to competitors.

The combination of benefits and price relative to other businesses will determine the competitiveness of a firm's offering. For example, a business may charge more than rivals and still be competitive, provided it offers more benefits. A business can offer fewer benefits than rivals and still be competitive, provided its prices are lower.

However, if a business offers less or the same benefits as rivals and charges a higher price it will be uncompetitive. Ideally a business might want to offer high benefits and a low price but this can be difficult to do as providing more benefits usually incurs additional costs.

The competitive and uncompetitive combinations are shown in Figure 9.7.

Price relative to competition		Benefits relative to competition		
		High		Low
High		High price and high benefits	High price and average benefits	High price and low benefits
		Average price and high benefits (Difficult to achieve as additional benefits usually increase price.)	Average price and average benefits	Average price and low benefits
Low			Low price and average benefits (Difficult to achieve as additional benefits usually increase price.)	Low price and low benefits
		Low price and high benefits (Very difficult to achieve as additional benefits usually increase price.)		

Key

☐ competitive   ■ uncompetitive   ☐ difficult to achieve

Figure 9.7 Benefits–price matrix

Managers will want to choose what combinations of benefits to provide and prices to charge and where they want to position the business in the market relative to who is already there. For example, should the business be a premium provider (Hilton Hotels) or a more basic provider (Travelodge)?

Influences on the positioning of a product

Influences on the positioning of a product include:

- The strengths of the business. If, for example, a business is particularly efficient in its processes it may aim to be a low-price provider. For example, the business may be large and have bargaining power over suppliers, it may be particularly good at negotiating or it may have good links with suppliers (or perhaps controls several stages of the supply chain). Businesses such as Walmart and Amazon

manage information very effectively, have developed very efficient processes and have huge buying power. This enables them to position themselves as a low-price provider.
- On the other hand, a business may be good at innovation, may have highly skilled employees and resources and systems that encourage the development of ideas. In this case a business may focus on providing greater benefits than rivals. Apple, Bang and Olufsen and Mercedes are not cheap but are innovative, well designed and have distinctive features.

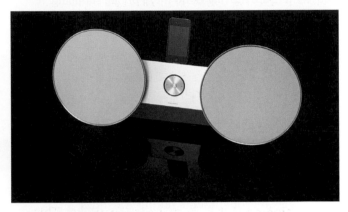

Figure 9.8 A Bang and Olufsen product: well designed and innovative

- Competitors. Where a business positions itself in a market may depend on what the established firms are already offering. Managers may produce a market map to identify what exists already in the market and what gaps exist. If it chooses to target a gap it must have the necessary strengths to do this well.
- Market conditions. External influences on positioning can be analysed using the PEST-C model we looked at in Chapter 7. For example, as the economy recovers, low-cost airlines such as easyJet have reconsidered their proposition and started to offer more benefits to meet customer needs.

Weblink

To keep up to date with Tesco's progress you can visit its website and go to the investor relations section: www.tesco.com

Business in focus: Tesco

Once regarded as the one of the most successful British companies of the century, Tesco has faced a number of problems in recent years. Its entry into the US market with the brand Fresh 'n Go was extremely unsuccessful and led to the company withdrawing in 2013. It also pulled out of Japan. Meanwhile it seemed to have lost its way in the UK market too, which was still by far the biggest part of its operations.

Tesco has let discounters, such as Aldi and Lidl, gain market share; it has misread market trends and invested too heavily in big hypermarket locations when customers are moving to do more online shopping. It also seemed to have lost its positioning in the market; it has tried to be all things to all people resulting in

confusion about where it fits in the market. It is neither a clearly premium retailer like Waitrose nor a discounter like Lidl. One of the challenges the company seems to face now is defining how it wants to be perceived in the market relative to its competitors. It then has to ensure it has the right products, promotions, prices, and physical environments and locations to reinforce this positioning. Tesco has brought in a new chief executive to lead the way forward.

Questions

1. Analyse the possible value to Tesco of having a clear positioning in the market.

2. To what extent do you think the difficulties at Tesco are due to internal issues rather than external?

ASSESSMENT ACTIVITIES

Sections (a), (b) and (c) of these assessment activities are relevant for students taking AS and A-level

examinations. The questions in section (d) are for A-level students only.

(a) Knowledge check questions

1 Explain what is meant by segmentation.

2 Grouping customers by their age is an example of .... segmentation.

3 Deciding which segments to focus on and operate in is called ....

4 State one benefit of segmenting a market.

5 What is the difference between segmenting and targeting?

6 What is meant by positioning?

7 State two factors that might influence the positioning of a business.

8 Explain one reason why a business might want to change its positioning.

9 Explain the difference between niche and mass marketing.

10 Identify which of the combinations of benefits and price in the chart below would be uncompetitive.

Price relative to rivals	Benefits relative to rivals	
	High	Low
High		
Low		

(b) Short answer questions

1   Explain how the holiday market may be segmented.   (5 marks)

2   Explain how targeting business customers rather than holidaymakers might affect the marketing of an airline.   (5 marks)

3   Ford is trying to develop cars that can be sold in the mass market across the world rather than adapting cars for each market. Explain one benefit of this mass market approach.   (5 marks)

4   Explain how a new breakfast cereal might be able to compete even if it has a relatively high price.   (5 marks)

5   Explain one benefit to a drinks business of focusing on a specific segment of the market.

(c) Data response questions

In 2014 the supermarket business Morrisons announced that it was going to be permanently cheaper, with price reductions on over 1,200 everyday essentials.

The price cuts, which on average are 17 per cent, are on their own brand and on well-known branded products that together make up a typical weekly shopping basket. The latest price drops follow earlier ones on milk, fresh meat, fruit and vegetables.

The Chief Executive of Morrisons said that although the company's products were now cheaper this does not mean that quality was reduced: the aim is to make food more affordable to keep and gain customers.

The company is also being very transparent about its pricing. It is launching a new website, powered by *mysupermarket.co.uk*, which gives customers the ability to view the pricing history of an item. The aim is to reassure them that prices are indeed lower.

The cheaper prices are being promoted via a campaign which has the title, 'I'm Your New Cheaper Morrisons'. This was launched on 1 May 2014 with heavy advertising in the commercial breaks during *Emmerdale* and *Coronation Street* on television.

Morrisons is the UK's second largest fresh food manufacturer and unlike its competitors it makes more than half of the fresh food it sells. It will be using this vertically integrated structure to maintain quality of products while keeping prices down.

1   Explain two benefits to a supermarket of segmenting the market.   (6 marks)

2   Analyse the factors that might influence a customer's decision to choose one supermarket rather than another.   (9 marks)

3   To what extent do you think changing its positioning is likely to be a good strategy for Morrisons?   (15 marks)

(d) Essay questions

1   To what extent is the process of segmentation and targeting and positioning useful to a business entering the retail clothing market?   (25 marks)

2   You are the managing director of an airline that is considering entering the holiday market by providing not only the flights but also running resorts. You are considering different destinations but also different customer experiences, such as family breaks or romantic getaways.

To what extent should your decision on which segment to target depend on the size of the market?   (25 marks)

Chapter

10

Using the marketing mix

Introduction

In this chapter we will introduce the marketing mix, examine the influences on the different elements of the marketing mix and consider how it is used in marketing decision making.

What you need to know by the end of this chapter:

- the elements of the marketing mix (7Ps)
- how to analyse the influences on and effects of changes in elements of the marketing mix
- the difference between industrial and consumer products
- the difference between convenience, shopping and specialty products
- the implications of the product life cycle and the Boston matrix for marketing decision making
- the influences on new product development decisions
- the influences on pricing decisions
- how to analyse the promotional mix, including branding
- how to analyse distribution decisions
- how to analyse decisions relating to people, process and physical environment
- the importance of an integrated marketing mix
- the value of digital marketing and e-commerce.

The elements of the marketing mix (7Ps)

The positioning of a business is a key part of the marketing planning of a business: it determines how managers want the product to be perceived relative to rivals. For example, if a business is deciding on launching a product it can analyse the market to identify the segments it wants to target and then decide on its desired positioning. Does a new sports retailer want to be regarded as a discounter (like Sports Direct) or more of a fashion business (like JD Sports)? In the case of an established product a manager may decide to change

the positioning of its product relative to competitors; for example, Waitrose supermarket has been trying to reposition itself so it is not seen as so expensive and Morrisons wants to reposition itself to compete more directly with the discounters such as Aldi.

Once a manager has decided on the positioning of the product or business in the market they can then organise the marketing activities to reinforce this position. For example, in a premium hotel you expect room service, a pool and excellent customer service, for which you would expect to pay a relatively high price. In a budget hotel you expect a basic room and a low price.

The combination of marketing decisions that influence a customer's decision to buy is known as the **marketing mix**. The nature of the mix will depend on the positioning.

Figure 10.1 The marketing mix

The marketing mix can be analysed using the 7Ps framework. The 7Ps are:

- The **price** of the product. This includes the prices charged for different versions of the product (for example for different-sized bottles) and payment terms – for example, whether a customer can pay in instalments.

- The **product** itself. This includes the physical features and specifications of the product (what does it do), what it looks like (its design), how reliable it is, how long it lasts, what guarantees are provided, what after sales service is provided.
- The distribution of the product (this is known as **place**). This refers to the distribution channel, that is how the ownership of a product moves from the producer of the product to the final customer. In some cases a customer buys direct from the producer and the distribution channel is known as '0 level' as there are no intermediaries. In other cases a product is sold to intermediaries such as retailers who then sell it on to the final customer.

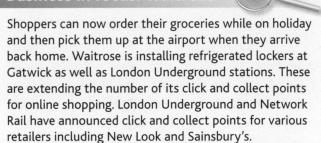

Business in focus: Waitrose

Shoppers can now order their groceries while on holiday and then pick them up at the airport when they arrive back home. Waitrose is installing refrigerated lockers at Gatwick as well as London Underground stations. These are extending the number of its click and collect points for online shopping. London Underground and Network Rail have announced click and collect points for various retailers including New Look and Sainsbury's.

Argos has signed a deal with eBay allowing people to pick up deliveries from 650 stores. Waitrose e-commerce director said, 'More and more people are adding an online shopping mission to their way of buying from Waitrose and we will continue to invest in making sure that we give them what they want when they want it.'

Source: Adapted from *The Times*, 8 August 2014

Questions

1. Analyse why companies such as Waitrose and Sainsbury's are seeking new types of distribution outlets.
2. To what extent do you think the growth of e-commerce means retailers no longer need high street outlets?

- The **promotion** of the product. This refers to the ways in which a business communicates about the product. This can be through a variety of ways such as:
  - advertising: this involves paid for communications, for example in newspapers or on billboards
  - public relations: this is when businesses try to get free coverage of their activities, for example if their chief executive gives an interview to the press
  - sponsorship deals, for example promoting the Premier League

- sales promotions: these are special offers such as 'buy one get one free' (BOGOF)
- sales teams: many businesses have salesforces to contact potential customers or distributors. This is especially important with industrial goods where a business is selling to other businesses and uses its salesforce to make the contacts.

What do you think?

In 2014, to promote the launch of its new Apple Watch, Apple gave away the new album from U2 via iTunes. Do you think this was a good way to promote the product launch? Do you think this was a good way for U2 to promote their new world tour?

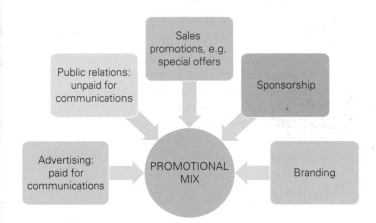

Figure 10.2 The promotional mix

- the **people** involved in the transaction, For example, the people who take your enquiry if you ring up about a product, the people who serve you in a shop, the people who change your tyre in the garage and who cut your hair at the hairdresser. Their skills and their attitudes affect your perception of the product.
- the **process**. This refers to how you actually buy the product. A customer's satisfaction with a good or service can be affected by the process that is involved in buying it or paying for it. Paying for car parking has got a lot easier with mobile phone payment and ordering your shopping has got easier by using your phone or your tablet; these sorts of changes have improved the customer experience. Equally you can have a bad customer experience if the website crashes when you want to make a booking, if the shop does not accept credit cards or you have to wait a long time because of the queuing system. Improving the buying process can therefore improve customer satisfaction.
- the **physical environment**. This refers to the physical premises of a business, (for example if you

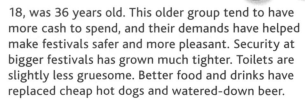

Business in focus: Music promotion

In 2014 Dolly Parton, an American country and western singer, played a set at Glastonbury, Britain's largest music festival. She was seen by 100,000 people at the festival and by a further 2 million television viewers. After this her album 'Blue Smoke' was near the top of the album chart for eight weeks. Her resurgence shows how festivals are reshaping Britain's music business.

The live music market is flourishing even as sales of recorded music have fallen. Between 2012 and 2013 the live market grew by a quarter, according to the Performing Rights Society for Music. Gig-goers now spend more than £1 billion a year on tickets and almost half that again on food, drink and the like while at the gig. Festivals make up a large part of this market. In the early 1990s Britain had few festivals but around 450 now take place each year. The festival season, once limited to July and August, now stretches until early autumn.

One boost was a change to the licensing laws in 2005 which made it easier to put on a show outdoors. The recession helped too: Britons who could no longer afford foreign holidays found a weekend of camping in a muddy field more attractive. Ageing crowds are another bonus. A survey in 2013 found that the average age of a reveller at Glastonbury, excluding those under

18, was 36 years old. This older group tend to have more cash to spend, and their demands have helped make festivals safer and more pleasant. Security at bigger festivals has grown much tighter. Toilets are slightly less gruesome. Better food and drinks have replaced cheap hot dogs and watered-down beer.

All this is changing the way the music industry works. Festivals are increasingly seen as a way to test whether big-name artists have enough fans to warrant arena tours. Newer names find them essential: Clean Bandit, a British band who brought out their first album in 2014, performed at over 20 festivals over that summer. And music executives are increasingly taking into account how successfully they think artists will perform at big outdoor gigs before deciding to sign them.

Source: The Economist, 23 August 2014
www.economist.com/news/britain/21613333-how-big-outdoor-concerts-are-changing-music-industry-muddy-tunes

Questions

1. Analyse the ways in which you would promote the next album of the band Arctic Monkeys.
2. To what extent do you think a festival is a good way to promote a new band? Justify your view.

---

go and buy a car, look around the car showroom) and how carefully it has been designed; the decor, the cleanliness, the design, the pictures, the state of the cars themselves and the reception desk all influence your perception of the business. The same is true when you go to the hairdressers: the signage, the layout of the salon, the music playing and so on all affect the positioning of the business.

Figure 10.3 A car showroom

What do you think?

You have decided to open an upmarket hairdressing salon in the West End of London. How might this positioning affect the 7Ps?

The decisions made about the 7Ps and the way the different elements of the marketing mix interrelate will affect the customer's overall perception of the product, whether they think it represents good value for money and how they think it is positioned relative to other products in the market.

Key term

The **marketing mix** is the combination of marketing choices that can be used by a business to influence consumers to buy products.

Study tip

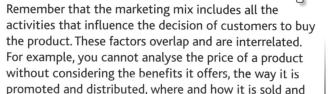

Remember that the marketing mix includes all the activities that influence the decision of customers to buy the product. These factors overlap and are interrelated. For example, you cannot analyse the price of a product without considering the benefits it offers, the way it is promoted and distributed, where and how it is sold and who sells it.

The relationship between the positioning of a business and the marketing mix can be seen by analysing Ryanair. Ryanair has been clearly positioned as a low-cost airline.

This means:

- The product is basic. The company focuses on short-haul flights to airports where it is cheap to land. It uses a standardised fleet of planes so that parts are standardised and staff only have to be trained to maintain and repair one type of aircraft, which keeps costs low.
- The price is low because it is positioned as a budget airline.
- The promotion focuses on the low-cost message and is via inexpensive methods. For example, boss Michael O'Leary has tended to get a lot of publicity for some of the things he says (such as threatening to charge customers to use the toilet on the plane!) – this gets the company's name mentioned without paying anything for advertising.
- The process focuses on online bookings to keep the costs down. If a customer makes a mistake in the booking it is their fault and they must pay for any necessary changes. This may be annoying but it keeps the price down and this is what the business is focusing on.
- The staff are expected to undertake many different tasks, which also helps keeps costs down.

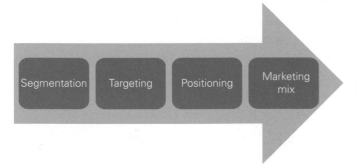

Figure 10.4 The stages of the marketing process

Compare this with MontBlanc, which is positioned as a luxury brand that offers products such as watches and pens, or 'writing instruments'. To match this luxury positioning the marketing mix includes:

- a product that is focused on craftsmanship
- high prices to reflect the brand's exclusivity
- limited distribution; the products are sold in premium outlets
- promotion that highlights quality; for example, advertising in upmarket publications
- the staff will place a high level of importance on customer service.

Figure 10.5 A Montblanc pen

What do you think?

The InterContintental Group of hotels is one of the largest in the world. It comprises several brands aimed at different customer segments as shown below. Explain why Intercontinental might have a range of hotel brands. Discuss how the marketing mix might vary for Holiday Inn and Crown Plaza.

Figure 10.6 The Intercontinental group owns several hotel businesses aimed at different market segments. The Holiday Inn aims at families and social travellers, whereas the Crowne Plaza attracts business guests.

Changes in the marketing mix

The positioning of a product is not fixed. It may need to change as internal or market conditions change. For example, following a disappointing financial performance in 2014, Ryanair's boss announced the

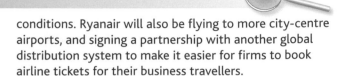

Business in focus: Ryanair

In 2014 Ryanair announced it was launching a business service in another move to reposition the business and catch up with travellers' demands for better treatment.

The airline said its 'business plus' fares would give customers flexible tickets, more check-in baggage, priority boarding and 'premium' seats – in the first five rows for quick boarding, or on exit rows with extra legroom. It said business passengers already make up more than a quarter of its customers and that the new fares, starting at €69.99 (or £59.99 for UK customers), were designed to get more of their business.

Ryanair admitted it had been 'asleep at the wheel' as customers got fed up with receiving bad service in return for low fares. Its rival, EasyJet, moved upmarket and launched a business package. Ryanair has recently introduced allocated seating, relaxed cabin bag restrictions, reduced charges, and loosened booking

conditions. Ryanair will also be flying to more city-centre airports, and signing a partnership with another global distribution system to make it easier for firms to book airline tickets for their business travellers.

In the past Chief Executive Michael O'Leary had made Ryanair's hidden charges and inflexible booking procedures a selling point to emphasise his cheap fares but consumers seem to have grown tired of this approach, prompting a change in strategy.

Source: The *Guardian*, 27 August 2014
www.theguardian.com/business/2014/aug/27/ryanair-business-class-service

Questions

1. Analyse the possible reasons why Ryanair is repositioning itself.
2. To what extent do you think the marketing mix of Ryanair will have to change as it repositions itself?

company would place more emphasis on customer service, for example allowing a second cabin bag on board, reducing the number of clicks to book online and having allocated seats. These efforts to improve customer service and enhance the benefits offered were an attempt to catch up with EasyJet, which had moved very successfully in this direction ahead of Ryanair.

Changes in the mix occur due to internal or external influences. Internal influences might be:

- changes to the financial position. This might affect investment in new product development or promotion.
- changes to staff bringing about new marketing opportunities. New signings at Arsenal might improve the team and lead to greater promotions or higher priced tickets.
- changes to operations. For example, greater efficiencies might enable lower prices. More innovation might lead to a wider range of products being offered.
- changes to objectives. New managers or owners may set new targets for the business. For example, there may be a target of faster growth. These new objectives for the business as a whole will have implications for each of the functions including marketing. New marketing objectives might include higher sales and this might influence the marketing mix.

External influences can be analysed using the PEST-C framework:

- **Political and legal** factors. For example, new European legislation might affect how products have to be labelled.

- **Economic** factors. For example, if the economy is growing, higher prices might be possible.
- **Social** factors. For example, greater environmental concerns might affect how the product is produced.
- **Technological** factors. For example, more people using the internet might make online promotion more effective.
- **Competition**. For example, greater competition might mean the benefits of the product have to be enhanced to match what they are offering.

Influences on the marketing mix

Types of product

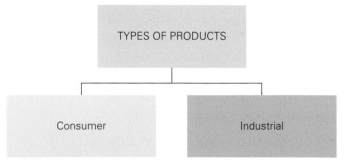

Figure 10.7 Types of products

There are, of course, many different types of products and the relative importance of different marketing activities and the nature of the marketing mix will vary for these. A common distinction when analysing products is to distinguish between **consumer** and **industrial products**.

Business in focus: Navigator photocopier paper

Navigator photocopier paper is sold mainly to businesses. The promotional information below is aimed at business buyers.

INCREASED PRODUCTIVITY

99.99 per cent paper jam free. A reduction in jams which leads to a lower cost per printed document.

IMPROVED SURFACE

Provides excellent printing quality while reducing toner consumption.

SILKY TOUCH

Extra smooth surface. Lower abrasiveness improves the lifetime of office equipment.

MULTIFUNCTIONAL

100 per cent guaranteed for all printers and copiers and any type of document.

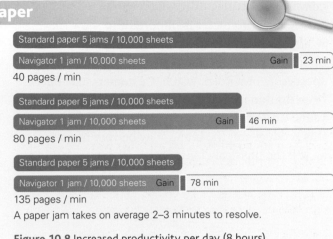

Standard paper 5 jams / 10,000 sheets
Navigator 1 jam / 10,000 sheets — Gain — 23 min
40 pages / min

Standard paper 5 jams / 10,000 sheets
Navigator 1 jam / 10,000 sheets — Gain — 46 min
80 pages / min

Standard paper 5 jams / 10,000 sheets
Navigator 1 jam / 10,000 sheets — Gain — 78 min
135 pages / min

A paper jam takes on average 2–3 minutes to resolve.

Figure 10.8 Increased productivity per day (8 hours)
Source: Navigator website
www.navigator-paper.com

Questions

1. Analyse the potential benefits to a business of buying Navigator photocopier paper.
2. To what extent do you think the product is the most important element of the marketing mix in the case of industrial products?

Consumer products are bought by individuals like you and me: we either consume them ourselves or give them to others to consume. This means that there may be many thousands or even millions of customers being targeted. As a result promotional activities may have to reach large numbers of people and may justify national advertising.

When targeting customers of consumer products marketing managers will bear in mind that consumers are not professional buyers. Although on occasion they may be rational and very logical in their decision making there will also be occasions where they are emotional and affected by all kinds of factors such as the brand image.

By comparison, **industrial products** are sold to businesses, which use them in their own processes. In this case a business may be dealing with professional buyers (that is, buying is their job) who:

- are probably less interested in packaging and branding in itself and more interested in having evidence of the technical performance of the product
- will want to understand exactly how the product represents value for money and how it helps their business improve their competitiveness.

Key terms

Consumer products are goods bought for consumption by the general public.

Industrial products are goods bought for use in business processes.

Types of consumer products

With the overall category of consumer products it is possible to analyse sub-categories:

- **Convenience items**: these are products such as milk and newspapers, which are very widely distributed. Customers will not usually travel very far to buy these products and if they are not available at one store customers will probably buy another brand. Ensuring the products are widely available is an important part of the success of these products.
- **Shopping goods**: these are products where customers compare features and price between different options and may take some time before deciding which one to buy. Shopping goods are the sort of products you might visit several stores before deciding which brand to buy (i.e. when out shopping or online). If you want to buy a washing machine or microwave you might want to shop around and

compare before deciding which model to buy. For this type of product it is important to show the relative benefits of your product compared to rivals.

- **Specialty products**: these are products such as a sports cars or a Rolex watch. Customers may have been thinking about buying these for months or even years. Customers will be willing to travel far to buy this product and the brand may be very important, as will the physical environment where it is sold.

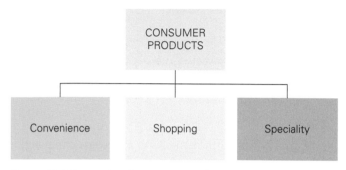

Figure 10.9 Categories of consumer products

	Convenience	Shopping	Speciality
Example	Chewing gum	TV	Sports car
Distribution (Place)	Very wide	Wide	Limited
Price	Not necessarily that important as usually relatively low	Important as customers shop around and compare	Not so significant as this is a special purchase
Product	Some brand loyalty	Some brand loyalty but comparison between brands	Strong brand awareness
Promotion	Aiming at large numbers of customers; aims to draw them into the store and in-store will use promotions to attract impulse buys	Will raise brand awareness	Very targeted
Process	Often impulse buy	May have payment and credit terms	May want payment terms
Physical environment	Not very significant	Relatively significant	Very significant
People	Limited importance	Important: want staff in store to know the strengths of the brand and particular model	Very important – staff in store reflect on the brand

Table 10.1 The marketing mix and different types of product

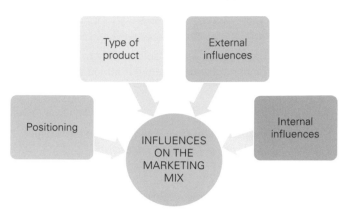

Figure 10.10 Influences on the marketing mix

Analysis of product decisions

The product lies at the heart of the marketing mix. After all it is the product that defines the benefits that the business provides. A product consists of:

- **the core benefit** it provides, for example a washing machine provides clean clothes.
- **the tangible product**: this refers to features such as its specifications, its reliability and its design. In the case of a washing machine, this would refer to the size, shape and look of the machine as well as features such as spin speed and energy usage. (Samsung have recently introduced a washing machine that will store a month's worth of washing powder and gradually release it as required; the washing machine decides how dirty the clothes are and how much powder is needed!)
- **the augmented product**: this refers to the 'extras' such as the brand name, the delivery and any guarantee and after-sales service provided. For example, a retailer may offer to take away your old washing machine and install your new one, to encourage you to buy from it.

What do you think?

What do you think are the core, tangible and augmented aspects of a Honda Prius?

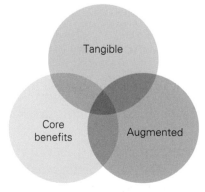

Figure 10.11 Features of a product

Features of a product

Managers will want to decide not only the features of a given product but also what products to offer (which markets to compete in) and how many versions to offer (for example what sizes, with what forms of packaging).

Figure 10.12 Different offerings for different market segments

Managers will want to:

- monitor the progress of individual products over time to decide whether to change the marketing mix – this can be analysed using the **product life cycle** model
- take an overview of how all the products fit together to decide whether some need more investment or whether some are no longer viable – this is analysed using **product portfolio analysis**
- decide whether to develop new products as markets change (new product development)
- how to develop the brand of a product.

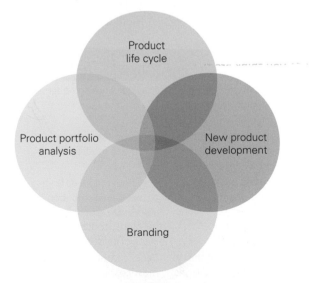

Figure 10.13 Aspects of managing products

Key terms

A **product life cycle** model shows the sales of a product over its life. Usually involves stages such as introduction, growth, maturity and decline.

Product portfolio analysis examines the market position of all of the products of a business, for example in terms of market share or market growth.

These aspects of managing products are examined below.

Product life cycle

As part of their decisions about the marketing mix, managers will review how products are doing over time and whether the mix needs to change. The different stages of a product's progress in terms of sales are shown on the product life cycle model in Figure 10.14; this model plots sales over time.

The stages of a typical product life cycle are:

- **Development:** this is the stage when a product is being developed. At this stage there is investment into research and development, products will be tested and assessed to see if they are worth launching. This means money is being invested into product development but given that there are no sales, cashflow is negative. Developing a new film, a new car or new TV series takes time and money. Products such as driverless cars are still at this stage.
- **Introduction:** this is when a product is launched on to the market. Sales may be relatively slow as awareness can take time to build. High levels of investment may be required to promote the new product. Cashflow may still be negative. Products such as Google glasses are at this stage.
- **Growth:** this when the sales begin to increase at a relatively fast rate. Customers are increasingly aware of the product and sales are building. Managers will still be investing to keep sales growing but by this stage cashflow should be becoming positive. Products such as the latest iPhone are at this stage.
- **Maturity:** this is when the rate of growth of sales begins to slow; this could be because competitors are entering the market taking away potential sales. Products such as BIC biros are at this stage. Note that sales may be high, it is just that they are not increasing rapidly, possibly because they are so high already.
- **Decline**: this is when sales are falling (the growth rate is negative), perhaps because new and better products are now on the market.

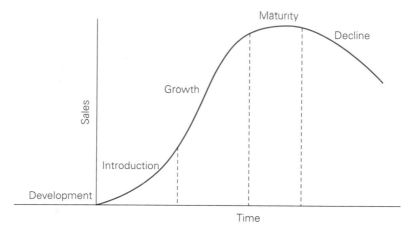

Figure 10.14 The product life cycle

What do you think?

What stage of the product life cycle do you think the following products are at? Why?

Product	Annual sales growth
A	−5 %
B	15 %
C	0 %

Table 10.2

What do you think?

What do you think the product life cycle for a new Harry Potter book by JK Rowling would look like? Explain your reasoning.

What about the product life cycle for:

- Facebook
- Manchester United
- the next James Bond film
- Heinz Tomato Ketchup
- record players?

The marketing mix will need to be adapted at different stages of the product life cycle. For example, when demand is growing the business may be able to maintain a relatively high price whereas if the product is entering the decline phase managers may have to reduce the price. When a product is introduced promotion may focus on making customers aware of the product; when competitors enter the market the promotion may focus more on why this product is different from others.

The value of the product life cycle model

The product life cycle model shows different stages a product may go through, from its conception to its withdrawal from the market. The actual duration and precise nature of each stage will vary from product to product. For example, a new restaurant may take months to establish itself; a new film may be popular as soon as it is released. A successful medicine may be on

Elements of the marketing mix	Introduction	Growth	Maturity	Decline
Price	May enter with low price to gain sales or high price if demand is high	May be able to maintain a relatively high price	Likely to consider cutting price to sustain sales	May cut price to boost sales
Product	Likely to be limited number of versions of the product as it is just launched	May develop other varieties/models	May start to focus on best sellers as demand is not growing fast any longer	Focus on the most profitable models
Distribution	May be limited as the product is not yet established	Will become wider as more businesses will want to sell the product	May focus on best-selling distribution channels	May find it more difficult to maintain distribution as stores may drop your product for more popular brands (this is called delisting)
Promotion	May focus on raising awareness of the product	Continuing to raise awareness	Focus on benefits of this product compared to rivals	Reduced to focus on the most cost effective methods

Table 10.3 The marketing mix through the product life cycle

Business in focus: Rainbow Loom

Figure 10.15 A Rainbow Loom

Rainbow Looms are one of the biggest crazes in recent years that have caught on with children around the world. The product was originally developed by Cheong Choon Ng in 2011 when he built a loom out of pins and wood. Mr Ng had noticed his daughters weaving with elastic bands just using their fingers and decided there must be a better way of doing it. (His background is in engineering.) The plastic loom he developed enabled more complex patterns and more intricate designs to be created. The success of Rainbow Looms has been

extraordinary and incredibly rapid. This success is due mainly to word of mouth and children seeing others making bracelets, and even clothes, with the looms and bands, and wanting to copy what everyone else seems to be doing!

However, the Rainbow Loom and loom bands are not without critics. Some people complain that they are bad for the environment because they are made of plastic and, when thrown away, the bands do not biodegrade but instead enter the food chain when they are eaten by fish. Others believe the bands are dangerous because animals can choke on them and children can cut off the blood supply to their fingers if they weave without the loom.

Typically products such as the Rainbow Loom have a relatively short product life cycle as children move on to the next craze. Will this be the case for loom bands and, if so, will Mr Ng move on to another product?

Questions

1. Analyse the possible reasons for the growth in sales in loom bands.

2. To what extent is a decline in sales of loom bands inevitable?

Figure 10.16 Different product life cycles: a fad product, a product that makes a return to the market and a product with a short life cycle

the market for over 15 years, whereas a new song may only be successful for weeks. From this we can see how decisions may vary over time as the sales of a product move into different stages. Just when these stages occur differs, but there are important lessons for marketing managers about what to expect at some point in the progress of a product over time. The problem is knowing exactly where you are at any particular moment; a slight fall in sales could be the beginning of the decline stage of the life cycle or a temporary drop. Managers need to be careful how they interpret the data before acting.

Extension strategies

An extension strategy occurs when a business attempts to prevent sales of a product from falling and avoid or delay the decline stage of the product life cycle. For example, a business might:

- increase promotional expenditure to renewed interest in the product or to increase usage of the product
- revamp the product in some way, for example new packaging, new flavours

- find new target market segments for the product, for example new countries to sell it in or target a new age group with the product
- find new usage occasions for the product. For example, cereal companies are keen to try and increase consumption at other times in the day apart from breakfast.

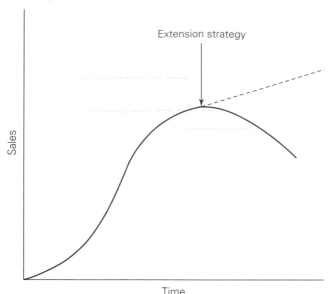

Figure 10.17 An extension strategy

What do you think?

How could Mattel, the producers of Barbie, extend its product life cycle?

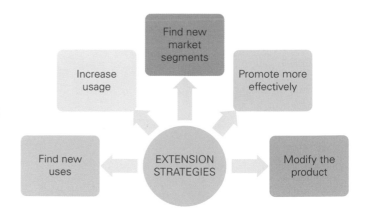

Figure 10.18 Extension strategies

The Boston Matrix

The product life cycle shows the progress of one product over time but most business have several products. This means they will want to analyse the overall position of the collection (or 'portfolio') of products before deciding what to do next; this is known as 'portfolio analysis'.

One well-known method of portfolio analysis is known as the **Boston Matrix**. It plots the position of each product in terms of its market share and the relative growth of the market. The size of the circle drawn to illustrate each product highlights the size of its turnover.

Business in focus: Candy Crush

Figure 10.19 Candy Crush

King Digital Entertainment is the producer of the world famous, and slightly addictive, Candy Crush games. The company's sales have shot up in recent years with the increased popularity of this game but, late in 2014, the

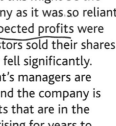

business announced a fall in its expected profits. This worried some analysts who thought this might be the beginning of the end for the company as it was so reliant on one product, even though its expected profits were still well over $2 billion. Some investors sold their shares and the share price of the company fell significantly. However, King Digital Entertainment's managers are confident that this is not the case and the company is here for the long term; new products that are in the pipeline will keep sales and profits rising for years to come.

Questions

1. Analyse the possible extension strategies King could use to prolong the life cycle of the Candy Crush brand.
2. To what extent should investors avoid mobile games businesses because of their short product life cycles?

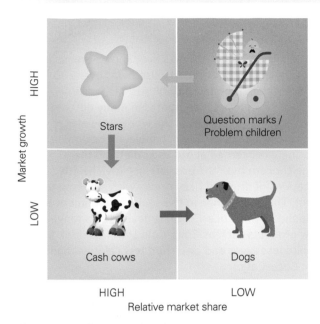

Figure 10.20 The Boston Matrix

In the Boston Matrix, products are given names according to which quadrant they are in.

- **Dogs**: these products with a relatively low share of a slow-growth market. Marketing managers must either invest to revitalise these products or let them decline and eventually remove them.
- **Cash cows**: these products are well established and so have a relatively high market share; however the market they are in is growing slowly, perhaps because it is mature and therefore not growing fast any more. These products do not need promoting as heavily as some others because they are well known and given their relatively high sales they generate a high level of funds for the business. Think of Heinz baked beans: the total sales of baked beans is probably quite large but not growing fast. Heinz baked beans is well established and should generate high profits that can help fund other projects for the business.
- **Problem children/question marks**: these are products that are in fast-growth (and therefore appealing) markets; however they are not yet established and only have a relatively small market share. They are problem children because they may turn out to do well but equally may not! Managers may want to invest to protect and grow these products.
- **Stars**: these are products that are in fast-growth markets and are doing well in terms of market share. It could be the leading brand in a new type of app, for example. Managers will probably need to keep

investing in, promoting and gaining more distribution for these products to ensure they remain stars.

The value of the Boston Matrix

The value of the Boston Matrix model is it helps managers categorise their products and take a view on what they should do next. For example:

- If all of the products of a business are cash cows managers might worry about the future success of the organisation because sales growth is slow. In this case managers may decide to invest to build some question marks and stars to help ensure future sales
- If all of the products of a business were dogs managers would definitely worry because they all have low market shares in slow growth markets. Drastic action may be needed.

What do you think?

Identify whether the following products are a cash cow, question mark, dog or star.

Product	Market share (%)	Market growth (%)
A	0.05	20.00
B	34.00	25.00
C	0.10	0.01
D	25.00	2.00

Table 10.4

In theory, a manager will aim for some well-established products (cash cows) to help fund the development and success of new products (question marks and stars). They will want a **balanced portfolio** in which the mature, established products help prepare the business for the future.

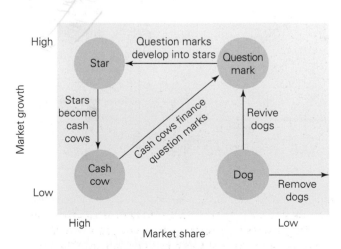

Figure 10.21 Boston Box with funding

Key terms

The **Boston matrix** analyses all of a firm's products in terms of their market share and the growth of the market.

A **balanced portfolio** is an appropriate mix of products in terms of their market shares and market growth.

What do you think?

Below, you can see some of Unilever's vast product portfolio.

Why do you think companies like Unilever, Pepsico and General Motors have built up their portfolios of products?

Figure 10.22 The extensive product portfolio of Unilever

What do you think?

Why do you think a business might sell off some products in its portfolio?

What might a business look for in a product when deciding whether to add it to its portfolio?

Look at the data below from Thomas Cook, the travel company. How might the company use this analysis of its holiday products?

Business in focus: Coca-Cola

Coca-Cola is one of the world's best known brands in its own right, but the company also owns over 200 other brands of carbonated drink such as Sprite and Dr Pepper. This means it competes in many different segments in markets all over the world. However, the company faces a problem; people are becoming increasingly concerned about their diet and there is some concern over the possible negative health implications of drinking fizzy drinks with a high sugar content. This is a change in the social environment and to respond to this Coca-Cola has developed a range of new products such as Coca-Cola Life. This drink has one-third less sugar and one-third less calories than classic Coca-Cola.

Coca-Cola has also looked for new growth markets to move into. For example, in 2014 it bought a 16.7 per cent share in Monster, the energy drinks business. This gave Coca-Cola a quick entry into the rapidly growing energy drinks sector as well as gaining access to brands such as Monster's Peace Tea and Hansen's Natural Sodas. These are potential growth areas for Coca-Cola and it has judged it more profitable to buy established brands than try to build its own competing brand from scratch. For Monster it has given the business access to Coca-Cola's huge distribution system.

Questions

1. Analyse factors which might affect sales of Coca-Cola.

2. Analyse the ways in which the Boston Matrix might help marketing decision making at Coca-Cola.

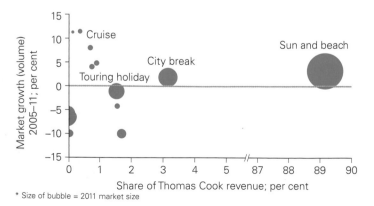

Figure 10.23 Thomas Cook's holiday products
Source: Thomas Cook's website
www.thomascookgroup.com/wp-content/uploads/2014/04/130313-no scriptv1G-FINAL-EMAIL.pdf

Analysis of new product development decisions

New product development involves investment to modify an existing product or replace it with a new one. It may take several months (for example for a new computer game) or several years (for example for a new model of car).

New product development may be required because:

- the existing products are coming to the end of their life cycle
- new opportunities are opening up do to changes in the market
- there is a desire to build on the strengths of the brand
- it is a way of achieving growth
- to match what competitors are doing.

However, new product development involves risk because:

- Many product ideas do not make it to actual production. This is because the idea proves not to be viable in terms of producing it and making a profit or because of technical problems along the way.
- Many products do not sell well and are withdrawn. This may be because the market has not been understood properly, promotional problems or competitor actions.

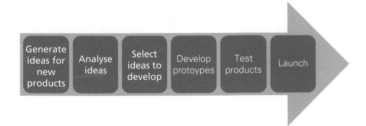

Figure 10.24 The process of new product development

When considering whether to invest in a new product, managers will consider the likely time it will take to recover the initial spending (this is called payback) and the rate of return on the investment.

What do you think?

What could managers do to increase the likelihood of success of a new film?

What do you think?

Figure 10.25 New product development at Apple Inc.

Apple has had several highly successful innovative products. What do you think determines the success of Apple's new product development?

Analysing pricing decisions

In addition to the features outlined in Figure 10.10 such as positioning, the stage of a product in the product life cycle and the competitive environment which influence all aspects of the marketing mix, when considering pricing decisions it is important to examine factors such as:

- The price elasticity of demand. If demand is price inelastic then it is possible to increase revenue by increasing price; this is because the price increase leads to a smaller percentage fall in quantity demanded. If demand is price elastic it is possible to increase revenue by reducing the price; this is because the percentage increase in quantity demanded is greater than the cut in price in percentage. Businesses will consider the price elasticity of demand before making price changes.
- **Costs**. For a business pursuing profit a manager will need to ensure that over time the price more than covers the cost per unit. In fact some businesses adopt an approach to pricing called cost plus: a plumber or road builder might estimate the cost of doing the work and add on a percentage. However, this method is not always appropriate. For example the cost per unit may vary according to how much is being produced and so managers may estimate expected sales at different prices and compare this with the expected costs. If a business installs a high-speed broadband network in an area

for example, this will involve high fixed costs to set up the system. The more users the business signs up the more it can spread these fixed costs and bring the unit cost down. This will enable the same profit margin to be achieved with a low price. By comparison, lower levels of sales may have higher unit costs and require a higher price to make a profit. The effect of price changes on revenue, sales and profit can be analysed using break-even charts (see page 220–21).

Business in focus: Dropbox

If at first you don't succeed ... try again; that seems to be the lesson learned from the story of Drew Houston who along with Arash Ferdowsi founded Dropbox, the online storage system, in 2007.

Mr Houston was studying at the world famous Massachusetts Institute of Technology (MIT) when he had a business idea to develop a programme to play online betting games. As a computer science graduate he seemed ideally placed to do this – except that his programme kept losing to the human players and had to be scrapped. However, like all great entrepreneurs, Mr Houston refused to be beaten and went on to his next idea, which was to develop online courses for students. Unfortunately, despite three years' work, this also failed to take off. A lesser man might have walked away from entrepreneurship but not Mr Houston.

Like so many fantastic business products, the idea for Dropbox came from frustration with what was available already. Mr Houston did not like having to remember to take USBs everywhere to carry his documents around. Storing files online seemed to be the solution and although some other businesses were starting to offer this solution few people were actually using the services because they were not very user friendly. The key to Dropbox's success was to make the service very simple to set up and use. Within 7 years the company had over 300 million users and growth remains rapid. The ease of the experience and the value of the service provided means that Dropbox's customer base grows largely from customers telling their friends about it and getting them to install it so they can share files easily.

So, what is it that makes a business successful? According to Mr Houston it is fairly simple – you just have to make something that people want. When companies fail, he argues, it is because they don't have enough customers; so to succeed, just make sure you provide something that lots of people want!

Questions

1. Analyse the possible reasons why new products often fail.

2. What do you think is the key reason why Dropbox has succeeded? Justify your answer.

What do you think?

The chart below is from Thomas Cook. What does it show us about the new product development process?

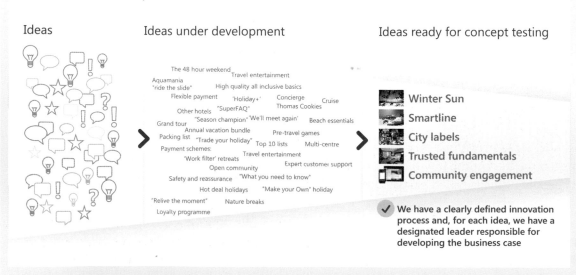

We have developed a full innovation funnel

Ideas	Ideas under development	Ideas ready for concept testing

Winter Sun
Smartline
City labels
Trusted fundamentals
Community engagement

✓ We have a clearly defined innovation process and, for each idea, we have a designated leader responsible for developing the business case

Figure 10.26 Thomas Cook's innovation process
Source: Thomas Cook's website
www.thomascookgroup.com/wp-content/uploads/2014/04/130313-no-scriptv16-FINAL-EMAIL.pdf

Influences on pricing

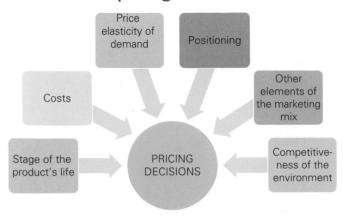

Figure 10.27 Factors that influence pricing

There are many different approaches to pricing that a business might adopt. These include:

- **penetration pricing.** This occurs when a business charges a low price to gain market share. This is most suitable when demand is sensitive to price (price elastic). A low price can gain high sales and enable the business to benefit from producing on a large scale (for example it may be able to gain lower prices from suppliers if it is buying materials on a large scale).
- **price skimming.** This occurs if a relatively high price is charged when a product is launched. For example, when a new iPhone is launched there are often queues outside the stores as some customers are so eager to buy it. Price skimming is most appropriate when demand is price inelastic; for example if the product is heavily branded.

Figure 10.28 Customers queuing for a new iPhone

- **dynamic pricing.** This occurs when prices are changing rapidly in response to changing demand conditions. For example, airlines and hotels can track the number of enquiries at any moment and the number of seats or rooms left and change the price accordingly. This means there is no 'one' price for a ticket or a room – it depends when you enquire and make the booking.

Business in focus: Uber

Uber is a new business in the taxi market. Customers can identify the nearest Uber car and use an app to order it and it should turn up in minutes. However, although the convenience of this service is appealing to customers they have been less pleased with Uber's dynamic pricing model. When demand is high, such as at the weekends, Uber pushes up prices to many times more than its normal fares.

Uber was launched in San Francisco in 2010 and it lets passengers call drivers from their smartphones. Uber has a number of carefully checked cars and drivers; customers can even see who is picking them up and what their rating has been in the past from their customers. Generally, Uber's prices are slightly cheaper than a taxi you stop in the street but when demand is high 'surge prices' kick in. On New Year's Eve, for example prices can be seven times normal levels, and minimum fares of up to $175 can apply.

Like many technology companies Uber is an intermediary. It links independent cab drivers with customers wanting a ride, in the same way that Google links searchers and advertisers or eBay links sellers and bidders.

Source: Adapted from *The Economist*, 29 March 2014
www.economist.com/news/finance-and-economics/21599766-microeconomics-ubers-attempt-revolutionise-taxi-markets-pricing-surge

Questions

1. Analyse the influences on the price of an Uber taxi ride.
2. To what extent is Uber's pricing policy ethical, in your opinion? Justify your answer.

Analysing promotional decisions

In addition to the features outlined in Figure 10.10 which affect all aspects of the marketing mix, when considering the appropriate mix of promotions a manager will examine factors such as:

- **the target audience.** Who is the business trying to communicate with? It is vital to understand the target group to understand how best to reach them. For example, day time television would not be useful if you are trying to target people who are out at work during the day. Google advertising would not be effective if your target group does not use the internet much.

- **the promotional budget** (how much money there is to spend). Some methods of promotion are relatively expensive (for example television advertising) and therefore would not be possible on a small budget.
- **the message**. For example, Red Bull has been keen to associate itself with sports and high energy activities and has done this through sponsorship of extreme sport type events.

Figure 10.29 Red Bull sponsors sports

- **technology**. The growth of online businesses has created many new forms of promotional opportunities which are transforming the promotional strategies of many businesses. Whereas you can never be sure who sees an advertisement on a billboard or in the newspaper, you can target online advertising much more effectively. With Google adwords, for example, a business can ensure its advert only appears if people enter certain search terms; they can also define in which regions it will appear, at what times and on what types of devices. They can assess the effectiveness of such advertising by measures such as CTRs (click-through rates) which measure how many people click through an advert to a company's website once it appears on their screens. This is much more targeted promotional activity with much more measurable results than in the past. Businesses are also making much use of **social media**; for example by creating their own blogs, contributing to other blogs linked to their products and using **viral marketing** to generate a buzz about their products.

Key terms

Social media refers to the social interaction among people where they create, share or exchange information and ideas in virtual communities.

Viral marketing is a marketing technique that uses social media and networks to raise brand awareness and boost sales by getting users to recommend the promotional campaign (such as a blog or advert) to others.

Influences on the promotional mix

Figure 10.30 Influences on the promotional mix

What do you think?

It is estimated that by 2020 there will be 50 billion 'connected devices' in the world – that is seven times more than there will be people. How do you think this will affect the promotional activities of business?

Analysing branding decisions

A **brand** represents a promise made by a business to provide a specific set of benefits. As customers we recognise brands and believe that they each represent certain values and so buying a branded product will deliver a certain set of features and/or services to us. We take a view of different brands and whether or not we want to be associated with them and want what they provide. We recognise a brand by its name, symbol/logo, slogan or anything else that is used to identify and distinguish it from the competition.

A brand is recognised by customers and has various associations for them. A brand has a promise of an experience. For example, if someone asked what you thought of Nike, Apple, Mc Donalds, Primark, Marks & Spencer and Beats you would have various thoughts about all of them: what the brand stands for, what it represents and what it means to you. These values can make you loyal to the brand because you want to be associated with it and because the brand acts as an assurance of the nature of the product and the service you will receive. A brand conveys something to the customer: it may be exclusivity, excellence of customer service or ethics. A brand is, therefore, a reputational asset, that is the reputation of the brand is something that has value to the business.

The values of a brand are not created immediately; the associations and trust tend to build over time. And a brand is not safe forever: brands are also vulnerable and can be severely damaged if something happens that conflicts with its values.

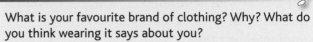

What do you think?

According to brand specialists Interbrand, the biggest European brands of 2013 were as follows.

Rank	Company	Revenue in 2013	Change from 2012
1	H&M	$18,168	New to top 10
2	Ikea	$13,818	New to top 10
3	Zara	$10,821	New to top 10
4	Carrefour	$10,299	+0 %
5	Tesco	$9,042	−16 %
6	M&S	$5,633	−14 %
7	Auchan	$3,697	+7 %
8	Boots	$3,376	+2 %
9	Aldi	$2,940	+1 %
10	Sephora	$2,143	+20 %

Table 10.5 The biggest European brands of 2013 by revenue

Source: Interbrand website

http://interbrand.com/assets/uploads/Interbrand-Best-Retail-Brands-2014-3.pdf

What do you associate with the brands above?

Key term

A **brand** is a promise to deliver certain benefits and services. It can be identified via a recognisable name, symbol, slogan, logo or anything that is used to identify and distinguish a product or business from competitors in the market.

If a brand is strong this may mean that:

- demand is likely to be more price inelastic
- customers may become brand ambassadors, telling others about the brand and convincing them to try it

- customers may be more open to other products launched under the same brand name
- it may be difficult for other brands to enter the market or gain market share.

What do you think?

What is your favourite brand of clothing? Why? What do you think wearing it says about you?

According to Warren Buffett, one of the richest men and most successful investors in the world, it takes 20 years to build a reputation. Do you agree with this?

Can you think of a brand whose reputation has been damaged in recent years?

Analysing distribution decisions

In addition to the features outlined in Figure 10.10 that affect all aspects of the marketing mix when considering distribution decisions, a manager will also examine factors such as:

- **the degree of coverage.** Does the business intend to target customers globally? Nationally? Or locally? The broader the spread of customers the more a business may have to use intermediaries to reach them rather than try to distribute directly to them.
- **the costs of different distribution strategies**. Setting up your own distribution network (for example your own chain of retail outlets across the country) may be expensive and take time. However, online sales opportunities mean businesses can now be global easily rather than having to open stores around the world.
- **the nature of the product.** For example if you have a high value product that sells in relatively

Business in focus: Top youth brands

According to a recent Marketing Week survey the following brands are the most popular with 18-to-24-year-olds:

1. YouTube
2. Amazon
3. Google
4. BBC
5. Ben & Jerry's
6. Cadburys
7. Facebook
8. Pringles
9. Wikipedia
10. Channel4

Source: Marketing Week

Questions

1. Explain why two of these brands might appeal to a youth audience.
2. Analyse how the fact these brands are popular with 18-to-24-year-olds might affect their marketing.

low quantities it may be realistic to distribute these products direct to the customer. However, if the product is relatively low-value and sells in high quantities (such as chewing gum) a business is likely to use intermediaries such as wholesalers and retailers. Convenience items need to be widely distributed whereas specialty items can be focused on fewer outlets that reinforce the brand.

- **the degree of control a business wants over the way its products are priced and promoted.** If an intermediary is used, for example, this business may gain ownership and therefore control how the product is displayed, promoted and priced. Companies such as Aston Martin, Rolex, Gucci and Chanel keep very close control of the outlets that sell their products because they want to protect the brand.

- **how customers expect to access the product and what technology allows a business to deliver.** Increasingly, shoppers are expecting **multichannel distribution**. This means they want to access a product in many ways. For example, businesses such as Tesco offers its products:
  - in out of town hypermarkets and supermarkets
  - in more local city stores
  - online.

Many businesses are having to respond to the demands from customers for greater flexibility by developing more distribution routes. Technology is revolutionising distribution in many industries and changing the value and nature of physical stores.

Key term

Multichannel distribution means that customers can buy the product in several ways, for example in store, online or 'click and collect'.

Study tip

Remember when discussing the elements of the marketing mix that it is essential to consider the requirements of the specific product being considered. There are not set answers to the best price to set, the best way to promote or the best way to distribute: it depends on the product and the particular objectives and environment in which it operates.

Business in focus: Hay fever

Many of us choose to buy a brand we know because we find it reassuring and because it reduces the risk of the purchase. We feel we understand the values of particular brands and we know we can rely on their quality. This can make buying quicker and less worrying. As a result of this, well-known, trusted brands may be priced more highly because we, as customers, are willing to pay for reassurance. A good example of this can be found in the pharmaceutical industry. When a company develops a new drug it can protect it with a patent. This prevents it being copied by others for a certain period of time and so allows the pharmaceutical company time to recover its investment costs. This also gives the brand time to become established in the market without competition. If successful this product becomes the brand we associate with curing a particular condition and so turn to it when we want treatment.

Once the patent expires the drug can be copied and produced by other businesses and these can be sold under their own labels. Whilst competitors do create new cheaper options which customers buy, the branded products often continue to sell well too. For example, Clarityn is a product to relieve the symptoms of hayfever. It contains the active antihistamine ingredient Loratadine which prevents the body creating the histamine that causes inflammation in the nose and throat. Clarityn sells for nearly £3.50 in high street chemists such as Boots. However, Boots also sells its own label product of anti-hayfever tablets called Allergy Relief; these also contain Loratadine but sell for under £3. Products such as Nurofen and Lemsip also have own-label equivalents but still command higher prices and sell well as some customers prefer to buy a brand name.

Questions

1. Analyse the possible reasons why people are willing to pay more for a branded product.

2. To what extent do you think the brand is more important than the actual product?

People, process and the physical environment decisions

In the past the marketing mix was often studied as the four Ps: price, place (distribution), promotion and product. However, as the service economy has grown other marketing activities have become important such as:

- **the people.** Those providing the service, advising and carrying out the task. The expertise and skills of your hairdresser, accountant, doctor and dentist are all important influences on your decision to use their services. Training, education and awareness of customer requirements are all important parts of marketing. Have you ever praised the helpfulness of a store? Ever criticised one for having staff who do not seem interested in you as a customer? If so you can see the importance of people. What influenced your first impression of your school? Inevitably it was the people you met, such as the teachers, the Head and the administrative staff. Managers will have to decide on staffing levels, investment in training and how to reward staff. These decisions will depend on factors such as how the business is positioned (we expect more personal attention and interaction at a four-star restaurant than at a McDonald's for example) and the nature of the product (for example, we may want more advice and information for shopping goods compared to convenience items).

- **the process.** Part of the customer experience in the whole process of buying. Do you have to wait for a long time in a queue? Are there seemingly endless forms to fill in? Can you order easily online? All these features will affect the buyer. Stores may compete by making the process easier: buy online and collect in store, 24-hour home delivery, online check-in and swiping your credit card rather than having to enter your code are all examples of how the process can make a business more competitive. Companies such as Disney appreciate that the process is a very important part of the mix: they manage queues at their theme parks carefully by flagging how long you have to wait, making sure you can always see the end of the queue so it does not seem far away, having entertainers distract you and allowing you to have a set time to go on a ride so you don't need to queue. Technological changes in particular have enabled businesses to improve their process.

- **the physical environment.** When you first walk into a leisure centre or the beauty salon you get an impression. The way it is designed, what is on the walls, what facilities there are all give signs that tell us something about the service. Marketing managers will want to consider how this fits in with the brand. Just think of any new buildings around your school – what messages do they convey in terms of design – are they modern in feel? Practical? Safe? What does the physical environment tell you about what the school values. The same is true for businesses – their head office, their offices generally and their stores all convey something. Managers will consider factors such as where to locate them, how to design them and how much to invest in them. This will again depend on factors such as the brand, the nature of the product and positioning.

Figure 10.31 Foxton's estate agents place great importance on making the physical environment in their branches appealing to customers.

The importance of an integrated marketing mix

The marketing mix refers to all the activities that might affect a customer's decision to purchase and indeed their experience of the product and whether they return to buy again. To be effective, the different aspects of the mix must work together and reinforce each other, that is they must be integrated. For example, if you walk into a shabby cafe on the outskirts of town you might be reluctant to pay high prices; the price and physical environment do not match. If you book a five-star hotel for your honeymoon you expect the service and the staff to be outstanding; the people have to match the product.

The different elements of the marketing mix must therefore complement each other to reinforce the brand values. The mix must also be developed to be appropriate for the given context. For example, the marketing mix must take account of:

- the position in the product life cycle; for example, in the decline stage the price may need to be lowered
- the Boston Matrix; there may need to be investment in more distribution for the star products, for example to build on their success
- the type of product; the price must be competitive with rivals for shopping goods, for example, but it is possible to charge higher prices than rivals for specialty products provided the brand is strong enough
- the marketing objectives; for example a desire to increase sales significantly may require more investment in promotion

- the target market; for example the promotional mix may need to be digitally based for a youth market and use social media but these methods are unlikely to be as effective for buyers aged over 80
- competition; for example a business may want to differentiate itself from rivals and so developments in their products may require more investment in new product development to keep pace
- positioning: for example, a business such as Ikea wants to provide well designed furniture at low prices. This affects aspects of the marketing mix such as:
  - the product, which has to be designed and produced in a way that is cheap. Customers assembling their own furniture and enabling it to be stored flat packed in a warehouse environment (which has only basic features) keeps costs down
  - the physical environment. Ikea stores are located outside of town in low cost locations. They are designed so that once you enter them it is difficult to leave without seeing everything. It has the products kept in a warehouse environment which is cheap to build and maintain.

Figure 10.32 IKEA store

- the process. Customers identify what they want and then find it in the warehouse. They take it to their car themselves and assemble themselves.
- the people; staffing levels are kept low.

The positioning of the business influences all aspects of its integrated marketing mix.

The value of digital marketing and e-commerce

In recent years developments in technology have significantly affected most aspects of business not least marketing. For example, digital marketing has enabled businesses to:

- gather more information about customers and process it more quickly and more effectively. This has provided much more insight into markets and customers
- build relationships with customers more effectively by being able to track their buying habits and recommend other products they might like
- target very specific segments. A business can now set up online quite cheaply and focus on quite a small segment of the market. It does not have to sell stock that may not sell: it can produce to order.
- involve customers more in the marketing process; customers can provide reviews of products to help other potential buyers; customers can also contribute designs and ideas online and the business can produce these if there is enough interest
- target global markets 24 hours a day.

Key term

E-commerce is the buying and selling of products through an electronic medium such as the internet.

Of course the value of digital marketing and **e-commerce** depends on how fast and how well a business adopts it. Morrison's was slow to go online and therefore lost market share: to Morrison's e-commerce proved a threat. HMV struggled as customers opted to download music rather than buy in-store; although the company tried to respond by changing its product mix it could not generate enough sales. By comparison, businesses such as eBay, Alibaba and Amazon have flourished through digital marketing and e-commerce.

It should not be assumed that these technological developments benefit every business. Traditional print newspapers have struggled as customers read online. Traditional television producers have struggled as customers want to watch online as and when they want. The key for marketing managers is to watch the trends in the market and make sure the business is adapting accordingly.

Business in focus: Location targeting

Walk along the street and look at all the places where advertising is placed – on bus stops, on billboards, on posters on the wall, on the backs of buses and the sides of cars. Advertisers are trying to communicate messages about their products in many different ways. The problem for the companies trying to promote their products is that these adverts are not very targeted – they may be seen by large numbers of people but the products or messages may not be relevant to most of them so a great deal of money spent on advertising is wasted. But what if the advertisers knew who was walking past at any moment and could change their adverts and messages accordingly? This means they could target their messages very precisely.

Developments in technology are making this possible – companies are able to track where you are via your phone and then change their adverts accordingly. For example, Esri is a company that specialises in location data mapping. It brings location data gained from a range of sources such as Wi-fi, phone masts, GPS and card transactions, and combines this with other data such as social media to enable companies (Esri's customers) to identify where their potential customers are at any moment and advertise accordingly. This kind of targeted marketing is much more efficient but acquiring the data obviously comes at a cost.

Questions

1. Analyse the benefits of location targeting for businesses.
2. To what extent is location targeting ethical?

Element of the marketing mix	Technology
Pricing	Businesses can adjust price according to the time when people are searching, where they are searching from and their previous behaviour; regular changes in price as demand conditions change is known as 'dynamic pricing'. It is not appropriate these days to ask for 'the price' of a plane ticket – it depends on when you ask.
Promotion	Online advertising can be much more targeted than, say, print advertising. If you place an advert in a newspaper or magazine you cannot easily be sure who sees it or what they do as a consequence. If you advertise online you can target the advert to show up in response to particular search terms at specific times from specific locations; you can also measure how many people then request more information or visit your website.
Distribution	By offering products online it Is possible to reach people around the world 24 hours day
Process	An online presence designed for e.g. PC, tablet and phone allows customers to find information and order whenever and wherever they want
Physical environment	Some businesses are adopting an online presence to complement their physical stores. For others the business is their online presence and so the web design reflects the brand rather than a store.

Table 10.6 The marketing mix and technology

Business in focus: Technology

Some analysts believe that technology has hit an inflection point where it has become so all embracing that there is no going back. The world today is multichannel. Every retailer has to be online. However, that does not mean the traditional store will no longer be needed but that stores may perform a very different function. People like to shop and shops help with engagement. Stores are likely to continue to be wanted but their functions may move towards distribution and 'click and collect' centres. They may well become shop windows from which you order products to be delivered later.

Retailers have to get used to thinking about many different channels, not just one – for example, the PC, the phone, the tablet as well as the physical store. They need to understand how to market in a digital world. It is also a world in which data is plentiful and what will matter is how that data is used. Businesses have to be careful with data – they could, for example, find all kinds of different segments but which ones do they actually want to target?

Questions

1. Explain what is meant by multichannel distribution.
2. To what extent is e-commerce likely to lead to the end of retail outlets?

Study tip

To develop its marketing mix a business needs a clear understanding of its target market segment. It can then adapt its mix accordingly.

Business in focus: Funerals

Some industries, like construction, are cyclical – they do well in times of booms and badly during recessions. Other sectors such as financial administrators that help recover money and close businesses down are contra cyclical – they do better when the economy is doing badly. Other businesses are not as vulnerable to the economic climate because they provide the essentials. The funeral industry is one of these. Whatever else is happening in the world people are born and people die, so the funeral industry should have a steady demand. However, that does not mean that the market never changes. For example, changes in society can affect whether people want to be buried or cremated. The availability of land can affect where and how people are buried. Also, technology is now having an impact on the funeral industry: people are choosing to record messages to be played when they are gone and readable

QR codes will be placed on their headstones so visitors can play a message from the deceased; and it is even possible to set up a messaging service to text everyone you know when you are dead. Further technological innovations include having personalised coffins and the option of having your remains sent into outer space. A company called Celestis, for example, charges around £3,000 to send your remains around the Earth. No market, it seems, can ignore changes in the macro-environment.

Questions

1. Analyse the ways in which technology is benefiting customers of funeral businesses.

2. To what extent do you think price is an important element of the marketing mix for a funeral?

Business in focus: Online sales as a percentage of retail sales in the UK

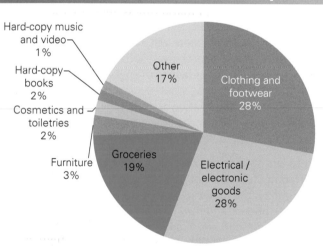

Figure 10.33 Types of products bought online

Source: Mintel, E-commerce, July 2014

The data above shows the trends in online retailing, that is the proportion of retail sales that are made online. It also shows the percentage of sales made online for different product categories such as electrical and electronic goods.

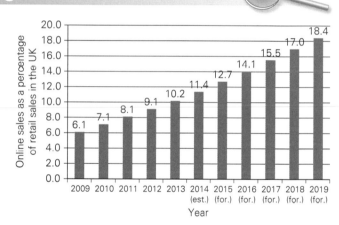

Figure 10.34 Online sales as a percentage of retail sales in the UK

Source: Mintel, E-commerce, July 2014

Questions

1. Summarise the trend in the data above.

2. Analyse the possible reasons for the growth in internet retailing in the UK.

3. Analyse the possible implications of the data above for the marketing decisions of retailers.

ASSESSMENT ACTIVITIES

Sections (a), (b) and (c) of these assessment activities are relevant for students taking AS and A-level examinations. The questions in section (d) are for A-level students only.

(a) Knowledge check questions

1   Distinguish between price penetration and price skimming.

2   State what is on the axes of the Boston Matrix.

3   State what is on the two axes of the product life cycle.

4   Identify the four stages of the product life cycle.

5   What are the three categories of consumer products?

6   An attempt to prolong the decline of sales is known as an ……… strategy.

7   State one benefit to a confectionery business of having a well-known brand.

8   State two ways a business might try to prevent sales from falling in the decline stage of the product life cycle.

9   If a product has a high market share of a low-growth market the product is known as a cash cow. True or false? Explain your answer.

10   Price skimming is more likely when demand is price elastic. True or false? Explain your answer.

(b) Short answer questions

1   Explain one influence on the price of a new computer console game.   (5 marks)

2   Explain one way in which a balanced portfolio might benefit a soft drinks business.   (5 marks)

3   Explain one way in which a social networking site might respond to falling numbers of users.   (5 marks)

4   Explain how digital marketing is affecting the marketing mix of banks.   (5 marks)

5   Explain one way in which the marketing mix of a tyre manufacturer differs from that of a hairdressing salon.   (5 marks)

(c) Data response questions

Google Glass

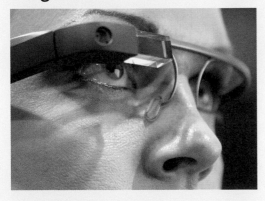

Figure 10.36 Google Glass

Google Glass is one of the latest products to be launched by the online giant and is another example of the company's desire to push forward the technological frontiers. Its Google X division is constantly seeking innovations that can transform the world within ten years.

Google Glass was launched in the UK in June 2014. Interestingly the product was priced relatively high at the time (at over £1,000) because it was, in essence, still in its development phase and was aimed at those who are real technology fans and are willing to pay premium prices to get the latest product early and experiment with it. Google wanted these early adopters to feedback to the company so it could continue to develop the glasses before targeting the mass market.

Google Glass has a small transparent display that is worn in front of the eye and can display information to the wearer. It is powered by Android and the wearer can access information such as websites, emails and numerous apps. Google Glass also has a camera and microphone built in so the wearer can take or play back film. Sound is communicated by vibrations, using a bone conduction transducer, through the wearer's head.

Although there has been a great deal of media interest in Google Glass it is not yet certain how popular the product will be with the general public. There is definitely a move towards mobile technology that we wear but it is not yet certain what form will win out – will it be similar to a watch or will the Google Glass approach prove more appealing?

There is also some resistance to the product from businesses that are reluctant to have people wandering around possibly filming others. For example, some cinemas have banned cinema goers from wearing Google Glass in case they video the latest releases. Some coffee chains are banning the Glass as well because they don't want an invasion of other customers' and staff's privacy.

The cost of producing Google Glass is estimated to be around $150. When Google feels ready to target the main market, it should be able to cut the price significantly making it more of a mass market product.

1 Explain the factors that might influence the price of Google glasses. (6 marks)

2 Analyse the ways in which the marketing mix may change over the life cycle of Google glasses. (9 marks)

3 To what extent do you think the price of Google glasses will ultimately determine its success? Justify your answer. (15 marks)

(d) Essays

1 To what extent is price the most important element of the marketing mix these days? (25 marks)

2 To what extent is the product life cycle a useful model for managers of decision making by the marketing managers of a perfume business? (25 marks)

Case study: Unit 3 Decision making to improve marketing performance

The Cambridge Satchel Company

Figure 1 A Cambridge Satchel Company satchel

The Cambridge Satchel Company is one of the great British business success stories of recent years. The company was set up in 2008 by Julie Deane and her mother Freda Thomas. It started with £600 invested to get the idea launched. The company is now known all over the world. It has even moved out of Deanne's kitchen to two prime locations in London!

The Cambridge Satchel Company (CSC) bags are all hand made in the UK and the Made in Britain feature is key part of the brand. The company's product range has grown from classic satchels to backpacks, handbags and small leather goods. Its awareness has increased by being featured on influential fashion blogs to being chosen as gifts for the cast members of the hit US TV show Mad Men as an end of series party gift; this high-profile status has helped to make the product be seen as a celebrity brand. The handmade bags have been bought by fashion celebrities such as Alexa Chung and have been seen on hit US TV shows such as Girls and the Good Wife. The company also featured as a case study in a Google advert campaign.

The Cambridge Satchel Company now makes 500 bags a day and in 2013 made pre-tax profits of £5 million on sales of £13 million.

In the early days the company gathered most of its market research data through bloggers. It would run a competition and for the price of giving away a handbag it would learn a lot from people interested in fashion and the company's products. This was a lot cheaper than commissioning research and at that time was all they could afford.

In 2014 Cambridge Satchel Company targeted more overseas markets after it announced that Index Ventures (a global venture capital firm) invested £13 million into the group. The company also recruited a number of senior employees who are experienced in the retail industry; for example it has recruited from Net-a-Porter and Marks & Spencer. Julie and Freda have realised the need to strengthen the management team as the business has grown. As well as overseas expansion through retail stores the company is building its digital presence. It is aiming to build the profile of The Cambridge Satchel Company as an internationally recognised online brand. It is now selling in over 100 countries around the world.

The investment from Index will help preserve British craft skills, with plans to double the 50-strong workforce at its Leicestershire factory. Its first factory opened in Wigston in 2011, but last year the company moved to larger premises. Apprentices will be taken on and taught traditional skills, easing youth unemployment and reinforcing the company's commitment to British enterprise.

The Cambridge Satchel Company has now created a multi-million pound, international brand, with its customers acting as ambassadors – as they carry the company's products around they are seen by others and this leads to more sales.

However, one problem the company now faces is counterfeits. This year alone Deane has uncovered 330 fake websites that claimed to sell Cambridge satchels. Some sites take the money and disappear, others send out poor imitations of the product, which damages the brand. The company is fighting hard to find and prosecute counterfeiters and protect its brand.

AS questions
(50 marks)

1 a Calculate the profit of the Cambridge Satchel Company as a percentage of sales. (2 marks)

   b Explain one way the business may try to increase this percentage. (3 marks)

2 Analyse the reason why the Cambridge Satchel Company is so eager to protect its brand. (10 marks)

3 To what extent do you think the way the Cambridge Satchel Company has conducted market research through blogs is a good one? (15 marks)

4 To what extent do you think the 'Made in Britain' feature is likely to be the most important feature of the company's marketing mix? (20 marks)

A-level questions
(70 marks)

1 Analyse the factors the Cambridge Satchel Company might consider when deciding which overseas markets to enter. (10 marks)

2 To what extent do you think the success of Cambridge Satchel Company has been due to luck? (15 marks)

3 Do you think the brand is the most important element of the Cambridge Satchel Company marketing mix? (20 marks)

4 Do you think the Cambridge Satchel Company will continue to grow over the next ten years? (25 marks)

Unit 4

Decision making to improve operational performance

Setting operational objectives

Introduction

Operations is one of the functions of a business: this department is responsible for the actual production of the good or service. In this chapter we will explain the meaning of operations management and outline the activities it involves.

What you need to know by the end of this chapter:

- what is meant by operations management
- the activities involved in operations management
- the factors in the environment that influence operations management
- how operations objectives are set
- how to analyse the relationship between operations and other functions
- how to analyse some of the differences between operations processes
- how to analyse the operations decision-making process.

Figure 11.1 Functions of a business

Operations management

Operations management involves managing the process of converting inputs into outputs. It transforms resources into goods and services. Goods are tangible

items such as cars, tablets, or mobile phones. Services are intangible, for example mortgages, transport, or education. Take the example of an airline: this transforms people by moving them from one location to another. To do this an airline needs a plane, an airport and an air crew. The process as a whole is made up of a series of smaller operations, such as checking in passengers and their baggage, getting them on and off the aircraft, feeding them, ensuring they are safe, flying the plane and ensuring passengers get the right bags at the other end. The overall operations process is therefore made up of a series of smaller operations processes. The same would be true at your school or college. Within the overall process of education there is a whole series of other operations that contribute to the whole, such as catering, maintenance, IT and sports and activities.

What do you think?

Can you think of other operations processes that occur within a school or college?

As with all aspects of business, operations management involves choices and decisions. For example, an airline must decide where to fly to, what sort of aircraft to use, what systems to use for booking in and for security, what sort of seats, entertainment and food to provide and how best to provide it.

Operations management is at the very heart of the organisation: it is what it actually does. Operations management affects all aspects of our lives: everything you read, use, consume, watch, listen to or wear has been produced as a result of operations management. It involves a transformation process which turns inputs into outputs.

What do you think?

Amazon is a huge online retailer. What operations activities do you think will be involved at Amazon?

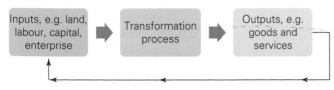

Figure 11.2 The operations process

The operations process is ongoing, as shown by the feedback loop. If the products do not sell then operations managers will review their activities. Similarly, if there are quality issues, environmental issues or changes in technology the operations process will be considered and changed. Just think about how over the years agriculture has changed, with investment in new equipment, new chemicals, new growing methods and new crops, and you can see how operations management evolves over time. How many people, even thirty years ago, would have imagined you would listen to music by streaming it as opposed to going to a shop to buy a record, or that we would buy our holidays online instead of through a high-street travel agent.

Operations management involves taking decisions, such as:

- the level of output a business needs to be able to produce. For example, if a small food producer wins a contract with a major national supermarket it will have to be able to produce on a much larger scale. This will involve investment in equipment and people, managing a more complex operation and coping with managing growth. Managers will want to assess whether this is possible and whether it was what they want. They will also want to consider the risk – what if the business expands and then the supermarket cancels the order?
- the range of products the business wants to offer, the level of customer service to provide and how flexible a business wants to be in relation to customer demands. For example, how many versions of the product and how many different product categories does a business want to provide? How much choice should the customer have?
- how best to produce the good or service. For example, is it better to use mainly labour – which is known as a **labour intensive** process – or to invest more in equipment and have a **capital intensive** process?
- how best to provide the good or service to the customer. For example, is it better to sell clothes online or via high street stores? Or both?

- how much of a process managers want a business to provide itself and how much they want to use suppliers. For example, Zara produces its own clothes, whereas most clothes retailers buy them from other suppliers. The decision about how much of the process to undertake has implications in terms of resourcing, quality and costs. Producers may move 'upstream' which means going towards the raw materials and taking on more of these activities, or 'downstream' which means undertaking more activities that are moving towards the customer. All the activities involved in taking the initial resources to providing the final product are collectively called the **supply chain**. Managers will decide how much of the supply chain to directly control and how much they will manage through other providers.

Key terms

Operations management describes the activities, decisions and responsibilities of the managing production and delivery of products and services.

A **labour intensive** operations process means a relatively high proportion of labour in the production is used compared to capital equipment, for example hairdressing.

A **capital intensive** process uses a relatively high proportion of capital equipment relative to labour, for example a bottling process.

The **supply chain** is the series of activities involved in taking the initial resources to providing the final product.

What do you think?

Can you think of any labour intensive operations processes?

Stages of operations

When you buy a product in a shop there may well have been hundreds of businesses involved in the process of making this transaction happen: suppliers of components, manufacturers, transportation businesses, retailers, advertising businesses and packaging businesses.

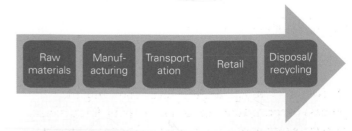

Figure 11.3 The stages of operations

This highlights that every operations process has a series of stages and that there are several stages and businesses involved in a supply chain. Note how the operations process can continue until after consumption, when a product may need disposing of or recycling. For example in the UK, retailers of household electrical goods and electronic equipment must provide free written information to their customers on how they can return goods if they are faulty or not what they wanted; and on how they can reuse and recycle electrical and electronic equipment, why this waste needs to be separated from other waste and the damaging effects of not recycling electrical and electronic equipment. Throughout any operations process, business activity impacts on society and on stakeholder groups. Operations managers have to consider how they want to deal with the impact on stakeholders, for example, whether they just want to act to meet the minimum requirements of the law, or whether they want to do more than they have to save the environment and act ethically.

What do you think?

Consider the possible impact on society throughout the operations process involved in extracting, refining, transporting and selling petrol.

How might these operations activities affect different stakeholders?

Adding value

Operations management is based on transforming resources. It turns inputs into outputs. Ingredients with a recipe, a chef and cooking utensils become a meal. A group of musicians with a conductor, a rehearsal space and musical instruments become an orchestra. An idea, a script, a director, a producer, actors and a film crew becomes a TV series. Whatever type of operations process is undertaken the aim is to add value (that is, for the outputs to be worth more than the inputs used up to produce them). The value created can be measured in many ways – is it financially worth it? Is it worth it in terms of its impact on society? What about in terms of how enjoyable it is? While many businesses make profit one of their key targets, a prison might be interested in preventing reoffending, a charity may be focused on saving lives, a football club may be interested in winning matches and a school in improving academic achievement. The important thing is to make sure the process does add enough value and to look for ways of

increasing the value being added. For example, your school will often review results and look for ways of improving the teaching and learning even more. Like any operations processes managers are eager to measure what is being achieved and how to improve it further. If no value is being added the business would be better reallocating resources and providing something else.

What do you think?

Why might the concept of opportunity cost be important when managers are considering whether they are adding enough value?

Business in focus: Ryanair

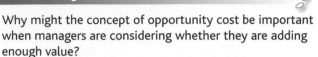

FACT AND FIGURES

EUROPE'S NO 1 CUSTOMER SERVICE AIRLINE
EVERY MONTH, RYANAIR PUBLISHES ITS CUSTOMER SERVICES STATISTICS

DID YOU KNOW, RYANAIR...

- Will carry over 87m passengers this year
- Carries more international passengers than any other airline
- Has an unblemished 30 year safety record
- Has a fleet of 300 Boeing 737-800 aircraft
- Operates in 30 countries
- Operates to/from 186 airports
- Has 69 bases across Europe and North Africa
- Operates over 1,600 routes
- Operates over 1,600 flights per day

HOW WAS SEPTEMBER?

WE CARRIED OVER...

8.5m	51.000	90%	0.51	0.47	99%
PASSENGERS ON	FLIGHTS, AND HAD	OF FLIGHTS ON TIME, WITH	COMPLAINTS PER 1,000 PAX.	BAGGAGE COMPLAINTS PER 1,000 PAX	OF COMPLAINTS HANDLED WITHIN 7 DAYS

PAX = passengers

Figure 11.4 Ryanair facts and figures

Source: Ryanair website
www.ryanair.com

1. Outline three operational decisions that managers at Ryanair might have to make.
2. Why do you think Ryanair measure the percentage of flights that are on time, the number of complaints and the number of complaints handled on time every month?

The nature of operations management

The nature of operations management will vary enormously from business to business.

For example, operations can involve:

- gathering, analysing and distributing information (for example search engines such as Google)
- storing and transporting products (for example delivery businesses such as FedEx)

- transforming people (for example plastic surgeons and psychotherapists)
- producing goods (for example car manufacturers)
- bringing products and customers together (for example retailers such as IKEA).

Some operations processes will be very labour intensive, for example architecture, advertising or financial advice, whereas other processes will be capital intensive such as a bottling process. Dell used to be proud of the fact that almost no human hands touched the computer in its assembly whereas the production of an Akubra hat, which takes almost one month, involves two hundred pairs of hands.

Figure 11.5 A Dell computer

Figure 11.6 An Akubra hat

Weblink

To find out more about the traditional production of Akubra hats (an Australian product) visit www.akubra.com.au/

Study tip

Remember that each operations process will have its own demands and requirements, Make sure your response relates directly to the specific operations process in terms of the operations issues such as capacity, unit costs and quality.

These different operations process can be analysed in terms of the 4Vs model:

- The **Volume** of output – compare the relatively small output of a business making hand-made shoes with the amount of cans of drink that Coca-Cola produces every day.
- The **Variety** of output – bottled water production, for example, is high volume with relatively little variety in what is being produced (as is fast food) whereas for a dentist or doctor every patient is different and therefore there is a high level of variety.
- The **Visibility** of production – this refers to how visible staff are in relation to the final customer. Some operations have little if any direct contact with the final customer. For example, businesses producing car parts sell these to the car producers rather than the person buying the car. By comparison a service business such as a retailer has a high level of interaction with the customer and therefore high level of people skills are important for employees.
- The **Variability** of demand. The demand for newspapers may be relatively constant from one day to the next. Demand in accident and emergency wards may vary much more depending on the day and time of day and whether any major accidents have occurred.

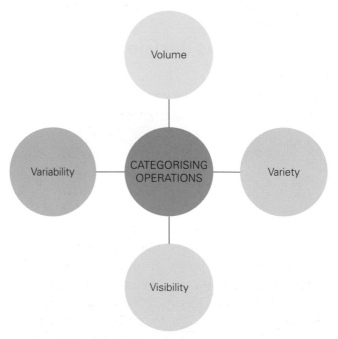

Figure 11.7 The 4Vs

Where an operation sits in relation to these 4Vs will affect the nature and challenges that operations managers face.

What do you think?

The UK is increasingly producing services rather than goods. What do you think might be different in managing the operations of services compared to manufacturing?

Low		High
Likely to be high unit costs Employees likely to be multi skilled Little repetition of tasks	**Volume**	High repeatability Low unit costs Capital intensive
Stable Routine Predictable High capacity utilisation	**Variation in demand**	Changing levels of capacity utilisation Need to try and predict demand Need flexibility
Limited customer service skills Time lag between production and consumption	**Visibility**	Good customer service skills needed Flexible in terms of information and communications to customer
Routine operations Standardised processes Low unit cost	**Variety**	Flexible Quite complex operations to manage High unit cost Can meet customer needs precisely

Table 11.1 Results of low and high 4Vs

The operations decision-making process

Figure 11.8 The operations decision-making process

The operations decision-making process involves:

- identifying the operations objectives
- analysing the existing position of the business in relation to operations
- choosing what actions need to be taken to achieve the objectives.
- implementing these decisions
- reviewing to see if they are on target and taking actions if not.

This process will be iterative, meaning that managers may move backwards and forwards between different stages. For example, when they gather operations data they may go back and revisit their objectives. If they have problems putting decisions into effect, they may revisit the decisions.

What do you think?

Can you think how the internet and information technology might be affecting operations decision making?

Ethics, the environment and operations decisions

Like all decisions in business, operations decisions will include an ethical element. Managers will have to decide what they think is right or wrong in any given circumstances. For example, there will be ethical issues involved in:

- how to reward and treat employees. Increasing employees' workloads may improve the amount produced but place high levels of stress on employees.
- where to locate the business. Should the business locate in a low-wage location? This will be good in terms of costs and profits but is it exploiting the workforce?
- safety features. Should the business avoid adding some safety features to the product (that they do not have to have by law) because they would add significantly to costs?
- the environment. Should the business worry about the environmental costs of their suppliers' operations or of the way in which supplies are transported to them? This last example highlights an area of particular concern in operations, which is impact of the activities of a business on the environment.

Managers will want to assess this impact (for example, in terms of noise, pollution and emissions) and may want to take this into account when making decisions.

What do you think?

Can you think of three ethical issues or environmental issues involved in the operations management of running a football club?

Operations, competitiveness and the competitive environment

As we have seen, the competitiveness of a business depends on the benefits it can offer relative to the price it charges compared to its rivals. If it can offer excellent value for money it is competitive. Much of this depends on operations. Operations delivers the actual goods and services, and the extent to which they provide benefits for the customers relates to operations activities. The operations also account for the majority of the costs in a business and so again operations management is vital to competitiveness. Visit the website of almost any company and you will see how strongly they cite 'operational excellence' as the key to success.

To maintain this excellence usually involves on-going improvements. The competitive environment is such that if you are not launching a new or modified product, your competitors are doing so, and therefore you will probably need to do the same fairly soon to keep up. Take a product such as paint and you might imagine the market does not change much. However, visit your local DIY store and you will find matt paint, gloss paint, quick-drying paint, non-drip paint, odourless paint, in all sizes and types of containers alongside paint brushes, rollers and paint sprayers: there is regular innovation as technology improves. The value offered by competitors is likely to be improving constantly, putting pressure on all businesses to review and develop their operations, in the same way as your school is constantly trying to develop its teaching and learning to keep moving forward.

Setting operational objectives

The **operations objectives** that a business sets must fit with the overall competitive strategy of the business. The operations objectives it sets must be linked to where it wants to achieve its competitive advantage.

For example, a business such as Poundland or the 99p store is competing by offering products at a low price and this means it will have a low costs objective. Its operations processes must then be able to deliver this and still enable the business to be profitable. Some breakdown recovery companies compete by stressing how quickly they can be with you if you break down: they will set targets relating to their response time and again the operations process must be developed to enable the business to do this. An investment fund business that offers expert advice or a hairdressing salon that promotes its 'expert stylists' will set service objectives and will then have to make sure these are delivered. Operations objectives therefore support the competitive strategy of the business.

Figure 11.9 Typical operational objectives

Typical operations objectives include:

- **Quality**. Operations managers have to decide what they think customers want and expect – in liaison with marketing – and then set appropriate targets. For example, a quality target for an insurance company might aim to process a given number of claims accurately per day. A quality operation is one that has the resources and systems in place so it can meet these key targets consistently. The better the quality of an operation the more competitive a business might be as customers will recommend it and use it again. McDonald's is a very high-quality operation. For example, it has set targets for how long food should be cooked, how it should be laid out on a tray and what staff should say to customers: it hits these targets consistently, meaning that on an operations measure the quality is high.

Study tip

Remember that quality has a specific meaning in operations relating to whether or not the business meets its operations (for example is the product the right weight, colour, dimensions)? This is different from the way the word 'quality' is sometimes used elsewhere when it refers to 'premium products'. A low-price product that meets its operations targets can have a quality operation, whereas an expensive product that has variability in its processes would not meet quality operations criteria. Imagine an upmarket restaurant where customers experienced amazing food on some occasions but poor food on others: this is not quality.

- **Speed of response.** Businesses may compete by providing their goods or services faster than their competitors. For example, if the managers of a restaurant decide no customer should wait more than five minutes to have a seat and must be served within one minute of sitting down this may be appealing to customers and win business. The operations targets relate to the speed of response. However, setting such a target will have resource implications in terms of the number of seats, the level of staffing, the nature of the menu, training and equipment. Similarly, if an optician decides to provide glasses within one hour, or a pizza company decides to deliver within 30 minutes, this will require resourcing and have cost implications but is a potential source of **competitive advantage**. Direct Line home insurance recently advertised that it could replace stolen items within eight hours of a claim being made: a clear use of a time target to provide additional benefits to consumers.

What do you think?

Can you think of any other businesses that compete on speed of response?

- **Dependability**: this refers to the ability of a business to deliver reliably on time. A delivery business may set an objective that 95 per cent of its deliveries are picked up and arrive at the set time. Provided it can deliver, this it is likely to be popular, assuming this level is better than that of rivals. Similarly, if a bus company ensures its buses leave and arrive on time,

this should meet customer requirements, as will repair businesses or telecommunications companies that arrive at the time agreed, or businesses that complete their projects on schedule.

- **Costs.** If a business can produce at lower costs than rivals it can make profits with the same price or it may enable businesses to reduce its price and be competitive on that basis. A business may therefore set cost objectives to enable it to control prices.
- **Flexibility.** If a business can meet customer needs more precisely than others this may give it an advantage. A tailor may make a suit to fit your figure precisely; Marks & Spencer sells suits 'off the rack'. A business may therefore have targets relating to the range of products it provides.

Other operational objectives include:

- **Environmental objectives**. Greater awareness of the environmental impact of operations decisions and greater interest in the impact of decisions by stakeholders has raised the profile of such objectives in recent years. These objectives might focus on recycling materials, reducing waste or reducing emissions.
- **Defect rates**. Operations managers may measure the proportion of products that are thrown away, have to be reworked or are sent back by customers for being faulty.
- **Safety targets**. Operations managers may set targets to limit the health risk to employees. For example, they may aim to eliminate accidents or injuries.

Key term

An **operations objective** is a target set for the operations function such as to improve the proportion of deliveries on time by five per cent within two years. Like all objectives these should be SMARTER: specific, measurable, agreed, realistic, time related, evaluated and reviewed.

Airline	Car manufacturer	Retailer
Proportion of planes leaving and landing on time	Number of cars produced per day	Speed of processing transactions
Proportion of bags lost in transit	Number of defects identified in production	Customer satisfaction
Time taken to get passengers on to the plane	Delivery time to car dealerships	Not having unsold stock
Environmental targets	Environmental targets	Environmental targets
Turnaround time at airports	Flexibility to customer orders	Reducing queues

Table 11.2 Examples of operations objectives

Setting operational objectives will have resource implications. For example, to be more flexible may require more investment in technology and training.

The relative importance of these operational objectives will vary from product to product and will depend on the target market and customer requirements. For example with airlines, business fliers want speed to get to and from meetings as fast as they can; the time taken may be more important than cost. Holidaymakers may not be so bothered if the journey takes one hour longer if it brings the price down. In the delivery business sometimes what matters most is that a parcel is delivered on time; at other times it is more important that it is delivered safely; sometimes there is no time or security pressure and you want a low price.

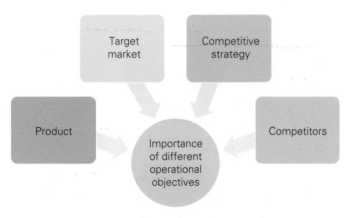

Figure 11.10 The importance of different operational objectives

The relative importance of the different operational objectives will also depend on how managers want the business to compete. For example, McDonald's focuses more of the speed of service and less on flexibility (try asking for your burger to be cooked differently!) whereas a top restaurant may be slower but have more flexibility. Choices have to be made on how to compete. The Emma Maersk is one of the world's biggest container ships that moves millions of products around the world; for example, importing products from China to the UK. Given the huge volumes it carries the unit cost per item is relatively low. However, the transportation is relatively slow. If you want the Emma Maersk to travel faster, this will increase energy consumption and increase costs. So there is a trade-off in this case between cost and speed. It may not be possible to be the cheapest, fastest, most flexible and most dependable provider: managers will need to make choices.

Figure 11.11 The Emma Maersk

Key term

A **competitive advantage** is a way in which a business offers superior value to its competitors.

Using polar diagrams to illustrate operations objectives

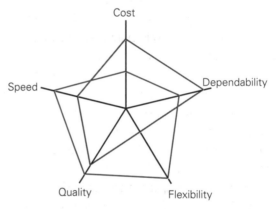

Key
— Taxi service
— Bus service

Figure 11.12 Polar diagram comparing bus and taxi services

The polar diagram in Figure 11.12 shows how important different aspects of operations might be in the taxi industry and the bus industry. The relative importance of the five operations criteria are shown by how far away from the centre the point is. The further away the line is from the centre the more significant customers think this factor is in this industry.

For buses:

- It is essential the bus sticks to its set times (dependability is important).
- Relatively low costs are expected.
- Buses are not expected to leave their set route, that is flexibility is not expected to be high.
- Buses are not expected to be especially fast.

For taxis:

- Flexibility is essential to take you from one location to another.
- Taxis are expected to be relatively expensive.
- You understand a taxi may be a little later than promised due to traffic so dependability is less signficant.

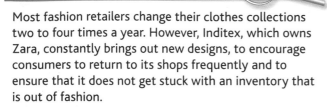

What do you think?

Can you plot a polar diagram for: trains, airlines, coaches?

Business in focus: Inditex

Most fashion retailers change their clothes collections two to four times a year. However, Inditex, which owns Zara, constantly brings out new designs, to encourage consumers to return to its shops frequently and to ensure that it does not get stuck with an inventory that is out of fashion.

Inditex has about half of its clothes produced in Spain or nearby countries, so it is able to react quickly to changing trends. This costs more but helps to ensure it stays in touch with changes in fashion. Most of Zara's rivals buy their clothes from Asia to keep costs lower. However, this slows down the response time to changes in customer tastes because of the distances involved.

Amancio Ortega, the founder of Inditex, says that selling fashion is like selling fish. Fresh fish sells quickly and at a high price. Yesterday's catch must be discounted and may not sell at all. The same is true with fashion: as soon as it becomes out of date you have to discount it. This is why Zara holds little inventory and changes it regularly.

However, other businesses do it differently. Uniqlo, for example, produces large quantities of relatively few product lines and changes these relatively rarely. The aim is to reduce costs through bulk buying.

Source: Adapted from *The Economist*, 24 March 2012 www.economist.com/node/21551063

Questions

1. Analyse how the speed of response and flexibility helps Zara to compete.
2. Explain how the Uniqlo approach reduces costs and analyse how low costs may help Uniqlo to compete.

Internal influences on operational objectives and decisions

Operations managers do not operate in isolation. All operational decisions will have implications for other areas of the business such as human resources,

marketing and finance. These other functions will also provide internal influences on operations decisions.

For example:

- Marketing activities may determine what actually has to be produced, how it is produced (for example customers may want free-range eggs or organic food) and what quantities are required.
- Human resources may determine what is possible. The number and skills of staff may influence what can be provided. The skills and experience of the members of your football team may determine how you play, for example.
- Finance. The finance available may affect the level of investment in technology which may affect what can be produced.

Figure 11.13 All the other functional areas influence operational objectives

What do you think?

How can the operations process affect the other functions of a business?

Study tip

Remember that to be successful any operations decision will depend on having the necessary resources. It will also have an effect on all the other functions.

Business in focus: Amazon

Technological innovation drives the growth of Amazon.com to offer customers more types of products, more conveniently and at lower prices. Since 1995, Amazon has significantly expanded its product selection, international retail websites, and worldwide network of fulfilment and customer service centres. Today, Amazon retail websites offer everything from toys and video games to MP3 downloads and collectible items. The company entered the e-book hardware industry in 2007 with the release of the original Kindle reader. The Kindle family has now grown to include Kindle Fire HD 4G LTE Wireless, with HD display, Dolby Digital Plus, and 4G connectivity; and Kindle Paperwhite, the world's most advanced e-reader.

Amazon has teams across the world working on behalf of its customers at fulfillment centres, which provide fast, reliable shipping directly from Amazon's retail websites, and Customer Service Centres, which provide 24/7 support. In addition, Amazon's technology teams are located in Seattle and in International Development Centres designed to tap the world's best technical talent.

Source: Amazon website
www.amazon.com/Careers-Homepage/b?ie=UTF8&node=239364011

Questions

1. Outline the different operations activities at Amazon.
2. 'Amazon has the objective of being the most customer-focused business in the world.' Analyse the ways in which operations management at Amazon can help it achieve its objective.

External influences on operational objectives and decisions

Figure 11.14 External influences on operational objectives

Like all aspects of business the environment in which operation decisions are made is changing all the time. These external influences can be examined using the PEST-C framework:

- **Political and legal factors.** Greater legal regulation and concerns over health and safety. This may place restrictions on what can be produced, how it can be produced, where it can be produced and who it can be produced for. For example, some countries ban gambling, which means that online gambling businesses cannot offer their services to people based there.

- **Economic factors.** Greater globalisation enables businesses to source supplies more easily from countries all over the world and/or produce globally. The removal of many barriers to trade, such as many taxes (tariffs) on foreign goods and improvements in technology and communications have enabled more global operations.

- **Social factors.** There is now greater demand for choice and variety. Customers can search more easily for alternatives as so much is now online; they also have more choice as buying from abroad is cheaper and faster than it was. This means operations managers have to watch what competitors are doing worldwide.

- **Technological factors.** With technological advances it becomes quicker to develop, test and launch new products. To keep pace managers will want to consider how much they invest in new product development and how to develop a business that encourages successful innovation. Technology is also enabling new operations to exist (believe it or not computer games, apps, online university courses and music streaming are not very old!) and enabling new processes to develop (such as paying for parking with your mobile, ordering products online or using new lightweight materials for aircraft). Technological change can completely disrupt an industry: just think of the impact on operations for publishers of e-books, for newspapers of online news services, for the music industry of streaming, for the computer industry of cloud computing, for watchmakers, mapmakers, producers of smartphones and for banks of online banking. Some of the biggest businesses in the world, such as Google, Apple and Facebook are undertaking operations that did not even exist twenty years ago. Radical changes are affecting what it is that businesses actually do and how they provide their services. This is affecting the skills required, the way businesses are competing and what operations management involves.

- **Competition**. There is greater demand for better customer service as customers realise their power to demand more or they will switch to other providers. This means business are trying to offer more while also keeping costs down – this can be a difficult balance

What do you think?

What factors make a business innovative? Can you think of examples of how legal regulations may affect operations activities?

Figure 11.15 Self-service check outs

Business in focus: Tesla

Figure 11.16 A Tesla car

Tesla Motors was founded in 2003 by a group of Silicon Valley engineers who set out to prove that electric vehicles could be awesome. **The Tesla Roadster** hit the streets in early 2008 as a sports car that can go from 0 to 60 mph in 3.7 seconds and travel for 245 miles per charge.

Model S arrived in 2012. A premium sedan that goes from 0 to 60 mph in 4.2 seconds and travels for 265 miles per charge.

Model X, set to enter volume production in 2015, is a crossover utility vehicle that blends the best of an SUV with the benefits of a minivan.

Tesla's batteries and powertrains will help lessen global dependence on petroleum-based transportation and drive down the cost of electric vehicles. By cooperating with other car manufacturers, we hope to put more electric cars on the road.

'Our long-term plan is to build a wide range of models, including affordably priced family cars. This is because the overarching purpose of Tesla Motors (and the reason I am funding the company) is to help expedite the move from a mine-and-burn hydrocarbon economy towards a solar electric economy, which I believe to be the primary, but not exclusive, sustainable solution.

Critical to making that happen is an electric car without compromises, which is why the Tesla Roadster is designed to beat a gasoline sports car like a Porsche or Ferrari in a head to head showdown. Then, over and above that fact, it has twice the energy efficiency of a Prius. Almost any new technology initially has high unit cost before it can be optimized and this is no less true for electric cars. The strategy of Tesla is to enter at the high end of the market, where customers are prepared to pay a premium, and then drive down market as fast as possible to higher unit volume and lower prices with each successive mode... In keeping with a fast growing technology company, all free cash flow is ploughed back into R&D to drive down the costs and bring the follow on products to market as fast as possible. When someone buys the Tesla Roadster sports car, they are actually helping pay for development of the low cost family car.

So, in short, the master plan is:

1. Build sports car.

2. Use that money to build an affordable car.

3. Use that money to build an even more affordable car.

4. While doing above, also provide zero emission electric power generation options.

Don't tell anyone.'

Elon Musk, Co-Founder and CEO of Tesla Motors
Source: Telsa Motors' website
www.teslamotors.com/fr_CH/blog/secret-tesla-motors-master-plan-just-between-you-and-me

Questions

1. Explain the long-term objective of Tesla Motors.

2. Do you think its long-term plan is a good one? Justify your answer.

These external pressures influence operations managers who have to produce better products, with more flexibility at lower costs. To maintain competitiveness, operations managers have to work ever harder and ever smarter. To do this they must review all aspects of the operations process such as how they produce, what technology they are using, who they work with, where they source materials and what controls and systems they have in place to check and improve standards.

What do you think?

How do you think the operations of supermarkets have changed in recent years?

Changing operational objectives

The operational objectives set by a business will depend on what the managers believe is important and what they think is the best positioning of the business and the best way of competing against rivals. This will be influenced by what rivals are doing and the resources of the business, for example its capacity and the skills of employees.

Operational objectives may change as the values and strategy of the business change. For example:

- After a terrible oil spill in 2010, referred to as 'Deepwater Horizon', BP's managers made safety a higher priority to prevent it happening again.
- After much criticism for the way they took huge risks to try and boost profits, banks such as Barclays have stated that they want to be much more ethical in their operations and try to benefit the community.
- After a disappointing financial performance, Ryanair decided to put more emphasis on customer service.

Figure 11.17 The Deepwater Horizon oil spill

Business in focus: LEGO

Figure 11.18 Lego

Product development is extremely important at LEGO® as 60 per cent of their annual sales are accounted for by new products. The company has a large team of trained designers from around the world who are based at their Denmark headquarters. LEGO® produce 4,200 unique elements that come in a variety of different colours and finishes.

LEGO® manufacture their products in factories in Europe and Mexico, which are close to their main markets in Europe and the USA.

The number of LEGO® elements produced each year is enormous – equivalent to 68,000 elements per minute. Precision is incredibly important; LEGO® bricks must fit together perfectly and also easily break apart. The

production process relies on high temperatures (up to 310°C), high pressure and moulds that are accurate to within 0.005 mm to ensure the level of accuracy for each brick is high. So you can rely on the fact that any LEGO® product you buy is compatible with any other, even if they were made as long ago as 1958!

LEGO® have objectives for the different parts of their business and their operations objectives consist of the following:

- No product recalls ever – LEGO® don't want any substandard products released to the market
- Top 10 on employee safety by 2015
- Support the learning of 101 million children in 2015
- Use 100 per cent renewable energy and remove reliance on fossil fuels by 2020
- Zero waste – LEGO® want to reduce or recycle the waste they produce.

Source: LEGO® website

Questions

1. Analyse the reasons why Lego has set the operations objectives shown above.
2. To what extent do you think the success of Lego depends on its operations management?

ASSESSMENT ACTIVITIES

Sections (a), (b) and (c) of these assessment activities are relevant for students taking AS and A-level examinations. The questions in section (d) are for A-level students only.

(a) Knowledge check questions

1 State two resources that might be used in an operations process.

2 State two possible operational objectives.

3 Outline three operations decisions that would need to be made to manage a retailer such as H&M.

4 Outline three operations decisions that would need to be made to manage an apps business such as Snapchat or Instagram.

5 State two internal influences on operational objectives.

6 State two external influences on operational objectives.

7 State two ethical or environmental considerations when making operations decisions.

8 Which of the following do you think are directly linked to operations management? Explain your answer.
   ● choosing suppliers
   ● installing new technology
   ● advertising the product
   ● selling shares
   ● reducing waste

9 When a high proportion of labour is used relative to machinery the operations process is known as labour ....

10 When transforming inputs into outputs operations management aims to .... value.

(b) Short answer questions

1 Explain two external factors that might influence the operational objectives set by a catering business.   (5 marks)

2 Explain how the operations activities of an online retailer can affect its competitiveness.   (5 marks)

3 Explain how operations management can add value for a coffee shop chain.   (5 marks)

4 Explain one internal influence on the operational objectives of a train company.   (5 marks)

5 Explain one ethical issue that may be involved in the operations of a clothing manufacturer.
                                                  (5 marks)

(c) Data response questions

German supermarket chains Aldi and Lidl came first and second respectively in YouGov's Brandindex Buzz brand perception survey in January 2015. John Lewis and BBC iPlayer took the third and fourth spots.

Aldi and Lidl are often called discounters and as family incomes have been squeezed over the last few years more and more people have been visiting them. They offer a no-frills shopping experience – they don't provide plastic bags, and they only stock approximately 2,000 lines compared to up to 20,000 in the Big Four supermarkets (Tesco, Asda, Sainburys and Waitrose). Many of their products are also own brand and they only stock branded items where they can use their purchasing power to obtain big discounts from their suppliers.

However, their success isn't just about price. They have made it their mission to attract an increasingly middle-class customer base by combining affordability with quality. They want people who would never previously have considered shopping there. Although they only stock a limited range of items, they have increased this since their first entry into the UK market and they've introduced premium ranges. The two supermarkets have received various accolades for the quality of their products. For example, in 2014 Lidl won Wine Supermarket of the Year (with Aldi a close runner-up) and its premium own-brand range won Own Brand Range of the year.

At the moment Aldi only has a 4.9 per cent market share of the UK grocery industry and Lidl 3.5 per cent, compared to Tesco's 28.7 per cent. However, they plan to double their numbers of stores and their profits over the next ten years.

Source: adapted from various news sources

1 Explain how food retailers add value for customers. (6 marks)

2 Analyse the factors that might influence the operations activities of retailers such as Tesco, Sainsbury, Aldi and Lidl. (9 marks)

3 To what extent do you think the success of Aldi and Lidl is due to their operations? (15 marks)

(d) Essays

1 To what extent do you think operations management is the most important factor in the success of social networking sites such as Facebook? Justify your answer. (25 marks)

2 To what extent does the competitiveness of a chocolate producer such as Cadbury depend on its operations? Justify your answer. (25 marks)

Analysing operational performance

Introduction

In this chapter we examine how to analyse the operations performance of a business in order to decide how to improve it.

What you need to know by the end of this chapter:

- how to calculate operations data
- how to interpret operations data
- how operations data is used in decision making.

Calculation of operations data

Analysing the operational performance of a business involves measuring how an organisation is performing in relation to its operations objectives. A business will review progress against these targets in the same way as you might measure your academic progress against target grades: if you are far away from targets you will hopefully take action to improve your performance.

Quite what a business sets as its operational objectives will depend on its operations and how it wants to compete, but typical measures of operational performance include the following.

- **Labour productivity.** This measures the output per employee. It can be calculated using:

$$\text{Labour productivity} = \frac{\text{total output}}{\text{number of employees}}$$

For example, if output is 3,000 units in a given period and the number of employees is 300 then:

$$3{,}000 / 300 = 10$$

So, labour productivity is 10 units per employee.

Operations managers may influence labour productivity in many ways such as the way they train and organise employees and how they reward staff.

- **Unit costs.** This measures the cost per unit (and is sometimes called the 'average costs'). It can be calculated using the equation:

$$\text{Unit cost} = \frac{\text{total costs}}{\text{total output}}$$

This is measured in pounds. For example, if a business produces 2,000 units and the cost is £50,000 then:

$$£50{,}0000 / 2{,}000 = £25$$

So unit cost is £25 per unit.

Operations managers may influence the **unit costs** in many ways. For example, they can consider what suppliers to use, what resources to use, how to make the operations process more effective and how to reduce waste. However, when trying to control costs managers must consider the possible knock-on effects for the business: cheaper resources or less flexibility, for example, may affect the customer's experience of the product.

Controlling unit costs is important because it influences the price a business can charge and still make a profit.

Maths moment

(a) To calculate the unit cost you need the total costs and the number of units produced.

  Total costs = fixed costs + variable costs

  Unit costs = total costs / output

(b) If unit costs are given, then total costs are worked out by multiplying the unit cost by the number of units. For example, if the unit cost is £5 and 30 units are produced then the total cost is £5 × 30 = £150.

  (i) Fixed costs are £20,000, variable costs are £2 per unit and output is 6,000 units. What is the total cost? What is the unit cost?

  (ii) If the unit cost is £4 and output is 4,000 units what are total costs?

  (iii) If the unit cost is £30 and output is 5,000 units what are total costs? If fixed costs are £12,000 what are the variable costs per unit?

Key terms

Total costs are made up of fixed costs and variable costs.
Unit or **average costs** are the cost per unit, that is total cost/number of units.

What do you think?

Units	Fixed costs	Variable costs*	Total Costs	Unit costs
	£	£	£	Total costs / output £
10	100	200	300	30
20	100	400	500	25
30	100	600	700	23
40	100	800	900	23
50	100	1,000	1,100	22

Table 12.1 Unit cost falls as output increases
*Variable cost per unit is £20.

In the table above the unit cost falls as output increases. Why do you think this is? What are the implications for pricing?

● **Capacity**. The capacity of a business measures the maximum it can produce given its existing resources. For example, the capacity of a restaurant may depend on staffing, kitchen space and number of tables. The capacity of accountancy business may be limited by the number of staff it has. The capacity of an airline may be determined by the number of pilots and cabin crew, the number and type of planes and the number of landing slots. The capacity of a call centre may depend on the number of operatives and the number of phone lines they have. At any moment the capacity of a business is fixed, as there are a given level of resources.

Figure 12.1 A call centre

Over time the capacity of a business can change as more resources become available. More staff can be employed, more land can be acquired and more equipment bought.

However this may take time, for example increasing the scale of your chemical processing plant or building more nuclear power plants will take years. Increasing capacity is an investment and managers will want to consider the cost, the likely returns and the risk.

The desired level of capacity will depend on the expected level of sales.

Study tip

Make sure you think about the most appropriate units to use when measuring capacity. A restaurant may measure the maximum number of meals it can produce and sell. Managers of a football stadium may measure the maximum crowd. Managers of an airline may refer to the maximum number of passengers. It is important to apply your understanding to the context.

● **Capacity utilisation.** Capacity utilisation measures existing output as a percentage of the maximum possible output.
It is calculated by the equation:

existing output / maximum possible output × 100

For example, if an hotel has 50 rooms occupied out of a total of 150 rooms its capacity utilisation is:

(50 / 150) × 100 = 33.3%

The higher the capacity utilisation the more resources are being fully utilised.
A low-capacity utilisation may be a concern to a manager because:
● it suggests that demand is relatively low
● the cost per unit is likely to be high. This is because the fixed costs of the business are not spread over many units. This means there is a high fixed cost per unit, which may result in low profit margins or even a loss on each unit. This is why businesses are often eager to achieve a high capacity utilisation. This is because it allows them to spread their fixed costs over more units and bring down the unit cost, enabling them to be profitable.

Output	Fixed costs £1000	Variable costs £10 per unit	Total costs	Unit costs	Capacity utilisation %
100	1,000	1,000	2,000	2,000/100 = £20	25
200	1,000	2,000	3,000	3,000/200 = £15	50
300	1,000	3,000	4,000	4,000/300 = £13.30	75
400 capacity	1,000	4,000	5,000	5,000/400 = £12.50	100

Table 12.2 Unit cost falls as capacity utilization increases

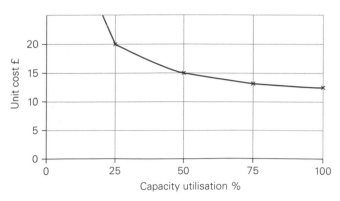

Figure 12.2 Graph showing how unit costs fall as capacity utilisation increases

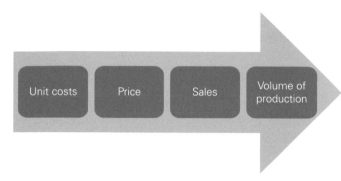

Figure 12.3 The potential benefits of high-capacity utilization

Maths moment

Output	Fixed costs	Variable costs £10 per unit	Total costs	Unit costs	Capacity utilisation %
100	£500				
200					
300					
400					

*Variable costs = £10 a unit

Table 12.3

Complete the table above. What is happening to unit costs as capacity utilisation increases? Why do you think this is?

Key terms

Capacity is the maximum output of a business at a moment in time given its resources.

Capacity utilisation measures the existing output over a given period as a percentage of the maximum output.

What do you think?

How might a business respond to low-capacity utilisation? In 2013 the world car industry had the capacity to produce 107 million cars but only produced 83 million. What do you think are the possible implications of this data for car companies?

What do you think?

Most businesses only use 30 per cent of their server capacity. Why do you think this is?

The use of data in operational decision making

By analysing the operational data, managers may be able to identify problems or opportunities. This enables them to analyse different courses of action and decide what to do next. Operations data therefore informs operations decision making and planning. For example:

- If labour productivity is low managers can analyse this further to identify the cause. They may then consider whether it is necessary to invest in training, review reward systems or change the way work is undertaken.
- If unit costs (average costs) are higher than expected managers will analyse the cause. Is this due to supplier costs? Low labour productivity? High levels of defects? Again this will lead to actions being taken

Business in focus: Energy shortages

According to The Royal Academy of Engineering there is an increasing risk of power shortages in the UK over the next few years. The closure of older power plants and the fact that decisions to build new ones are regularly delayed means the system might soon be over-stretched because it lacks sufficient capacity.

Until fairly recently the supply of energy in the UK was about 16 per cent higher than demand but this could fall

to 2 per cent by 2015, according to the National Grid and the energy regulator, Ofgem.

Questions

1. What could the government do to help ensure there is not a shortage of energy?
2. What might the consequences of a shortage of supply of energy in the UK be?

to improve the situation, such as negotiating with suppliers.

- If capacity is too low, managers may want to consider whether it is worth investing to expand. This would depend on factors such as the costs, the likely returns and the risks involved.
- If capacity is too high, managers would consider whether they can increase demand (perhaps by improving the promotions or the product) or whether the business should 'downsize', that is reduce capacity by closing part of the facilities.

When making operations decisions, managers will consider the costs, the profits, the risks, the impact on competitiveness and the effect on other functions and stakeholders. Some decisions may be relatively quick to implement, for example discussing lower prices with suppliers. Others may take a significant period of time, for example changing suppliers or changing capacity.

Developments in technology have enabled operations managers to track data more effectively and hopefully make better decisions.

Business in focus: BP

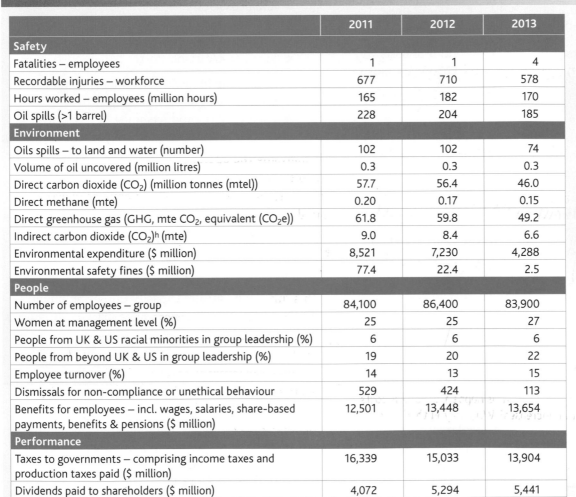

	2011	2012	2013
Safety			
Fatalities – employees	1	1	4
Recordable injuries – workforce	677	710	578
Hours worked – employees (million hours)	165	182	170
Oil spills (>1 barrel)	228	204	185
Environment			
Oils spills – to land and water (number)	102	102	74
Volume of oil uncovered (million litres)	0.3	0.3	0.3
Direct carbon dioxide (CO_2) (million tonnes (mtel))	57.7	56.4	46.0
Direct methane (mte)	0.20	0.17	0.15
Direct greenhouse gas (GHG, mte CO_2, equivalent (CO_2e))	61.8	59.8	49.2
Indirect carbon dioxide (CO_2)[h] (mte)	9.0	8.4	6.6
Environmental expenditure ($ million)	8,521	7,230	4,288
Environmental safety fines ($ million)	77.4	22.4	2.5
People			
Number of employees – group	84,100	86,400	83,900
Women at management level (%)	25	25	27
People from UK & US racial minorities in group leadership (%)	6	6	6
People from beyond UK & US in group leadership (%)	19	20	22
Employee turnover (%)	14	13	15
Dismissals for non-compliance or unethical behaviour	529	424	113
Benefits for employees – incl. wages, salaries, share-based payments, benefits & pensions ($ million)	12,501	13,448	13,654
Performance			
Taxes to governments – comprising income taxes and production taxes paid ($ million)	16,339	15,033	13,904
Dividends paid to shareholders ($ million)	4,072	5,294	5,441
Contributions to communities ($ million)	103.7	90.6	78.8

Table 12.4 BP operations data

Source: BP's website http://www.bp.com/en/global/corporate/sustainability/bp-and-sustainability/bp-in-figures.html

Question

1. Table 12.4 shows some operations data for BP. Analyse the possible significance of the changes in the operational data over the period shown.

ASSESSMENT ACTIVITIES

Sections (a), (b) and (c) of these assessment activities are relevant for students taking AS and A-level examinations. The questions in section (d) are for A-level students only.

(a) Knowledge check questions

1 What is meant by labour productivity?

2 If labour productivity is eight units and there are six employees, what is the total output?

3 If output is 48,000 units and the number of employees is 70, what is the labour productivity?

4 Total costs are £44,000 and output is 11,000 units. What is the unit cost?

5 Capacity utilisation is 40 per cent and present output is 600 units. What is the capacity?

6 If output increases total costs and unit costs will inevitably rise. True or false? Explain your answer.

7 State two factors that might influence operational objectives.

8 Which of the following is most likely to be true?
- Increasing capacity utilisation will leave total costs unchanged.
- Increasing capacity utilisation will reduce total costs.
- Increasing capacity utilisation will increase total costs.
- Increasing capacity utilisation will increase unit costs.

9 Which of the following is the equation for unit cost:
- Total cost/output
- Total cost/labour
- Total costs/total revenue
- Fixed cost/variable cost?

10 Which of the following statements is true?
- Capacity can never be changed.
- High-quality products must be expensive.
- A business with 80 per cent capacity utilisation must be producing more than a business with 20 per cent capacity utilisation.

(b) Short answer questions

1 Explain one reason why a farm might want to increase productivity.   (5 marks)

2 Explain one factor that might influence the labour productivity of a checkout assistant.   (5 marks)

3 Explain the factors that determine the capacity of a bank.   (5 marks)

4 Explain one way a football club may react if it consistently has low capacity utilisation of its stadium.   (5 marks)

5 Explain why greater capacity utilisation might decrease the unit costs of a cinema.   (5 marks)

(c) Data response questions

Center Parcs

Center Parcs is a holiday business which opened its first village in the UK at Sherwood Forest in July 1987. It provides short break holidays in the forest on a year-round basis. Center Parcs now has five villages across the UK: Whinfell Forest in Cumbria, Sherwood Forest in Nottinghamshire, Elveden Forest in Suffolk, Woburn Forest in Bedfordshire and Longleat Forest in Wiltshire.

The data in Table 12.5 shows the performance of Center Parcs in a number of areas of the business:

	2012/13	2011/12
Occupancy (%)	97.2	97.1
Sleeper nights (m)	6.0	5.9
Number of guests (m)	1.7	1.6
Capital investment (£m)	39.9	41.4
Revenue (£m)	303.5	291.7
Profit before tax and exceptional items	18.6	31.9
Average daily rate (£) (net of VAT)	148.36	140.73
Accommodation bookings (% of total)	79	79
Guest satisfaction (% of guests ranking their break as excellent or good)	96	95
Brand awareness (%)	99	99
Employee turnover (%)	23	20

Table 12.5 Center Parcs performance data

Source: Center Parcs website
http://www.centerparcs.co.uk/images/pdfs/annual_review_2013.pdf

1 Explain what is meant by a 97.2 per cent occupancy rate. (3 marks)

2 Explain what is meant by capital investment. (3 marks)

3 Analyse how the operations performance of the business has changed between 2011/12 and 2012/13. (9 marks)

4 To what extent do you think measuring operational data is likely to be useful for Center Parcs? (15 marks)

(d) Essays

1 What do you think is the best way for a restaurant to respond to low-capacity utilisation? Justify your answer. (25 marks)

2 To what extent should reducing unit cost be the key operational objective these days? (25 marks)

Chapter 13

Increasing efficiency and productivity

Introduction

In Chapter 12 we analysed operational data including **labour productivity** and unit costs. In this chapter we will examine the ways in which managers might improve the productivity and **efficiency** of the business.

What you need to know by the end of this chapter:

- the meaning and significance of efficiency
- the importance of capacity
- how to utilise capacity efficiently
- the meaning and significance of productivity
- how to improve productivity and efficiency
- the benefits and difficulties of lean production
- the meaning and significance of 'Just in Time'
- the meaning and significance of labour and capital intensive production
- how to analyse difficulties increasing efficiency and productivity
- what is meant by the optimal mix of resources
- how to use technology to improve efficiency.

Efficiency

Operations managers may want to make their operations process more efficient. Increasing efficiency involves getting more output from a given level of inputs. Alternatively it can be seen as using less resources to achieve a given level of output and quality. A more efficient process will have lower unit costs because it is using its resources more effectively.

The importance of efficiency

Businesses are constantly trying to improve their efficiency because if they can drive down unit costs they can bring the price down or make higher profits with the same price. In a highly competitive business

world, greater efficiency is important to be able to at least match what others are doing. Ways of improving efficiency include:

- using capacity more efficiently
- choosing the optimal mix of resources
- increasing labour productivity
- introducing lean production
- using technology.

Each of these methods will be examined in this chapter, along with the difficulties involved in using them.

Key terms

Labour productivity is the amount of output per employee.

Efficiency is measured by the inputs used to generate output. If a process becomes more efficient it uses fewer inputs to produce a given output and the unit cost should fall.

Improving efficiency: using capacity efficiently

The capacity of the business is determined by its resources at any given moment, that is the amount and quality of its employees, capital and land. This determines the maximum that can be produced at the time by the business itself. This is important because if this capacity is not used fully resources are being wasted. This is likely to increase the unit cost because the fixed costs are not being spread over as many units as they would be if the business was at 100 per cent capacity. It is the role of marketing to generate more sales and achieve higher levels of capacity utilisation. It is inefficient if resources are not utilised fully. On the other hand, if the capacity is being fully utilised the business is unable to accept new orders and produce them itself. This might lead to customers finding alternative providers and moving to them.

It is important, therefore, for a business to have the right level of capacity to meet demand and to be looking ahead to what demand might be in the future; it can then prepare accordingly by increasing or decreasing its scale over time, or making alternative arrangements.

What do you think?

If capacity utilisation is 10 per cent, what does this mean? What might be the cause?

If capacity utilisation is low this is inefficient and so a manager might:

- try to improve their marketing to boost sales. For example, it might reduce price, spend more on the promotional mix, widen distribution or change the product.
- reduce its capacity. This is known as rationalising or downsizing. This may take time to do (for example to close and sell off stores) and may not be possible (for example, it may not be possible to close part of a production line or part of a chemical factory without shutting the production down). This may be a major strategic decision that is difficult to reverse and therefore will be taken with care.

If demand is too high for the existing capacity a business might:

- outsource to other producers. This may take time to negotiate and is likely to be more expensive than doing the task in house. Also the business that is outsourcing may be concerned about the quality of the work: if it is poor this will reflect on the business that has overall responsibility for the order. Businesses that have a strong brand or way of doing things (for example a management consultancy or firm of architects) may be wary of outsourcing a service task to an alternative provider that may do things differently.
- find a way to reduce demand in the short term. This might be through pushing the price up. Dynamic pricing occurs when businesses such as airlines change the prices regularly in response to demand conditions. When demand is getting higher they can raise prices to match supply more closely. Alternatively a business might start a waiting list and provide the service or good when it does have capacity.

Increasing efficiency: increasing labour productivity

Another way of increasing efficiency is to improve the output per employee. The output per employee is called labour productivity.

Labour productivity is measured by:

$$\text{Labour productivity} = \frac{\text{total output}}{\text{number of employees}}$$

If a business can achieve more output from a given number of employees, then assuming the wages and salaries stay the same, the cost per unit falls. For example:

100 employees produce 200 units with a labour cost of £2,000:

- Labour productivity = 200 / 100 = 2 units per employee.
- Unit cost of labour = £2,000 / 200 = £10 per unit.

If 100 employees produce 400 units with a labour cost of £2,000:

- Labour productivity = 400 / 100 = 4 units per employee; productivity has increased
- Unit cost of labour = £2,000/400 = £5 per unit; the labour cost per unit has fallen as productivity has increased.

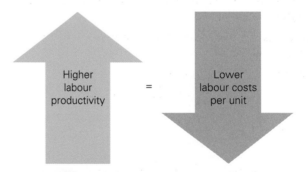

Figure 13.1 Higher labour productivity results in lower unit costs.

Study tip

Measuring output per worker may be relatively straightforward in some businesses. Managers could measure the number of cars produced and divide this by the number of employees to calculate the cars per employee. However, in other businesses there may be other indicators of performance. For example, in an estate agency or retailer the sales per employee may be measured. It is important to think of the context and refer to an appropriate measure of labour productivity when analysing a given situation.

Maths moment

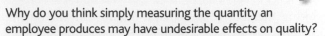

$\dfrac{1+b}{c}=3$

Employees	Wage costs £	Units	Labour productivity (number of units)	Wage cost per unit £
1	100	10		
2	200	30		
3	300	60		
4	400	100		
5	500	200		

Table 13.1

(a) Complete the table above.
(b) What does it show about the relationship between labour productivity and the costs of a unit?

To increase labour productivity a manager may:

- invest in technology so employees have access to more equipment to help them complete their tasks more effectively
- improve training of employees so staff have more skills to do their jobs
- change the way the work is organised and the design of jobs to improve the flow of work and reduce time waiting to complete tasks
- change the way employees are rewarded to provide more incentive.

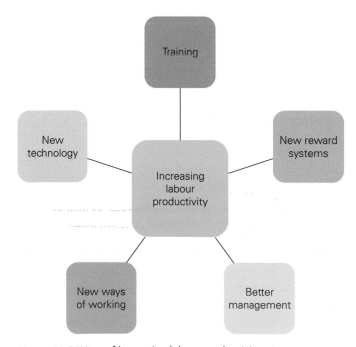

Figure 13.2 Ways of increasing labour productivity

What do you think?

Why do you think simply measuring the quantity an employee produces may have undesirable effects on quality?

Why do you think measuring productivity might be difficult in some businesses such as healthcare, teaching and financial advice? What do you think should be measured in these cases to assess employee performance?

Difficulties in increasing labour productivity

Although increasing productivity is in itself a desirable target for managers this must be achieved without a negative impact elsewhere. Imagine you are rushing to get homework done more quickly: this might increase your productivity on a given day but the quality may suffer. Imagine setting productivity targets in the health service: this might mean more patients are treated but the quality of treatment may suffer. Higher productivity targets for a call centre may mean more calls are taken but less time is taken with each customer, so sales and customer satisfaction may fall. Managers need to be aware of 'unintended consequences' whereby setting one target leads to undesirable behaviour and effects in other areas.

Also, while introducing ways of achieving higher levels of labour productivity is desirable for the business (because output per employee is higher), this may be resisted by employees. This is because if the demand for a product does not increase but productivity does, fewer employees will be required to produce the output required. If demand is 100 units and output per employee is 5 units this means 20 employees are required. If productivity is 25 units only 4 employees are required to produce the same total output. This means higher levels of productivity may be associated with staff being moved to jobs elsewhere in the organisation or being made redundant. As a result employees may resist attempts to increase productivity because they want to retain jobs.

Alternatively, employees may demand higher pay in return for higher productivity on the basis that they deserve more. This is because higher productivity means more output can be produced with the same number of employees, which can lead to more sales and revenue. It is not unusual therefore for employees and managers to negotiate pay deals linked to increases in productivity. However if the pay increase is too high it may offset any efficiency gains from the higher productivity and therefore the business will not have benefited.

Increasing efficiency: choosing the optimal mix of resources

The resources available to a business include land, labour and capital. The combination of resources used by a business will depend very much on the nature of the operations process. Running a logistics business like UPS that delivers parcels across the world is different from running an online retailer, which is different from running a bottling plant. Each process brings with it its own challenges and different combinations of resources.

Some processes are quite capital intensive: this means they involve a relatively high level of capital equipment (such as machinery). Airlines and oil refineries and chemical plants are capital intensive. By comparison, website design, nail parlours and hairdressers are relatively labour intensive. The best (or optimal) combination of resources will depend on:

- the process itself, for example what kinds of processes are involved. High-volume repetitive tasks may be able to be undertaken by machinery, whereas very creative, ideas-type work may not.

Business in focus: Productivity

Figure 13.3 A Best Buy store

Companies such as Best Buy have increasingly recognised that work is not a place where you go but rather something you do. To get the most out of its corporate workforce, the company has adopted a 'results-only work environment,' which gives workers big targets but lets them meet these goals in any way they see fit. This approach has improved worker productivity by as much as 35 per cent in departments that have deployed it.

Transforming process flows will also unlock new kinds of productivity. Companies such as Cisco and IBM are aggressively developing approaches (from social networks to video-conferencing) that tear down silos and reinvent how far-flung employees collaborate and exchange knowledge. UK grocer Tesco, for example, saved up to 45 per cent of the travel budgets of key departments by substituting video-conferencing for long-haul travel. The Hong Kong apparel supplier Li & Fung now uses video-conferencing to connect clothing designers with fabric suppliers around the world, dramatically speeding up the design process.

Another factor that should affect productivity is how the growing amounts of information are used. Although the volume of data created is expected to increase fivefold over the next five years, best-guess estimates suggest that less than ten per cent of the information created is meaningfully organised or deployed. That number will only shrink as the rate of information production goes up. Enter business analytics software, which increasingly allows companies to make sense of data 'noise', helping them 'de-average' data to eliminate waste, more closely target customers, and identify new opportunities. In general, companies that are aggressive adopters of business analytics are proving twice as good at predicting outcomes and three times as good at predicting risk as those that are not.

The Swiss telecom operator Cablecom, for example, improved customer retention nearly tenfold through the better use of customer information. Both Amazon and Google have developed predictive models that use enormous amounts of data to figure out what products customers might like, based on past searches and clicks. Companies that deploy technology more successfully to get more from the higher-quality employees they attract will gain large business model advantages, as well as driving substantial growth and productivity gains.

Source: McKinsey & Company website, authors of article: Peter Bisson, Elizabeth Stephenson and S Patrick Viguerie, June 2010
www.mckinsey.com/insights/growth/the_productivity_imperative

Questions

1. Analyse how a 'results only' environment might improve productivity.
2. Analyse how transforming process flows can improve productivity.

- what is affordable and achievable. It may be that the funds or space are not available to justify investment in new equipment. It may be that the scale of operations does not merit it. A small farm may not be able to afford some of the farming equipment because it would use it relatively little, as its scale is small. It therefore may have to rent the equipment for short periods of time, which is relatively expensive (although cheaper than buying it and having it sit idle for most of the time). A large farm may have the scale required to justify such equipment as the initial costs can be spread over high volumes and therefore be more efficient.

Getting the optimal mix of resources will affect the quality of the work done but also the efficiency. A business that is operating without the latest technology because it cannot afford it may be inefficient, for example. A business that meets extra demand by simply bringing in staff because there is not time to invest in capital equipment may also be inefficient.

Increasing efficiency: adopting lean production

With greater pressure to keep prices low due to greater competition, **lean production** has been adopted by more businesses seeking to remain competitive in recent years. Lean production aims to reduce waste throughout the organisation. It seeks to reduce time wasted, material wastage and final products that are wasted due to defects.

Being lean aims to reduce waste by:

- improving quality and so reducing the number of items that need to be reworked, thrown away or fixed.
- reducing the amount of inventory held as this reduces costs of protecting and storing it; it also reduces the risk of the inventory going out of date or not being sold. Some businesses aim to order in supplies only when they are needed. This is known as 'Just in Time' production and involves holding as close to zero stock as possible. Lean production requires good communication with suppliers and the ability

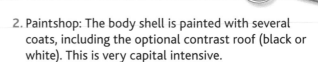

Business in focus: BMW Mini

Figure 13.4 The Mini assembly line

At BMW in Oxford more than 4,700 associates work three shifts, seven days a week, to produce as many as 700 Minis per day. The production process involves:

1. Bodyshell production: this is where metal is mainly welded together to form the body of the MINI. This is a very capital intensive process using 230 robots and with a quality standard of 0.05 mm standard.

2. Paintshop: The body shell is painted with several coats, including the optional contrast roof (black or white). This is very capital intensive.

3. Assembly: All 2,415 different inner and outer parts of the Mini that come from 200 suppliers are mounted to the painted bodyshell. This involves relatively high levels of labour as it is quite skilled.

About half of the £100 million investment at Plant Oxford has gone into modernising and increasing the capacity of the paint shop. The paintshop took one million man-hours to build, and is held together by over 250,000 bolts. Its construction in 1996/97 was the second-largest building project in Great Britain in that year (after the Millennium Dome).

There are 372 different interior trim and 319 different exterior options for the new Mini.

Questions

1. Why do you think the nature of the operations varies from the bodyshell, paintshop and assembly parts of the overall operations process?

2. How do you think BMW would measure the success of its operations at BMW Mini?

of suppliers to produce and deliver quickly. It also assumes good relations with employees and a reliable operations process because if anything goes wrong (for example a dispute with employees) there are no inventories as a back-up.

- reducing the time items are waiting for something to happen to them; this is because if items are idle they are not being sold and generating profits. This may be done by changing the layout or the way a process is carried out.
- reducing the time when items are moving from one stage of process to another; again this represents a waste of resources.

Key term

Lean production occurs when managers reduce waste and therefore operations become more efficient.

What do you think?

Why do you think suppliers and employees are crucial to the success of lean production?

To become leaner a business may adopt a number of processes such as:

- Kaizen: this is an approach which emphasises the value of continuous improvement. Major changes over time can occur as a result of relatively small changes made regularly. Employees are encouraged to work in kaizen groups to focus on their area of work and come up with ideas on how processes can be improved and made leaner. The idea is that those doing the work are more likely to know how to do the work more efficiently.
- Andon: On a process an andon cord is present above the process. If there is a problem the andon cord is pulled and production stops. Flashing lights highlight where the problem has occurred and everyone goes to this point to understand what happened. The andon approach involves transparency and ensuring that when a problem happens everyone in the organisation learns from it and becomes more efficient as a result.
- Changes to the layout of a store or factory and changes to the process used to make it more efficiently.

Figure 13.5 shows how changes to a system in a fast-food business can make a process leaner and more efficient. It shows in number order the stages and movements in fulfilling an order, both before and after changes that were made to improve efficiency.

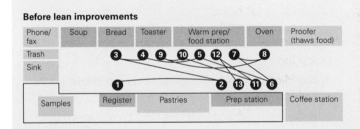
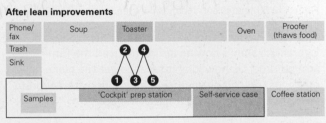

Figure 13.5 Developing a leaner approach to making sandwiches in a shop

Business in focus: Amazon

Kaizen is a powerful tool for improvement that is used at Amazon. The founder Jeff Bezos requires all senior managers to work in customer service at least one day a year. This allows managers to experience what it is like on the front line, to understand the problems that occur and to find solutions.

Each improvement from kaizen may be small but they add up to major change overall. For example, on one day when Bezos was on the front line he discovered that some suppliers were sending boxes that were incorrectly labelled or badly packed. In one instance bottles were broken, which was dangerous for employees and if they ever got to the customer would obviously be returned. Bezos introduced a 'three strikes' policy.

The first time there is a problem, suppliers are reminded of the packing rules, the second time anything happens they get a warning, and the third time they are dropped as suppliers.

The ideal kaizen teams for Amazon include frontline workers, engineers, and a few managers who are going to question and look for ways of improvement.

Adapted from McKinsey & Company website, author of article: Marc Onetto www.mckinsey.com/insights/operations/when_toyota_met_e-commerce_lean_at_amazon

Questions

1. Explain what is meant by 'kaizen'.
2. Analyse how kaizen might help Amazon be more competitive.

Business in focus: Lean operations at Airbus

Turnaround time between flights

	Average	Best practice	Potential reduction	Lean techniques
Unload passenger	6:14	4:38	1:36	Stricter controls on carry-on bags, fewer passengers moving back in aisle to find bag
Wait for cleaning crew to board aircraft	0:24	0:18	0:06	Cleaning crew in position ahead of time
Clean aircraft	11:48	9:40	2:08	Standardise work flow, timing and methods, such as cleaning supplies in prearranged kits
Wait for transmission to gate of cabin crew's approval to board	4:11	0	4.11	Visual signal from cabin crew to agent when plane is ready to board, e.g. light flash at top of ramp
Wait for first passenger to board	4:06	0	4:06	
Load passengers	19:32	16:00	3:32	Active management of overhead storage bins by flight attendants
Wait for passenger-information list	1:58	0:13	1:45	Passenger-information list delivered by agent following last passenger to board
Close aircraft door	0:57	0:09	0:48	Agent ready at aircraft to close door
Detach boarding ramp	1:39	0:43	0:56	
Total time (including initial steps)	52:18	33:11	19.07	

Figure 13.6 Minutes and seconds per step for Airbus A320 single-aisle, medium-range airliner

Source: McKinsey & Company www.slideshare.net/xtalentcat/next-frontiers-for-lean-32065239

Figure 13.6 shows how an airline reduced the turn-around time, i.e. how long it takes to get the plane ready for take-off again once it has landed, for an Airbus through a series of small improvements.

Questions

1. Analyse how the improvements shown above would benefit an airline.
2. Analyse the possible reasons why employees might resist kaizen groups.

Lean organisational structure

Being lean can affect every aspect of the business including its structure. Peter Drucker, a management writer, once wrote that 'much of what we call management consists of making it difficult for people to work'! What he means is that management can create so many forms, so many rules, have so many meetings and have so many procedures that making decisions, getting things done and actually getting on with work can be difficult. Lean organisations, therefore, try to ensure that the systems and rules in place are the essential ones, that meetings are productive and do not take up too much time and that there is not so much communication that people spend most of their time responding to emails.

What do you think?

How would you ensure that meetings are productive?

The difficulties of adopting lean production

Although lean production can provide greater efficiency it can also mean a business is more vulnerable because there is no inventory if there is ever a disruption to production. If employees strike, for example, or if suppliers fail to deliver, the business will have to halt operations. This means that working closely in partnership with stakeholders is essential to keep operations going. Even then the business is vulnerable to unpredictable events. For example, a major earthquake and tsunami in Japan in 2011 disrupted the production of many lean producers that relied on the production from there; they simply did not have the inventory they needed. This made companies such as Honda review their 'one supplier' policy because although it helped build up a strong partnership with that supplier it left the business very vulnerable to any disruption in supply.

Introducing lean production can also be difficult. Employees are expected to take a more active role in checking their own work to ensure that any problems are discovered early and that mistakes are not repeated. Employees need to be engaged, have the skills and training to improve the quality of their own work and be willing to send work back to others in the organisation if it is not good enough. Some employees will resist these changes, preferring to keep their jobs as they are and not want to train or take on extra responsibility.

Lean production also requires excellent links with suppliers so they know exactly what is needed and when. This may require investment in communications and technology.

What do you think?

What do you think are the advantages and disadvantages of using one supplier rather than many for any given input?

Weblink

Toyota is famous for its lean production process. To find out more about its process visit: www.toyota-global.com/company/vision_philosophy/toyota_production_system/

Using technology to improve operational efficiency

Technological developments improve not just what is produced but how it is produced. Think of how you do your homework and compare it to how your grandparents did theirs: not only are the nature of the tasks likely to be different but there will be radical differences in how you do your work. You research online, word process, produce presentations on a computer and share ideas online with friends. Your grandparents didn't do any of these. And what about the way you are taught: with interactive whiteboards, video clips, websites, virtual learning environments, email, blogs and social media. Your parents are emailed reports and updates from the school and may be able

to log in to see what you are doing, how you are doing, what your attendance is like and so on. This is a very different world from when your grandparents were at school! Many of the products and processes we take for granted: online ordering of tickets for the cinema, downloading music, using sites that recommend other products we might like or enable us to compare prices from different businesses and click and collect, simply did not exist 20 years ago because the technology was not there.

Technology continues to move forward businesses and their operations, improving the quality and improving their efficiency. Whether it is information technology, robots, computer-aided manufacturing or transportation developments, technology is reducing unit costs as well as helping organisations become more flexible and more competitive. Technological developments enable businesses to:

- be more flexible to customer needs: with technology they can track customer behaviour more effectively, target specific groups more easily and provide more personalised products
- reduce costs by having more efficient processes with less errors; for example online booking and ordering means you enter your own details, saving the business time and money and meaning there is less to change if the wrong details are put in. Technology enables processes such as computer-aided design, which enables prototypes and models to be developed and tested on screen rather than actually built.
- be innovative; for example enabling you to download and watch films as and when you like: this should increase customer satisfaction

However, managers have to:

- have the finance to invest; new technology may be needed just at the moment when the business is struggling and lacking finance to buy new equipment
- have the training to use it effectively
- understand and manage the impact on other functions; for example technology may change people's jobs and managers have to ensure staff understand why this is happening, have the necessary skills to adapt and do not resist this change if it is needed
- be able to judge which technology will be useful in the long term rather than trying to adopt every new development that comes along.

Business in focus: Technology and airlines

One of the key considerations when designing an aircraft is the weight. The heavier the plane the more fuel it will use, thereby increasing fuel costs. Attempts to increase fuel efficiency and improve the aerodynamic design of new aircraft have led designers to stop using aluminium. The most modern planes, for example Airbus's A350, use lightweight carbon fibre; this is a very strong and very light composite material. The use of composite materials can reduce the weight of an aircraft by 20 per cent. Each kilogram reduction in the weight of an aircraft can save the airline flying it around $1m (£603,000) in costs over the lifetime of the aircraft.

Using these composite materials is also creating other possible savings. For example, an A380 super-jumbo has about six million parts – but in future this could be reduced considerably as some of the parts can be moulded together to form one part and be manufactured at the same time. With fewer components, manufacturing time will be reduced, therefore saving more money.

Designers are also looking at improving the shape of the aircraft to improve its aerodynamics. One recent

development has been the trailing edges of the wing of Airbus's latest plane, the A350 shown in Figure 13.7.

Figure 13.7 The Airbus A350

Questions

1. Analyse the benefits to airlines of this new technology of carbon fibre.

2. Analyse the benefits to customers of this new technology of carbon fibre.

ASSESSMENT ACTIVITIES

Sections (a), (b) and (c) of these assessment activities are relevant for students taking AS and A-level examinations. The questions in section (d) are for A-level students only.

(a) Knowledge check questions

1 An operations process that has little waste is known as .... production.

2 What is the difference between total output and productivity?

3 You employ 20 employees who produce a total of 700 units per week. What is the labour productivity?

4 Explain one reason why managers may be eager to increase labour productivity.

5 Explain what is meant by kaizen.

6 In 'Just in Time' production, businesses hold high levels of inventory. True or false? Explain your answer.

7 State two ways a business might try to improve labour productivity.

8 State one reason why employees may resist attempts to increase productivity.

9 State two possible benefits of higher efficiency.

(b) Short answers

1 Explain how a leaner approach to operations might benefit a food retailer.   (5 marks)

2 Explain one way in which a car manufacturer might improve productivity.   (5 marks)

3 Explain one possible way in which increasing efficiency might help the growth of a restaurant business.   (5 marks)

4 A business employs 20 people with a productivity of 500 units per person. The wage rate is £2,000 per person. What is the labour cost per unit?

(3 marks)

5 If productivity rises by 20 per cent at the business in Question 4, what is the labour cost per unit? (4 marks)

6 Explain one reason why managers in a car factory may face resistance from employees when trying to increase productivity. (5 marks)

(c) Data response questions

Working hours and productivity

Research increasingly seems to suggest that working fewer hours a week can actually increase labour productivity. Although managers often assume that working more hours leads to more output there seems to be little correlation between hours worked and productivity. A recent study showed that employees in Germany work almost 45 per cent fewer annual hours than Greece, but are 70 per cent more productive, while annual German salaries are higher. It may be that improving the work–life balance actually improves performance at work and output. This may be particularly true these days in a service-based economy where new ideas and innovation are critical for success.

Environmentalists are also in favour of a shorter working week because of its impact on traffic congestion and pollution. Less time is wasted on commuting and less time in spent sitting at your desk, which is bad for your health.

And of course, it is better for morale, which is good for both employees and employers, who will have to deal with less labour turnover and a more motivated workforce. This is important for businesses that are seeking to maintain their competitiveness. Companies such as Google and Facebook are always looking to ensure they keep their staff engaged to keep productivity high. However, companies generally seem reluctant to take the decision to move to a four-day working week. They are worried about not having staff there when others do.

Richard Branson at Virgin Group recently announced that staff at the Head Office could decide how long to take on holidays and when to take them, without permission from their bosses. Some think this may actually lead to higher productivity.

Of course, productivity is not just down to working patterns and whatever managers do with working hours: they need to ensure that other factors such as training and investment are not neglected.

1 Explain how online businesses such as Google and Facebook might measure productivity. (6 marks)

2 Analyse how working fewer hours might increase productivity. (9 marks)

3 To what extent do you think a shorter working week is a good idea in all businesses? (15 marks)

(d) Essays

1 To what extent do you think that adopting lean production is guaranteed to lead to higher profits? Justify your answer. (25 marks)

2 Some of the most successful businesses these days are online, for example, Amazon and Google. To what extent do you think productivity is a useful operations measure for online businesses? Justify your answer. (25 marks)

Chapter 14

Improving quality

Introduction

In this chapter we examine the concept of quality in operations. We analyse what is meant by quality, how it can be achieved and the dangers of poor quality.

What you need to know by the end of this chapter:

- the importance of quality
- how to analyse methods of improving quality
- how to analyse the benefits of improving quality
- how to analyse the difficulties of improving quality
- how to analyse the costs of poor quality.

Quality

Operations managers will set targets that determine what they are trying to achieve for their customers. For example:

- A bottling plant may set a target for how many of the bottles produced should contain between 4.99ml and 50.01ml.
- An insurance company may set a target for how many claims are processed accurately.
- A call centre may set targets for how many calls are answered per hour.
- A supermarket may set a target on how many items are scanned per minute on average.
- A restaurant may set a target for how long it takes to prepare a meal.
- An airline might set a target for the proportion of passengers' bags that are lost (hopefully a low target!).

The business will have determined how it wants to compete and what it wants to provide. Managers will then have set targets, such as those listed above, to ensure the business is competitive. The **quality** of an operation is measured by the extent to which a business meets these targets consistently. A good-quality operations process delivers exactly what it is intended to produce and meets the targets that have been determined

by the customer requirements; a poor-quality operations process fails to achieve these targets or does so inconsistently. Imagine you have set yourself the target of getting an A in A-level Business Studies and your teacher says to do this you need at least 75 per cent on each piece of work. You listen in class, you study, you research, you plan, you take care with your work and you read over your work. You consistently achieve 80 per cent and you clearly have a quality process. Compare this to a student who sometimes gets 90 per cent and sometimes 30 per cent and who has no system in place to do the work: sometimes they spend the appropriate amount of time on it, sometimes they don't, sometimes they research, sometimes they don't. This is not a quality process.

To achieve its targets and develop a quality process a business must develop appropriate systems. It must also monitor what is happening to ensure the targets continue to be achieved. If the targets are met then this is a quality process.

What do you think?

What business you know would you say had a quality operations process? Why?

A quality process

For a business to have a quality operations process requires:

- a clear definition of what its targets are; these should be set to meet customer requirements
- systems to achieve these targets
- training of employees so that they have the necessary skills

- ongoing measurement of what is achieved relative to the targets
- action to be taken if performance does not meet the targets.

Edward Deming is a major contributor to thinking on quality. He introduced the PDCA cycle:

- **Plan:** Plan what you have to achieve and how to achieve it.
- **Do:** Put into action the necessary processes and systems.
- **Check**: Check the results. Measure outcomes: are you achieving your targets consistently?
- **Act:** If you are hitting targets then set more demanding quality targets; if you are not achieving targets consistently then review why and take action to do so.

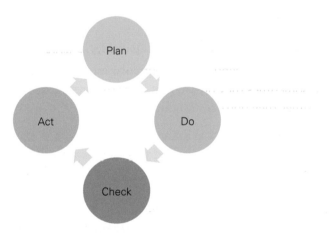

Figure 14.1 The PDCA cycle

Quality is therefore very much linked to data: it involves specific targets that define what is trying to be achieved and the efforts focused on achieving them. It is also an ongoing process. If you are consistently getting 80 per cent in work then it is time to up the standard and aim for 81 per cent. You need to review how you could do this, introduce change, measure what happens and see if you can consistently achieve 81 per cent. When you can do this the standard should move up again. Quality is a journey not a destination: you should always be trying to improve.

What do you think?

What targets would you set for the operations of:

- a school
- a hospital
- a hotel
- a retailer?

The importance of quality

Achieving quality is important to remain competitive. Why would customers choose a business that is unreliable, does not deliver what it promises or does not meet the agreed requirements? It is easier for customers to choose alternative businesses with more organisations being online and with developments in technology making it easier to source materials. As competitors keep improving the quality of what they do, businesses need to improve and offer better quality to their customers to retain them and gain their loyalty.

To improve quality, managers will want to develop processes to ensure that their targets are hit. For example, this might involve:

- using market research to ensure the requirements of customers are clearly met and that what the business is trying to achieve is appropriate relative to what competitors are doing
- the careful selection of suppliers
- training employees to check the work they receive and make sure it is acceptable, to do their job properly and check their own work
- investment in technology to help ensure the process does what it is supposed to
- reviewing the way the work is done to see if the systems can be improved. This should be done with the employees who undertake the work as they are in the best position to improve it. This is where kaizen groups (see Chapter 13) may be used.

Figure 14.2 Ways to achieve quality

Quality assurance

One approach that is designed to prevent mistakes occurring and to ensure targets are hit is called a **quality assurance** process. A quality assurance system refers to the activities involved to ensure an operations process meets the requirements of its customers. The aim is to make sure mistakes do not occur and to achieve zero defects. Think of all the measures and systems that are in place to make sure a plane takes off and lands safely. Staff have been trained, technology is used, processes are in place to make sure everything works before the plane takes off. It is no good a plane being 'nearly safe' – it has to be absolutely right. This is the same approach many other business are now trying to adopt: they want employees to think of what steps can be taken to get it right and avoid errors.

Consider a car production line. Traditionally, employees on the production line simply wanted to produce as many cars as possible. Once the car was produced it was up to the sales and marketing team to find someone to buy it. If an employee found a problem on the production line they would simply do their work and move the faulty car on to the next stage. It was not their job or responsibility to fix it and they did not have the training to do so. The car would move along the line without anyone doing anything about the faults until it got to the end. At that point a 'quality team' would inspect and try and find the faults that had been built in. This is known as **quality control**. Products are inspected to find faults. If anything, staff on the production line did not want to solve any mistakes because it would remove the need for quality control and therefore some employees would be made redundant.

Nowadays, car companies train staff to identify faults and expect employees to highlight them and stop the production line rather than pass them on to the next stage. Every employee is held responsible for any errors they pass on to the next stage. The aim therefore is to make everyone feel responsible for quality and able to improve it in their part of the process. It is also intended to reduce waste and lead to fewer items being returned as faulty. The intention is to make sure that targets are hit at each stage and the final car does not even need checking: it must meet quality standards as it has reached the end of the process.

Key terms

Quality assurance is the maintenance of target quality by attention to detail at every stage of the process.

Quality control is a system of maintaining standards by testing or inspecting the output against standards.

The benefits of improving quality

The main benefit of improving quality is that it means a process is under control. It is doing what it should be doing and consistently delivering what it should be delivering. This means operations managers can feel comfortable that they can meet the set targets. Assuming these targets have been set at an appropriate level the business will be competitive. It will be providing its service fast enough and reliably enough in a manner it has promised. It says it will deliver the gift within three days and does. It says the hair dye will last 20 washes and it does. It promises to deliver the flowers between 9a.m. and 11a.m. and it does. It says that 90 per cent of its produce is sourced locally and it is. This helps the brand image, leads to customer satisfaction and generates goodwill through word of mouth.

Difficulties in improving quality

While improving quality seems an obvious target that everyone would agree with, that is not always the case. For example, employees might:

● believe the business is doing well enough as it is and not see the need to set higher targets over time. They may resent this and even perceive it as a criticism of what they currently do
● see improving quality as extra work and not understand why they should bother unless they are paid more
● be unwilling to suggest improvements, believing this is management's job not theirs
● be unwilling to undertake all the administration required to measure and check progress.

From the business perspective improving quality will require:

● discussing the issues with employees and getting them to agree to the process
● investing in training
● possibly changing suppliers
● developing a culture (that is, a state of mind) where getting it right first time and continually measuring performance is the norm. This may be difficult to achieve due to employee resistance and difficult to sustain and ensure this remains the way people think, rather than just a short-term initiative.

The consequences of poor quality

Philip Crosby, a famous writer on quality, argues that getting quality right is cheaper than paying to fix things when they go wrong. He stated that the four absolutes of quality are:

1. Quality is conformance to requirements (quality is about meeting targets).
2. Preventing defects is preferable to inspection and correcting mistakes (quality assurance is better than quality control).
3. Zero defects should be the target (don't accept failure of any kind and keep aiming for better).
4. The cost of quality should be measured in terms of the costs of not conforming.

   This last point is important: managers should not just focus on the cost of achieving quality but on the costs incurred if they do not achieve quality.

Poor quality is expensive because:

- It costs money to recall faulty products and recall them. In recent years companies such as Toyota and General Motors have had to recall significant numbers of cars due to production problems.
- It can damage a brand's reputation.
- It costs money to rework faulty items
- There may be legal costs if customers sue the company.

ASSESSMENT ACTIVITIES

Sections (a), (b) and (c) of these assessment activities are relevant for students taking AS and A-level examinations. The questions in section (d) are for A-level students only.

(a) Knowledge check questions

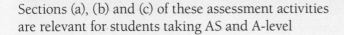

1 What is meant by quality?

2 State one reason why improving quality is important.

3 State one difficulty of improving quality.

4 What is meant by quality assurance?

5 State two ways in which a business might try to improve the quality of its operations.

6 State two costs of poor quality.

7 'Quality is a journey not a destination'; what does this mean?

8 'A quality product' is the most expensive one in the market. True or false? Explain your answer.

9 State one benefit of high quality.

10 What is quality control?

(b) Short answers

1 Explain one way in which improving quality might help the competitiveness of a hotel.   (5 marks)

2 Explain why an airline might invest in marketing research as part of its efforts to improve quality.   (5 marks)

3 Explain how a hospital might measure its quality.   (5 marks)

4 Explain one cost of poor quality in an online bank.   5 marks)

5 The Principal of a world-famous university has told staff that it is important the organisation improves the quality of its service, given how much students now pay. Explain one reason why staff might resist attempts to improve quality at this university.   (5 marks)

(c) Data response questions

The car company Toyota was once recognised for its focus on quality. However in recent years there have been a number of problems with Toyota cars, leading to product recalls. The reason for this seems to have been a focus on rapid growth. Mr Toyoda, the company's President, has acknowledged that the company's decision to focus on growth meant that Toyota placed real pressures on its operations systems and lost its focus on quality. What had made it great was making sure it met customer requirements but in recent years it concentrated more on generating sales and producing high volumes of cars.

Arguably the problems began in 2002, when Toyota set itself the goal of increasing its global market share from 11 per cent to 15 per cent. To achieve this volume of sales the company had to work with unfamiliar suppliers.

The majority of Toyota's problems have almost certainly been due to its suppliers. The automotive industry has a complex supply chain. The carmakers (who are known as original equipment manufacturers, or OEMs) are right at the centre. Next come tier-one suppliers, such as Bosch, Delphi, Denso, and Continental, who supply integrated systems directly to the OEMs. After them are the tier-two suppliers, who provide individual parts or assembled components either directly to the OEM or to tier-one suppliers.

The tier-three suppliers often make just a single component for tier-two suppliers. There are thousands of tier-two and tier-three suppliers globally, although their numbers have fallen in the last decade as the OEMs and the tier-one firms have focused on fewer key suppliers.

Toyota went as far as making some suppliers the sole provider of some products. Its aim was to build long-term, trusting relationships. By comparison, Western car companies tended to use many suppliers on short-term contracts to make them compete against each other.

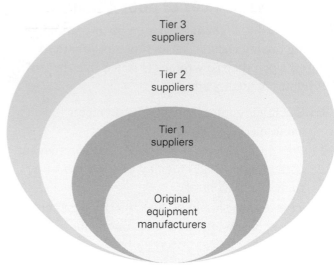

Figure 14.3 Tiers of suppliers to equipment manufacturers

Most large car firms now follow Toyota's approach and collaborate with key suppliers on new product developments. Rather than just looking at the initial costs of a component from a supplier, car companies now consider the possible costs if suppliers were delayed or faulty.

Toyota's rapid expansion meant that it had to use suppliers who did not necessarily have the same focus on quality. Given its single sourcing approach it was highly vulnerable to mistakes being made.

1   Analyse the possible consequences of poor quality for Toyota.   (9 marks)

2   Do you think using one supplier is good for quality? Justify your answer.   (15 marks)

(d) Essays

1   To what extent do you think better quality should be the priority for all businesses in the increasingly competitive markets in which they operate?   (25 marks)

2   Is improving quality within a car manufacturer inevitably going to be expensive? Justify your answer.   (25 marks)

15 Managing inventory and supply chains

Introduction

Inventory (or stock) refers to the materials held by a business; for example, there may be inventory of supplies or finished goods. In this chapter we examine the types of decisions managers might make in relation to inventory such as when and how much to order. We also consider how managers may respond to having too much or too little demand and how managers manage the supply chain.

What you need to know by the end of this chapter:

- ways of improving flexibility, speed of response and dependability
- the importance of inventory
- how to analyse the factors influencing how much inventory to hold and order
- how to examine the factors that might influence which suppliers are used
- how best to match supply to demand
- how to manage the supply chain effectively and the value of doing so
- how to evaluate the benefits and disadvantages of outsourcing.

Improving operational performance

In the last few chapters we have analysed how a business might achieve some of its operational targets such as greater efficiency and better quality. However, there are other objectives that managers may also be trying to achieve. These include:

- **speed of response**. In some industries speed of response has been used as a competitive weapon – the speed with which a recovery vehicle will get back to you if you break down, the speed with which any exam script will be re-marked if you appeal the grade, the speed with which a product

can be delivered to you. These are all attempts to be more competitive. To improve the speed may involve reviewing the process to find time savings – for example, can some activities be carried out simultaneously rather than one after another. Have you ever eaten your breakfast while getting dressed, doing your teeth and finishing your homework? If so you have been undertaking activities simultaneously and saving time! Increasing the speed of response may also involve investment in new technology. However, speed does not always need to be the key operational objectives. You may be more concerned that your plane leaves at the time stated rather than whether it is 10 minutes faster than a rival company's. You might be more concerned that the items ordered online arrive in perfect working order rather than whether they arrive one day earlier, but broken.

- **dependability**. This refers to a process starting and finishing at the stated time. This may be very important in the travel sector or in project work where you may need to be sure that it starts and ends on time. For example, you are on holiday for two weeks and in that time need the outside of the house repainted. You may choose a builder that guarantees it can be done in that time. When exams are being marked it is vital the marking finishes in time for the results to be published on the set date. Greater dependability may therefore be more important in some industries than others. To achieve it may involve new processes, investment and training.

- **becoming more flexible**. Some businesses might want to offer greater flexibility to their customers. Made-to-order sandwiches at a cafe, any combination of A-level subjects in a sixth form and your own personalised picture on your credit card are all examples of greater flexibility. Technological developments are making this flexibility easier. If you buy a BMW Mini, for example, you choose the colour, the wheels, the radio, the type of roof, the upholstery, the interior trim and various other features from different lists. Your car is then produced for you and BMW claim no two Minis are exactly the same. The use of technology to produce on a large scale while adapting the individual items to meet individual customer needs is called **mass customisation**. Greater flexibility may lead to more customer satisfaction but there is a trade-off – it may be more expensive to produce many different versions of a product and it may be a more difficult process to manage. Your school may not want to offer all A-level subjects in any combination because it would be very difficult and expensive to provide this. Most fast-food restaurants have a relatively limited menu so that staff do not need much training, the restaurant does not need to hold lots of different inventory and they can buy ingredients for these items in bulk. Being more flexible would not fit with this low-cost, fast approach.

Operations managers will, therefore have to decide what the key operational objectives are in their business. In some industries, speed may be the key; in others dependability may be more important. If flexibility is the priority it may involve holding more inventory to enable a business to provide more choice.

Inventory

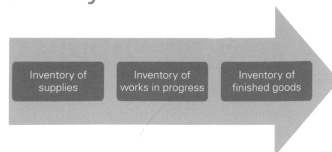

Figure 15.1 The different forms of stock inventory

The **inventory** of a business refers to the goods that it holds; it is also called stock. Inventory may take several different forms:

(a) Inventory of materials and supplies may be held by the business. For example, a car producer may hold vehicle parts ready to use in production.

(b) During a production process, semi-finished items may be held ready for the next stage of the process.

(c) Finished products may be held ready for distribution or sale. Think of how much inventory many retail outlets hold on their shelves.

Figure 15.2 Inside a distribution centre

Key terms

Mass customisation is the term for producing on a large scale while still enabling individual customer preferences to be met.

A company's **inventory** is the goods or stock it holds.

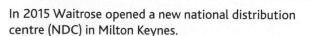

Business in focus: Waitrose distribution centre

In 2015 Waitrose opened a new national distribution centre (NDC) in Milton Keynes.

The NDC is the size of about twelve Premiership football pitches and will be able to deal with the distribution of around 25,000 nationally available grocery and home department product lines that are sold in Waitrose branches and online at Waitrose.com.

The NDC will deliver these products via Waitrose's four regional distribution centres (RDCs). It will also simplify the supply chain and improve the efficiency of handling national product lines that in the past have been sent between RDCs. This should enable more manageable growth. The company has plans to open 38 shops next year and expand its online sales.

Questions

1. Explain the purpose of a national distribution centre.

2. Analyse how a distribution centre could affect the performance of Waitrose.

Why hold inventory?

Inventory is held to ensure that production can take place immediately (as opposed to having to wait for supplies to arrive) and to ensure that customer orders can be fulfilled quickly (without having to wait for items to be produced).

Influences on the amount of inventory held

Managing the amount of inventory held is important for these reasons:

- Holding inventory uses up resources. For example, managers may need to invest in warehousing space or security measures to protect the items and prevent damage and theft.
- Holding inventory has an opportunity cost; that is, the money invested in producing products could have been used for something else. Just think of how much money is invested in inventory when you visit a car showroom – hundreds of thousands of pounds worth of cars may be sitting on the forecourt. This is why managers are often eager for the inventory to 'turn over' relatively fast as this frees up funds and generates a profit to expand the business.
- Inventory may go out of date and become worthless if held for too long. When England went out of the World Cup a lot earlier than expected in 2014 many shops were left with unsold England merchandise that had to be discounted to sell it.

Figure 15.3 England football team merchandise

To manage inventory, managers will want to measure how much of an item is held at any time, what the likely usage rate is going to be and how quickly it can be replaced. Technology is enabling much more efficient inventory control.

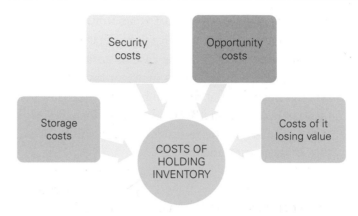

Figure 15.4 The costs of holding inventory

When managing inventory, therefore, a manager will want to make sure that enough inventory is held to ensure that production and sales can continue and meet customers' requirements quickly. However, managers will not want to hold too much inventory because of the costs involved.

What do you think?

What do you think will determine how much inventory a retailer holds?

Inventory control charts

The management of inventory can be analysed using inventory control charts.

The key elements of this type of chart are:

- **The buffer inventory.** This is the minimum amount of inventory a business wants to hold. Buffer or safety inventory is held to ensure production can continue in an emergency and/or customers can continue to be supplied. The amount of buffer inventory may depend on how difficult and expensive it is to store and how likely it is that there will be problems with inventory arriving on time.
- **The lead time.** This is how long it takes from an order being placed with suppliers and the items arriving. It is measured in days, weeks or months. The lead time determines when an order has to be placed in order to arrive in time to prevent the inventory falling below the buffer (safety) stock level.
- **The re-order level.** This is the level at which a new order must be placed for supplies. This will depend on the buffer inventory, the rate at which materials are used up and the lead-time.

● **Re-order quantities.** This is the amount a manager orders of a particular item. It might depend on factors such the cost and the ease of storage and the usage rate. The more often a manager re-orders, the less the quantity that needs to be re-ordered, if other factors are unchanged. The less often a manager orders, the bigger the re-order quantity will be, if others factors are unchanged.

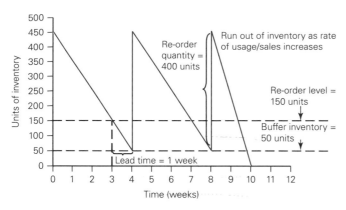

Figure 15.5 Inventory chart

Problems with inventory control might arise if:

● supplies are delayed and do not arrive on time; in this case the business will use up its buffer inventory for as long as it can
● the usage rate is faster than usual; perhaps because of an increase in demand
● there is a failure to reorder inventory. Increasingly, orders are done automatically but in some areas this is still done manually and can be forgotten.

If a business does run out of inventory it may have to halt production and let customers know there will be a delay. This may cause customer dissatisfaction and lead to lost orders.

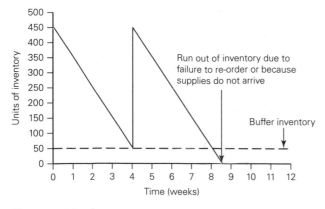

Figure 15.6 Stock out

What do you think?

How do you think a business might react if it runs out of stocks due to problems at the suppliers?

Study tip

In some cases a business can operate with almost no inventory; in other situations managers may want to hold inventory, for example to show customers. Avoid making assumptions about the 'right level' of inventory until you understand the context of the case and its operational objectives. A retailer may want to display a wide range of products and hold high levels of inventory, whereas a web design business may have relatively little inventory, probably consisting of general supplies such as print cartridges.

Technology and inventory control

Developments in technology are enabling managers to keep a better track of what inventory they have. The use of Electronic Point-of-Sale scanners in stores, for example, enables the business to know what it has available and when an item needs reordering. Better marketing databases also mean the business can forecast likely sales more easily and therefore be able to have items in place, avoiding the danger of running out.

Communications links with suppliers have also improved making 'Just in Time' more possible. As items are running out, orders can be placed directly with suppliers, reordering them as and when needed. This helps improve efficiency as businesses are not left with unwanted products that they then have to discount or discard.

Managing supply to match demand

An important aspect of operations management is to ensure that the supply of a product can match the demand. In some industries demand may be relatively stable and therefore the required output is also fairly predictable. For example, assuming demand is constant, managing a soft drinks factory will involve keeping the existing process running continuously.

However, in some businesses demand will vary enormously on different days of the week (for example, retailers may be busier on a Saturday), at different times of the year (for example, a ski resort) or even at different times of the day (for example, an accident and emergency unit at a hospital or a car breakdown service). Think back to the 4Vs of operations (in Chapter 11): the degree of variability of demand differs significantly from one sector to another.

To match supply to demand there are various methods an operations manager may adopt:

- employing a flexible workforce: by ensuring employees are multi-skilled and have flexible contracts, managers may be able to move staff to where they are needed and increase hours to meet any sudden peaks in demand. Managers may also make use of **part-time** or **temporary staff** to enable them to increase or decrease the workforce as required.
- using queuing systems or introducing waiting lists to manage high levels of demand
- outsourcing production to other businesses to meet high levels of orders
- increasing prices to reduce demand
- accepting orders to produce for others if demand is low
- producing to order. This occurs when a business only produces when the actual order is placed rather than producing items and hoping they will sell. This reduces any risk of being left with unsold stock but requires a flexible production process.

Weblink

The furniture company Made.com collects customer orders and only produces the furniture when it has enough orders. One of the reasons the company can keep prices down is there are no warehouse costs to pass on to the customer.

Key terms

Part-time staff work less than a full working week, for example 20 hours a week.

Temporary staff work for a limited period of time, for example for the summer only.

The supply chain

Take a look at your phone and think of all the producers who will have been involved in producing and delivering this final product to you. One business may have designed it and then used suppliers to produce parts such as the screen, the handset, the memory card, the camera and so on. Then there will have been businesses involved in assembling all the parts, distributing the phones to retailers and promoting the products. A large number of businesses will therefore have been involved in the overall process of developing and producing this final product.

Business in focus: RAC Breakdown

Figure 15.7 RAC breakdown vehicles

'RAC Breakdown, our roadside assistance service, has more than 7 million roadside assistance customers – 2.2 million individual members and 5.4 million corporate customers. Our breakdown assistance centres operate 24 hours a day, seven days a week, 365 days a year and handle around four million calls a year which, at peak times, can mean two calls every second. RAC has around 1,800 patrols that attend around 2.5 million rescue breakdowns each year. RAC Breakdown also includes our overseas development of roadside and related products and services, through RAC Europe. Through a wide network of contractors and partners across continental Europe RAC provides breakdown assistance to members when they're abroad.'

The number of breakdowns may vary enormously at different times of day and at different times of the year. Consider the problems this creates and how the RAC can cope with such variability.

Source: RAC website
www.rac.co.uk/about-us/rac-products-and-services

Questions

1. Explain the factors that affect the demand for RAC breakdown services.
2. Analyse the operations decisions facing RAC.

Managing relations with all the other partners involved in the supply process is therefore an important aspect of a business.

Key term

The **supply chain** of a business refers to all of the providers of resources (such as money, people, finance, machinery, equipment) at different stages of the operations process.

Managing the supply chain

Managing a **supply chain** involves taking decisions about:

- what to produce yourself and what to buy from others
- which other businesses to work with
- a supplier strategy, in terms of how many suppliers to work with; is the aim to build a long-standing relationship with one supplier or get different suppliers to compete for business regularly
- setting out the terms and conditions of the supplier relationship, for example penalty clauses for any delays
- deciding on the assurances from the supplier on their operations e.g. in terms of treatment of employees, where they source their resources. A business that wants to protect its brand and its image needs to be careful who it is buying from and will want to ensure it is not likely to be affected by a scandal at its suppliers. Businesses such as Marks and Spencer and The Co-operative that promote an image of behaving very responsibly would not wanted to be associated with suppliers who did not
- how much direct involvement to have with suppliers – will the business insist on a Code of Conduct with suppliers? How rigorously will this be enforced and how? This has become an important issue in many industries where there are important ethical and environmental issues.
- how centralised purchasing should be; for example, do all offices around the world have to buy their supplies from a company list, or are they able to choose who they want to work with?

Effective management of the supply chain will ensure:

- the right supplies arrive on time
- a fair price is paid for the items
- the products are produced in a way which is acceptable to the business.

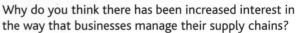

Figure 15.8 The supply chain

What do you think?

Why do you think there has been increased interest in the way that businesses manage their supply chains?

Business in focus: Ford

'We continue to work to strengthen our global supply base. As part of this process, we have been reducing the global number of production suppliers from 3,300 in 2004 to about 1,200 at year-end 2013. We have identified plans that will take us to a target of about 750 suppliers, and we are confident that our consolidation efforts will result in a stronger and healthier supply base. We continue to work closely with our suppliers to address any near-term capacity constraints as we continue to ramp up production. In addition, our move to global vehicle platforms increases our ability to source to common suppliers for the total global volume of vehicle components resulting in a smaller number of suppliers receiving a greater volume of purchases to support our global vehicle platforms and allowing us to gain greater efficiencies.'

Source: Ford website
http://corporate.ford.com/doc/ar2013-2013_ford_annual_report_mr.pdf

Questions

1. Analyse how Ford's choice of suppliers can affect its performance.
2. Analyse the possible reasons why Ford is reducing the number of suppliers it is working with.

The value of managing the supply chain effectively

The way in which the supply chain is managed will affect:

- the extent to which suppliers meet the requirements of the business reliably
- the costs of the business
- the ability of the business to be flexible to customer requirements.

Managing the supply chain also involves ethical issues. For example, a business may buy supplies from a business that is paying low wages or that has working conditions that do not meet the standards in the home country. This may keep costs down but leave a business open to criticism for working with that supplier.

The dangers of not managing your supply chain properly can be seen in the horsemeat scandal in 2013. Some meat labelled as beef burgers in UK supermarkets was found to be horsemeat, so consumers had been misled. The pressure to keep costs down led to some business in the supply chain switching cheaper meat for beef.

In some cases businesses will take control of their supply chain by owning more of the stages within it. **Vertical integration** occurs when businesses start producing at different stages in the production process, for example they buy their suppliers or set up their own business to supply themselves. This gives them greater control over their supply chain. IKEA, for example, controls the whole process from design to production to sale. This means the designers understand how the products have to be moved, stored and used by consumers.

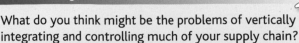

What do you think?

What do you think might be the problems of vertically integrating and controlling much of your supply chain?

Key term

Vertical integration is the combination of two or more stages of production normally operated by separate companies.

Influences on the choices of suppliers

When choosing a supplier, many factors may be considered by a manager. For example:

- the cost of materials and quality. All managers will be conscious of costs although at the same time they must consider whether the supplies meet their requirements, that is they must be aware of the quality of the supplies. Managers will want value for money
- dependability. Managers will generally want supplies to arrive as and when they are ordered to arrive. However, this may increase costs and so, as ever,

Business in focus: Fair Trade

'When you buy products with the FAIRTRADE Mark, you support farmers and workers as they work to improve their lives and their communities. The Mark means that the Fairtrade ingredients in the product have been produced by small-scale farmer organisations or plantations that meet Fairtrade social, economic and environmental standards. The standards include protection of workers' rights and the environment, payment of the Fairtrade Minimum Price and an additional Fairtrade Premium to invest in business or community projects.

Fairtrade works to benefit small-scale farmers and workers, who are among the most marginalised groups globally, through trade rather than aid to enable them to maintain their livelihoods and reach their potential.

For certain products, such as coffee, cocoa, cotton and rice, Fairtrade only certifies small-scale farmer organisations. Working through democratic organisations of small-scale farmers, Fairtrade offers rural families the stability of income which enables them to plan for the future.

For some products such as bananas, tea and flowers, Fairtrade also certifies plantations – companies that employ large numbers of workers on estates. Our Standards for such large-scale production units differ and protect workers' basic rights; from keeping

them safe and healthy, allowing them freedom of association and collective bargaining, to preventing discrimination and ensuring no bonded or illegal child labour. They also require employers to pay wages that progress towards living wage benchmarks. Ensuring decent working conditions and strong worker rights is central to Fairtrade's work.

The producers themselves decide how the Fairtrade Premium should be invested. The premium is the additional sum of money paid on top of the Fairtrade minimum price that farmers and workers receive which can be invested in social, environmental and economic developmental projects to improve their businesses and their communities. In real terms, it means investment in schools, transport, health care, sanitation, an improved environment and better business equipment and practices.'

Source: Fairtrade website
www.fairtrade.org.uk/en/what-is-fairtrade/what-fairtrade-does

Questions

1. Explain why Fairtrade might be necessary to protect small producers.
2. Analyse why a business might want to use Fairtrade products.

Business in focus: Nike

In the early 1990s news hit the headlines, as the conditions in the factories of some of Nike's suppliers to whom they outsourced their manufacturing were criticised. Low wages and poor working practices revealed by the media resulted in many people boycotting Nike's products.

However, since the 1990s Nike has changed the way it works with suppliers. In 1996, working with other organisations and the US government it established the Apparel Industry Partnership, and drew up a code of conduct for factories. In 1999 the Apparel Industry Partnership established the Fair Labor Association, which aimed to improve working conditions in factories around the world. In 2005 Nike was the first firm in the apparel industry to publish a full list of the suppliers it worked with. Nike now has a large corporate responsibility team that works with suppliers to ensure codes of conduct are enforced.

Although it is now common for businesses to have a code of conduct governing working practices in supplier factories, it can be difficult to ensure these are enforced. Corruption and bribery mean it is not always easy to get a clear picture of what is going on in a factory. Auditors can be bribed and records can be faked. It may even be that workers are complicit in poor working practices, wanting to maximise their pay by working long hours or feeling that if they were to reveal the true situation they may lose their jobs.

However, Nike feel that improving relationships with suppliers is worth it. They say that productivity and profit have risen since new rules and procedures have been enforced and that labour turnover has also fallen.

Source: adapted from various news sources

Questions

1. Explain what is meant by social responsibility in relation to suppliers.
2. Do you think that a business should take responsibility for its suppliers? Justify your answer.

---

there will be a trade-off. In the case of a major project working to tight deadlines with a Just-in-Time approach for example, dependability will be absolutely key. It may be less important in other situations.

- ethical considerations. Organisations are increasingly being held responsible for the behaviour of their suppliers. Businesses need to decide on how much responsibility they need to accept, what their standards are and how they will ensure they are achieved.

Key term

Corporate social responsibility refers to the extent to which a business takes into account its stakeholder views and accepts its obligations to society over and above the legal requirements.

The changing supply chain

Managing the supply chain effectively has become more important and more complex in recent years because many customers increasingly want to know more about how and where a product is produced. Managers need to be able to track back more of their supplies to know the answers to these questions. This may mean investigating not just their immediate suppliers but their suppliers and their suppliers and so on. If you buy a tin of John West fish, for example, you can now research where and when the fish was caught using the code on the tin. Managers are being held accountable for more and more of the supply chain and there are greater demands for transparency at all stages. An ethical business should ask questions not only about what it does but what its partners are doing as well.

Figure 15.9 John West fish

However, greater globalisation means that it is easier to find suppliers around the world and to move materials. Managers searching for the best value for money may be using suppliers thousands of miles away and their suppliers will also be global. The supply chain can therefore be very complex in terms of tracking who is involved and coordinating activities around the world.

Improvements in technology are enabling better tracking systems but equally supply chains are often involving more organisations and may be stretched around the world.

Developments in technology are also changing the nature of the supply chain in some industries. Customers can now access more products directly from the provider without as many intermediaries. For example, only two years after the release of the Kindle, Amazon.com now sells half of its books electronically for the titles it offers customers in both bound and digital formats. The Kindle is removing the entire physical supply chain of going to a bookshop to buy a book that has been produced by a publisher, printed by printer and physically sent to a store.

Outsourcing

Outsourcing occurs when a business uses another provider for some of its goods or services. For example, a school may outsource the provision of food at lunchtime and the security of the premises out of school hours.

> ### Key term
>
> **Outsourcing** is when a business uses an outside supplier.

The value of outsourcing

The benefits of outsourcing are that:

● It enables the business to make use of specialist skills and services; this may mean they get a better quality of work provided more efficiently.

● It can increase the capacity of the business by getting some aspects of its provision provided by others.

However, outsourcing can bring disadvantages and difficulties. For example:

● A business will be affected by the work undertaken by other businesses in terms of the costs and quality of their suppliers. If the supplier's quality is poor this may adversely affect the reputation of the business itself.

● A business may also be held accountable for the actions of its suppliers; for example if the supplier behaves unethically the business buying its services may be criticised for using its services.

● A business will have to pay enough for the products for the supplier to make a profit. This may be more expensive than doing the work in-house.

> ### What do you think?
>
> Do you think businesses are more or less likely to outsource in the future? Why?

ASSESSMENT ACTIVITIES

Sections (a), (b) and (c) of these assessment activities are relevant for students taking AS and A-level examinations. The questions in section (d) are for A-level students only.

(a) Knowledge check questions

1 Explain the difference between flexibility and dependability as operational objectives.

2 What is meant by mass customisation?

3 State two problems of holding inventory.

4 State two factors that might influence the buffer level of inventory.

5 What is the difference between the re-order quantity and the re-order level?

6 The time taken for supplies to arrive from the time of them being ordered is known as .... time.

7 State one possible benefit of outsourcing.

8 State one possible problem of outsourcing.

9 State two factors that might influence the choice of a supplier.

10 State two benefits of effective supply chain management.

(b) Short answer questions

1 Explain one factor that might influence the level of inventory held by an upmarket restaurant. (5 marks)

2 Explain one factor Starbucks might consider when choosing which coffee farmers to work with. (5 marks)

3 Explain one factor a furniture store might consider before deciding whether to buy in materials or produce them itself. (5 marks)

4 Increasingly, customers want to be reassured about the way in which a product is made and how it is sourcing its supplies. Explain one possible impact of changes in these areas on a business. (5 marks)

5 Explain one way in which a theme park might respond to having consistently high queues for its rides. (5 marks)

(c) Data response questions

Figure 15.10 Ben & Jerry's ice cream

Using our ingredients and the power of our purchasing decisions to support positive change not only makes sense – it makes our ice cream taste sensational!

Caring Dairy

When you think about it, Ben & Jerry's wouldn't be Ben & Jerry's if it weren't for the family farms supplying the high quality dairy ingredients we depend on. Caring Dairy™ is a unique program that's helping farmers move toward more sustainable practices on the farm.

Cage Free Eggs

The eggs we buy for Ben & Jerry's ice cream in the United States come from hens on Certified Humane cage-free farms. Certified Humane cage-free standards ensure that laying hens have wholesome, nutritious food, access to clean water, and adequate space to engage in normal behaviors, among other criteria crafted by veterinary professionals.

Brownies

If you've ever had our Half-Baked™ or Chocolate Fudge Brownie ice cream flavors, then you've already had a taste of the greatness that comes from Greyston Bakery. Greyston Bakery is as committed to providing jobs and job training for individuals who face barriers to employment.

Fairtrade

Fair trade is about making sure people get their fair share of the pie. The whole concept of fair trade goes to the heart of our values and the sense of

right and wrong. Nobody wants to buy something that was made by exploiting somebody else.' (Jerry Greenfield, Ben & Jerry's Co-founder)

Non-GMO

Ben & Jerry's is proud to stand with the growing consumer movement for transparency and the right to know what's in our food supply by supporting mandatory GMO labeling legislation.

Climate Change

All businesses have greenhouse gas emissions associated with their operations – at Ben & Jerry's, we have ours. We know our footprint, are working throughout our operations to reduce it, and we report on progress annually.

Productive Waste

With an eye towards closing loops in our supply chain, we even send the dairy waste from our Vermont plants back to two of the farms that supply us with fresh dairy ingredients. Our waste is put into methane digesters with other farm waste – where it generates energy to power the farms.

Cleaner Greener Freezer

We make ice cream in the nicest way possible, and now the freezers we put it in are, too! Our 'Lean & Green' freezers are more climate-friendly and energy efficient!

Responsibly Sourced Packaging

Our paperboard packaging is Forest Stewardship Council certified, which means forest wildlife, biodiversity and sustainability is protected from the start.

Source: Ben & Jerry's website
www.benjerry.com.sg/values/how-we-do-business?v=%3C!-

1 Explain the factors Ben & Jerry's might consider when choosing a supplier. (6 marks)

2 Analyse why Ben & Jerry's is so concerned about the suppliers it uses and the way it produces. (9 marks)

3 To what extent is producing reports on its environmental impact useful for Ben & Jerry's? (15 marks)

(d) Essays

1 To what extent is effective supply chain management essential to gain market share these days? (25 marks)

2 To what extent is outsourcing a good idea for a business wanting to be more competitive? (25 marks)

Case study: Unit 4 Decision making to improve operational performance

IKEA

Figure 1 An IKEA store

The mission of IKEA is to provide a range of well-designed home furnishings that are affordable to large numbers of people. It sells through large out-of-town stores. IKEA says it wants to help people lead a better life by providing them with well-designed, low-price furniture.

The IKEA name combines the initials of IKEA founder, Ingvar Kamprad, (IK) with the first letters from the names of the farm and village where he grew up – Elmtaryd and Agunnaryd (EA).

When designing furniture IKEA works closely with its suppliers from the very start of the process. This is to ensure that costs are minimised and that the products are designed to be flat packed in stores. Customers wander around the store – which is carefully designed so once inside you have to tour the whole store before leaving, to make sure you see everything – and select their items. They then pick their items from the warehouse and take them to the tills. At home customers assemble their products. By involving the customer in selecting and taking their products to the till and in home-assembly the business keeps costs low. It aims to work with suppliers to develop the most cost-efficient and creative ways of turning their ideas into products for the home. IKEA has around 1,000 suppliers in 53 countries.

All of the materials used in IKEA's products are tested rigorously during the product development phase. The company studies closely how customer use their furniture to influence future designs and products are tested and assessed at the two IKEA Test Labs in Sweden and China; these are also used as training centres for co-workers and suppliers.

The company sells worldwide and promotes itself online, through apps as well as print and other media advertising.

Sales growth

IKEA recently reported a rise in its annual sales and gained market share in almost all its markets. Global sales have increased 3.1 per cent to 27.9 billion euros ($37.8 billion; £23.6 billion) in the 12 months. Like-for-like sales, which remove the impact of new stores, rose 1.8 per cent in the same period. Growth was particularly strong in China, Russia and the US. IKEA, which has its headquarters in Sweden, said some of the strongest growth was in Russia and China, and that it had also made significant progress in North America during the year. The chain opened five new stores last year, two of which were in China. The company's marketing objective is to double sales to 50 billion euros by 2020. Its stores are already visited by 690 million people per year. The privately owned firm has 303 stores globally at the moment. It said it is now looking for the right location for its first Indian store.

Forced labour

However, there has been some controversy over IKEA's use of forced labour in the past. It has been revealed that 25 to 30 years ago IKEA used political prisoners in communist East Germany to produce its products. The company has said that it deeply regrets this. It says that better processes are now in place to monitor working conditions at suppliers. The company carries out more than 1,000 audits every year to make sure suppliers are complying with its code of conduct.

Source: www.ikea.com/ms/en_GB/this-is-ikea/about-the-ikea-group/index.html

345
IKEA stores

345 IKEA stores in 42 countries were open and operating by the end of business year 2013.

1958	2010	2011	2012	2013
1	316	325	338	345

IKEA stores

775 million
IKEA store visits

IKEA stores were visited 775 million times during the year.

1958	2010	2011	2012	2013
0.05	699	734	776	775

IKEA store visits in millions

29.2 billion
in sales turnover

IKEA retail sales totalled EUR 29.2 billion.

1958	2010	2011	2012	2013
0.003	23.8	26.0	27.5	29.2

IKEA sales turnover in billion Euros

151,000
IKEA co-workers

The majority of the 151,000 IKEA co-workers work in IKEA stores.

1958	2010	2011	2012	2013
100	145,000	151,000	151,000	151,000

IKEA Co-workers

9.9 million
retail square metres

The area of all IKEA stores combined was 9,883,241 m^2.

1958	2010	2011	2012	2013
0.007	8.7	9.0	9.5	9.9

Retail square metres in millions

9.7 million
application downloads

The 2013 "IKEA Catalog" application was downloaded close to 10 million times.

1958	2010	2011	2012	2013
-	-	3.5	5.7	9.7

Application downloads in millions

Figure 2 IKEA statistics

Source: IKEA website
www.ikea.com/ms/en_GB/this-is-ikea/the-ikea-concept/index.html

AS questions

(50 marks)

1 Explain two operations issues that may be involved in running an IKEA store. **(5 marks)**

2 Analyse the operational factors IKEA might consider when choosing its first location in India. **(10 marks)**

3 To what extent is involving the customer in its operations a key part of the IKEA approach? **(15 marks)**

4 To what extent do you think suppliers are an important element of the success of IKEA? **(20 marks)**

A-level questions

(70 marks)

1 Analyse the operational objectives IKEA might set. **(10 marks)**

2 To what extent do you think it is important for IKEA to have a code of conduct for suppliers? **(15 marks)**

3 What do you think might be the major operations issues involved in IKEA opening a store in India? Justify your answer. **(20 marks)**

4 To what extent do you think IKEA is safe from other competitors taking its market share in the future? **(25 marks)**

Unit 5

Decision making to improve financial performance

Chapter 16

Setting financial objectives

Introduction

This chapter is the first of four which consider how managers can take decisions to improve a business's financial performance. Setting **financial objectives** is the first element of the decision-making process in relation to financial issues: deciding what financial objectives a business should pursue. Later chapters in this unit will look at the subsequent stages in the financial decision-making process, such as financial analysis and taking financial decisions.

What you need to know by the end of this chapter:

- the value of setting financial objectives
- the distinction between cash flow and profit
- the distinction between gross profit, operating profit and profit for the year
- the meaning of revenue, costs and profit objectives
- how cash flow objectives are set
- how objectives for investment levels are set
- how capital structure objectives are set
- the external and internal influences on financial objectives and decisions.

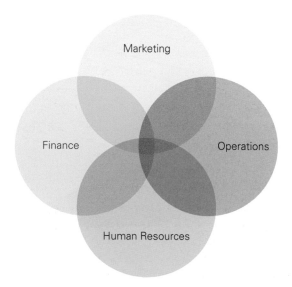

Figure 16.1 Functions of a business

The value of setting financial objectives

Financial objectives can be described as goals or targets that relate to the business's financial performance. It is common for financial objectives to contain a specific numerical element and also a timescale within which they are to be achieved. The financial objective will be set by the managers responsible for finance in the business, but will be consistent with other functional objectives and also contribute to the achievement of the business's corporate objectives.

Key terms

A **financial objective** is a goal or target pursued by the finance department (or function) within an organisation.

Profit measures the extent to which revenues from selling a product over some time period exceed the costs incurred in producing it.

Cash flow is the movement of cash into and out of a business over time.

Businesses can derive great benefits from setting financial objectives. It enables managers and owners to judge the performance of the enterprise from when it is first established. Newly established businesses may be vulnerable to running out of cash. Thus setting objectives for cash flow can assist managers to avoid this particular pitfall. Similarly, many established businesses (especially public limited companies) are judged by the level of profits that they make over a financial year. The level of profits achieved by a business impacts upon other aspects of the business's financial performance, such as its share price and its ability to negotiate loans with banks and other financial organisations.

Financial objectives are also valuable to managers as a measure of performance because most businesses are judged on their financial attainments by other stakeholders. We saw in earlier chapters that managers will take decisions designed to maximise profits or to control costs. Because businesses are judged in this way by many of their stakeholders it makes perfect sense for managers to set themselves objectives in these areas to try to maximise the business's financial performance.

What do you think?

Which of a public limited company's stakeholders would be interested in the profits earned by the business over a financial year? Why would they be interested?

The use of financial objectives enables managers to identify aspects of the performance of the business that are causing problems at the earliest possible stage. For example, managers may receive early warning that costs are higher than expected, or profits lower, if they have set objectives for these aspects of financial performance. As an example, a comparison between actual costs and the figures set out in the objective encourages corrective action, such as seeking cheaper supplies or eliminating waste, to bring costs under control before they cause too much damage to the business.

Finally, setting financial objectives, or any other objectives for that matter, can be very motivating for employees at all levels within the business. Having a financial goal may encourage employees to work conscientiously or creatively to achieve this goal, thereby enhancing their performance and that of the business as a whole.

The distinction between cash flow and profit

Cash flow and profits are two very different concepts:

- **Profit.** As we saw in Chapter 1, a business makes a profit if, over a given period of time, its revenue is greater than its expenditure. A business can survive without making a profit for a short period of time, but it is essential that it earns profits in the long run to provide a return for the business's owners.
- **Cash flow.** This relates to the timing of payments and receipts. Cash flow is important in the short term, as a business must pay creditors (people and organisations to whom it owes money).

Just because a business is profitable, it does not mean that it will hold large sums of cash, or even have enough cash. There are several reasons why this situation might arise.

First, the business might sell large numbers of goods or services at profitable prices by offering customers 60 or 90 days' grace before they have to pay. This will mean that the business has to find cash to buy supplies and pay employees several months before the cash from the sale of the product flows into the business. This problem can be made more serious if the business pays its suppliers promptly.

Alternatively, a business such as a jeweller might hold large amounts of expensive inventories (or stock) for customers to view before making a choice. This will entail large amounts of cash being tied up in the form of stocks, and not available to the business for other purposes.

A business may have paid for assets such as property or vehicles and used large sums of cash to do so. These assets may support the business over many years, and will lead to future inflows of cash. However, the outflow of cash may place pressure on a firm's finances initially.

So, a profitable business may find itself short of cash and possibly unable to settle its bills as they fall due. This could lead to the firm becoming insolvent and having to cease trading. A cash crisis is a major reason why many businesses fail.

In the long term, however, a business has to make a profit to satisfy its owners. The owners will have invested funds into the business, quite possibly by purchasing shares, and expect to see a return on their investment. This is only possible if the business makes a profit in the longer term. A business may survive for some time without making profits if its owners are prepared to be patient, but cash has to be managed carefully in the short term to ensure that bills can be paid on time.

Study tip

The distinction between profit and cash flow is vital. You should use these terms with care, remembering that they have quite different meanings. It is useful when answering financial questions to consider the short-term effects of any action on cash flow and the long-term effects on profits.

Different measurements of profit

It may seem surprising that there is more than one way of measuring profit. However, this is the case and having different ways of measuring profit assists managers in assessing a business's financial performance and in making good decisions.

At its simplest, profit is what remains from revenue once costs have been deducted. However, the managers of a business may calculate several different types of profit relating to a business's performance over a financial year. These are recorded on the business's **income statement**.

1. **Gross profit.** This form of profit is calculated by deducting **direct costs** (such as materials and shop-floor labour – also known as cost of sales) from a business's sales revenue. This gives a broad indication of the financial performance of the business without taking into account other costs such as **indirect costs** or overheads.

2. **Operating profit.** This type of profit takes into account all earnings from regular trading activities and all the costs associated with those activities. However, operating profit excludes any income received from, or costs incurred by, activities that are unlikely to be repeated in future financial years. It also excludes profit from any joint ventures or non-trading activities such as investments. Finally, it does not include certain expenditure a business may undertake such as paying interest on loans or taxation on its profits.

3. **Profit for the year.** This measure of profit takes into account a business's income from all of its sources, trading and non-trading and the full range of costs incurred including taxes on profits and interest charges. A business's managers can decide how to utilise its profit for the year. They may decide to pay some to the owners of the business (dividends to shareholders in the case of companies) or retain it within the business to invest in assets, provide a source of cash or as savings.

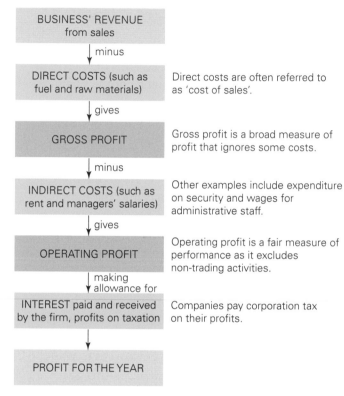

Figure 16.2 Types of profit

Figure 16.2 summarises the relationship between the three types of profit we have explored. However, not all businesses measure and record all three types of profit. Companies are more strictly controlled by laws in the UK on how they have to present financial information for stakeholders. However, companies do publish their financial information in slightly different ways despite the strict legal rules.

Financial objectives

The managers responsible for a business's finance department or function may set a range of objectives, including those discussed below. These objectives will contribute towards the business achieving its overall or corporate objectives.

Business in focus: Johnson Matthey's profits

Johnson Matthey plc manufactures chemicals and related products including catalytic converters, ingredients for the pharmaceutical industry and fuel cells. It also refines and distributes precious metals such as gold, platinum and palladium. The company's profits rose between 2013 and 2014, as shown in Table 16.1.

Item	2014 (£m)	2013 (£m)
Revenue	11,152.2	10,728.8
Cost of sales	10,356.1	10,024.5
Gross profit	799.1	704.3
Operating profit	406.6	381.8
Profit for the year	338.7	271.8

Table 16.1 Key financial data for Johnson Matthey, 2013–2014

Source: Johnson Matthey plc website

www.matthey.com/documents/pdfs/2013_14/annual-report/jm-ar-2014.pdf

Johnson Matthey plc's existing and potential shareholders consider the company's financial performance when making judgements about buying and selling its shares. They may be particularly interested in the level and growth of its operating profit.

Questions

1. Explain why Johnson Matthey plc's profit for the year may have risen in 2014, compared with 2013.
2. Do you think that Johnson Matthey plc's shareholders will be particularly interested in the level and growth of the company's operating profits between 2013 and 2014?

Key terms

Revenues are the earnings or income generated by a firm as a result of its trading activities.

Objectives are medium- to long-term goals established to coordinate the business.

1. Revenue, cost and profit objectives

(a) Revenue objectives

Businesses commonly set themselves objectives in terms of earning a certain amount of revenue over a financial period. Many new businesses set such an objective to assist them in building a customer base and establishing themselves within their chosen market. A **revenue objective** may be used more widely by businesses that aim to grow: setting a challenging objective in terms of revenue can help to achieve growth. Businesses that sell products with short product life cycles who wish to maximise the short-term selling opportunities that are available may also opt for revenue objectives. They may also be particularly relevant for charities who aim to maximise the revenues they can generate to support their chosen cause.

Revenue objectives can relate to an aspect of the business rather than the entire business. For example, *Mail Online*, the internet element of the *Daily Mail* newspaper has a revenue objective of £5 million a month, or £60 million a year from advertising.

In the five months to the end of February 2014 the revenue received by *Mail Online* was £23 million (or an average of £4.6 million a month), just failing to reach its objective.

What do you think?

What actions might the managers at *Mail Online* take to increase the website's revenue?

A more aggressive type of revenue objective can also be set. This is one which requires a business's revenue to grow at increasing rates over time. Thus, a business may aim to generate revenue amounting to £4 million next year, £4.5 million the following year and £5.3 million in the year after. This means that the rate at which revenue is increasing is rising from £0.5 million per year to £0.8 million. The revenue objective could also be expressed as percentage increases.

Maths moment

$\frac{1+b}{c} = 3$

In the example above, calculate the percentage rate of increase in sales revenue:

(a) from next year to the year after
(b) from the second to the third year.

Revenue objectives can be based on a business reducing its prices in the expectation of making a large number of additional sales and therefore increasing its revenue. This may be appropriate for businesses such as supermarkets where demand for products can be sensitive to prices (or price elastic, as discussed in Chapter 10). In these circumstances a price reduction could boost revenue from sales. In contrast, other businesses face inelastic demand, where customers make buying decisions on a range of factors and price may be relatively unimportant. In this case a revenue objective may be based on increasing prices and relying on a relatively small proportion of customers stopping buying the products.

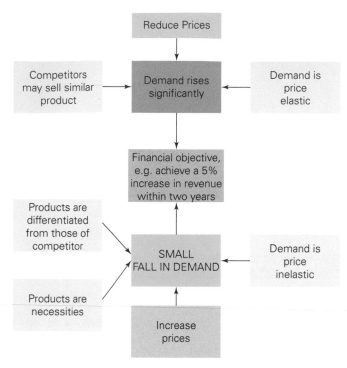

Figure 16.3 Price changes with a revenue objective

Of course revenue objectives do have disadvantages. They do not necessarily increase a business's profits. Indeed a challenging revenue objective might only be achieved by increasing costs for advertising, for example, which may result in lower profits. Revenue objectives that entail reducing prices to increase revenue can also be risky as competitors may respond by reducing prices too, resulting in a loss of revenue for all businesses involved but a pleasing situation for customers.

(b) Cost objectives

Businesses can pursue two different types of cost objective. Some businesses may set themselves an objective of reducing costs by a given percentage or amount within a stated time period. The intention may be to maintain the business's profits if it is operating in a market in which prices are falling. In 2014 the growth of Aldi, Lidl and other low-price grocery retailers placed great pressure on established supermarkets such as Morrisons, Tesco and Asda to reduce prices to compete. To do so the supermarket either has to reduce costs or accept lower profits. We look at this scenario more fully in the Business in Focus feature about Morrison's.

Maths moment

How much revenue was generated in the grocery market in 2014? Use the data in the box in the Business in Focus feature about Morrison's to carry out this calculation.

Business in focus: Morrison's looks to achieve cost objectives

Morrison's, one of the UK's largest supermarket groups, has set itself tough cost objectives as it seeks to compete with low-price rivals such as Lidl and Aldi. Both of the low-price supermarkets (known as 'discounters') have achieved impressive growth rates in revenue recently.

Company	Revenue, Jan–March 2014 £m	Annual revenue growth, 2013–14	Market share, 2013	Market share, 2014
Aldi	1,140	35 %	3.4 %	4.6 %
Lidl	857	17 %	2.9 %	3.4 %

Source for data: *Sunday Express*, 9 April 2014

www.express.co.uk/finance/city/469414/Supermarket-Aldi-has-hit-record-sales-as-its-marketshare-surges-despite-challenging-time

Morrison's management team has pledged to invest £1 billion into cutting its prices as part of a 'bold plan' to respond to the discounter supermarkets. This plan is being implemented at a time when the supermarket is making a substantial loss – £176 million in the financial year ending in February 2014 and the loss is forecast to be larger over the 2014–15 financial year. Morrison's share price has fallen by 12 per cent recently.

Morrison's plans to reduce its expenditure on assets such as vehicles, technology and property from £1.1 billion to £550 million and cut its operating costs by £1 billion per year to enable it to lower its prices.

Questions

1. Explain the possible reasons why Morrison's share price 'has fallen by 12 per cent recently'.

2. Will Morrisons' cost objective result in the company enjoying higher profits in the future?

Some businesses pursue objectives of cost minimisation. By minimising costs managers are able to offer the lowest possible prices, which can represent good value to consumers. This financial objective has become well known over recent years due to the publicity given to low-cost or budget airlines, for example EasyJet, and their policies of minimising costs. A financial strategy of cost minimisation entails seeking to reduce to the lowest possible level all the costs of production that a business incurs as part of its trading activities. In the case of the budget airlines this has extended to minimising labour costs (some require employees to pay for their own uniforms), reducing administrative costs by, for example, using the internet for booking and using 'out of town and city' airports to reduce landing and take-off fees charged by airport authorities.

The financial objective of cost minimisation has clear implications for the management of other functional areas within the business. Clearly, the managers responsible for the other functions should aim to operate with minimal expenditure in order to support the fulfilment of this financial objective. Such a financial objective is likely to support corporate objectives such as profit maximisation or growth.

Study tip

Do consider the effects of the pursuit of financial objectives on other functions such as operations and marketing, within the business. This can help you to develop powerful lines of argument.

(c) Profit objectives

It is very common for a business to have a profit objective. As with cost minimisation, this is frequently an objective for the entire business and not just its finance function or department.

Profit objectives can be expressed in several different forms.

- **As a simple figure**. This figure will be based on profits generated in previous years and take into account any expected changes in business activity over the foreseeable future. The International Airlines Group (IAG) which owns British Airways and the Iberia airline has a profit objective for 2015 of €1.8 billion, a rise of 15 per cent on its objective for 2014.

- **As a percentage increase in profits**. This is usually a yearly target representing a certain percentage rise on the previous year. In 2014, Europe's biggest tour holiday business Tui Travel plc was targeting an objective of a 7–10 per cent increase in annual operating profit.

Figure 16.4 An attractive long-haul destination

What do you think?

Why might the management team at Tui Travel plc have set a financial objective of rising profits?

- **As a percentage compared to sales.** This is called a profit margin, which we will consider in detail in the next chapter. Tesco, the UK's leading retailer has pursued a profit objective whereby profits are 5.2 per cent of its revenue from sales. This approach to a profit objective allows the company's revenue to change, but its profits must alter in line with it.

Profit objectives have the advantage of being simple to understand and measure and can help to motivate employees across an organisation. However, they can be risky as well. If a business suffers an unexpected change this can result in it recording profits lower than forecast which can be damaging because it provides very clear, and possibly public, evidence of under-performance. This may result in falling share prices and nervousness among banks and other financial institutions that have lent the business money. In May 2014, Petrofac, a company that provides services to oil companies, announced that its profits for 2013–14 would be between $580 million and $600 million, well below its objective of $650 million. In consequence its share price slumped by 16 per cent.

Cash flow objectives

For many businesses cash flow is vital and an essential element of success. Without cash any business is unable to meet its financial commitments as they fall due. If a business is unable to meet its financial commitments it cannot continue trading. This is especially true of businesses that face long cash cycles. A cash cycle is the time that elapses between the outflow of cash to pay for labour and raw materials for a products or service and the receipt of cash from the sale of the product. House builders, oil companies and pharmaceutical firms can face long cash cycles.

The American oil and gas exploration company, Encana Corporation, exceeded its cash flow objectives in 2014. It achieved a positive cash flow amounting to $3.5 billion against its objective of $2.95 billion. Discovering and retrieving oil and gas reserves can take many years and exposes companies such as Encana to very long cash cycles. Thus it is important for Encana to manage its cash carefully and setting objectives for cash flow is an important part of this.

Banks require a steady inflow of cash from depositors to enable them to engage in lending activities. The difficulties experienced over recent years by banks in the UK and other countries has, in part, been due to a lack of cash being available to these organisations. Without cash, banks do not have the necessary funds to avail themselves of profitable lending opportunities.

Other businesses that may establish financial objectives in terms of cash flow may include those that are growing and need regular inflows of cash to finance the purchase of increasing quantities of inputs such as labour and raw materials. Failure to set such objectives may result in a business facing financial problems because it runs short of cash as its expenditure or outflow of cash 'runs ahead' of inflows of cash. Such a situation is described as overtrading.

Objectives for investment levels and returns

Setting objectives for the level of investment (or capital expenditure)

Many businesses set goals for the level of **investment** they wish to undertake over specific future periods. Investment entails the purchase of assets that will

remain with the business over the long term and for at least a period of one year. This type of asset is called a **non-current asset**. Investment objectives are also called **capital expenditure** (or capex) objectives. They are most commonly set by businesses which purchase and use large quantities of non-current assets.

Key terms

Investment is the purchase of assets such as property, vehicles and machinery that will be used for a considerable time by the business.

Non-current assets are items that a business owns and which it expects to retain for one year or longer.

Capital expenditure is spending undertaken by businesses to purchase non-current assets such as vehicles and property. It is another term for investment.

A business may seek to achieve a certain level of capital expenditure over a financial year, possibly to support a wider objective of growth. By undertaking a given level of capital expenditure the business will increase its size, its value and its ability to supply products to its customers. A retailer might, for example, set itself a capital expenditure objective of £25 million each year for the next three years to fund the purchase of new stores across the UK. This financial objective would support objectives set for the whole business such as achieving specified rates of growth in sales or a targeted market share.

A business may set itself an objective of lowering its capital expenditure to reduce the amount it has borrowed if it considers that its debts are too high. In this situation the management team may divert funds that would have been invested into buying non-current assets to repaying loans. This can reduce the interest payments that the company is liable to pay and increase profits in the long term. In 2014, Sam Walsh, the chief executive of the multinational mining company Rio Tinto, reported to the company's shareholders that it was reducing its capital expenditure objective. The objective for 2014 has been adjusted to $9 billion, $2 billion below its original target. Rio Tinto has set a capital expenditure or investment objective of $8 billion a year from 2015. In part this decision is possible because the company has already invested heavily in improving and modernising its facilities and has closed some older copper and iron ore mines. The company's profits have risen recently.

Figure 16.5 Rio Tinto invests heavily in non-current assets but has recently set a lower financial objective in this area.

Capital expenditure objectives can be difficult to achieve principally because the business may encounter problems in raising sufficient capital to fund its planned investment programme. It may be easier to raise capital for investment if:

- the business has not borrowed excessive amounts already, reassuring lenders that it will be able to repay any borrowings
- the business is purchasing non-current assets (such as property) that will retain value and could be sold if necessary to repay a loan
- the business is a company and can sell additional shares to raise funds.

Setting objectives for returns on investment

An alternative way of setting financial objectives for investment or capital expenditure is to set a target for the return on an investment. This objective expresses the annual return in the form of operating profit as a percentage of the amount that was invested. The calculation is fairly simple, using the formula set out below:

$$\text{Return on investment} = \frac{(\text{operating profit} \times 100)}{\text{capital invested}}$$

Suppose an entrepreneur purchases a corner shop for £100,000 and in the first year of trading earns a profit of £6,000. The return on capital for this first year of trading would be 6 per cent.

A higher figure is preferable in this case and in most circumstances. However, it might be that the corner shop will earn higher profits (and a higher return on the investment) in future years.

Many investments are long-term projects and it may be too simplistic to make a judgement against an objective over a single year. Some investments (for example, in property) are designed to produce returns over many years and may not meet the percentage return that is the objective for some considerable time.

In setting objectives for returns on investment, managers may want to consider the alternative uses for the capital concerned. A financial objective should, in the long-term at least, seek to exceed alternatives, taking into account differences in the degree of risk. Thus managers may set a lower objective if the choice is relatively safe. They may make the judgement that the project with the higher returns represents too great a risk and opt for the safer alternative.

Capital structure objectives

Decisions made by managers in relation to the business's **capital structure** can be important in both the short and long term. Basically there are two types of capital that a business may use for its operations and growth. Managers may opt to borrow funds, normally over a long-term period, to finance capital expenditure. This commits them to paying interest on these loans until they are repaid. However, managers in companies have another option. They can choose to sell shares to fund their capital expenditure. The company may have to pay dividends to the new shareholders, but only if the company makes sufficient profits. However, if a company sells too many additional shares the existing owners may lose control of the business. We will look at sources of finance for all businesses more fully in Chapter 18.

A business's capital structure is the balance between these two types of capital which are termed loan capital and share capital. Figure 16.6 illustrates two companies with contrasting capital structures.

Key term

Capital structure refers to the way in which a business has raised the capital it requires to purchase its assets.

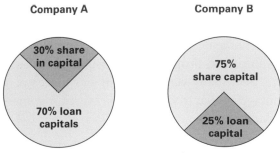

Company A

- 30% share in capital
- 70% loan capitals

- More than 50% of capital is borrowed
- Considered to be 'highly geared'
- May be at risk of increasing interest payments

Company B

- 75% share capital
- 25% loan capital

- Less than 50% of capital is borrowed
- Considered to have 'low gearing'
- Original owners may have lost control of the company

Figure 16.6 Contrasting capital structures

Businesses that have capital structures with high levels of borrowing (normally more than 50 per cent) as in the case of Company A in Figure 16.6, are referred to as 'highly geared'. Such companies may be at risk of rising costs if interest rates rise and, in any event, are committed to interest payments, even if their revenues decline.

Maths moment

A company has a total capital of £1,200,000. It has raised 42 per cent of its capital from the sale of shares. What is the value of its loans?

There are a number of influences on the capital structure objectives set by businesses. The cost of borrowing is one. At the time of writing, interest rates in the UK, and much of Europe, are at all-time lows, so borrowing is very cheap and repayments on loans will be relatively low. This will encourage companies to pursue capital structures with higher proportions of loan capital than at times when interest rates are higher. Some companies set capital structure optimisation objectives. This objective aims to minimise the cost of raising capital for the company without affecting its overall value. In 2014 Nokia, the telecommunications equipment company, announced that it was buying back shares to the value of €1.25 billion from its shareholders to achieve its optimal capital structure.

In a time of inflation companies may opt for capital structure objectives that contain a higher proportion of borrowing. In a situation in which prices are rising

at, say 5 per cent a year, the value of money (and a business's debts) will be falling by the same percentage. Borrowing relatively heavily in this situation may be sensible as the value of what is owed and repayments will be falling.

During prosperous times, when incomes are rising, share prices may be buoyant. This means a company opting for a capital structure with a higher proportion of share capital may be able to raise a greater amount of capital by selling a specific number of shares. At such times capital structure objectives may be more reliant on share capital.

The internal and external influences on financial objectives and decisions

A management team will be subject to a range of factors when setting its financial objectives. Some of these influences arise from within the business, while others are external.

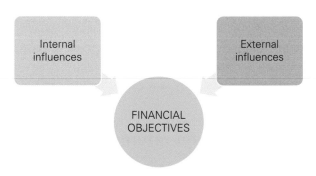

Internal influences

External influences

FINANCIAL OBJECTIVES

Figure 16.7 Influences on financial objectives

Internal factors

- **The overall objectives of the business**. This might be the most important internal influence on a business's financial objectives. A financial objective must assist the business in achieving its overall or corporate objectives such as growth. The corporate objectives are set first, followed by functional objectives such as financial objectives that are designed to complement them. A business that has profit maximisation as its primary corporate objective may operate a financial objective of cost minimisation. Reducing costs as a financial objective should assist the business in maximising its profits.

- **The nature of the product that is sold**. The type of product can be a major influence on financial objectives. Businesses with long cash cycles (such as the American oil company Encana Corporation, mentioned earlier) are much more likely to set cash flow objectives as this should be a major focus of their management of finance. Alternatively, if a product's demand is sensitive to price (if its demand is price elastic) it may be more likely to persuade managers to implement and pursue a financial objective related to costs. This financial objective may allow price reduction with a positive impact on future sales and the business's sales revenue.

- **The objectives of the business's senior managers.** If the managers of the business hold large numbers of shares, perhaps as a result of founding the business, then pursuing a profit objective may be appropriate as this may increase share prices and the value of their holdings. On the other hand, managers may seek the recognition that accompanies the successful achievement of a corporate objective of growth. In such circumstances a financial objective of achieving substantial increases in revenue may be more appropriate.

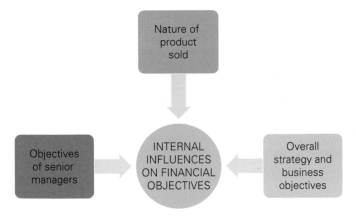

Figure 16.8 Internal influences on financial objectives

Study tip

Remember that financial objectives are not set in isolation from the rest of the business. They will be a part of the creation of objectives for the entire business as well as the objectives of the remaining functions within the business.

External factors

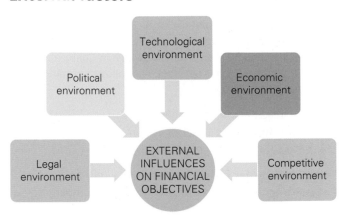

Figure 16.9 External influences on financial objectives

- **The competitive environment**. A business will be unlikely to ignore the actions of its competitors when establishing its financial objectives. For example, a retailer operating in a highly competitive market might consider establishing an objective of increased levels of investment to provide it with new and improved locations for its stores to attract greater numbers of customers. In contrast, a business wanting to achieve a profit objective may seek to form alliances with its rivals or to develop a USP for its products to allow it to charge premium prices.

- **The economic environment.** Even though the UK economy is showing clear signs of recovery from the financial crisis of 2008 and the subsequent recession, many businesses continue to experience difficulty in arranging loans. If a business is experiencing difficulty in raising capital then financial objectives are more likely to centre on profits. Achieving specific returns in terms of profit will assist in reassuring potential shareholders or investors as to the safety of their investments and the level of expected returns. It will also provide a source of capital for future investments.

  The state of the economy has implications for consumer spending and the growth rates of the markets in which businesses trade. If the market for the business's products is expanding it may lead a business's managers to set more expansive financial objectives, such as higher figures for profits or cash flow. In contrast, in a market in which sales figures are stable or declining, financial objectives may be more cautious. Financial objectives such as cash flow targets may be deemed more appropriate in these circumstances.

Business in focus: The Adidas group's financial objectives

Herbert Hainer, the chief executive officer (CEO) of the sportswear group Adidas set out the company's financial objectives until 2015 in a recent speech in California. For 2015 the company has set itself the following financial objectives:

- global revenue of €17 billion
- profits amounting to €1.87 billion
- Adidas brand sales of €12.8 billion.

The company has revised these financial objectives upwards since they were originally set. The company's CEO explained that certain sports, for example golf, had proved to be surprisingly popular, boosting sales more than expected. He argued that the company's success was based on its innovative products and its ability to meet the changing needs of its customers.

Adidas faces intense competition from other multinational sportswear producers such as Nike and new firms are emerging, for example Li-Ning in China, as well. Rising incomes, especially in some countries in Asia could boost sales for sportswear products. Adidas is targeting three key markets: the USA, China and Russia to achieve its ambitious financial objectives and overall growth.

Questions

1. Explain the possible implications of the company's ambitious financial objectives for its marketing and operations functions.

2. Do you think that the actions of other businesses was the main influence on the financial objectives set by the Adidas Group?

- **The technological environment.** Many businesses operate in environments in which technology is changing rapidly and these can influence financial objectives. For example, an increasing number of supermarket checkouts in the UK are no longer operated by an assistant, similarly many transactions in banks no longer require a cashier. Such developments may encourage managers to set challenging objectives for costs and increase long-term profit objectives.
- **The political and legal environment.** Political and legal changes can have considerable implications for the financial performance of businesses and

the objectives they set themselves. The expansion of the EU to include Eastern European and Balkan countries has resulted in considerable levels of immigration into the UK from countries such as Latvia and Bulgaria. This has created a supply of relatively cheap labour, enabling businesses to control costs and cash flow more effectively and influencing these and other financial objectives. Research by the London School of Economics has suggested that the impact of immigration on wage costs is greatest for those businesses that employ large numbers of semi-skilled and unskilled workers, and especially those that operate in the services sector.

ASSESSMENT ACTIVITIES

Sections (a), (b) and (c) of these assessment activities are relevant for students taking AS and A-level

examinations. The questions in section (d) are for A-level students only.

(a) Knowledge check questions

1 What is meant by the term 'financial objective'?

2 Distinguish between profit and cash flow.

3 Is the following statement true or false: *'Revenue minus cost of sales gives gross profit'*?

4 The following financial information relates to a company:

- revenue = £ 750,000
- operating profit = £125,500
- gross profit = £140,000
- profit for the year = £40,000.

Which of the following figures is the company's direct costs?

i) £625,000	**iii)** £710,000
ii) £610,000	**iv)** £165,000.

5 Is the following statement true or false? 'Reducing price when demand is price inelastic may help a business to achieve a revenue objective.'

6 A business has set itself a financial objective of cost minimisation. State two implications of this objective for other functions within the business.

7 Identify two categories of business that may set themselves cash flow objectives.

8 What is meant by the term capital expenditure?

9 Name the two types of capital that a business may use to purchase its non-current assets.

10 State two factors that might influence a business's choice of capital structure.

(b) Short answer questions

1 Explain why a profitable business may run out of cash. (4 marks)

2 Explain the disadvantages of a business in a highly competitive market setting itself revenue objectives. (5 marks)

3 Explain why a public limited company might decide to reduce its capital expenditure. (5 marks)

4 Explain why a business that is growing quickly should set itself financial objectives. (6 marks)

(c) Data response questions

Mark Ford established a farm growing chilli peppers in Suffolk last year – it is a very seasonal business with most sales in the summer. His business has had a relatively successful first year although it didn't make a profit – Mark can afford to be patient though. The business has just won a contract with a major food manufacturer to supply chilli peppers for a range of chilled meals. It is a large order but the price is lower than Mark normally receives. There is the possibility of further, even larger orders. The manufacturer will pay Mark 60 days after the peppers are delivered. Mark will have to borrow money to invest in expanding production to fulfil the contract.

Mark is keen to set financial objectives for the next three years as part of his plan to expand his business to enable it to supply the food manufacturer. He plans to set objectives for cash flow and revenue for the next three years. His accountant has advised against

setting objectives for revenue and suggests profit objectives for each of the years.

Mark faces increasing competition from established chilli producers. One local rival has reduced her prices and has arranged to supply a chain of organic shops. However, he is determined to pursue his objective of growth for the new business and to accept low profits or even losses in the short term.

1 Explain the possible reasons why the accountant advised against setting revenue objectives for the next three years. (6 marks)

2 Analyse why Mark thought setting objectives for cash flow were more important than profit objectives. (9 marks)

3 To what extent are external influences likely to have a greater impact on the company's financial objectives than internal influences? (15 marks)

(d) Essays

1 Is setting financial objectives of greatest value for a business that is growing quickly? Justify your decision. (25 marks)

2 Do you think that financial objectives have any relevance for social enterprises and other not-for-profit businesses? Justify your view. (25 marks)

Chapter 17 Analysing financial performance

Introduction

This chapter continues our consideration of how managers can take decisions to improve a business's financial performance. It looks at techniques of financial analysis, such as budgeting and break-even analysis, which might provide managers with crucial information to support the decision-making process. Subsequent chapters will consider the nature of financial decisions that are taken by the managers of a business.

What you need to know by the end of this chapter:

- how to construct and analyse budgets and cash flow forecasts
- the value of budgeting
- how to construct and interpret break-even charts
- how to calculate and illustrate changes in key variables on break-even charts
- the value of break-even analysis
- how to analyse profitability data
- how to analyse timings of cash inflows and outflows
- the use of data for financial decision making and planning.

Budgets

Budgets are financial plans for a future period of time. Businesses forecast their revenue and expenditure (or costs) using budgets. Budgets are usually drawn up on a monthly basis, over the period of a financial year.

Later in this chapter we will consider cash flow forecasts, which are also financial plans and a different type of budget. Sometimes they are called 'cash budgets'. However, for the moment we shall concentrate on budgets relating to earnings, expenditure and profits.

Key term

Budgets are financial plans that forecast revenue from sales and expected costs over a time period.

Types of budgets

1. **Revenue or earnings budgets**. These set out the business's expected revenue from selling its products. Important information here includes the expected level of sales and the likely selling price of the product. It may be relatively straightforward for an established business to forecast its revenues based on past performance. In contrast a start-up business may have more difficulty and cautiously predict relatively low revenue budgets during its first few months of trading.

2. **Expenditure budgets**. These are also called cost or production budgets. Businesses need to plan their expenditure on labour, raw materials, fuel and other items that are essential for the process of production. These set out the expected expenditure on a monthly basis for these items.

3. **Profit budgets**. By combining sales revenue and expenditure budgets it is possible to calculate expected profits. The profit budget is an important piece of information for managers and would be of interest to many of the business's stakeholders.

Setting budgets helps the business achieve its financial and wider objectives. If, for example, a business has growth in sales as a major objective, the budgets will reflect this, with higher revenues being forecast but also higher costs of production planned.

The construction of budgets

Before businesses can start to construct budgets for the coming year, they need to carry out some research. This may involve:

- analysing the market to predict likely trends in sales and prices to help forecast revenue

- researching costs for labour, fuel and raw materials by contacting suppliers and seeing if they can negotiate price reductions for prompt payment or ordering in bulk
- considering government estimates for wage rises and inflation and incorporating them into future sales revenue and expenditure budgets.

Once a business has collected the necessary data, it is normal to draw up expected revenues from selling products – the revenue or sales revenue budget – first. This is the first budget because, once a firm knows its expected sales, it can plan production and therefore forecast expenditure. This enables the business to forecast the costs associated with producing enough to match planned sales. It is vital when constructing budgets that expenditure is sufficient to allow production to match expected demand or sales. It is impossible for a business to increase its sales without producing more of its goods or services to supply customers.

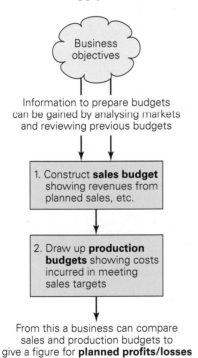

Figure 17.1 Constructing budgets

Once production budgets and sales budgets are completed, it is possible to compare revenues and expenditure. This allows managers and entrepreneurs to forecast profits (or losses) for the future trading period.

Sources of information for budgets

A major source of information for budgets is previous trading records on which to base revenue and expenditure figures. Clearly, if a business has traded for several years, much of the budgeting process can be based on the outcomes of previous financial years adjusted for expected future events. Among other things, this enables managers to predict trends in sales and seasonal effects with a greater chance of accuracy. This source is not, of course, available to entrepreneurs who are starting a new business.

So, what other sources of information are available to managers who are constructing budgets? Managers are likely to rely heavily on the results of market research to predict likely sales, especially in markets that are subject to change. In fashion or technology markets, where products' life cycles can be short and where tastes and fashions may change quickly, market research may play a vital role. Similarly, managers are likely to research the costs of supplies that they require as part of the production process. Developments in technology, most obviously the internet, have made it easier for managers to collect and analyse large amounts of data relating to consumers' needs and spending behaviour.

Government agencies can also provide managers with helpful information when constructing budgets. The UK Government operates a website (see weblink below) designed to provide the owners and managers of businesses with a great deal of information as well as links to other potential sources of advice.

Study tip

When writing answers to questions on budgets it is important to consider the links that exist with other functions within a business. One such link is between revenue budgets and marketing. Market research may play an important part in forecasting sales and therefore also in revenue. Equally, sales revenue is likely to be affected by the actions of competitors and the success of the new business's promotion.

Weblink

Find out more about advice and information provided to businesses by the UK government by going to www.gov.uk, then clicking on the tab for 'business and the self employed'.

Business in focus: Vixen soaps Ltd

Vixen Soap Ltd is due to start trading in two months' time. The company's owners are planning to manufacture a range of hand-made soaps. It intends to produce a range of soaps including those made from olive oil, lavender and camomile, as well as organic soaps. The intention is to sell these products using the internet and an effective website has been developed to promote the new company and its products as well as to provide a method of selling the soaps.

A detailed business plan has been prepared including sales, expenditure and profit budgets for the first year of trading. They conducted primary and secondary market research, which suggested that the company's unique range of high-quality products will prove popular and sales are expected to rise steadily. However, initial costs are expected to be high as the company builds up a stock of products ready for sale and it will have to negotiate a large loan from its bank.

The starting point of constructing budgets was estimating the company's sales using the market research data. By combining the likely volume of sales with the expected prices, the sales revenue budget was developed. For example, the company's managers have forecast that in January the company would sell 5,000 bars of scented soap at £1.49 each, giving a sales revenue of £7,450.

Once the level of forecast sales was decided, it was possible for the company to calculate its expected costs of production. As with many start-up businesses, production costs are initially high. The company has to build up a stock of its full range of soaps to enable it to supply customers promptly. At the same time, production costs have to reflect likely sales. So, variable costs of production are forecast to rise in February and March as sales increase.

The company's sales revenue, expenditure and profit budgets for its first three months of trading are shown in Table 17.1.

	January £	February £	March £
Sales of scented/flavoured soaps	7,450	12,560	17,500
Sales of organic soaps	2,765	3,400	4,125
Total sales	**10,215**	**15,960**	**21,625**
Purchases of raw materials	19,500	14,010	15,550
Packaging	1,215	1,105	1,350
Wages & salaries	3,000	2,850	2,995
Marketing & administration	2,450	2,400	2,450
Other costs	975	1,100	1,075
Total costs	**27,140**	**21 465**	**23,420**
Profit/Loss	**–16,925**	**–5,505**	**–1,795**

Table 17.1 Vixen Soap Ltd's budgets

Questions

1. Explain why it may be difficult for the managers of a start-up business to construct its first budgets.
2. Do you think that the managers of Vixen Soaps should be worried by the figures shown in the budget in Table 17.1? Justify your view.

Difficulties in constructing budgets

Constructing a budget is not always an easy exercise. Here are some of the reasons why this may be the case.

- **It may be difficult to forecast sales accurately.** Managers may find it difficult to estimate their sales when setting the revenue budget. Most businesses are highly dependent on market research to forecast sales and revenue. If this research is inaccurate, sales forecasts will probably prove incorrect. Changes in tastes and fashions can occur rapidly, and consumers' incomes may rise or fall, making accurate forecasts more difficult to achieve. Similarly, the pace of change in high technology industries, such as personal computers, makes the process of planning sales very tricky.

- **The risk of unexpected changes.** Forecasting events for the next year is fraught with difficulty. A business may face an unforeseen rise in costs – for example, oil prices rose from $104 to $116 a barrel between April and June 2014. The price of oil affects nearly all businesses and would alter the costs of many components and services as well as transportation. This can increase expenditure above the budgeted figure, reducing their accuracy and effectiveness in planning finances.

- **Decisions by governments and other public bodies**. These can make it difficult to set accurate budgets. In January 2011 the UK Government increased the rate of Value Added Tax (VAT) from 17.5 per cent to 20 per cent. This is likely to have increased the costs of most businesses. The Bank of England is expected to start to increase interest rates in the autumn of 2014 or in 2015. The timing

Business in focus: The Cambridge Satchel Company

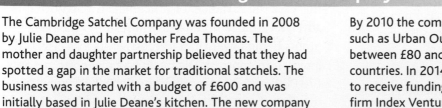

The Cambridge Satchel Company was founded in 2008 by Julie Deane and her mother Freda Thomas. The mother and daughter partnership believed that they had spotted a gap in the market for traditional satchels. The business was started with a budget of £600 and was initially based in Julie Deane's kitchen. The new company was only able to produce and sell one satchel a week as her initial budget only allowed her to make eight satchels.

The company has not developed as Julie Deane expected. Her original target market was parents who wanted to purchase a good quality leather bag for children. However, the company's satchels were judged to be fashion items, and benefited from favourable coverage in the fashion media, becoming a popular celebrity accessory. Realising that her company's products appealed to the fashion market Julie Deane began experimenting with colours. The company is growing very quickly – in 2012 its sales exceeded £1 million for the first time.

By 2010 the company was selling to popular retailers such as Urban Outfitters and the satchels, priced between £80 and £130, sell in more than one hundred countries. In 2014 the company announced that it was to receive funding of £13.25 million from venture capital firm Index Ventures, backers of global brands and fashion retailers including ASOS, Moleskine, and Net-a-Porter. The finance will be used to fund expansion into China and the USA.

The Cambridge Satchel Company employs over 100 staff, and has its own factory in Leicestershire.

Questions

1. Explain why setting a budget is important for a start-up business such as the Cambridge Satchel Company.
2. The Cambridge Satchel Company is growing very quickly. Is this the most important reason for it to set budgets? Justify your view.

and the extent of the change are uncertain, meaning that this could affect expenditure budgets as well as revenue budgets for businesses that sell products that are often bought using borrowed money – house builders and car manufacturers are obvious examples.

Analysing budgets

Constructing budgets is the first stage in the budgetary process. Once a business has planned its sales revenue and expenditure, it is essential to analyse the data by comparing the budget figures with the actual figures resulting from the business's trading.

What do you think?

The owners and managers of many small businesses do not use budgets. Why might this be the case?

Budgets can provide a wealth of information to help managers take decisions on how to improve the financial performance of the business:

1. **Analysing budgeted and actual expenditure**. This provides information on how successful the businesses is at controlling its costs. The analysis of budgets makes it possible for managers to judge the ability of different parts of a business to manage expenditure against given targets. If one area of a business is regularly overspending

its budgets, managers may take action to reduce expenditure and, by so doing, increase profitability. Relevant actions might include addressing issues such as poor motivation of employees, problems with quality or not using capacity fully. Of course, if a business, or part of a business, fails to meet expenditure budgets regularly it may be because the budgets are too low to be achievable.

2. **Analysing revenue data**. A business that fails to meet its revenue budgets for one or more of its products may need to consider why this is occurring. Prices may be too high when compared with those of competitors, the business may not be advertising sufficiently or not targeting the correct market segments, or the quality and/or design of the product may be inadequate. Effective managers will use the information from analysing budgets to make decisions to improve the business's sales performance.

3. **Analysing profits budgets**. Profits below the budgeted figure are likely to be a cause of concern for most businesses. These can be caused by excess expenditure, by revenue falling short of expectations, or by a combination of these factors. This scenario may prompt managers to examine means of cutting expenditure as well as boosting revenue from sales.

Variance analysis

The process used for analysing budgets is known as **variance analysis**. A variance occurs when an actual figure for sales or expenditure differs from the budgeted figure. Actual revenue and cost figures can either be higher or lower than planned and these differences fall into two categories. The two categories of variance are shown in Table 17.2.

Key term

Variance analysis is the process of investigating any differences between forecast data and actual figures.

Favourable variances	Adverse variances
A favourable variance exists when the difference between the actual and budgeted figures will result in the business enjoying higher profits than shown in the budget.	An adverse variance occurs when the difference between the figures in the budget and the actual figures will lead to the firm's profits being lower than planned.
Examples of favourable variances include: • actual wages less than budgeted wages • budgeted sales revenue lower than actual sales revenue • expenditure on fuel less than the budgeted figure.	Examples of adverse variances include: • sales revenue below the budgeted figure • actual raw material costs exceeding the figure planned in the budget • overheads turn out to be higher than in the budget.
Possible causes of favourable variances: • wage rises lower than expected • economic boom leads to higher than expected sales • rising value of pound makes imported raw materials cheaper.	Possible causes of adverse variances: • competitors introduce new products winning extra sales • government increases business rates by an unexpected amount • fuel prices increase as price of oil rises.

Table 17.2 The two categories of variance

Revenue/cost	Budget figure (£)	Actual figure (£)	Variance
Sales revenue	840,000	790,000	£50,000 – adverse
Fuel costs	75,000	70,000	£5,000 – favourable
Raw material costs	245,000	265,000	£20,000 – adverse
Labour costs	115,000	112,000	£3,000 – favourable

Table 17.3 Calculating variances

The process of calculating a variance is simple, as shown in Table 17.3. It simply involves a comparison between the budgeted figure and the actual figure. The business had forecast that its sales revenue would be £840,000. However, the actual figure was £790,000. In this case the variance (or difference) is £50,000. It is an adverse variance because it will result in the business's profits being lower than forecast, or its loss larger than forecast. In contrast, the business's fuel costs are only £70,000 – £5,000 less than the budgeted figure. In this case this is a favourable variance because this will result in the business's profits being larger than forecast (or a smaller loss than budgeted).

Carrying out regular variance analysis can give a business advance notice that its financial forecasts are inaccurate and allow managers to take timely decisions to improve financial performance. Variance analysis can be carried out each month and will show before the end of the financial year that the firm's finances are not as planned. This allows the business to take action to reduce expenditure or increase revenue at an early stage. Figure 17.2 summarises the range of actions that businesses may take in response to adverse and favourable variances.

Managers may also need to respond to favourable variances. Production costs that are lower than planned may be regarded as beneficial. But revenue that is greater than anticipated might be caused by the firm selling more products than planned. In these circumstances, the business might not have sufficient supplies to meet future customer requirements. This could result in the loss of long-established customers and should be avoided.

There are internal connections in budgets that are important to understand. For example, if a business experiences a rise in output and sales revenue above expectations it will affect expenditure. If a product becomes unexpectedly popular and sales rise, the business may have to purchase more raw materials and hire additional labour. This is likely to result in adverse expenditure variances. Similarly, sales below those set out in the budget may lead to favourable variances for costs as expenditure falls as less is produced.

Other factors leading to adverse and favourable variances

It may be that variances are not the result of unexpected developments and changes in the markets in which businesses operate. Poor forecasting techniques can also result in unexpected revenues and expenditures and therefore variances.

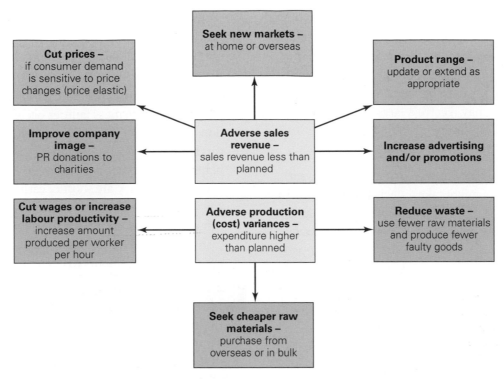

Figure 17.2 Responding to adverse variances

Managers may make insufficient use of market research to forecast sales revenue. This can lead to adverse or favourable revenue variances. It may also result in inaccurate budgets for expenditure as the managers will not have forecast correctly the amount of labour and other resources that the business needs to satisfy customers' needs. Inaccurate budgets are also the result of inexperience on the part of managers and variances will be more common when a business is new to a market and has no financial records on which to base forecasts.

The value of budgeting

The advantages of budgeting

Budgets are used to control finances effectively and enable managers to make informed and focused decisions to improve financial performance. Production or expenditure budgets allow managers to ensure that a business does not overspend. Senior managers receive their own budgets and can allocate them between the various parts of the department or area for which they are responsible. As long as each individual budget holder makes sure that they do not spend more than the agreed figure, the business's overall expenditure should remain under control.

Budgets allow senior managers to direct extra funds into important areas of the business. So, if a business is concerned that its product range is not selling well, it may increase its budgets in the areas of market research, promotion and product research and development.

Budgets can be used to motivate staff. Employees can gain satisfaction from being given responsibility for a budget, and from keeping within it. As a result, their level of motivation and their performance may improve, benefiting the firm as a whole. (We look at motivation in more detail in Chapter 23.)

Revenue budgets can also be used as targets for employees. Employees may be motivated to improve their performance by the existence of targets in the form of sales revenue budgets. If successful this can increase the business's revenue and possibly its profitability.

The disadvantages of budgeting

If a business intends that some of its employees should manage budgets (known as delegating budgets), then training will be required. The cost of the training could be substantial, depending on the skills of the workforce. Furthermore, there could be teething problems in the form of errors or delays as employees adjust to the new roles and responsibilities.

Allocating budgets fairly and in the best interests of the business is difficult. Some managers may be skilled at negotiating large budgets for the areas for which they are responsible. This might be at the expense of more worthy areas. So, for example, a manager responsible for the sales force may receive a large budget allocation, while insufficient funds are given to the manager responsible for production.

Budgets normally relate to the current financial year only. So, managers might take a decision to keep within the current budget, which is not actually in the longer-term interest of the business. For example, a decision to reduce the size of a workforce for budgetary reasons might result in competitors gaining more of the market over the next few years because the business is unable to supply sufficient quantities of the good or service.

Effective budgeting

The process of budgeting is more likely to be effective if the budgets are constructed to assist the business in achieving its financial and wider objectives. Thus a business with a growth objective may require expenditure budgets that facilitate expansion. Effective budgeting may also require that managers set demanding targets for employees to encourage them to work as efficiently as possible which should assist the business in achieving ambitious targets.

Finally, effective budgeting requires that managers review budgets as frequently as possible to assess their effectiveness. The budgets should be challenging but achievable. Reviewing budgets allows managers to adjust them as necessary in the light of their experience.

Cash flow forecasts

There are two main reasons why a manager might forecast the **cash flow** for a business.

1. **To support applications for loans.** Almost all businesses require loans to enable them to trade successfully. Short-term loans may be required to purchase supplies and businesses negotiate longer-term loans to finance major projects such as purchasing property. Banks and other financial institutions are far more likely to lend money to a business that has evidence of financial planning. It is reassuring for the bank that the management team understands the importance of cash and has

planned carefully to avoid cash flow crises. Cash flow planning gives the bank more confidence that the business will be able to make the repayments of the loan as and when they are due.

2. **To help avoid unexpected cash flow crises.** A high proportion of business failures occur because of cash flow difficulties. Constructing **cash flow forecasts** can help avoid such difficulties. Cash flow planning helps to ensure that businesses do not suffer from periods when they are short of cash and are unable to pay their debts. By forecasting cash flows, a business can identify times at which it may not have enough cash available. This allows managers to make the necessary arrangements to overcome this problem.

Key terms

Cash flow is the movement of cash into and out of a business over a period of time.

Cash flow forecasts state the inflows and outflows of cash that the managers of a business expect over some future period.

Constructing cash flow forecasts

The structure of a typical cash flow forecast is illustrated in Figure 17.3.

		January	February	March
1 Cash in	Cash sales			
	Credit sales			
	Total Inflow			
2 Cash out	Raw materials			
	Wages			
	Other costs			
	Total outflow			
3 Net monthly cash flow	Net monthly cash flow			
	Opening balance			
	Closing balance			

Figure 17.3 A typical format for a cash flow forecast

Although cash flow forecasts differ from one another, they usually have three sections, as shown in Figure 17.3, and are normally calculated monthly. An essential part of cash flow forecasting is that inflows and outflows of cash should be included in the plan at the time they take place.

1. **Cash in.** The first section forecasts the cash inflows into the business, usually on a monthly basis. This section includes receipts from cash sales and credit sales. Credit sales occur when the customer is given time to pay: normally 30, 60 or 90 days.

2. **Cash out.** The cash out (or expenditure) section will state the expected expenditure on goods and services. Thus, a typical section might include forecasts of expenditure on rent, rates, insurance, wages and salaries, fuel, and so on. At the end of this section the total expected outflow of cash over the time period in question would be stated. The net monthly cash flow is calculated by subtracting the total outflow of cash from the total inflow.

3. **Net monthly cash flow.** The final section of the forecast has the opening balance and the closing balance. The opening balance is the business's cash position at the start of each month. This will, of course, be the same figure as at the end of the previous month. The net monthly cash flow is added to the opening balance figure. The resulting figure is the closing cash balance for the month. It is also the opening balance for the following month. Figure 17.4 shows an example of the calculation of opening and closing balances.

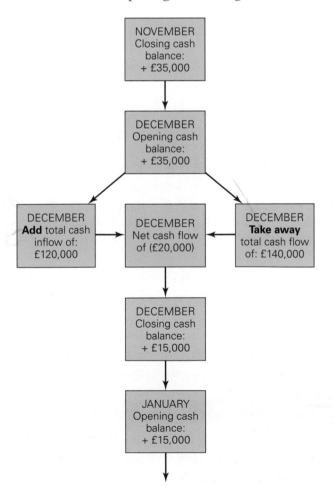

Figure 17.4 Opening and closing balances

Maths moment $\frac{1+b}{c}=3$

Suppose, in the example given in Figure 17.4, that the cash outflow forecast for December is £160,000. What would be the closing balance for December in these circumstances?

Study tip

With cash flow forecasts it is important that you understand how they are constructed as this understanding will enable you to more easily identify potential problems and propose possible solutions.

Analysing cash flow forecasts

Timing is the key issue underpinning the management of cash flow and should guide managers when making decisions in this area. Essentially a business should seek to ensure that it has sufficient cash inflows prior to cash outflows taking place.

The cash flow forecast drawn up by the managers of Marshall Books Ltd and shown in Table 17.4 illustrates many of the key principles.

Net monthly cash flow and closing balances

An important figure for each month is shown in the row entitled 'Net monthly cash flow'. This simply records the balance between the inflow and outflow for the month. In Table 17.4 the month of June provides a good example of how this operates. In June, Marshall Books Ltd expected to receive £5,750 from book sales, in addition to the £75,000 loan. At the same time it planned to spend £94,500 on an initial stock of books as well as supplying the local college's order, but also to spend on marketing, wages and rent. So, in June the managers expected the net cash flow (cash inflows less cash outflows) to be minus £13,750 (£80,750 – £94,500). In cash flow forecasts, negative figures can be shown in brackets or with a minus figure in front. Hence, the figure entered for net monthly cash flow in June could be (£13,750).

A negative figure for net monthly cash flow for a month can cause problems for a business if it does not have sufficient cash to cover it. The new branch of Marshall

Business in focus: The new bookshop

The managers at Marshall Books Ltd are planning to open an additional bookshop in a growing town near to the company's four existing bookshops. The company will require a loan from its bank to finance the purchase of its new branch and understands that the bank is unlikely to advance a loan unless it constructs a cash flow forecast for the new enterprise.

The managers at Marshall Books Ltd have made the following forecasts about the new branch for the first four months of trading from June until September:

- The company has raised £75,000 from a bank loan to buy the lease on a property and to purchase a stock of books. This money will be used to pay the new branch's marketing costs.

- The new branch is forecast to have a cash balance of £2,000 at the start of June.

- Cash sales will rise steadily for each of the four months (from £5,750 to £9,215) as the new branch becomes better known. The branch has already received an order to supply books to a local college. The order is for £10,000. Payment is expected in September, but the branch will buy the books in June at the same time as the initial stock is bought.

- Each month the company orders books for this new branch to replace stock that has been sold.

- The new bookshop will be staffed by one full-time and one part-time employee. Wages normally amount to £1,500 each month.

- Other costs, including rent, rates, heating and lighting amount to £1,500 each month in June and July, but are higher in August and September.

The cash flow forecast for the new bookshop is shown in Table 17.4.

	June	July	August	September
Cash in:				
Savings & borrowings	75,000	0	0	
Cash sales	5,750	7,500	8,475	9,215
Credit sales	0	0	0	10,000
Total cash inflow	**80,750**	**7,500**	**8,475**	**19,215**
Cash out:				
Purchase of lease on shop	30,000	0	0	0
Purchase of books	59,000	4,500	5,000	6,100
Wages	1,500	1,500	1,500	1,500
Marketing costs	2,500	1,500	975	400
Other costs, e.g. rent	1,500	1,500	1,605	1,630
Total cash outflow	**94,500**	**9,000**	**9,080**	**9,630**
Net monthly cash flow		**−1,500**	**−605**	**9,585**
Opening balance	2,000	−11,750	−13,250	−13,855
Closing balance	−11,750	−13,250	−13,855	

Table 17.4 The cash flow forecast for the first four months of trading for the new bookshop

Questions

1. Calculate the following figures for the cash flow forecast for the new bookshop:
   - the net monthly cash flow for June
   - the closing balance for September.
2. Do you think that this cash flow forecast will be valuable to the managers at Marshall Books Ltd? Justify your view.

Books Ltd only had £2,000 available in the form of cash and so the managers will have to make other arrangements to cover the deficit of £11,750 (which is shown as the closing balance for the month). If the company is unable to do this it may face severe problems.

Payables and receivables

Payables is a term that relates to the amount of time taken by a business to pay its suppliers and other creditors. It is normally expressed in terms of days. Thus, a business might take an average of 42 days to settle its bills. Receivables is a matching term that relates to the time taken by a business's customers (or debtors) to pay a business for the products that is has supplied. Once again this is normally stated in days, for

example, 45 days. Managers take decisions on how long to allow customers before payment is due. The notion of allowing customers time for payment is referred to as **trade credit** and offering trade credit can help a business to win customers as it reduces the pressure on customers' cash flow if they have additional time to pay.

Key term

Trade credit is the period of time given by suppliers before customers have to pay for goods and services.

One useful way of analysing a business's cash position is to compare the number of days for payables and receivables. If the figure for receivables is higher, this could cause the business to incur cash flow problems. This tells managers that, on average the business pays its suppliers earlier than it receives payment from its customers. The business is generally incurring an outflow of cash before it receives inflows and a cash shortage may result.

In the example shown in Table 17.4 Marshall Books Ltd has, in effect given three months trade credit to the local college. It is buying £10,000 worth of books in June (when the cash outflow will occur) and payment will not be received until September, 90 days later. In effect the company's figure for receivables here is 90 days, while that for payables is 0 days. This does not represent good management of the company's precious cash.

Identifying potential crises

One important aspect of analysing cash flow forecasts is to highlight when the business may be short of cash. This allows managers to take appropriate decisions to avoid the problem and may prevent some vulnerable businesses from failing.

The cash flow forecast set out in Table 17.4 illustrates this. The new bookshop will be short of cash during June, July, August and, to a lesser extent, September. The closing balances for these months indicate that the new branch will require a maximum of £13,855 of additional cash (in August) to enable it to pay rent, wages, and so on. Knowing this in advance means that managers can take steps to avoid a cash crisis, possibly by agreeing an overdraft with its bank.

Break-even analysis

At **break-even output** a business's sales of its products generate just enough revenue to cover all its costs of production. Therefore, at the break-even level of output, a business makes neither a loss nor a profit.

Managers may use break-even analysis for a number of reasons:

- to help to decide whether the business idea will be profitable and whether it is viable
- to help to decide the level of output and sales necessary to generate a profit
- the results of break-even analysis can be used to support an application by a business for a loan from a bank or other financial institution
- to assess the impact of changes in the level of production on the profitability of the business
- to assess the effects of different prices and levels of costs on the potential profitability of the business.

Key terms

Break-even output is that level of output or production at which total costs exactly equal revenue from sales.
Contribution is the difference between revenue and variable costs.

Calculating break-even output

Contribution is an important part of calculation break-even output. Contribution is the difference between sales revenue and variable costs of production. This is illustrated in Figure 17.5 on page 218.

Business in focus: Newport County Football Club's cash woes

League Two football club Newport County is blaming its cash flow problems on a recent period of poor weather in South Wales. The club has had five of its last six matches postponed with severe consequences for its cash inflows; the postponements are also damaging the club's prospects of achieving promotion to League One.

The club's chief executive, Dave Boddy, estimates that each postponed match results in a loss of cash inflow amounting to £36,000. He said 'It's devastating for everybody at the club, frustrating is not the word. It's killing us on all fronts – on the cash flow front we're now £180,000 down just on the gates for the five games we've had postponed.'

There may be further bad news in store for Newport County Football Club – its next home match against AFC Wimbledon is at risk because of the weather too. If it is postponed the club will lose a further £36,000 of cash inflows.

Questions

1. Explain why having five home matches postponed might damage Newport County Football Club's cash flow, but not necessarily its profits.
2. Does the example of Newport County Football Club show that there is little point in constructing cash flow forecasts? Justify your opinion.

Contribution is calculated through the use of the following formula:

contribution = revenue – variable costs

Contribution can be used to pay the fixed costs incurred by a firm. Once these have been met fully, contribution provides a business with its profits.

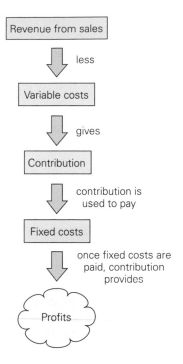

Figure 17.5 Contribution, revenues, costs and profits

Contribution can be calculated in two different ways:

● If a manager decides to produce more than one product, they may calculate the contribution made by each product to paying fixed costs and providing profits. Using contribution avoids the need to divide up fixed costs between the firm's various products. This assists managers in assessing the financial performance of each of their products.
● Contribution can be calculated for the sale of a single unit of a product. This is known as contribution per unit. It is calculated by using the formula: contribution per unit = selling price of one unit of output – variable cost of producing that unit.

It is this second method of calculating contribution that is useful when calculating break-even output.

A manager wishing to calculate break-even point will require the following information:

● the selling price of the product
● the variable cost of producing a single unit of the product
● the fixed costs associated with the product – remember, fixed costs do not change as the level of production alters.

This information is used within the formula set out below:

break-even output = fixed costs/(selling price per unit – variable cost per unit)

This formula can be rewritten, given that contribution is the result of taking away variable cost from the selling price of a product:

break-even output = fixed costs/contribution per unit.

Using break-even analysis: a case study

Hazel Foods plc owns and operates 112 restaurants throughout the UK. One of its restaurants is in Soho, West London – it is called *The Holly*. This restaurant needs refurbishing and there is potential to expand it as it is currently very small. The company can provide much of the finance for the project to upgrade, although it would need to borrow some money.

Sarah Patel is the manager responsible for the company's restaurants in London and is providing the financial analysis for the decision on whether or not to refurbish The Holly. She has analysed the likely effects of the refurbishment and has produced the figures set out in Table 17.5. Break-even analysis is just one of the financial methods Sarah plans to use to help her to make a decision on whether to refurbish the restaurant.

Type of cost or revenue	Amount
Average selling price per meal at The Holly	£60
Variable costs per meal – ingredients, fuel, wages	£35
Monthly fixed costs of the restaurant, for example interest charges & business rates	£10,000

Table 17.5 Sarah's analysis for The Holly

Using this information, Sarah is able to calculate how many meals the company would need to sell (or how many diners it has to attract) in the restaurant if the refurbished restaurant is to break even.

break-even output = fixed costs/contribution per unit

Sarah knows that the refurbished restaurant fixed costs will be £10,000 each month and this figure is entered into the top of the formula. To fill in the bottom, Sarah has to take away the variable cost of producing a meal from the price the customer pays for a meal. The contribution earned from each meal at The Holly is £25 (£60 – £35), so the calculation looks like this:

Monthly break-even output   = £10,000/£25 = 400 diners

So, Sarah knows that, if the plan for The Holly is to break even, it will need to attract at least 400 customers each month. If it attracts more than 400 customers, the project will make a profit. Hazel Foods plc operates all its restaurants for 25 evenings each month and The Holly would, therefore, break even if attracted an average of 16 customers each night.

While this calculation gives Sarah a quick guide to the number of customers The Holly will need to break even, it says little more about the level of profit or loss the restaurant might make. A break-even chart is one way to work out the level of profits the business will generate if her forecast is proved to be correct.

We can use a break-even chart to analyse the financial position relating to The Holly once it is refurbished.

Study tip

In order to gain a full understanding of break-even you should practise both drawing charts and using them to illustrate the impact of a change in price or change in costs on both the break-even point and profit. This will involve drawing new lines for revenue, variable or fixed costs onto individual charts.

Constructing a break-even chart

The first stage in constructing a break-even chart is to mark scales on the two axes. Sarah knows that The Holly can seat a maximum of 30 customers per night and that it normally opens for 25 evenings each month. So the maximum number of customers each month is 750 (30 customers x 25 nights). So the scale on the horizontal axis runs from zero to 750.

The vertical scale on a break-even chart records costs and revenues. Normally, revenues are the highest figure. So Sarah has to calculate the highest possible revenue the restaurant could earn. At most The Holly could attract 750 customers paying an average of £60 each. So the highest revenue it could possibly receive is (£60 x 750) = £45,000. If she marks the vertical scale from zero to £45,000, Sarah will have an appropriate range of values.

Having marked the scales, the first line to be drawn onto the chart is fixed costs. This is relatively simple as fixed costs do not change whatever the number of customers. So Sarah marks a horizontal line on the chart to show the monthly fixed costs the company will have to pay – £10,000. This is illustrated in Figure 17.6.

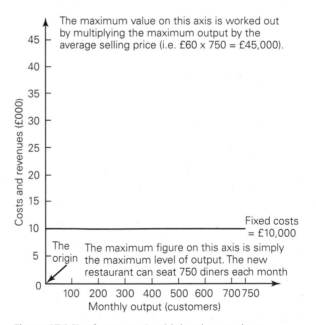

Figure 17.6 Fixed costs on Sarah's break-even chart

The next stage is to include variable costs. As variable costs are expenditure on items such as components and raw materials, these costs will rise along with output. If there are an increasing number of people dining at The Holly it will need to buy more food and the wage bill will also rise.

Variable costs always start at zero – the origin. It is not necessary to plot variable costs at each level of production. Sarah can simply calculate variable costs for the highest possible level of output. This would occur if The Holly was full every night and the restaurant had 750 customers each month. So, the highest variable costs Sarah could encounter are to provide 750 meals each having a variable cost of £35. The highest variable cost would therefore be £26,250 (£35 x 750). Sarah marks this point onto her break-even chart as shown in Figure 17.7 and draws a straight line from this point to the origin.

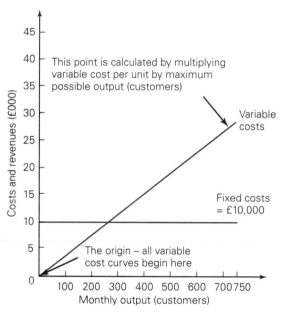

Figure 17.7 Adding variable costs to Sarah's break-even chart

The next task for Sarah in drawing the break-even chart is to add together fixed and variable costs. The results can be entered onto the chart as total costs. Sarah will calculate total costs at zero output and maximum output (750 customers per month). She can mark these two points onto the break-even chart and join them with a straight line.

- If The Holly has no customers in a month, it will not incur any variable costs. At zero output, total costs are the same as fixed costs. In Sarah's case, this will mean a total costs figure of £10,000 per month.
- At the other extreme The Holly might be full, with 750 customers each month. Sarah will add together fixed costs (still £10,000, of course) and variable costs at full capacity (750 customers' meals each

having variable costs of £35) equal to £26,250. So, total costs for the restaurant in these circumstances will be £36,250 (£10,000 + £26,250).

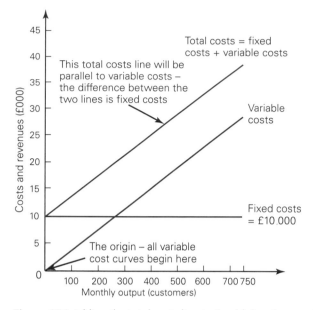

Figure 17.8 Adding the total costs line to Sarah's break-even chart

The line connecting these two points is equal to total costs. If it is drawn correctly, it should be parallel to the variable costs line.

The last stage in constructing the break-even chart is to add on a line showing the revenue The Holly will earn. Sarah has already calculated that an average customer spends £60 on a meal in her restaurant. Following the approach we used for costs, Sarah works out the revenue if the restaurant has no customers and if it is full every evening during a month.

- The first situation is easy. If The Holly does not have any customers, it will not have any revenue. So the revenue line begins at the origin.
- If the restaurant is full, Sarah expects each of the 750 customers to pay £60 on average. If The Holly attracts this level of custom, it will earn £45,000 (£60 x 750).
- The revenue line can be constructed by drawing a straight line to link the origin and the point where a vertical line drawn up from 750 customers cross a horizontal line drawn across from £45,000.

Figure 17.9 shows the break-even chart with the revenue line included. To make the chart easier to read, the variable costs line has been left out in this case.

The break-even chart tells Sarah that she needs 400 customers each month if The Holly is to break even when it is refurbished. This confirms the calculation we carried out earlier. However, a break-even chart provides much more information. Sarah can use it to read off the level of profit or loss her new restaurant will make according to the number of customers it attracts. Figure 17.10 summarises how to construct a break-even chart.

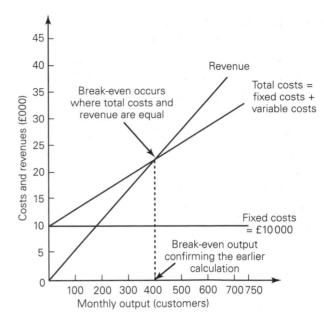

Figure 17.9 The full break-even chart

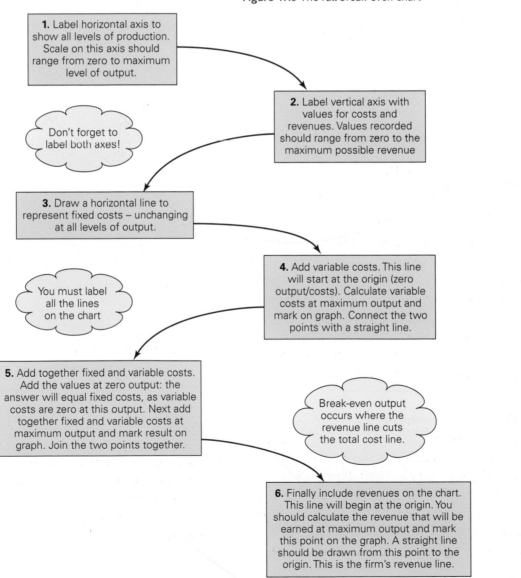

Figure 17.10 In summary: constructing break-even charts

Interpreting break-even charts

Figure 17.11 shows the break-even chart for The Holly. We have indicated on the chart the following scenarios:

1. **Attracting 200 customers each month**

    If The Holly attracts 200 customers each month, the restaurant will make a loss when it is refurbished as this figure is less than break-even output. The financial position of the business will be:

    Revenue (200 customers paying £60 each)

    = £12,000

    Total costs [costs of £10,000 + (200 x £35)]

    = £17,000

    With 200 customers The Holly will make a loss

    = £5,000

    This loss is illustrated on the vertical axis.

2. **Attracting 600 customers each month**

    If The Holly attracts 600 customers each month when the refurbishment is complete, the restaurant will make a profit, as this figure is greater than break-even output. The financial position of the business will be:

    Revenue (600 customers paying £60 each)

    = £36,000

    Total costs [costs of £10,000 + (600 x £35)]

    = £31,000

    With 600 customers The Holly will make a profit

    = £ 5,000

    The amount of profit at this level of output is shown on the vertical axis.

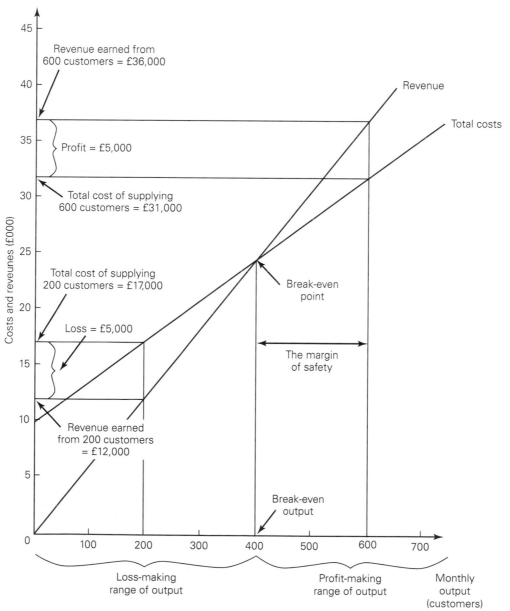

Figure 17.11 Interpreting break-even charts

It is, of course, possible to read off the level of profit that Sarah's restaurant will make, whatever the number of customers it attracts each month.

This is one way in which a break-even chart is of value to managers. It can be used to read off the expected profit or loss at various levels of output. If the manager believes that they can achieve a certain level of sales, this technique will provide guidance on whether this is likely to be profitable or not.

The margin of safety

A break-even chart can be used to show the **margin of safety**. The margin of safety is the amount by which a firm's current level of output exceeds the level of output necessary to break even.

Key term

The **margin of safety** measures the amount by which a business's current level of output exceeds break-even output.

If The Holly is successful and attracts 600 customers each month, the margin of safety will be 200 customers. This means that, in these circumstances, The Holly could lose 200 customers monthly before it began to make a loss.

Changing variables and break-even analysis

Break-even analysis can assist managers in taking a range of decisions relating to their businesses. Break-even analysis can identify the number of sales a business needs to make to generate a profit at certain levels of costs and prices. However, break-even can also deal with more complex circumstances including:

- analysing the impact of changing costs and/or prices on the profitability of the business
- deciding whether to accept an order for products at prices different from those normally charged.

In spite of its relative simplicity, break-even provides managers with an effective and clear method of analysis and can assist in making decisions, such as setting prices or accepting one-off orders.

Break-even analysis can show the consequences for a business in terms of changing profits (or losses) that may result from changes in fixed and variable costs or alterations in the firm's selling price. This is important for the planning of new businesses or projects for existing firms and also for businesses that operate in environments which change frequently. It is too simplistic for managers to assume that costs will remain constant or that prices in their markets will not alter over a period of time. Using break-even analysis for a number of 'what if?' scenarios can increase the value of the technique in financial planning and decision-making.

Table 17.6 illustrates the general effects of changing costs and prices on the break-even point of a business. To calculate the precise effect of changes at a particular level of production, it is necessary to conduct calculations or to construct a break-even chart.

Change in business environment	Effect on break-even chart	Impact on break-even output	Other effects
Rise in variable costs	Total cost line pivots upwards	Greater output necessary to break even	Due to rise in costs greater revenue (and so more customers and sales) are necessary to break even.
Fall in variable costs	Total cost line pivots downwards	Smaller output required to break even	Each sale incurs lower costs so that a smaller number of customers is needed to cover costs.
Rise in fixed costs	Fixed cost line and total cost line move upwards in a parallel shift	Greater output required to break even.	Business incurs greater costs before earning any revenue, so more sales will be required to cover costs and break even.
Fall in fixed costs	Fixed cost and total cost lines make parallel shift downwards	Smaller output is necessary to break even	The business's overall costs are lower and hence fewer sales will be required to break even.
Rise in selling price	Revenue line pivots upwards	Break-even is achieved at a lower level of output	Each sale will provide the business with greater revenue while costs are unaltered. Hence fewer sales will be necessary to break even.
Fall in selling price	Revenue line pivots downwards	Break-even is reached at a higher level of output.	Every sale will earn the business less revenue so, as costs are unchanged, more sales will be required to earn sufficient revenue to break even.

Table 17.6 The effects of changing costs and prices on a business's level of break-even output

Case study: the continuing story of the refurbishment of The Holly

Sarah is conscious that the cost of construction work on older properties in London is rising rapidly. She is concerned that the planned alterations to The Holly will cost significantly more than she originally forecast and that this will increase the fixed costs as the company will have to pay more interest on the loan it will need. If this happens this will reduce the profitability of the restaurant. Sarah is concerned that a substantial rise in fixed costs (to say £12,500 each month) might make the business unattractive in financial terms.

Sarah's other fear is that The Holly may be forced to reduce its prices because of increasing competition from other restaurants in west London. She believes that it may be necessary to cut the average price of a meal at The Holly from £60 to £55 as part of her analysis. Sarah recognises that if the restaurant has lower prices it will need to attract more customers to break even. At the same time, the level of profit earned from a given number of customers will fall. The effects of reducing prices by £5 per meal are shown in Figure 17.13. This assumes that all costs are unchanged.

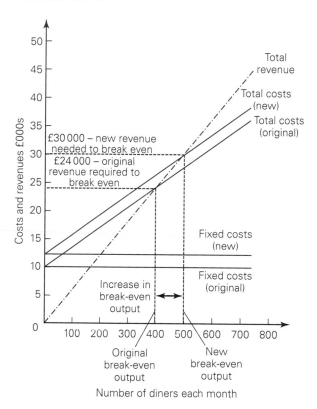

Figure 17.12 Break-even output and rising fixed costs

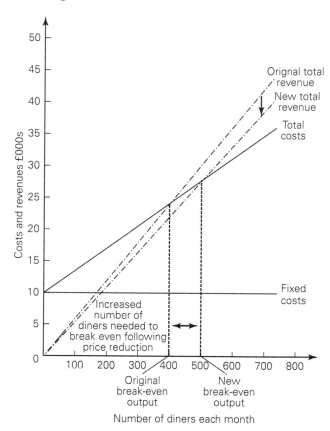

Figure 17.13 Break-even output and reduced prices

Figure 17.12 illustrates the effect of a rise in fixed costs on The Holly. The chart highlights that a rise in fixed costs results in The Holly requiring a greater number of diners (500 rather than 400) to break even. This occurs because given the increase in costs faced by The Holly, the restaurant will need to earn higher revenue to cover its costs. Originally, with fixed costs at £10,000 a month, a revenue of £24,000 was sufficient to break even. With the increased level of fixed costs, Sarah needs to attract sufficient diners to give the restaurant a monthly income of £30,000 and a contribution of £12,500 to ensure that break-even is achieved.

Managers can take actions to reduce the level of production or output necessary to break even. So if a business is able to increase its price, fewer units of output will need to be sold to break even. A reduction in fixed or variable costs will have a similar effect.

What do you think?

Would an increase in price always increase the chance of a business actually breaking even?

Break-even and non-standard prices

A similar analysis would have resulted if Hazel Foods plc had been approached by a customer and offered the chance to provide a large number of meals at a price below the normal average of £60 in The Holly if it is refurbished. Suppose a local theatre offered a contract to fill the restaurant one night each week as part of its 'View & Dine' package. The theatre may only offer a fixed price of £50 per diner, but guarantee a minimum of 25 diners on that evening. Sarah could take this into account in her business planning and decide whether it is an attractive offer using break-even analysis.

In this case she may be tempted. Assuming her fixed costs for one night are £334 (£10,000/30) and that her contribution per unit is now £15 (£50 – £35), The Holly would break even on this offer with (just over!) 22 diners and the contract is for 25 as a minimum. Sarah might also think that this is a good way of publicising The Holly. If they enjoy the experience, diners might return and pay full price, or tell friends about it.

The value of break-even analysis

Most techniques of financial analysis have advantages and disadvantages, and break-even analysis is no exception. Assessing its value entails considering the advantages and disadvantages offered by break-even analysis in specific circumstances.

The advantages of break-even include the following:

- By using break-even charts a business can forecast the effect of varying numbers of customers on its costs, revenues and profits. Break-even analysis can also be used to analyse the implications of changing prices and costs on the enterprise's likely profitability. These 'what if' analyses are arguably the greatest potential benefit to a business from using break-even analysis.
- It is a simple technique allowing most managers to use it without the need for expensive training. Because of this it is particularly suitable for newly established and small businesses and those that produce a single product.
- It is a technique that can be completed quickly, providing immediate results. This means that it can be used by managers at all levels within a business.

- Its use can be of value in supporting a business's application to a bank for a loan. It provides evidence of financial planning as well as evidence of whether the business is likely to make a profit.

However, break-even analysis has a number of shortcomings:

- It says nothing about the level of sales a business might achieve. In our case study earlier Sarah might have assumed that she will attract 600 customers each month. She will order the necessary food and hire sufficient staff. However, if only 500 turn up, she will not make the profit indicated for 600 customers on the break-even chart.
- It is a simplification of the real world. Businesses do not sell all their products at a single price and calculating an average is unlikely to provide accurate data.
- The technique is also difficult to use when a business sells a number of different products. This would require managers to divide up the business's fixed costs and allocate them between its products. This would be difficult to do accurately.
- Costs do not rise as steadily as the technique suggests. As we have seen, variable costs can rise less quickly than output because of the benefits of buying in bulk.
- A break-even analysis will only be as accurate as the data on which it is based. If costs or selling prices are incorrect, then the forecasts will be wrong.

So break-even analysis offers some support to a manager when making a decision and to entrepreneurs looking to start a business. However, it is only a guideline and its value should not be overstated. Perhaps most importantly, managers should bear in mind that the value of the technique depends on the use of reliable data for costs, prices and expected sales.

Business in focus: Blackberry targets break even

Blackberry, the Canadian smartphone manufacturer, which has suffered from severe financial difficulties recently, will break even in the 2013–14 fiscal year, its chief executive, John Chen has stated. It is renewing its focus on selling phones to its traditional customers such as those working in big businesses and government. Mr Chen said that while the company would not try to make cheap phones for emerging markets, it would maintain its position by going back to the key features that drove its former success and not sell cheap phones.

'What Blackberry does the best is security and productivity and communications,' he said. 'We have to make it competitive but we're not going to play the $75 phone game.'

He claimed that by looking at specific markets, the company could end up producing highly targeted devices. 'Eventually we could build a phone for the healthcare industry,' he said. Selling higher priced phones is the company's intention.

Although BlackBerry's share price has declined sharply in recent years, John Chen's strategy has seen it regain ground. 'Looking at profitable niche markets would allow BlackBerry to address new opportunities,' he said.

Launching two new mid-range phones, one with a keyboard, John Chen said the company's previous strategy under his predecessor had allowed the company to lose focus by neglecting core business customers. 'We have done some damage to our enterprise focus,' he said. 'That is not going to happen anymore. We got ourselves spread a little too thin.'

Source: Adapted from *The Daily Telegraph*, 25 February 2014

www.telegraph.co.uk/technology/blackberry/10660037/BlackBerry-looking-at-a-phone-for-medics.html

Questions

1. Explain how selling products at high prices might help Blackberry to break even.
2. To what extent is break-even a useful concept for the management team at Blackberry?

How to analyse profitability

We saw in Chapter 1 that profit is calculated by deducting total costs from the total revenue received by a business over a given time period. Profit is a very important objective for many businesses and it is one way of measuring the success of a business. Managers will analyse the performance of a business in terms of profits and use this information to guide decisions. A simple analysis of profit data would consider whether a business's profits have risen or fallen and the rate of change. Such an analysis would also examine the trend in the business's profits over a period of some years. Many public limited companies produce financial data to cover a five-year period.

Table 17.7 shows the operating profit for Unilever, a multinational company that supplies a range of consumer goods. Although the company's operating profit has grown over the five-year period, the rates of growth have varied considerably. The company's managers may regard 2010 as a relatively successful year, while operating profits grew much less quickly in the following year.

	2013	2012	2011	2010	2009
Operating profit (£m)	7,517	6,977	6,420	6,325	5,006

Table 17.7 Unilever plc's annual operating profit, 2009–2013

Source: Unilever website

www.unilever.com/images/ir_UNI_10-Year_Charts_2013_030314_tcm13-384260.pdf

However, a simple profit figure is not as revealing as it might appear. It is simple to assume that if one firm makes a larger profit than another, it must be more successful. This might not be the case. It is important to consider two factors when making a judgement on a business's profits:

- What level of sales was necessary to generate the profits? If a firm achieves a high level of profits from a relatively small number of sales, it may be considered very successful.
- How much money was invested into the project to produce the profits? Obviously, a larger investment would be expected to result in a higher level of profits. We looked at the concept of a return on an investment in the previous chapter but will focus on comparing profits and revenues here.

We can make a more meaningful judgement about a business's performance if we compare its profits with something else in a simple calculation. Calculating ratios that compare profits to revenue allows us to make more informed assessments of a business's performance.

Key terms

Profitability is a measure of financial performance that compares a business's profits to some other factors such as revenue.

A **profit margin** is a ratio that expresses a business's profit as a percentage of its revenue over some trading period.

Profit margins

A **profit margin** compares a business's profit to its sales revenue and expresses the outcome as a percentage. Thus, profit margin = profit x 100/revenue. The calculation of this simple ratio can provide a more informed analysis of a business's financial performance and it can take several forms depending on the type of profit that is used in the calculation.

It is possible to calculate a profit margin for a single product, or for the business's entire output. For a business that sells a single product at a standard price, these two figures should be the same. However, in reality the majority of businesses sell a range of products at a variety of prices.

Analysing the relative performance of the two businesses set out in Table 17.8 appears straightforward.

Company	Profits
Company X	£12.42 million
Company Y	£49.85 million

Table 17.8 A comparison of the profits of two companies

Company Y's profits were approximately four times higher than those of Company X during the most recent financial year. Thus, it would appear that Company Y recorded a better financial performance. However, this comparison may not be between two similar-sized businesses with equal access to resources.

By introducing more information into a financial analysis of a company's performance, it is possible to gain greater insight. Table 17.9 shows information on the revenue earned by the two companies and enables us to calculate two profit margins for comparison.

Business	Profits for last financial year	Revenue for last financial year	Profit margin
Company X	£12.42 million	£101.96 million	12.18 per cent
Company Y	£49.85 million	£603.16 million	8.26 per cent

Table 17.9 A comparison of the profit margins of the same two companies

By including information on the revenues generated by the two companies we are able to improve the quality of our analysis and to make a better quality judgement. The use of profit margin reveals that, even though Company Y achieves a higher profit it is from a much higher level of sales. Company Y's profits were about four times as high as those of company X, but its sales were about six times greater. As a consequence the percentage of Company Y's revenue that is profit is only 8.26 per cent, whereas the equivalent figure for Company X is 12.18 per cent. So, although Company X is smaller, it can be argued that its financial performance is superior.

Maths moment

(a) Assume that Company X in Table 17.9 above generated a revenue of £98.5 million in the last financial year. Calculate its profit margin.

(b) Assume Company Y's profit was unchanged, but that its profit margin was 9 per cent. What was its revenue for the year?

Types of profit margins

It is possible for a business to calculate several different profit margins. There are three profit margins that are commonly calculated.

1. Gross profit margin

Gross profit is a business's revenue minus its direct costs or cost of sales. The gross profit margin can be calculated using the formula below:

Gross profit margin = gross profit × 100 / revenue

The gross profit margin does allow comparisons to be made between different businesses or over different time periods. However, it has limited value as a measure of financial performance as the calculation of gross profit does not include all of a business's costs – for example it excludes indirect costs, interest payments and taxation. A negative figure for gross profit (that is, a gross loss) will lead to a negative profit margin.

We can calculate the gross profit margin for Burberry plc for the financial years ending in 2013 and 2014, which are shown in Table 17.10. Burberry plc is based in the UK and is a global retailer of luxury fashion products including clothing, cosmetics and perfumes.

Item	2014 £m	2013 £m
Revenue	2,329.8	1,998.7
Cost of sales (direct costs)	671.3	556.7
Gross profit	1,658.5	1,442.0
Operating profit	445.4	345.8
Profit for the year	322.3	259.2

Table 17.10 Selected profit data for Burberry, 2013 and 2014

Source: Burberry plc's Annual Report, 2014

www.burberryplc.com/documents/ar-13-14/burberry-annual-report-2013-14.pdf

Between the two years Burberry plc's gross profits increased by £216.5 million or 15.01 per cent to £1,658.5 million which looks to be a good performance by the company. We can calculate the company's gross profit margin for the two years, as shown below.

2013: £1,442.0m x 100/£1 998.7m = 72.15 per cent

2014: £1,658.5m x 100/£2 329.8m = 71.19 per cent

The company's gross profit margin has declined slightly despite its rise in revenue. It may be that Burberry has been slightly less effective in controlling its direct costs. Burberry plc's direct costs would include the wages of its employees and the cost of purchasing its distinctly branded clothing and other products.

2. Operating profit margin

A business calculates its operating profit by deducting direct and indirect costs of production from its revenue. The operating profit figure is useful to managers and others interested in the performance of a business, but more so when compared to the sales revenue the firm received in the sale trading period.

The formula for calculating the operating profit margin is shown below.

$$\text{operating profit margin} = \frac{\text{operating profit} \times 100}{\text{sales revenue}}$$

If the firm makes an operating loss, then its operating profit margin will be negative.

In general, higher profit margins are preferable to lower ones, as a higher profit margin is likely to lead

to greater overall profits. This should meet with the approval of the business's owners, assuming that their objective is to make the largest profits possible.

However, the pursuit of increased overall profits can lead to a fall in a business's profit margin. Managers may decide to reduce prices to attract additional sales in the hope of gaining higher profits. This may be effective, but only because the business earns a lower profit on each of a larger number of sales to generate the increased level of profits. Such a situation is illustrated in Table 17.11.

	Units sold	Sales revenue £	Total costs £	Operating profit £	Operating profit margin %
Scenario 1	100,000	2,400,000	2,000,000	400,000	16.67
Scenario 2	110,000	2,585,000	2,620,000	415,000	16.05

Table 17.11 A rise in profits, but a fall in the operating profit margin

Operating profit margins do reflect a business's financial performance more fully as operating profit takes into account both direct and indirect costs and therefore the resulting profit figure is a better measure of performance.

We can use the data in Table 17.10 to calculate the operating profit margin for Burberry plc for 2013 and 2014.

2013: £345.8m x 100/£1,998.7m = 17.30 per cent

2014: £445.4m x 100/£2,329.8m = 19.12 per cent

This piece of analysis is more revealing. The company's operating profit margin has risen by nearly 2 per cent over the two years. As operating profit is normally regarded as a better measure of a business's financial performance than gross profit, this rise may be a satisfying result for the company's management team. It suggests that the company has managed to control its indirect costs (or expenses) well and perhaps more so than its direct costs. The management team may seek to control direct costs such as inventories and employee wages more tightly over future financial years.

3. Profit for the year

Profit for the year is a measure of a business's profits that takes into account a wider range of expenditures and incomes including taxation. It is possible to calculate a margin based on profit for the year by using the formula below:

Business in focus: Profits at British Sky Broadcasting Group plc

British Sky Broadcasting Group plc (usually called BSkyB) is a British satellite television broadcasting company that also supplies telephone and broadband services throughout the UK and Ireland. BSkyB is the market leader for pay-for TV services in the UK.

The company reported a slight fall in its annual profits in July 2014 despite a 5.5 per cent growth in revenue. The company also announced that it was increasing its dividends by 7 per cent and would be paying 32 pence per share to its shareholders. The company commented that it was on target to meet its objectives and had achieved a 33 per cent growth in customer numbers during the year.

Item	2014 £m	2013 £m
Revenue	7,632	7,235
Cost of sales (direct costs)	4,616	4,329
Gross profit	3,016	2,906
Operating profit	1,275	1,330
Profit for the year	865	979

Table 17.12 Selected profit data for BSB Group plc, 2013 and 2014

Source: Yahoo Finance website

https://uk.finance.yahoo.com/q/is?s=BSY.L&annual

Questions

1. Calculate BSkyB plc's gross and operating profit margins for 2013 and 2014.

2. To what extent do you think that BSkyB plc's shareholders will be satisfied with the company's financial performance during 2013 and 2014?

Profit for the year margin $= \dfrac{\text{profit for the year} \times 100}{\text{revenue}}$

Finally, the data in Table 17.10 can be used to calculate profit for the year margins.

2013: £259.2m x 100/£1,998.7m = 12.97 per cent

2014: £322.3m x 100/£2,329.8m = 13.83 per cent

This final ratio shows an improvement over the two years, possibly because the company paid less interest on its loans or because it generated more profit from non-trading activities. It does mean that the company's management team is in a position to pay shareholders an increased dividend if this is judged to be in the company's best interests.

The use of data for financial decision making and planning

We saw in Chapter 4 that data is the basis of scientific decision making and that many managers avoid taking decisions without relevant data to analyse. Using data to support decisions has also become more straightforward and cost-effective due to developments in technology. It is becoming increasingly possible for many businesses to analyse enormous quantities of information (the so-called **big data**) to support decision making.

Managers use a range of financial information to plan their enterprise's future activities and to take decisions about these activities. Budgets, including cash flow forecasts, are a central part of financial planning. Managers and other stakeholders (such as investors) use this information to make judgements about the future viability of a business or a specific project. If managers require loan capital to support the activity, financial planning of this type will be essential. Banks and other investors will regard a loan as very high risk if they have not been able to view such financial plans. Break-even analysis is also used, particularly by managers, to model 'what if?' scenarios. This can play a vital part in planning and also in decision making. Break-even analysis could provide important evidence to assist managers in deciding whether to increase prices or to continue production following a substantial rise in fixed or variable costs.

A well-known quotation says that a manager should not take a decision without considering relevant numerical data, but should not take one on the basis of quantitative data only. Financial data has an important role to play in decision making throughout a business. It will influence decisions taken in all departments or functions of a business.

Key term

Big data is a term used to describe a massive volume of both organised and non-organised information that is very large.

For example, managers would be unlikely to consider launching a new product without considering a number of financial aspects such as the following:

- Does the business have sufficient capital (possibly from past profits) to fund this new product?
- What will be the effect of launching this new product on the business's cash flow?
- Will the new product generate a profit and, if so, over what timescale?
- How might the return from investing in this new product compare with other possible investments the business could make?

Key term

Primary market research gathers data for the first time for a specific purpose.

Is the data reliable?

Making decisions on the basis of financial data can improve the quality of such decisions, but it does depend on the reliability of the data. Financial data is often underpinned by assumptions about future customer buying behaviour, which determines revenue forecasts. It is not easy to forecast revenue accurately. The reliability of the data may depend on the quality of research used to provide it. Recent, relevant and well-focused **primary market research** is more likely to result in reliable revenue data and therefore good quality decisions by managers.

For example, historical data on a company's recent profits is likely to be accurate, but that does not necessarily make it reliable. Historical data is not always a good indicator of future performance, especially for businesses that operate in changing environments. In 2013 Tesco plc, the UK's largest retailer, announced that its operating profits had declined by 23.5 per cent after many years of trading during which its profits had risen and it had grown to be the UK's dominant retailer.

Managers have to make a number of judgements about data. They should consider whether it is accurate, whether it is reliable and whether it is relevant to the decision they are to take. If the answer to all these questions is yes, then they can consider how it should influence their decision.

ASSESSMENT ACTIVITIES

Sections (a), (b) and (c) of these assessment activities are relevant for students taking AS and A-level examinations. The questions in section (d) are for A-level students only.

(a) Knowledge check questions

1 Is the following statement true or false? 'Sales volume and average selling price are key pieces of information needed to construct a budget.'

2 Drawing up budgets involves a series of activities. Place the four activities below in the correct order.
   a) Construct expenditure budgets.
   b) Construct revenue budgets.
   c) Establish the business's objectives.
   d) Analyse markets and previous years' budgets to gather information.

3 State two reasons why a manager might analyse an expenditure budget.

4 Polly Ltd's recent budget contained the following information:
   - Budgeted expenditure on fuel: £37,500
   - Actual expenditure on fuel: £42,000
   - Previous month's budget: £39,000.

   Which of the following is the correct variance for this budget?
   i)   £3,000 adverse
   ii) £4,500 favourable
   iii) £4,500 adverse
   iv) £3,000 favourable.

5 For which two of the following reasons might businesses construct cash flow forecasts?
   i) to increase the profit made per unit of production
   ii) to support applications for loans
   iii) as a means of forecasting future profit margins
   iv) to avoid financial problems during periods when they may be unable to pay suppliers.

6 If Pip Ltd has an opening cash balance in April of £24,750 and a net cash flow for the month of (£14,250) which one of the following will be its opening balance for May?
   i) £39,000   iii) £38,500
   ii) £24,750   iv) £10,500

7 If a business has a net cash flow for October of £35,000 and an opening balance of (£12,500), what is its opening balance for November?

8 Complete the following formula by filling in the missing word. 'Cash inflow per month minus cash outflow per month equals ....'.

9 Is the following statement true or false? 'Sales revenue minus contribution equals fixed costs.'

10 The selling price of Marley's hand-knitted sweaters is £90. The variable cost of each one is £40. His monthly fixed costs are £1,000. His market research suggests he will sell 16 sweaters per month. Should he start producing sweaters on the basis of this information?

11 Does the total revenue line pivot or shift when there is a fall in prices?

12 Is the following statement true or false? 'A fall in variable costs per unit will always reduce break-even output.'

13 Saxon Pharmaceuticals plc's revenue for the last trading year was £375.4 million; its cost of sales were £225.2 million and its interest payments were £19.8 million. Calculate its gross profit margin.

14 Is the following statement true or false? 'A reduction in prices can, in some circumstances, increase a business's revenue.'

15 A company made an operating profit margin last year of 12.5 per cent. Its revenue for the year was £1,500 million. What was the level of its operating profit?

(b) Short answer questions

1 Explain why a large, established company selling a range of well-known brands may have access to a large quantity of good quality information when constructing its budgets. (4 marks)

2 Explain why a multinational business selling price and income elastic products may suffer adverse variances on its revenue budgets (4 marks)

3 Explain the possible benefits to a business with a low profit margin of constructing budgets for all its activities. (5 marks)

4 Explain why managing payables and receivables carefully is important for a start-up business. (5 marks)

5 Explain why break-even analysis may be of limited value to a multi-product business selling in an intensely competitive market. (6 marks)

6 Explain why the managers of a small house building company may be less confident that data on which they may base decisions is reliable. (6 marks)

(c) Data response questions

Healthy Meals Ltd provides a range of low-calorie, organic ready-meals in Bristol; it is the only supplier, although a competitor (part of a large food company) is about to enter the market. Demand for healthy meals has a price elasticity of −0.45 in the city and the company has received much coverage in the local media. The company has been trading since 2011 and last year it enjoyed a very successful year, with its operating profit margin rising to 20.07 per cent.

The company's managers have started to look forward to next year's trading and primary market research has revealed the following:
• monthly fixed costs will be £15,000
• the average price of a meal is forecast to be £6.50
• continuing the company's policy of slowly increasing prices may be less successful
• the ingredients of an average meal will cost £2.50
• other variable costs will amount to £2.00 per meal.

The company is considering launching a new range of meals based on seafood. One manager believes that break-even analysis will be of great value in reaching a decision on whether or not to go ahead with this project. Despite its rising profits the 'Seafood Project' will require a large loan from the company's bank.

1 Calculate the company's break-even level of production for the next year.   (6 marks)

2 Analyse why the company's operating profit margin might have increased over the last year.   (9 marks)

3 To what extent do you think that the company will benefit from the use of break-even analysis in taking a decision on the 'Seafood Project'?   (15 marks)

(d) Essays

1 Budgets offer the greatest benefits to decision-makers in large businesses. Do you agree? Justify your view.   (25 marks)

2 To what extent should managers rely less on financial data and more on data from other functions of the business (such as marketing) when taking decisions on whether or not to launch a new product?   (25 marks)

3 Decisions relating to cash flow are more important than other aspects of financial planning and analysis for start-up businesses. Do you agree? Justify your opinion.   (25 marks)

Chapter 18

Sources of finance

Introduction

This chapter builds on earlier ones and looks at a key decision that a business's managers have to make – that of deciding upon the most appropriate source of finance. It considers the various sources that are available to managers from inside and outside the business. The next chapter will look at other important decisions on how to improve profits or strengthen cash flow.

What you need to know by the end of this chapter:

- the internal and external sources of finance that are available to managers
- the advantages and disadvantages of different sources of finance for short- and long-term uses.

A number of sources of finance are available from which managers can select, but the one chosen will depend upon several factors:

- the amount of money required by the business
- the purpose for which the finance is required

- the time period over which the loan is required
- the legal structure of the business
- the financial position of the business.

We shall look at a range of sources of finance in this section and consider how factors such as those listed above may influence a business's choice of sources of finance.

Internal and external sources of finance

A source of finance refers to the way in which a business raises the finance that it needs for some activity. Sources of finance can be classified in a number of ways. **Internal sources of finance** already exist within a business and it only requires a decision about how to use it. Profits held over from previous years (known as retained profits) are an example of an internal source. **External sources of finance** are funds that are injected from outside the business. A bank loan is a prime example of this category of source of finance.

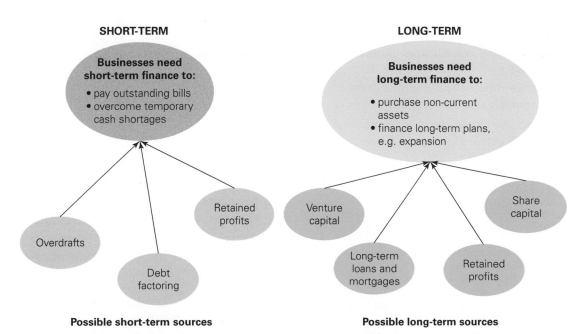

Figure 18.1 Why businesses need short- and long-term capital and how they meet those needs

It is also possible to classify sources of finance as short and long-term. A business may need **short-term finance** to pay its bills and to keep its suppliers happy, possibly covering a temporary shortage of cash. Sudden increases in the costs of raw materials can also create a need for short-term finance. Short-term finance of this kind is usually repayable within a one-year period.

However, businesses also need to purchase major capital assets such as land and buildings or to expand or to take over other businesses. To do this they will require **long-term finance**, which will be repaid over a period of time in excess of one year and on many occasions, much more than one year.

Table 18.1 classifies a range of sources of finance according to whether they are short- or long-term and internal or external.

	Internal sources of finance	External sources of finance
Short-term sources of finance	● Retained profits	● Overdrafts ● Debt factoring
Long-term sources of finance	● Retained profits ● Sale of assets	● Bank loans, mortgages & debentures ● Venture capital ● Share capital

Table 18.1 Classifying sources of finance in terms of time scale and source

Key terms

An **internal source of finance** is one that exists within the business

An **external source of finance** is an injection of funds into the business from individuals, other businesses or financial institutions.

Short-term finance is finance needed for a limited period of time, normally less than one year.

Long-term finance are those sources of finance that are needed over a longer period of time, usually over a year.

Internal sources of finance

An internal source of finance is one that exists within the business. The major internal sources of finance are retained profits and sale of assets.

1. Retained profits

This remains a major source of finance, particularly for smaller businesses. Businesses can use profits from the current trading year or profits from previous

trading years (technically these are called retained profits) as sources of finance. By using profits for reinvesting, a business avoids paying interest on a loan and this can avoid heavy interest charges if the loan required is a large one. Furthermore, using this source of finance may avoid the need for a company to sell further shares, enabling existing shareholders to retain control if they continue to hold a majority of the shares.

But using retained profits can have substantial opportunity costs – that is the business may lose out from not using these profits in another way. Reinvesting retained profits may not be popular with shareholders, who are likely to receive a lower dividend as a result. Alternatively, the business may lose out on interest it may have received if it held the money in an interest-paying bank account.

This method of finance is only available to firms making a profit. Even then the profits may not be sufficient to purchase expensive capital assets. In 2014 EDF, the French-owned energy company, announced that it was reinvesting a sum equivalent to its £863 million operating profit from the current year, but this was insufficient to finance the £1.1 billion it invested into its nuclear and coal-powered electricity generating facilities. The company has invested £3.5 billion of its retained profits over the 2011–2014 period.

2. Sale of assets

Firms can raise finance by selling assets that they no longer require – normally these are **non-current assets**. The sale of some assets can raise large amounts of finance for businesses. Thus a business might have land, buildings or other assets that not required and they may decide to sell to raise capital. Shell, the multinational oil company, announced that it is to sell $15 billion of its assets in the 2014–2015 financial year to fund, among other things, its trading activities in North America.

Raising finance in this way offers a key benefit in that the business is not committed to a stream of future interest payments, nor might its shareholders suffer dilution of control. However, the business would normally lose access to the assets it has sold.

But what if the assets will continue to be required by the business? A popular technique of raising funds in recent years has been sale and leaseback. Under this arrangement firms sell valuable assets and lease them back again. This means that they have the capital from the sale of the assets as well as the continuing use of these assets, so that their business is not disrupted. The major drawback is that the business now has to pay for the use of assets that previously were freely available. This may have a negative impact on its long-term profits as well as its cash flow position.

Key term

Non-current assets are items that a business owns and which it expects to retain for one year or longer. Examples include property and vehicles.

External sources of finance

When individuals, other businesses or organisations such as banks or governments provide capital to a business, this is an external source of finance. Businesses are more likely to use external sources of finance when:

● a large sum of finance is required (as they will find it more difficult to raise such sums internally)
● the level of risk associated with the source of finance is low encouraging outsiders to invest or lend money
● the company's profit levels are relatively low reducing the possibility of the use of retained profits.

Key terms

A **bank loan** is an amount of money provided to a business for a stated purpose in return for a payment in the form of interest charges.

An **overdraft** exists when a business is allowed to spend more than it holds in its current bank account up to an agreed limit.

Venture capital is funds advanced to businesses thought to be relatively high risk in the form of share and loan capital.

Share capital is finance invested into a company as a result of the sale of shares in the business.

The first three external sources of finance we consider are all types of loan capital – finance that is borrowed. The major difference between them is the timescale of the borrowing. An overdraft may be taken out for just a few weeks whereas a business mortgage could last for up to fifty years. Loan capital can be attractive to a business as a source of finance because it does not lead to any loss of control by the owners of the business.

Study tip

A knowledge of the advantages and disadvantages of the various sources of finance will help you suggest and justify suitable sources in specific circumstances.

Business in focus: The Thomas Cook Group

The Thomas Cook Group plc is a British registered company that sells holiday products to over 19 million customers worldwide each year. The company's management team has announced its intention to reduce the amount of debt the company holds and has been seeking the best source of finance to do this. The company operates with the primary aim of achieving sustainable, profitable growth.

In 2012 the Thomas Cook Group agreed a number of sale and leaseback deals for some of its non-current assets.

● It raised £11.5 million by selling its offices in Ghent in Belgium to Koramic Real Estate and leasing them back again.
● The Group signed a sale and leaseback deal with several other companies. This resulted in the sale and immediate leaseback of 19 aircraft, resulting in the company raising £182.9 million.

In 2014 the company announced further sales of assets. It received £13.5 million from selling its corporate travel business and a further £14.3 million from selling Elegant Resorts, its luxury travel enterprise. The Thomas Cook Group's share price has risen from 16.5 pence in May 2012 to 127.8 pence in August 2014.

Questions

1. Explain why the Thomas Cook Group might have wanted to reduce the amount of debt (or borrowing) that it had.
2. Evaluate whether sale and leaseback is the best choice as a source of finance for Thomas Cook Group plc in these circumstances.

1. Overdrafts

An **overdraft** is perhaps the best-known method of short-term finance. An overdraft is a facility offered by banks allowing businesses to borrow up to an agreed limit for as long as it wishes. Overdrafts are a very flexible form of finance as the amounts borrowed can vary so long as they are within an agreed figure. They are also simple to arrange – established business customers can often arrange, or increase the limit, without completing any forms.

However, overdrafts can be quite expensive with interest being charged at between 4 and 6 per cent over the bank's normal lending rate on a daily basis. This is not a problem unless a business seeks to borrow on overdraft over a long period of time. In these circumstances it might be better for a business to convert their overdraft to a longer-term method of finance. A further drawback of using overdrafts as a source of finance is that banks can demand immediate repayment.

2. Debt factoring

Debt factoring is a service offered by banks and other financial institutions. If businesses have sent out bills (also termed invoices) that have not yet been paid they can 'sell' these bills to gain cash immediately. Factoring debts in this way provides up to 80 per cent of the value of an invoice as an immediate cash advance. The financial institution then organises the payment of the invoice and makes a further payment to the business concerned. It is usual for the financial institution to retain about 5 per cent of the value of the invoice to cover its costs in debt collection. The process is summarised in Figure 18.2.

Many small firms believe that to lose up to 5 per cent of their earnings makes factoring uneconomic – this can eliminate much of their profit margin. Their customers are also likely to be aware that the debts have been factored, which may cause them to worry about the business's ability to manage its short-term finance. They may seek other suppliers if they believe the business is financially unstable.

However, debt factoring does offer a number of benefits.

- The immediate cash provided by the factor means that the firm is likely to have lower overdraft requirements and will pay less interest.
- Factoring means businesses receive the cash from their sales more quickly.

Debt factoring has become more popular for businesses, especially small and medium-sized ones (SMEs) as overdrafts have become more difficult to arrange. We consider this development further in the Business in Focus feature about UK banks.

3. Bank loans, mortgages and debentures

Bank loans can usually be arranged if the business that is seeking the credit is financially sound and has a satisfactory financial history. The financial institution advances the business a set figure and the business makes repayments over an agreed period of time. If the bank lending the capital considers the loan in any way risky, then it is likely to charge a higher rate of interest. Small businesses, in particular, suffer from this effect. Normally banks charge about 2 per cent over their base rate of interest for loans such as these. Interest rates can be fixed or variable.

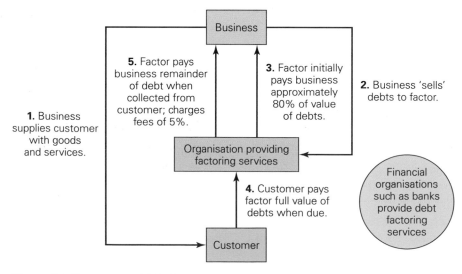

Figure 18.2 The process of debt factoring

Business in focus: UK banks withdraw overdraft facilities

Small and mid-sized enterprises (SMEs) have traditionally relied heavily on overdrafts, which account for half of the financial products traditional banks have offered to SMEs. They were popular due to them being able to be arranged easily, being cost effective and being a flexible way of borrowing money. Research from Platform Black, a finance company, suggested that 56 per cent of businesses surveyed had relied on their overdraft facility in the last two years.

However, the same research suggests that traditional lenders have been withdrawing overdraft services for SMEs. In 2011 overdrafts accounted for 25 per cent of all finance used by SMEs but by 2013 this had fallen to 16 per cent. Lending via overdraft to small and mid-sized enterprises fell by £800 million in December 2013 alone.

The withdrawal of overdrafts by banks can be devastating to SMEs, especially because banks can do it at very short notice. In the absence of being able to secure sufficient overdrafts, businesses have been relying on other forms of finance including credit cards, bank loans and hire purchase.

Source: adapted from various news sources

Questions

1. Explain why having short-term sources of finance available is important for small and medium-sized businesses.
2. Do you think that overdrafts are the best short-term source of finance available to businesses? Justify your opinion.

Key terms

Mortgages are long-term loans, repaid over periods of up to fifty years, and used to purchase property.

Debentures are loans with fixed interest rates that are long-term and may not even have a repayment date.

Banks will often require security for their loans and this will usually be in the form of property. Such security is often termed 'collateral'. If the business defaults on the loan the bank sells the property or other collateral and recoups the money that was lent. In this way the bank lowers the degree of risk it incurs in making loans to businesses.

There are different types of loans available to businesses.

- **Mortgages.** Mortgages are simply long-term loans granted by financial institutions solely for the purchase of land and buildings. The land or building in question is used as security for the loan – they act as collateral and will be sold to recover the money lent, if the borrower stops repayments. These loans can be for long periods of time – often in up to fifty years. Mortgages can have fixed or variable rates of interest and are particularly suitable when a business wishes to raise large sums of money.

Some businesses may choose to remortgage their premises to raise capital. A remortgage either increases the existing mortgage or establishes a mortgage where one did not exist before. This is a source of finance particularly popular with small businesses.

- **Debentures.** Debentures are a special type of long-term loan to be repaid at some future date, normally within fifteen years of the loan being agreed. The rate of interest paid on debentures is fixed. In some circumstances debentures may not have a repayment date, representing a permanent loan to the business. This is an irredeemable debenture. Debentures are normally secured by using the business's non-current assets as collateral. Debentures are a form of loan capital and holders of debentures do not have voting rights in the business.

The All England Lawn Tennis Club has issued debentures to help it to fund improvements to centre court and its other facilities at Wimbledon. These are particularly popular with tennis fans as tickets for the Wimbledon tennis tournament are included in the deal.

4. Venture capital

Venture capital is an important source of finance for small enterprises and for businesses that are considered to be risky and therefore in some danger of failing. It is normally a mix of loan and share capital. Financial institutions, for example merchant banks, provide venture capital as well as individuals (who are known as business angels).

Organisations and individuals providing venture capital frequently wish to have some control over the organisation for which they are providing finance. The business's owners may need to sell some shares in their companies (generally a minority stake) to the person or organisation providing the venture capital. Providers of venture capital may seek a non-executive director role in the business in which they are investing. Venture capital investors not only provide capital, but experience, contacts and advice when required, which distinguishes venture capital from other sources of finance.

A significant drawback is that providers of venture capital will not advance huge amounts to businesses. It is unusual for venture capitalists to lend in excess of £500,000 in a single deal. Despite this, Pinterest, an image-sharing social website, has raised $425 million from a number of venture capital companies to finance its expansion online. The size of this deal reflects the potential that venture capitalists believe lies in Pinterest.

Weblink

Find out more about venture capital by visiting the website of the British Venture Capital Association at www.bvca.co.uk/

5. Share or equity capital

This is a very common form of finance for both start-up companies and for established ones. Companies raise capital by selling, quite literally, a share in their business to investors. A share is simply a certificate giving the holder ownership of part (or a share) of a company. The shareholders purchases shares and by selling large numbers companies can raise significant sums of capital. Issuing shares can be very expensive, which means it is only appropriate for raising large sums of capital.

Share capital is a source of finance for both private limited companies and public limited companies. However, in the UK, it is much easier for public limited companies to sell shares for two reasons:

1. They can sell shares on the Stock Exchange. This is an efficient international market which brings together buyers and sellers of shares and sets share prices.
2. Unlike private limited companies, public companies do not need the permission of other shareholders to sell shares. Equally existing shareholders can sell their shares freely.

Both these factors make it easier to buy and sell shares in public limited companies and encourage shareholders to buy shares in the first place.

There are several benefits from the selling of shares or equity as a source of finance. Although the companies will be expected to pay an annual return to shareholders (dividends) the level of this payment is not fixed and in an unprofitable year it may be possible for the company to avoid making any payment. It can be used to raise large sums of capital, as in the case of UK airline group flybe. In February 2014 flybe announced that it was to offer shares for sale to the value of £155.1 million to finance the company's expansion plans. The company is investigating 100 new possible routes for its aircraft to fly.

However, there are disadvantages of using share capital as a source of finance. Clearly it is only available to companies. Private limited companies have to seek approval from existing shareholders before issuing further shares. The most significant disadvantage is the potential for loss of control. If a business issues too many shares it may dilute the control of the existing owners to the point where new shareholders have a majority, and controlling, interest in the business.

Business in focus: Crowdfunding – a different source of finance

Figure 18.3 Crowdfunding can finance expansion

George Christakos owns and manages a restaurant in Nova Scotia in Canada and, facing the normal difficulties in raising capital, decided to use his business's customers as a source of finance. He wanted to enlarge the restaurant in the town of Halifax, a restaurant that he co-owns with his father, Leo. George's first choice as a source of finance, the Bank, decided not to lend him any money.

Not dismayed, George and his father decided to use crowdfunding to raise the finance they needed. This is a source of finance that invites small contributions from a large number of people.

Mr. Christakos' crowdfunding effort was unique, but entirely suitable for his business, and comprised three options for his customers. For investing $50, a customer was rewarded with lunch for two and two T-shirts. The option of a four-course dinner for two for $100 proved to be the most popular. For customers with larger sums to invest, George offered two dinners a year for the rest of the restaurant's life.

Using crowdfunding as a source of revenue, the restaurant raised $23,000 from 115 contributors, 80 per cent of whom lived close to the restaurant. Crowdfunding campaigns can take many different forms. Some involve donations, while others, such as Mr. Christakos' effort, involve the pre-purchase of goods or services. In any event the goal is to raise capital.

Source: Compiled from a variety of sources including the *Financial Post*, 22 October 2012

http://business.financialpost.com/2012/10/22/equity-crowdfunding-source-of-innovation-capital-for-startups/

Questions

1. Explain why a loan from the Bank might have been George Christakos' first source of finance.

2. Discuss the major advantages and disadvantages for George of using crowdfunding as a source of finance.

6. Other sources of finance

The increasing role and importance of the internet has acted as a catalyst for the development of new sources of finance. It has allowed the owners of businesses to communicate with a large number of people and to appeal directly for finance for their enterprises. The Business in Focus feature about **crowdfunding** illustrates an example of a restaurant raising a relatively small sum of capital.

There are also more established businesses operating online with the intention of providing a source of finance for businesses. These are termed peer-to-peer lenders and raise money from large numbers of private investors to lend to businesses for specific projects. The peer-to-peer lenders undertake some assessment of the risks entailed with the loan and administrate the process in return for fees. Funding Circle and Zopa are among the UK's best-known examples of peer-to-peer lenders.

Weblink

Find out more about Funding Circle by using the link below and clicking on the 'about us' tab.
www.fundingcircle.com

Key term

Crowdfunding is practice of funding a project or venture by raising many small amounts of money from a large number of people, typically via the internet.

Choosing a source of finance

In the previous sections we have seen that all sources of finance, whether internal or external, short or long term, have advantages and disadvantages. These are summarised in Table 18.2 on page 240.

Source of finance	Advantages	Disadvantages
Overdrafts	• A flexible way of funding day-to-day financial requirements. • Interest is only payable on the actual amount borrowed.	• Interest rates are high. • Bank may ask for repayment at any time. • May not be available to some SMEs.
Debt factoring	• It allows businesses to receive cash almost immediately a sale is made. • It may reduce a business's overdraft and interest charges.	• It can reduce or even eliminate a business's profit margin, if it is small. • Customers may be aware if debts are factors and could lose faith in the supplier.
Bank loans	• Can be negotiated to meet a business's precise requirements. • Managers can plan for repayments within budgets.	• They are inflexible and businesses may pay interest on funds they are not using. • Businesses may be required to offer collateral.
Mortgages and debentures	• These are ideal sources of finance for very long-term projects. • They avoid the owners losing any control over the business.	• Managers will have to offer property as collateral for mortgages. • Businesses can pay large amounts of interest on very long-term loans.
Retained profits	• They are a 'free' source of finance as they do not incur interest charges. • They do not involve any potential loss of control by a business's owners.	• The owners of the business (e.g. shareholders) may wish to receive the profits. • The business may lose out on valuable alternative investments.
Share capital	• It can be used to raise very large amounts of capital. • The company is not committed to fixed interest payments.	• This source of finance is only available to companies. • Private limited companies can only sell additional shares with shareholder approval. • Existing owners may lose control of the company.
Venture capital	• Can bring expertise into the business as part of the deal. • Avoids having to pay interest on the entire amount of finance.	• Some entrepreneurs and owners may not wish to have venture capitalists involved in decision-making. • Usually only able to raise small amounts of finance.
Crowdfunding	• Can be a relatively cheap source of finance • Increasingly relevant as UK banks reduce short-term lending.	• Unfamiliar source of finance for many managers. • May not be suitable to raise very large amounts of capital.

Table 18.2 Some advantages and disadvantages of selected sources of finance

Managers can select the most appropriate source of finance by considering the advantages and disadvantages of each available source and making a decision on which is most appropriate for their circumstances. There are a number of factors that managers will need to take into account, as summarised in Figure 18.4.

Figure 18.4 The factors that influence managers' decisions on sources of finance

The influences on decisions on sources of finance

1. The business's legal structure

The legal structure of a business is a major influence of the sources of finance that are available to a business.

Start-up businesses, many of which may be sole traders or partnerships, normally have a more limited range of sources of finance to draw upon as they represent a greater risk to potential investors and have few, if any, internal sources of finance for use.

In contrast a public limited company has a greater range of sources of finance that it can use and, in particular in the UK, they benefit from being able to raise capital by selling shares on the London Stock Exchange.

2. The cost of the source of finance

The costs incurred by firms raising capital can take a number of forms.

Legal form of business	Possible sources of finance	Key issues for consideration
Sole trader	Owner's savings, banks, suppliers, Government grants and loans.	• Security for those lending funds • Loss of control by owner • Evidence that business has potential to develop • Financial history of business/owner
Private Limited Company (Ltd)	Dependent upon the size of the private limited company, suppliers, banks, Government grants and loans, venture capital institutions, private share issues.	• Disagreement among existing shareholders • Difficulty finding suitable shareholders • Loss of control by existing shareholders • Lack of collateral and security for those lending funds • Element of risk in the loan
Public Limited Company (plc)	Suppliers, banks, Government grants and loans, venture capital institutions, public share issues via the Stock Exchange.	• State of economy and stock market • Ability to move to area receiving government aid • Recent financial performance • Reputation of company and senior managers

Table 18.3 The legal structure of a business, possible sources of finance and key issues

(a) **The rate of interest.** The rate of interest charged by organisations granting loans can be a significant influence, especially if the loan is a large one. This will depend on the level of risk that the loan represents to the lender and the time period of the loan. A short-term loan to a high-risk business might be charged at a high rate of interest.

(b) **The costs of selling shares.** For a public limited company a share issue can be an attractive option, although this can be an expensive method of raising capital as it entails considerable administration and promotion and, on occasions, a form of insurance if the sale is not successful. When shares are first sold by a company it has to use the services of other expert organisations to organise the sale. It is common for companies to use merchant banks for this purpose.

Public limited companies sometimes use rights issues to sell new shares. A rights issue entails selling additional shares to existing shareholders in proportion to the number of shares already owned. For example, existing shareholders may be offered the opportunity to buy one new share for each eight already held. Because of the relatively low cost of issuing shares in this way it is usual for them to be sold at a slight discount to encourage purchases.

Key term

Opportunity cost is the next best alternative that is foregone.

Study tip

Do not confuse the sale of new shares and second hand ones. Firms sell newly issued shares directly to the shareholders. In contrast, second-hand shares are sold mainly through the Stock Exchange. When second-hand shares are sold on the Stock Exchange it is not a source of finance for the company whose shares are sold – it is merely a means of the shareholder recovering the investment by selling the shares to another person or organisation.

(c) **Opportunity cost.** A decision to use a particular source of finance may have a cost in terms of what has to be given up as a consequence of the decision. For example, using retained profits for reinvestment into the company entails an opportunity cost which can be measured in terms of the reduction in the amount of profits that can be paid to shareholders (these are known as dividends).

For many businesses, accessing sources of finance at the lowest possible cost is the most important factor.

3. Flexibility

Some sources of finance are highly flexible and can be adapted to meet a business's precise needs. The most obvious example is an overdraft. This source of finance allows a business to overspend in its current account (or not) according to its needs (but subject to an overall limit). Thus a business can use its overdraft only when it is necessary and can avoid any interest charges at times when its finances are stronger. This flexibility has a price however: overdrafts are an expensive source of finance.

4. Control

Some sources of finance may result in the original owners of the business losing some, or even complete control of it. Certain forms of finance are only available if the person or organisation investing gains a say in how the business is managed. This is perhaps most obvious in the sale of shares. If a private or public limited company makes a succession of share issues it may be that the number of new shares issued is greater than the number of 'original' shares. In this case the new shareholders may gain control of the company.

However, it may be possible for the company to issue shares that do not carry full voting rights. This can allow the original shareholders to retain control though, of course, it makes the issue of new shares much less attractive to potential shareholders.

Smaller businesses that do not trade as companies can also lose some degree of control if they opt to use certain sources of finance. For example, venture capitalists may only agree to provide finance to what

may be considered a risky business if a part of their investment is in the form of shares and they have a say in the management of the business.

5. The purposes for which the finance is needed

Some sources of finance are suitable in certain situations. Thus, for example, a business that is seeking to raise finance to purchase property and has to rely on loan finance will probably consider taking out a mortgage. A mortgage is a long-term loan (and can be available at relatively low rates of interest) and the combination of these two factors makes it an ideal source of finance to purchase property, which can be very expensive.

In contrast, if the finance is being raised to fund a risky start up then an entrepreneur may experience difficulties in finding investors willing to put capital into the business. In this situation a venture capitalist may be the best choice as this source of finance specialises in investing in relatively high-risk enterprises and may also provide support and guidance to novice entrepreneurs.

ASSESSMENT ACTIVITIES

Sections (a), (b) and (c) of these assessment activities are relevant for students taking AS and A-level examinations. The questions in section (d) are for A-level students only.

(a) Knowledge check questions

1 State the difference between a short-term and a long-term source of finance.

2 Is the following statement true or false? 'A major consideration when deciding whether or not to use retained profits as a source of finance is opportunity cost.'

3 What is meant by the term overdraft?

4 State two reasons why a manager might be reluctant to use debt factoring as a source of finance.

5 State two features of a bank loan.

6 Is the following statement true or false? 'Venture capital is not suitable as a source of finance for start-up or small businesses.'

7 State two types of businesses that can use share capital as a source of finance.

8 State two possible advantages of using retained profits as a source of finance.

9 State two disadvantages of using overdrafts as a source of finance.

10 State two factors that might influence a manager's decision on which source of finance to use.

(b) Short answer questions

1 Explain the circumstances in which a business may decide to use an overdraft as a source of finance. (4 marks)

2 Explain why a company in a very competitive market with low profit margins may decide not to use debt factoring as a source of finance. (5 marks)

3 Explain why the management team of a successful public limited company might decide not to use retained capital as its source of finance. (5 marks)

4 Explain why a first-time entrepreneur might choose to use venture capital as a source of finance. (6 marks)

(c) Data response questions

Bowles Foods plc is one of the UK's largest food-processing and manufacturing companies and is highly successful – its profits for the year have averaged £360 million over the last two years. It is well managed and has a reputation for paying shareholders high and increasing dividends.

It owns factories across the UK and is planning to expand its operations into eastern Europe. This requires the company to raise £750 million. Initially the company planned to use its profits over the next three years as the major source of finance, but has opted to use share capital to finance the entire sum. The CEO has stated that it will sell the new shares at an attractive price. The company owns a number of assets including a derelict factory site in east London.

Some the of the company's directors have opposed this decision and have recommended that the company uses a mix of sources of finance, particularly aiming to use share capital, profits and loan capital. They see significant advantages in this approach, even though interest rates in the UK are forecast to rise steadily over the next few years.

1 Explain the disadvantages of using profits to finance the proposed expansion. (6 marks)

2 Analyse the possible implications for the company's shareholders of using share capital to finance the expansion. (9 marks)

3 Do you agree with the decision to raise the £75 million solely by using share capital? Justify your opinion. (15 marks)

(d) Essays

1 To what extent do you think that it is true to say that it is always easier for a profitable business to raise capital? (25 marks)

2 'A well-managed business should not need to use any external sources of short-term capital.' To what extent do you agree with this statement? (25 marks)

Chapter 19

Improving cash flow and profits

Introduction

In previous chapters in this unit we have looked at the financial objectives that managers might set for their businesses, the techniques they might employ to analyse the financial position of the enterprise and some of the decisions they may take to achieve their objectives. This chapter concludes this unit by considering two other key aspects of financial decision making: selecting the most appropriate methods of improving a business's cash flow position and its profitability.

What you need to know by the end of this chapter:

- the methods used to improve a business's cash flow position
- the methods used to improve a business's profits and profitability
- the difficulties managers face in improving a business's cash flow and profit.

Improving cash flow

The first stage in improving a business's **cash flow** is to identify why the business is encountering difficulties in this area. Having identified the cause of the problem it is possible to apply the most appropriate remedy.

Causes of cash flow problems

Arguably the major cause of cash flow problems is lack of planning by managers. Many businesses, once established, do not forecast in this way and are thus at risk of unforeseen problems.

A number of other factors can contribute to cash flow difficulties:

1. **Overtrading**. This occurs when a business expands quickly without organising funds to finance the expansion. Rapid growth normally involves paying for labour and raw materials several months before receiving payment for the final product. If this occurs over a prolonged period, a business can face severe cash flow shortages.

2. **Allowing too much trade credit.** Most businesses offer **trade credit**, allowing customers between 30 and 90 days to pay. This helps to win and retain customers. However, if a firm's trade credit policy is too generous, it may lead to cash flow difficulties as cash inflows are delayed. In such a situation a business may find itself unable to pay its bills when they are due as it has not received payment from its customers.

3. **Poor credit control.** A business's credit control department ensures that customers keep to agreed borrowing limits and pay on time. If this aspect of a business's operation becomes inefficient, cash inflows into the firm may be delayed. In some cases, a customer may not pay at all (this is known as a 'bad debt'). In such circumstances it is highly likely that a firm will encounter problems with its cash flow.

4. **Inaccurate cash flow forecasting.** It is unlikely that managers will always forecast cash flow accurately. Inaccurate forecasting can lead to a business not believing that it will face cash flow problems and possibly not monitoring its forecasts to confirm that they are correct. Inaccurate forecasting may occur because of inexperience on the part of managers, unexpected costs, perhaps

due to an unforeseen rise in the price of fuel or raw materials or simply over-optimistic assumptions about the level of future revenue from sales.

The importance of monitoring cash flow

Monitoring cash flow is an essential and ongoing element of managing cash flow effectively and on improving a poor position. The process of comparing actual and forecast cash flows is called variance analysis. (We considered variance analysis in Chapter 17.) If a manager can spot a looming cash flow problem at an early stage by comparing forecast and actual cash flow on a monthly basis then it is possible to take prompt and decisive action. These actions, which we consider below, may rectify the problem before it becomes too severe.

Steve Marshall's cash flow forecast – June	Budget	Actual
Cash in		
Savings & borrowings	75,000	75,000
Cash sales	5,750	5,230
Credit sales	0	0
Total cash inflow	**80,750**	**80,230**
Cash out		
Purchase of lease on shop	30,000	29,500
Purchase of books	59,000	60,000
Wages	1,500	1,450
Marketing costs	2,500	2,400
Other costs, e.g. rent	1,500	1,500
Total cash outflow	**94,500**	**94,850**
Net monthly cash flow	**(13,750)**	**(14,620)***
Opening balance	2,000	2,000
Closing balance	(11,750)	(12,620)

*Subject to change to purchases of books

Table 19.1 Monitoring Steve Marshall's cash flow

In Chapter 17, we saw that the managers at Marshall Books ltd had drawn up a cash flow forecast as part of their financial planning for the opening of the company's newest bookshop. Table 19.1 shows the actual cash movements that took place during his first month of trading in comparison with the forecast. It is apparent that the bookshop's cash position is slightly worse than forecast. The managers expected to have a closing balance of (£11,750) whereas it is (£12,620). This may mean that they need to increase the overdraft above the amount they originally thought that would be needed.

Maths moment $\frac{1+b}{c}=3$

An entrepreneur had forecast that her business would have a cash balance of (£250,500) at the end of last month. Her opening balance for the month was (£130,795) and her net cash flow for the month was (£111,425).

(a) What was her cash balance at the end of the month?
(b) Was it worse or better than she expected?

Managers need to assess the significance of any unexpected figures when analysing forecast and actual cash figures. There are a number of possible causes when considering cash variances:

- It might be a one-off occurrence that will not happen again – such as a cancelled order (or an unexpectedly large one).
- It could be due to seasonal variations such as high levels of sales at Christmas or over the summer period – this can be important for certain types of businesses such as toy shops or garden centres.

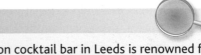

Business in focus: PBR Leisure Ltd

PBR Leisure Ltd operates seven bars and hotels in the North East of England and Belfast. It is facing severe cash flow problems partly reportedly caused by a fall in demand over recent months as well as fierce competition in the leisure market. The company's businesses include the Prohibition cocktail bar on Greek Street in Leeds, which is continuing to trade as usual while a solution is sought to the business's cash flow problems.

However, other elements of the business have been hit hard. The company has made 46 employees redundant following the closure of two of the company's other venues: Blu Bambu in Newcastle and Beach in Belfast. The decision has also been taken to make eight other PBR Leisure employees redundant.

The Prohibition cocktail bar in Leeds is renowned for its American-style design, offering corporate and private hire as well as membership, regular dining events and an affordable menu and its popularity may have saved it from closure.

Questions

1. Explain how 'a fall in demand' might have resulted in PBR Leisure Ltd suffering cash flow problems.

2. To what extent might closing two of PBR Leisure Ltd's venues weaken the company's cash flow position?

- More critically, it may be part of a continuing trend – whether sales are rising or falling steadily, there will be cash implications.
- It could be self-correcting – a surge in demand followed by a slump, and in this case no action will be required.

Methods of improving cash flow

Identifying potential cash flow problems is only part of the solution. Managers have to decide what actions to take to improve the cash position of their business. A number of techniques can be used to improve cash flow.

1. Improved control of working capital

Working capital is the finance available to the business for its day-to-day trading activities. Working capital is available to a business when its customers pay for the goods or services they have received. Working capital is used to pay wages, and for fuel and raw materials. There are a number of techniques set out below that a business may use to improve its working capital.

2. Negotiate improved terms for trade credit

Most firms receive some trade credit from their suppliers. This means they are given 30 or 60 days to pay for supplies. If a business can persuade suppliers who have previously been reluctant to offer trade credit to do so, it will improve its cash position. Remember, cash flow management is a matter of timing – delaying payments always helps. Another important move might be to extend existing trade credit agreements from, say, 30 to 60 days, or from 60 to 90 days.

3. Offer less trade credit

Similarly, a business can help its cash flow position by offering its customers less favourable terms for trade credit. This may require all customers to pay for products within 30 days, whereas in the past trade credit was for 60 days. However, this decision may result in a loss of customers as they move to competitors who offer more favourable credit terms.

4. Debt factoring

Debt factoring is a service offered by banks and other financial institutions. If businesses have sent out bills (also termed invoices) that have not yet been paid they can 'sell' these bills to gain cash immediately. Factoring debts in this way provides up to 80 per cent of the value of an invoice as an immediate cash advance. The financial institution then organises the payment of the invoice and makes a further payment to the business concerned. It is usual for the financial institution to retain about 5 per cent of the value of the invoice to cover their costs.

Many firms believe that to lose up to 5 per cent of their earnings means that factoring is uneconomic – it can eliminate much of their profit margin. However, factoring does offer the benefit that the immediate cash provided by the factor means that the firm is likely to have lower overdraft requirements and will pay less interest.

Debt factoring is generally used by small businesses. Businesses with a turnover above £1 million normally use an alternative technique (called invoice discounting) where the company retains the administration of the deal within the business. This way, its customers need not know that the company is using a debt factoring service. This can help a business to retain the confidence of its customers.

5. Arrange short-term borrowing

The majority of businesses have an agreed overdraft with their bankers, although small and medium-sized enterprises (SMEs) in the UK have faced problems in negotiating overdrafts over the last few years. An overdraft allows a business to borrow flexibly according to its needs, up to an agreed limit. Overdrafts can be expensive, but are reasonably economical and flexible when a business only borrows a set amount for a short period. As an alternative, a business may decide on a short-term loan to provide an injection of cash into the business. A short-term loan is likely to have a lower rate of interest and the option to pay the loan back over two years or so may be attractive to a business that is short of cash.

6. Sale and leaseback

This method of improving cash flow has been widely used by businesses over recent years. It entails a business selling a major asset – for example, a building – and then leasing it from the new owner. This provides a significant inflow of cash into the business, improving the cash position, but commits the firm to regular payments to lease the asset. In 2014 the Bannatyne Group announced an agreement with M&G Investments for the sale and leaseback of 39 of the company's Health Clubs. This allowed the Bannatyne Group to repay some loans and strengthen its cash position.

Business in focus: Sale and leaseback of business vans

'Cash flow poses problems for many businesses. But your vans could provide a much-needed cash using sale and leaseback. It's worth considering because access to cash is limited and expensive. Small and medium-sized businesses are being hit hard by late payers. Research in 2012 reported that average outstanding debt for a small or medium-sized enterprise (SME) was £36,000.

But sale and leaseback can help. How? You sell your van, or vans, to a leasing or fleet management company and they lease them straight back to you on a contract hire deal.

How a sale and leaseback works

You sell your vans to a leasing company.

The money is transferred to your business.

The leasing company then leases your vans back to you.

The vans remain in your hands at all times, so there's no disruption to your operations. You get an agreed price for the vans and you pay a set monthly rental to keep using them for an agreed period. You can pay for the lease company to handle all the maintenance too, if you want.

A big advantage is the cash sum, which you can use to improve cash flow. But there are other benefits. It can be cheaper than a bank loan. You don't have the hassle of disposing of the vans when it's time for them to leave your fleet. You also remove the risk of falling second-hand values. The leasing company handles disposal – subject to fair wear and tear conditions – and they take the hit if used van prices plummet.

Little wonder that sale and leaseback deals have been on the up since the financial crisis first occurred in 2008. But sale and leaseback is not suitable for every business.'

Source: Business Vans (Business Car Manager Ltd) website www.businessvans.co.uk/sale-and-leaseback-a-cash-injection-for-your-business-vans/2/

Questions

1. Explain why sale and leaseback of vans might be attractive to a business with cash flow problems.

2. Discuss the possible circumstances where sale and leaseback is not suitable to improve a business's cash flow position.

Cash flow and business performance

A business can benefit in a number of ways from effective and careful management of cash flow.

1. **Reduced borrowing costs.** If managers can predict periods of cash flow difficulty and take appropriate actions then it is likely that a business will not need to use its overdraft facility as fully as might have been the case. This can reduce interest charges significantly. If a business exceeds its overdraft limit then its bank is likely to impose penalty charges. Reducing interest charges means that a business will incur lower costs and enjoy higher profits.

2. **Good relations with suppliers.** Careful management of cash makes it more likely that a business will be able to pay suppliers promptly and in full. Many suppliers offer discounts for prompt payment and this can help a business to reduce its costs. Receiving a discount on supplies is also an effective way of reducing the business's costs.

3. **Public relations.** Businesses experiencing cash problems may lose the confidence of their customers, who doubt their ability to continue to supply goods and services. In such circumstances customers may no longer place orders; this is almost certain to exacerbate the problem and may result in the company being unable to continue trading.

Improving profits and profitability

A business can improve its profits if it reduces its costs or increases its revenues without any other changes occurring. However, increasing **profitability** requires managers to increase the amount of **profit** compared to some other measure such as revenue. We looked at the topic of profitability and profit margins in detail in Chapter 17.

Key terms

Profitability is a measure of financial performance that compares a business's profits to some other factors such as revenue.

Profit measures the extent to which revenues from selling a product over some time period exceed the costs incurred in producing it.

Improving profits

A survey by The Royal Bank of Scotland revealed that over 25 per cent of small businesses said that increasing profits was their 'main objective'. There are a number of methods that a business can use to achieve this aim.

1. Reduce costs of production

This is perhaps the first consideration of many managers when considering how to increase profits. If a business can maintain its prices while reducing its costs of production then profit margins will increase. So long as sales do not decline, its profits will rise. However, there are a number of risks in taking this action. First, the reduction in costs may result in lower quality goods or services being supplied. This could result in a loss of customers, which could prove counterproductive and ultimately reduce profits.

In 2014, Heineken, one of the UK's best-known brewers, announced that it was moving some of its operations from Scotland to Poland with the loss of 93 jobs. The company will be able to take advantage of substantially lower wage rates in Poland. However, these job losses have resulted in some adverse publicity for the company.

2. Increase prices

The other obvious option is to increase the price at which the business sells its products. An increase in revenue per unit with costs stable will boost profit margins. However, this is a risky option as an increase in price may lead to existing customers seeking alternative suppliers and potential new customers looking elsewhere. The success of this decision depends on the importance of price in the decision to purchase and thus on price elasticity of demand. The manager of a luxury hotel may be able to increase prices for accommodation and food with little effect on sales. In contrast, a small city-centre cafe may find a high proportion of its customers move elsewhere if prices are raised.

Business in focus: Wearable technology improves productivity

Figure 19.1 Participants in the study wear the Neurosky MindWave to track brain activity while they are working

Wearable technologies such as fitness bands and motion monitors can significantly increase employees' productivity in the workplace, according to a study. Researchers from Goldsmiths, University of London, studied the effect of wearable devices on workers' productivity and job satisfaction over a one-month period.

The findings of the Human Cloud at Work (HCAW) research revealed that employee productivity was boosted by 8.5 per cent, while job satisfaction improved by 3.5 per cent. 'Wearable technologies are arguably the biggest trend since tablet computing, so it's natural that employees and businesses will look to use these devices in the workplace,' said lead researcher Dr Chris Brauer.

Participants in the study wore Neurosky MindWave brain activity sensors, GENEActiv motion monitors and the Lumo Back posture coach to assess employee behaviour and allow them to improve upon it.

Additional findings also revealed that 29 per cent of UK firms and 63 per cent of US firms are undertaking some form of wearable technology project and that less than 5 per cent of employees raised concerns about wearing the devices.

The location, temperature and even mood data gathered from wearable technology in the workplace could potentially provide important insights into improving not only the worker's performance, but the overall efficiency of a company.

Source: *International Business Times*, 1 May 2014

www.ibtimes.co.uk/wearable-tech-improves-efficiency-workplace-1446949

Questions

1. Explain the possible financial benefits a business might receive from the productivity of its employees increasing by 8.5 per cent.

2. Assess the case for a multinational company requiring its employees to use wearable technology in all aspects of its operations.

Northern Rail introduced changes to its pricing structure in September 2014 that resulted in some fares during the evening period rising substantially. The decision resulted in claims that ticket prices could double. The company has received adverse publicity and the impact of the change on passenger numbers remains to be seen.

What do you think?

How much of a risk is it for a rail company to increase its ticket prices by a substantial amount?

3. Improve the business's efficiency

An efficient business uses a minimal amount of resources to produce its goods or services. Managers can take a number of decisions to increase the efficiency of their businesses and thereby reduce costs, with positive implications for profits.

4. Use capacity more fully

A business's capacity is the maximum amount that it can produce. If this capacity is used fully then the business's fixed costs are spread across more units of output, helping to reduce average cost. If prices are unchanged profits should rise as the business's profit margin per unit will rise. At the same time, more of the business's products are sold without incurring too many additional costs. This should increase revenue and profits.

Figure 19.2 A Jetstream 41 aircraft

Many small UK airlines operate Jetstream 41 aircraft, which can hold a maximum of 29 passengers. Profits from operating these aircraft can be increased if the aircraft is full, or nearly full, on flights. In this context a full aircraft means that the airline is using its capacity as fully as possible. The costs of operating a full aircraft are only a little higher (some additional fuel and meals) and more passenger fares will increase revenue.

5. Reduce the number of substandard products

If a business produces products that are not of the right quality, then it incurs additional costs. This is because it has paid to produce goods that it cannot sell. These must either be scrapped or reworked to make them saleable. In either case, costs rise. Any management decisions (for example, training employees to monitor quality) that help to reduce the number of poor-quality products will help to reduce costs of production and enhance profitability.

6. Improve methods of production

Decisions to improve the efficiency of the production process can help to reduce costs and to improve profitability. On the island of Jersey, a number of businesses have been encouraged by the island's government to recycle cooking oil for use to fuel vehicles. This helps to reduce disposal costs of the oil, as well as reducing expenditure on petrol or diesel.

7. Eliminating unprofitable aspects of production

A business can take decisions to close down certain aspects of its operations that are making a loss. This can lead to increased profits for the remaining parts of the enterprise as the business uses its resources in the most efficient manner. La Senza, a lingerie retailer, revealed in July 2014 that it is to close 12 stores with the loss of 130 jobs as it seeks to improve its profitability.

Study tip

Increasing profits illustrates how decisions by managers responsible for finance link with the work of managers responsible for other functional areas within a business. Figure 19.3 shows the actions that can be taken across the business to increase profits. You should look to consider all aspects of a business when tackling questions on this topic.

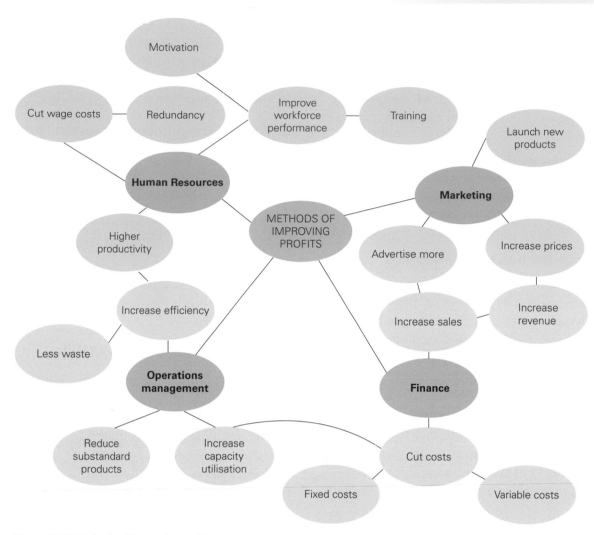

Figure 19.3 Methods of improving profits

Taking actions to improve profitability

Not all actions intended to increase profits will increase profitability and vice versa. For example, a decision to increase prices is likely to increase a business's profitability as it will probably result in a higher percentage of the selling price of a product being profit. However, if demand is price elastic it may result in a fall in overall profits. We saw earlier that Northern Rail has increased its early evening fares substantially. This action is likely to increase its profitability. The company will probably enjoy increased profits as well as profitability from this price rise as it does not face any direct competition and therefore demand for its services is likely to be price inelastic.

Most actions intended to cut costs have the potential to increase profits and profitability so long as the action does not reduce the value the consumer receives from the product. So, actions to reduce a company's waste should increase profits and profitability as they are unlikely to have adverse consequences for consumers.

Difficulties in improving cash flow and profit

Managers can face a number of difficulties when attempting to improve a business's performance in terms of cash flow and profits:

- identifying that there is a problem. This is not always simple to do in a timely fashion. It may take a business several months to uncover a cash flow problem, for example, especially if cash budgets are not carefully monitored.
- researching the cause of the problem. Identifying that there is a problem is the first difficulty. In many cases the management team will have

to research the cause before being able to take appropriate action. If a company suffers a large and sudden fall in sales and thus profits it may have to invest in primary market research to discover the reasons for the decline in consumer interest. This may be a rival offering similar products more cheaply or may be because its products are considered unfashionable. Once the cause is known suitable remedial action can be taken.

- coping with any adverse consequences in terms of the image of the business. Some decisions to improve cash flow or profits can have undesirable consequences. Heineken's decision to move some of its operations from Scotland to Poland has resulted in the loss of nearly 100 jobs. This is likely to have harmed the company's image, especially in the area where the redundancies occur.

- some decisions may have adverse consequences in the short term. A business may decide to invest more heavily in advertising to boost sales and improve profits. However, in the short term the increased cost of promotion may damage its profits until sales begin to rise.

In addition each method we have discussed to improve a business's cash flow or profits and profitability has particular difficulties associated with it. These are summarised in Tables 19.2 and 19.3.

Method of improving cash flow	Associated difficulties
Improved control of working capital	• The employment of additional staff to oversee the control will increase costs. • Customers may object to being pressured to pay and buy elsewhere.
Negotiate improved terms for trade credit	• This may be difficult for a firm with a poor payment record to achieve. • Discounts for prompt payment may be lost reducing profit margins.
Offer less trade credit	• Customers may move to other businesses offering more favourable trade credit terms. • Prices may have to be lowered in compensation.
Debt factoring	• Use of this technique can reduce profit margins by up to 5 per cent. • Customers may be unsettled by the realisation that a supplier is having cash flow difficulties.
Arrange short-term borrowing	• This can be expensive, especially if an overdraft is used. • The lender may gain some control over the business, either through holding collateral or by being able to withdraw credit at short notice.
Sale and leaseback	• The business may not receive a good price for the asset, especially if it is under pressure to sell it. • The business is committed to paying a rental on the asset permanently, which may reduce profits and impact on long-term cash flow.

Table 19.2 Difficulties associated with techniques to improve cash flow

Method of improving profits	Associated difficulties
Reduce costs of production	• This may result in lower-quality products if cheaper materials or less skilled employees are used. • It may entail redundancies upsetting customers and making it difficult to attract high-quality candidates in the future.
Increase prices	• May reduce sales and revenue substantially if demand is price elastic. • May result in criticism, particularly if the product is essential.
Improve efficiency	• May involve replacing labour with technology leading to redundancies. • May lose personal touch and lead to more standardised products.
Use capacity more fully	• May require a price cut, reducing revenue to some extent. • May be difficult to manage supply effectively to match demand, especially if it fluctuates.
Reduce the number of substandard products	• May require additional expenditure on employees or technology to identify faulty products. • May require more expensive inputs, increasing costs.
Improve methods of production	• This approach might require an investment in technology increasing the business's capital expenditure. • Staff training costs may increase in the short and long term.
Eliminate unprofitable aspects of production	• Possibility of redundancies resulting, with adverse publicity. • It may be difficult in some businesses to identify unprofitable aspects of production.

Table 19.3 Difficulties associated with techniques to improve profits and profitability

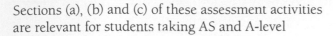

ASSESSMENT ACTIVITIES

Sections (a), (b) and (c) of these assessment activities are relevant for students taking AS and A-level examinations. The questions in section (d) are for A-level students only.

(a) Knowledge check questions

1   Is the following statement true or false? 'Drawing up detailed cash flow forecasts eliminates all risks of cash flow problems.'

2   State two factors that may cause a business to encounter cash flow problems.

3   What is meant by the term 'sale and leaseback'?

4   State one consequence of a business offering its customers less favourable terms for trade credit.

5   State two possible implications for a business of using debt factoring to improve its cash flow position.

6   Is the following statement true or false? 'An increase in price will always increase a business's profits.'

7   What is the difference between profits and profitability?

8   State two reasons why using capacity more fully should increase a business's profits.

9   State two difficulties a manager may face as a consequence of reducing costs of production to increase a business's profits.

10   State two general difficulties managers might encounter when implementing actions intended to improve cash flow or profits.

(b) Short answer questions

1   Explain how monitoring cash flow might help a rapidly expanding business to avoid cash flow crises.   (4 marks)

2   Explain how decisions on terms for trade credit may affect the cash position of a large and very competitive furniture retailer.   (5 marks)

3   Explain how effective management of cash flow might improve a business's profit margin. (5 marks)

4   Explain how a hotel chain might improve its profitability by using its capacity more fully.   (6 marks)

(c) Data response questions

Helix plc manufactures a range of components for high-technology products such as tablets and smartphones and is one of the largest firms in the industry. The company has its headquarters in London (which are valued at £95 million), but much of its manufacturing is carried out in Vietnam and Thailand. The company wishes to raise £125 million to finance expansion in Cambodia and to allow it to close its UK factories. This is forecast to lower its costs by 20 per cent and is judged essential to improve the company's very low overall profit margin of 1.9 per cent: some of its products have negative profit margins. It is considering taking advantage of the property boom in London by selling its offices and leasing them back again. Much of its capital has been raised through the sale of shares and it has low levels of borrowing.

The company supplies many major technology companies including Samsung and is noted for its price competitiveness in return for prompt payment. Helix plc's customers appreciate the quality of its products as well as its reliability. Demand for its products is surprisingly price inelastic. It places very large orders with its own suppliers and benefits from its scale.

1   Explain why a sale and leaseback deal might improve Helix plc's cash flow position but weaken its profitability.   (6 marks)

2   Analyse the possible reasons why Helix plc has a relatively strong cash flow position.   (9 marks)

3   Should Helix plc improve its profitability by moving production from the UK to Cambodia? Justify your opinion.   (15 marks)

(d) Essays

1   Any actions taken by an SME (small or medium-sized enterprise) to improve its cash position will inevitably damage its profitability. Do you agree? Justify your view.   (25 marks)

2   To what extent is price elasticity of demand likely to be the major factor determining whether a fashion clothing retailer's price cuts will improve its profitability?   (25 marks)

Case study: Unit 5 Decision making to improve financial performance

Voltaic plc announces new factory in Vietnam

The market

The market for manufacturing solar panels in the UK is subject to a number of influences. Demand is generally rising as an increasing number of solar panel farms are established and households and businesses are investing in their own source of renewable energy. IKEA, a retailer, has reacted to this growth by deciding to stock solar panels in all its UK stores and has 500,000 panels for sale in its shops worldwide. The UK Government offers a subsidy to those installing solar panels to encourage the expansion of renewable energy generation, although it has announced proposals to radically cut subsidies paid to encourage the development of solar farms. Demand for panels is thought to be price elastic.

The solar panel manufacturing industry is increasingly competitive with suppliers in Asia proving very efficient. There has been a series of takeovers in the industry with companies buying smaller rivals to gain market share. Prices for solar panels in Europe fell by 30 per cent over the past year and are expected to continue to decline slowly over the next few years. This decline in price may be accelerated if the latest research is converted into saleable products. Researchers at Liverpool University have replaced cadmium chloride, a toxic substance, in the production of panels with the much cheaper magnesium chloride. This development could make solar panels less expensive, more flexible and easier to use.

The world economy's recovery from the financial crisis is patchy and demand in markets in the UK and Europe for products such as solar panels has not risen as strongly as was forecast. Furthermore, interest rates in the UK are forecast to rise over the next few years, which may have a negative impact on consumers' spending power. However, economists have argued that, despite the expected rises, interest rates will remain very low by historical standards for the foreseeable future and inflation rates are also forecast to be low and stable.

The company

Voltaic plc manufactures a range of electronic products but its division that makes solar panels is its largest. It has grown quickly since 2010 and has financed much of its growth through loan capital; currently about 40 per cent of its capital has been raised through loans agreed with its bank and other organisations. Investors have been nervous about the company's financial performance at times, however, fearing it was at risk of overtrading.

Other aspects of the company's financial performance have caused concern for some of its stakeholders. In particular its operating profit margin at 6.4 per cent has been low in comparison to some other companies in the same market. One consequence of this has been that Voltaic plc's dividend payments have been low, leading to complaints from a vocal group of shareholders seeking short-term returns.

Its solar panels are forecast to sell for an average price of £5,500 next year, though this could alter as the market is changing, complex and difficult to predict.

The expansion plan

The company's management team believes that there is considerable long-term potential in the market for solar panels in Europe as well as the UK. It wishes to increase its production capacity. Voltaic plc's management team has developed a plan to open a new factory in Tuy Hoa, a coastal town in Vietnam, which will initially only manufacture solar panels. Typical monthly wage costs in Vietnam are about £100 a month, one-third of those in China and approximately 10 per cent of the company's UK pay rates. The new factory will operate alongside the company's existing solar panel factory in North Wales, although trade unions believe the jobs should be created in the UK and not overseas.

The company needs £74 million to finance the plan for the factory in Tuy Hoa and the director of finance has recommended that £58 million of this is raised by the sale of shares in the company. This will increase the total share capital of the company by 11 per cent.

Annual fixed costs	£4,500,000
Labour cost per solar panel	£875
Materials costs per solar panel	£2,900
Other variable costs per solar panel	£1,625
Production capacity	120,000 panels

Table 1 Financial data for the Vietnamese factory for its first year of production

AS questions

(50 marks)

1   Calculate the level of output required for the new factory in Vietnam to break even in its first year of production.   (5 marks)

2   Analyse the importance to Voltaic plc of setting cash flow objectives.   (10 marks)

3   To what extent do you agree with the company's decision to finance its expansion primarily through the sale of shares?   (15 marks)

4   Do you agree with the finance director's view that break-even analysis is of little value in judging the financial performance of the new factory in Vietnam?   (20 marks)

A-level questions

(70 marks)

1   Analyse the possible influences on Voltaic plc's capital structure targets following its expansion.
                                              (10 marks)

2   Assess the value of setting financial objectives to Voltaic plc.   (15 marks)

3   To what extent do you think that a decision to open a factory in Tuy Hoa will improve the financial performance of Voltaic plc?   (20 marks)

4   Is reducing costs always the best way for a business to improve its profits? Justify your view.   (25 marks)

Unit 6

Decision making to improve human resource performance

Chapter 20

Setting human resource objectives

Introduction

This chapter is the first of four that consider how managers can take decisions to improve a business's human resource (HR) performance. It also is the first element of the decision-making process in relation to human resource issues: deciding what HR objectives a business should pursue. Later chapters in this unit will look at the subsequent stages in the HR decision-making process such as analysing HR performance and taking HR decisions.

What you need to know by the end of this chapter:

- the value of setting human resource objectives
- internal and external influences on human resource objectives and decisions.

A business's human resource (HR) function or department is responsible for the use of labour within the organisation. Human resource management (or HRM) views activities relating to the workforce as integrated and vital in helping the organisation to achieve its overall or corporate objectives. People are viewed as an important resource to be developed through training. Thus, policies relating to recruitment, pay and appraisal, for example, should be part of a co-ordinated approach to human resources. HRM is an all-embracing integrated approach that aims to make the best use of human resources in relation to the business's overall objectives.

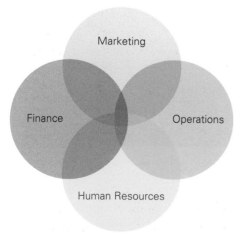

Figure 20.1 The functions of business

The value of human resource objectives

Human resource objectives are the goals or targets that a business's HR function or department seeks to achieve. The achievement of these targets should assist the business in attaining its overall corporate objectives. Tesco plc, the UK's largest retailer, has a vision statement which includes the aim of being 'a growing business full of opportunities.' The company's human resource function has set itself a number of objectives to allow the business to achieve its objective. For example, it had provided training to 250,000 staff by 2014, which allowed them to take advantage of the opportunities offered through employment with Tesco.

It is normal for HR objectives to contain a specific numerical element and also a timescale within which they are to be achieved. The HR target will be set by the managers responsible for human resources in the business, but will be consistent with other functional objectives and also contribute to the achievement of the business's overall or corporate objectives. Thus the management team at Tesco believes that having a well-trained workforce will aid it in fulfilling its vision of growth.

Businesses can derive great benefits from setting human resource objectives. It is one way in which managers and owners are able to judge the performance of an enterprise. It may be that managers set objectives relating to the amount employees produce each week, the quality of their work or to the feedback ratings received from customers. Such objectives can provide a target for managers and employees and can help to improve performance, especially if monetary or other rewards are offered for achieving the goals. It is possible to set HR objectives in relation to any measurable aspect of employee performance and to use these as a means of motivation.

Further, by comparing the actual performance of the business's workforce against these objectives it is possible for managers to assess the achievements of the workforce and to provide guidance on further actions that may need to be taken. In later chapters in this unit we will look further at how to analyse performance and the actions that can be taken subsequently to improve the performance of an organisation's employees.

Human resource objectives are also valuable to managers because many businesses are judged by customers on the basis of employee performance. By setting challenging but fair HR objectives, managers can set a standard for employee performance which will meet the needs and expectations of customers, who are a vital stakeholder group. It also helps the business's image if it is seen to have high and clear expectations of its employees and this can result in favourable publicity. One reason for the success of the John Lewis Partnership (which operates 42 department stores and 325 Waitrose supermarkets) is that customers value the knowledge and skills of the retailer's employees. Setting demanding objectives in terms of employee performance, involvement and training helped the business to achieve sales in excess of £9 billion for the first time in 2014.

Finally, the use of human resource objectives enables managers to identify those aspects of the performance of the business at the earliest possible stage that are causing problems. If particular divisions or parts of a business are failing to meet objectives for productivity, training or for developing the most talented employees it is possible to take suitable corrective action. Without objectives the diagnosis of the problem may be delayed until sales declined or customers decided to purchase products elsewhere. Such a delay in identifying the problem could result in the business suffering greater harm.

Employee performance is an important competitive weapon for many UK businesses that sell services. In hotels, restaurants, railways, airlines and shops, customers interact regularly with employees and the value they receive from buying the service will be determined to a great extent by employee performance.

Thus, those businesses whose employees provide better service to customers will offer greater value and may be able to charge higher prices and to use the **quality** of their service as a unique selling point (USP). A key element of achieving high standards of employee performance is to set clear HR objectives that ensure the business has the right number of suitably skilled and engaged employees in the right places and having values that accord with those of the business.

Types of human resource objectives

There are a number of HR objectives, the importance of which will vary according to the type of business, its products and the market in which it is trading.

> ### Key terms
>
>
>
> **Labour productivity** measures the output of a firm in relation to its number of employees.
>
> **Quality** is the extent to which a product meets customers' needs.

1. Labour productivity

Managers may set human resource objectives relating to the quantity of products that employees should produce, on average, over a specific time period. Such objectives may be more common in manufacturing and construction industries where it is more straightforward to measure the output of an individual employee, although they can be used widely. A BBC report in 2013 into working practices at the online retailer Amazon revealed that workers were expected to collect material for orders every 33 seconds. The attraction of setting **labour productivity** objectives is that it can assist businesses in controlling costs. If employees are efficient and produce a large number of units of output in a working day, the costs of producing an average unit will be controlled, enhancing the business's price competitiveness. We look at labour productivity more fully in Chapter 21.

2. The number and location of the business's workforce

It is normal for the labour needs of a business to change over time. A business might grow, move overseas, replace employees with technology or take decisions to produce new products. Each of these actions may mean that the business will require a different workforce. Technology-based businesses in London and the south east of England are expanding quickly as demand for their services rises. This growth is forecast to lead to the companies requiring an additional 46,000 employees by 2024. A number of high-profile technology companies have moved their operations to London, or have expanded existing workforces, as shown in the Business in Focus feature about Facebook.

Meeting this objective is essential because the business needs to have sufficient employees to ensure that it can meet the needs of its customers and to provide the best-quality goods or services possible. Having a workforce of the correct size and in the right place also assists the business in providing high-quality customer service. Ensuring that the business has the right number of employees to meet its customers' needs can be challenging for businesses that face seasonal demand and can be an important HR objective.

For example, the Royal Mail requires additional employees at certain times of the year such as Christmas, when demand for postal services is much higher. As a consequence one of the company's HR objectives will be to have a flexible workforce that can meet the changing demands of its customers. Fulfilling this objective requires ongoing action on the part of the company's HR function.

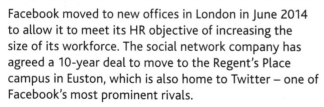

Study tip

Remember that HR objectives that are decided by a business's HR managers have to support the business in the achievement of its overall or corporate objectives. HR objectives can often be understood and their relevance judged in the light of the business's corporate objectives.

Developments in technology have had an impact on HR objectives in terms of location. Some businesses have opted to have a proportion of their employees teleworking. According to the UK Government, teleworking is an arrangement that allows an employee to conduct work during any part of regular, paid hours at an approved alternative worksite. This is feasible for many industries because electronic communications makes it possible for employees to communicate effectively with customers, colleagues and other stakeholders. Statistics from the Labour Force Survey suggest that the proportion of workers who work mainly at or from home in the UK has grown from 11.1 per cent in 2001 to 13.7 per cent in 2012. This trend is shown in Figure 20.2.

Business in focus: Facebook expands in London

Facebook moved to new offices in London in June 2014 to allow it to meet its HR objective of increasing the size of its workforce. The social network company has agreed a 10-year deal to move to the Regent's Place campus in Euston, which is also home to Twitter – one of Facebook's most prominent rivals.

The move will enable the company to expand its London workforce from 250 to 500. Nicola Mendelsohn, responsible for Facebook's British operations, said: 'Our new home will give us the space to double the number of people working at Facebook London and build on what we've achieved there over the past few years, including the only Facebook Engineering Centre in Europe.'

The number of UK users of Facebook has risen strongly over recent years. The company receives 26 million visitors daily, with users checking the website an average of 14 times each day. The company's HR managers have sought to hire software engineers and platform service

engineers to develop new apps. In part the expansion is due to Facebook's purchase of Parse. Parse provides cloud computing services allowing companies to develop software without using technology such as servers.

Facebook is reported to pay its software engineers in London annual salaries in the range of £49,000 to £150,000.

Source: *The Daily Telegraph*, 7 November 2013

www.telegraph.co.uk/technology/facebook/10433760/Facebook-to-double-London-staff.html

Questions

1. Explain how setting an HR objective of increased employment to meet demand might affect decisions by the finance function at Facebook.

2. To what extent is it particularly important for technology companies such as Facebook to set HR objectives?

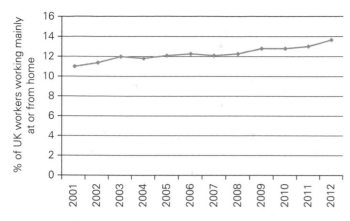

Figure 20.2 The proportion of UK workers working mainly at home, 2001–2012

Source: Office for National Statistics, Labour Force Survey

www.gov.uk/government/uploads/system/uploads/attachment_data/file/274633/UK_Broadband_Impact_Study_-_Baseline_Report_-_Jan_2014_-_Final.pdf

Permission for re-use of all © Crown copyright information is granted under the terms of the Open Government Licence (OGL).

What do you think?

Only about 14 per cent of employees in the UK work at home. Why don't all business try to benefit from technological developments and set an HR objective of having 33 per cent of employees working at home?

3. Employee engagement and involvement

There are numerous definitions of **employee engagement**. The Chartered Institute of Personnel and Development (CIPD) has defined employee engagement as 'being positively present during the performance of work by willingly contributing intellectual effort, experiencing positive emotions and meaningful connections to others.'

Key terms

Employee engagement describes the connection between a business's employees and its mission, goals and objectives.

Employee involvement exists in a business in which people are able to have an impact on decisions and actions that affect their working lives.

The CIPD believes that this definition gives three dimensions to employee engagement:

- intellectual engagement – thinking hard about the job and how to do it better

- affective engagement – feeling positively about doing a good job
- social engagement – actively taking opportunities to discuss work-related improvements with others at work.

Research by the CIPD and other organisations globally has shown that businesses benefit from having engaged employees in terms of improved performance. There is a positive relationship between how people are managed, employee attitudes and the business's performance.

Weblink

Find out more about the Chartered Institute of Personnel and Development (CIPD) and its work at: www.cipd.co.uk/

Employee involvement as an objective seeks to enable employees to contribute to the continuous improvement and performance of the business in which they are employed. Employee involvement is sometimes referred to as 'employee voice' and is normally management initiated. It can take a variety of forms.

- **Considering employees' ideas and opinions**. This can be achieved by using two-way communication channels or by establishing systems for employees to express their voice. The communication is directly between managers and employees. This may simply be the use of suggestions schemes or regular meetings between managers and employees to gather employees' opinions. Technological developments, especially in electronic media, have made this a simpler process and communication often takes place through email.
- **Employee representatives**. This type of employee involvement can occur through the appointment of employee directors or managers to provide the 'employee voice' on decision-making bodies or through employee forums where managers brief employees on matters of importance and invite feedback.

HR objectives in the areas of employee involvement and engagement are intended to improve the performance of employees and hence the business. They are also more likely to be set by managers and leaders who take a democratic view of leadership and take a 'soft' approach to human resource management (HRM). We look more fully at different approaches to HRM later in this chapter.

4. Training

Improving the work-related skills and knowledge of employees can be an effective way of improving employee performance. Many businesses have learning and development policies for their workforces in which **training** plays a central role. Learning and development policies set out the workforce capabilities, skills or competencies required, and how these can be developed, to ensure a sustainable, successful organisation. These can be a vital element of a business's HR objectives.

Key term

Training is a process whereby an employee gains job-related skills and knowledge.

Training is an important activity for UK businesses and research by the CIPD reveals that an average of £303 per employee per year was spent on training in 2013. Although setting targets for training as an HR objective can add to a business's costs it can provide a range of benefits. It can result in improved employee performance and can assist businesses in attracting the most talented and motivated employees. This can be particularly important for businesses in the service sector where employee performance can be a vital determinant of the business's performance and can provide a unique selling point.

Rapid developments in technology may mean that training as an HR objective has relevance for more businesses. The BBC offers more than 700 training courses to its employees, in part to ensure they are up to date with technological developments in broadcasting and the media.

5. Talent development

Talent development is different from training in that it focuses on fulfilling the potential of employees with the ability and potential to shape the business's future performance. Thus, some managers may believe that continued success for an organisation depends on its ability to retain these employees and to manage and develop their talents in the most effective manner.

The business case for setting talent development objectives is very strong. Many chief executives and senior HR managers have talent development and management as key priorities. Research has revealed that the increased interest in talent has arisen for a number of reasons. These include:

- overcoming the pressures of succeeding in increasingly competitive global markets
- coping with shortages of certain skilled employees
- growing need for highly specialist and creative employees.

The School of Management at Cranfield University operates a talent development programme for employees of other businesses. This includes modules on accelerating managerial performance and continuing development review. Businesses send employees on talent management courses to improve their performance and to provide a supply of able employees for promotion from within the business.

Key term

Talent development refers to the development and guidance of outstanding or star employees who have the potential to make a major contribution to an organisation's performance and success.

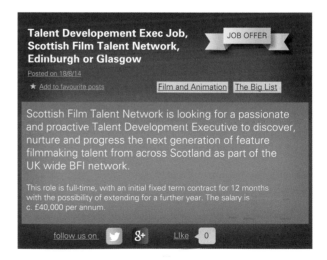

Figure 20.3 A job advert for a manager responsible for talent development. Talent development is an important HR objective for businesses in many industries including those who rely on creative abilities such as the film industry.

Source: Media Nation

www.medianation.co.uk/the-big-list/film-animation/talent-development-executive-job-scottish-film-talent-network-edinburgh-or-glasgow

6. Diversity

Businesses that have **diversity** as an HR objective will aim to treat people as individuals and will value the benefits that diverse individuals and groups in a workplace may offer to a business. Employee diversity could be based upon gender, race and ethnicity, disability, religion, sexuality, class and age.

Many organisations implement HR objectives for equality alongside those for diversity. Policies related to equality are intended to create a fairer society where all employees can contribute and fulfil their potential. One key aspect of this is to operate policies that allow all employees the opportunity to reach senior positions in a business, irrespective of their age, gender, ethnicity or sexual orientation. This is necessary as many minority groups are under-represented in senior positions in businesses, and this means that the skills and abilities of such employees are wasted.

Key term

Diversity, in an employment context, refers to recognising the differences between individual employees and also the differences that may exist between different groups of employees.

A number of governments have enacted employment legislation to ensure that businesses design and implement policies for diversity and equality. For example, the UK Government passed the Equalities Act in 2010. This offered protection to employees against:

- direct and indirect discrimination
- harassment
- victimisation.

Business in focus: Equality and diversity at the University of Cambridge

The University of Cambridge is one of the most famous universities in the world. It was founded in 1209 and has over 9,000 staff and 18,000 students from countries throughout the world.

The University of Cambridge is committed in its pursuit of academic excellence to equality of opportunity and to a proactive and inclusive approach to equality, which supports and encourages all under-represented groups, promotes an inclusive culture, and values diversity. The commitment applies to all protected groups and is underpinned by the University's Equal Opportunities Policy and Combined Equality Scheme (CES).

In recognition of the University's commitment to progressing equality and diversity, it has received awards from Stonewall, enei (the Employers' Network for Equality and Inclusion) and the Equality Challenge Unit's Athena Swan Charter.

Figures 20.4 a, b and c Stonewall's Top 100 Employers Award, enei and Bronze Athena Swan Charter logos

A new version of the E&D Essential online training module has been launched. It includes an introduction from the Vice-Chancellor and aims to help staff understand the main principles of equality and diversity, its impacts on the University and how members of staff and students can access support and other resources.

The module, which can be accessed on a variety of platforms, including tablets and laptops, is Cambridge-specific and takes about 30 minutes to complete.

Source: University of Cambridge website

www.admin.cam.ac.uk/offices/hr/equality/

Questions

1. Explain how training might assist the University in establishing equality and diversity as an HR objective.

2. To what extent might the benefits of the University of Cambridge's Equality and Diversity policy outweigh its costs?

The Act identifies a number of 'protected characteristics'. These are age, disability, gender reassignment, marriage and civil partnership, pregnancy and maternity, race, religion or belief, gender and sexual orientation.

The effect of legislation of this type is to encourage businesses to design and implement policies intended to encourage diversity and to promote equality.

Setting HR objectives for equality and diversity offers benefits to businesses. Drawing on all people within the local community when recruiting offers the best opportunity to employ the most talented employees, which will enhance the performance of the business. Similarly, promoting the most able employees, regardless of personal characteristics, secures the greatest level of talent for the business. Any other approach is likely to harm the business.

Establishing HR objectives to promote diversity can also bring benefit to the business. A diverse workforce may allow the business to understand the needs of a market, which may be comprised of diverse consumers.

This will assist the organisation in meeting the needs of its consumers more effectively. A business that acquires a reputation for operating an effective diversity and equality policy may become an attractive employer to potential employees. This process is called 'employer branding' and can help businesses to attract highly talented and skilled employees, whatever their personal characteristics.

7. Alignment of values

The American social psychologist Milton Rokeach defined an organisational value as 'a belief that a specific mode of conduct is preferable to an opposite or contrary mode of conduct'. Such values are sometimes referred to as 'core values'. An employee's core values will underpin the way they behave and influence the decisions that they make.

A business's core values should remain relatively unchanged over time and can provide a reference point for decisions made by managers as they respond to competitors' actions and other changes in the business's external environment. They can assist a business in establishing and maintaining a competitive advantage.

Business in focus: Sainsbury's values

Our five values provide the framework for how we do business at Sainsbury's. They guide us in everything we do – from key business decisions to day-to-day activities. Our values are part of what make us different from other supermarkets, so we see this as a strength, as well as a responsibility. In recent years we've transformed our business, and our five values have been integral to our success, drawing from our 144-year heritage. They are:

1. Best for food and health

We serve over 23 million customers each week and play a key role in helping them Live Well For Less. Being best for food and health involves making it economical and easy for our customers to enjoy a healthier, balanced lifestyle, providing specialist health services and promoting activity.

2. Sourcing with integrity

Consumers put their trust in us to do the right thing throughout our buying process, so sourcing with integrity is key in our dealings with farmers, growers and suppliers in the UK and around the world.

3. Respect for our environment

The scale of our business means we can make a massive difference by ensuring respect for our environment is embedded in our decision making. We aim to be the UK's greenest grocer and look to act sustainably, address climate change and conserve resources.

4. Making a positive difference to our community

We want to make a positive difference to the communities we're part of. With over 1,100 stores across the UK, 21 depots and 3 store support centres employing 157,000 colleagues, we set out to get involved and be a good neighbour.

5. A great place to work

Our success rests upon the 161,000 colleagues working in our stores, depots and offices who provide great service to our customers every day. Motivated, involved and engaged colleagues are fundamental to our continued success. We're committed to giving people the opportunity to be the best they can be.

Source: J Sainsbury plc's website

www.j-sainsbury.co.uk/responsibility/our-values/

Questions

1. Explain why 'motivated, involved and engaged colleagues are fundamental' to Sainsbury's continued success.

2. J. Sainsbury plc promotes its core values on its website. Do you think that it is more important for the company to publicise these values than to have them as an objective for all its employees to follow? Justify your view.

Core values support the business in attempting to fulfil its vision. For example, the core values of J. Sainsbury plc, set out in the Business in Focus feature, will guide the company's decision-makers in fulfilling its vision of 'being the [UK's] most trusted retailer where people love to work and shop'.

However, having and publicising core values is of little value to a business unless its employees hold similar values and therefore act and take decisions in the 'right' way. If a business sets an HR objective of aligning its employees' values with its own, through training and communication, it will assist the business in ensuring that its vision is pursued. Stakeholders will also see how the business's values are reflected in its decision making. This can reinforce the business's identity with its stakeholders and lead to the maintenance of customer loyalty. It will also help the business to attract suitable staff (with similar values) as potential employees are likely to research any likely employers as part of their application process.

Influences on human resource objectives and decisions

Managers responsible for human resources are subject to influences from inside the business as well as external factors when deciding on the objectives for their department and in taking decisions that relate to the management of human resources.

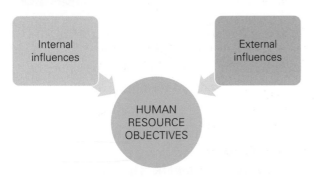

Figure 20.5 Influences on human resource objectives

Internal influences on HR objectives and decisions

Several internal factors may influence a business's decisions relating to human resources, including which HR objectives to adopt.

- **Corporate or overall objectives.** As with all functional objectives, those set by the HR

department must assist the organisation in achieving its overall objectives. Thus, if the business has a corporate objective of maximising long-term profits, the HR objective might set itself objectives concerned with reducing labour costs or making the most effective use of the workforce. The low-cost airline Flybe implemented a 'turnaround plan' of reducing costs and thereby remaining highly competitive in its particular market niche. In November 2013 it announced 500 redundancies to reduce its workforce to 2,200 employees and to save approximately £26 million annually.

Maths moment

Use the information on Flybe's costs in the paragraph above to answer the following questions.

(a) What was the average annual cost of employing one of the employees who is to be made redundant?

(b) Assume the employment costs of the 500 to be made redundant represent those of Flybe's entire workforce. What were the company's total labour costs before and after the redundancies?

- **Attitudes and beliefs of the senior managers.** The senior managers of a business can have an important influence on decisions relating to human resources. If they consider the workforce to be a valuable asset they may want a long-term relationship with employees and may set objectives such as developing the skills of the workforce to their fullest extent. Alternatively, they may see employees as an expendable asset to be hired when necessary and decide to pay the minimum rate possible. This can have considerable implications for the objectives that HR managers set and for the broader decisions that they take.

  There is not a single approach to human resource management (HRM). Different firms manage their human resources in different ways. These are summarised in Table 20.1.

- **'Hard' HR approach.** Some firms operate 'hard' HR policies, treating employees as a resource to be used optimally. Managers pursuing 'hard' HR policies regard employees as just another resource to be deployed as efficiently as possible in pursuit of strategic targets. Employees are obtained as cheaply as possible on short-term, zero-hour contracts.

	'Hard' HRM	'Soft' HRM
Philosophy	Employees a resource like any other available to the business	Sees employees as different, and more important, than any other resource available to managers
Time scale	HRM seen as a short-term policy: employees hired and fired as necessary	Takes a long-term view of using the workforce as efficiently as possible to achieve long-term corporate objectives
Key features	• Employees paid as little as possible • Employees only have limited control over working life • Communication mainly downward in direction • Employees recruited externally to fulfil human needs – giving short-term solution • Judgemental appraisal	• Managers consult with employees • Managers give control over working lives to employees through delayering and empowerment • Emphasis on training and developing employees • Employees promoted from within reflecting long-term desire to develop workforce • Developmental appraisal
Associated leadership style	Leaders operating this style of HRM more likely to be at the autocratic end of the spectrum of leadership	Leaders implementing 'soft' HRM more likely to be democratic in nature
Motivational techniques used	Probably mainly motivated by pay, with limited use of techniques such as delegation and teamworking	Delegation, empowerment. Heavy use of techniques designed to give employees more authority

Table 20.1 Approaches to human resource management

- **'Soft' HR approach.** Other firms use an HR system that is referred to as 'soft'. This approach is based on the notion that employees are the most valuable asset a business has and they should be developed to maximise their value to the organisation. This makes a long-term approach essential. Employees are seen as valuable resources and developed over time and in response to changing market conditions.

What do you think?

Will all businesses in the UK benefit in the long term from adopting a soft approach to managing their human resources?

- **Type of product.** If the product requires the commitment of a highly skilled labour force then objectives such as training and talent development may be most important. However, for businesses selling products which are mainly produced by machinery, and which require little in the way of skilled labour, minimising labour costs through having the fewest employees at any times may be a key HR objective. Some retailers with distinctive images (perhaps ethical) may focus on aligning the values of their workforces to those of the business as a prime HR objective because many of their staff have regular contact with customers and so the consequences of their 'values' are more apparent.

External influences on HR objectives and decisions

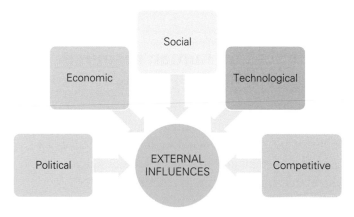

Figure 20.6 External influences on human resource objectives

External factors will have a significant impact on the decisions that are taken and the objectives that are set by HR managers.

- **The technological environment.** Advances in technology have had significant implications for managers responsible for HR. The effects can be separated into categories. Some developments have replaced labour. Many manufacturing businesses have opted to replace labour with technology as a means of strengthening competitiveness by reducing costs or by offering customers better service. Foxconn, the Asian manufacturer that makes many of Apple's products, announced in 2014 that it had an objective to replace up to 10,000 employees on the production line with robots. This decision may help Foxconn to retain the lucrative contracts to manufacture Apple's products. Technology has also changed working practices in other ways, such as allowing a steady increase in the proportion of employees working mainly from home. These changes will be reflected in the objectives pursued by HR managers.

Other developments in technology encourage the setting of HR objectives that may enhance customers' experiences. Online banking allows customers to have access to banking services at all times and book retailers are increasingly selling and distributing books online for use on e-readers. These developments may impact on HR objectives by, for example, increasing the importance of training and talent development to ensure that employees have the skills necessary to meet customers' needs in an increasingly technological environment.

- **The economic environment.** A growing or a declining market will have a significant impact on the HR objectives pursued by a business. Sales of many products have risen in the UK in recent times as the performance of the economy has begun to improve and wages have risen. In July 2014 unemployment in the UK fell to 2.02 million, 6.2 per cent of the workforce. These changes may have led HR managers to revise the number of employees that their businesses will require in the future as well as, possibly, their locations.

Asda, one of the UK's largest supermarkets, is implementing a five-year plan to develop 140 new supermarkets, 150 forecourt shops and 1,000 new click-and-collect points. This plan reflects a growing confidence by the company's managers in the state of the UK economy and, as it will create 12,000 new jobs by 2019, will have a significant impact on the business. It is likely to affect Asda's HR objectives in terms of skills and location of employees, training and talent development as well as the number of employees it plans to employ.

- **The social environment.** Ethical and environmental considerations are increasingly important for consumers in the UK. The market for ethical products in the UK grew by 12 per cent during 2012, according to research by *Ethical* consumer magazine. Many businesses respond positively to demands by consumers for ethical and environmentally friendly products and some seek to use this as a unique selling point.

Lush Retail Ltd is a private company that manufactures and sells hand-made cosmetics and is highly rated by UK consumers as an ethical business. It promotes its ethical stance, is strongly opposed to testing products on animals and will not buy supplies from companies that damage the environment. A key issue for HR managers at Lush will be to operate with HR objectives that align employees' values with those of the company and employee engagement and involvement.

Weblink

You can find out more about consumers in the UK and ethical issues by following the link below to the Ethical Consumer website.

www.ethicalconsumer.org

- **The competitive environment.** If competing businesses supply similar products, demand for a product is likely to be strongly price elastic (i.e. demand is very sensitive to price changes). In these circumstances it is more likely that a business will opt for HR objectives that allow it to reduce labour costs. This can be seen in the case of budget hotels. In 2013 the budget hotel provider, Travelodge, implemented a plan to divest itself of 49 less profitable hotels to reduce its debts and cut its costs. Reducing costs in this way would assist the company in remaining competitive against rivals such as Premier Inn. This decision had major implications for the company's HR objectives. However, if demand is price inelastic, a reduction in price is unlikely to lead to a substantial increase in sales and HR objectives may focus on issues other than costs.

- **The political environment.** The UK Government and EU authorities have passed a series of laws designed to protect labour in the workplace. The existence of such laws may encourage businesses to set HR objectives to develop the potential of their workforces as the law may make it difficult to hire and fire employees at will. In particular, a change in the law has an impact on the objectives that a HR department pursues. The Equalities Act (2010) offers protection to employees against discrimination, harassment and victimisation and has to be taken into account by managers when establishing HR objectives.

Business in focus: New diversity quotas possible for UK companies

Shadow Business Secretary Chuka Umunna has warned that unless there is progress in increasing diversity in the boardrooms of top British companies, Labour would consider introducing quotas if they win the 2015 general election.

This came after research by recruitment consultancy Green Park revealed a 'diversity deficit' amongst Britain's most important firms. The research looked at the backgrounds of 10,000 of the UK's most influential executives. It found that of the 289 people holding the roles of Chairman, CEO or CFO in FTSE 100 firms only 12 were women and only 10 were from an ethnic minority. Half of FTSE 100 companies have no non-white leaders at board level.

The study did indicate that there had been some progress in appointing ethnic minority and female

candidates as non-executive board members but progress for executive posts had been slower and the glass ceiling was still fully intact.

Chuka Umanna said: 'Increasing diversity adds to our international competitiveness as boards make better decisions where a range of voices drawing on different life experiences can be heard.'

Source: adapted from various news sources

Questions

1. Explain the possible benefits to large public companies of appointing more diverse teams of senior managers.

2. Do you think that the threat of legislation in this area is the most effective means of persuading UK companies to appoint more diverse teams of senior managers? Justify your view.

ASSESSMENT ACTIVITIES

Sections (a), (b) and (c) of these assessment activities are relevant for students taking AS and A-level examinations. The questions in section (d) are for A-level students only.

(a) Knowledge check questions

1 What is meant by the term human resource objective?

2 State two reasons why the number of employees needed by a business may change.

3 State the difference between employee involvement and employee engagement.

4 State two actions a business might take to fulfil an HR objective of employee involvement.

5 What is meant by the term talent development?

6 State two reasons why businesses have increasingly set an HR objective relating to talent development.

7 List three factors upon which employee diversity could be based.

8 Is the following statement true or false? 'An employee's core values will underpin the way they behave and influence the decisions that they make.'

9 Is the following statement true or false? 'The hard approach to HRM approach is based on the notion that employees are perhaps the most valuable asset a business has and they should be developed to maximise their value to the organisation.'

10 State two external factors that might influence a business's HR objectives.

(b) Short answer questions

1 Explain why an ethical retailer might set HR objectives to align its values and those of its employees.   (4 marks)

2 Explain the importance of setting HR objectives for talent development in large multi-national businesses.   (5 marks)

3 Explain how a soft approach to human resource management might influence the HR objectives set by a business. (5 marks)

4 Explain why a popular chain of fast-food restaurants may benefit from having clear HR objectives. (6 marks)

(c) Data response questions

Cargo plc is a car hire company that operates throughout the European Union. The market for car hire in the EU is extremely competitive and demand for smaller cars is more price elastic than for larger ones. Cargo plc is small in comparison to rivals such as Avis and Hertz and needs to establish and maintain a distinctive image to help it to be competitive. It operates 104 sites across the EU and demand for its services is seasonal and dependent upon the level of consumers' incomes. The company's sales have grown at an average rate of 19.4 per cent a year since 2012 and it focuses on hiring larger cars, luxury vehicles and 4x4s.

The company has set HR objectives for the number, skills and location of employees for some years, but a new senior director with responsibility for human resources has introduced a number of changes to the way employees are managed to support the company in achieving its overall objectives of growth. She is starting by establishing new HR objectives, focusing on training, talent development and alignment of values. These new HR objectives are expected to bring a number of benefits to the company, though

they are forecast to increase employment costs by 15 per cent within three years. Cargo plc has an overall objective of offering an improved service to its customers.

One of Cargo's rivals is ValueCar, a company noted for its very competitive prices. The major influence on the company's HR objectives and decision making is its 'hard' approach to managing its human resources. This has not always proved popular with the company's workforce. However, the company has a high market share in hiring smaller cars.

1 Explain why setting HR objectives for the number, skills and location of Cargo plc's employees continues to be important. (6 marks)

2 Analyse how ValueCar's hard approach to human resource management will affect the HR decisions taken by its management team. (9 marks)

3 To what extent might the setting of the new HR objectives for Cargo plc offer benefits that exceed the costs. (15 marks)

(d) Essays

1 The value of setting human resource objectives is greatest for businesses that sell high technology products such as tablets and computer software. To what extent do you agree with this statement? (25 marks)

2 Market conditions are always the most important factor influencing human resource decisions for small businesses. Do you agree with this view? Justify your decision. (25 marks)

Chapter

21

Analysing human resource performance

Introduction

This chapter continues our consideration of how managers can take decisions to improve a business's human resource performance. It looks at techniques that can be used to analyse workforce performance, such as calculating labour productivity and labour cost per unit, which might provide managers with crucial information to support the decision-making process. Subsequent chapters will consider the nature of human resource decisions that are taken by the managers of a business on the basis of this and other data.

What you need to know by the end of this chapter:

- how to calculate and interpret human resource data
- the use of data for human resource decision making and planning.

Calculating and interpreting human resource data

Before managers take decisions designed to improve the performance of a workforce it is important to analyse its current position. This analysis enables managers to take more informed, focused and effective decisions. If managers are dissatisfied with the overall performance of a workforce, identifying and analysing the precise cause of a problem will assist in deciding on the most appropriate course of action.

A range of data is available to managers to assess the performance of their employees.

1. Labour productivity

Labour productivity is perhaps the most fundamental indicator of the performance of a group of employees and has implications for a business's costs and hence the prices that it can charge. Productive workers produce larger quantities of output per worker per time period, and this is a measure that is relatively

easy to calculate and to interpret. In general, a higher productivity figure is preferable. Improvements in labour productivity allows businesses to enjoy increased profit margins or to reduce prices (while maintaining profit margins), hopefully leading to increased sales.

> Labour productivity = total output per time period / number of employees at work

For example, Nissan car factory in Sunderland produces up to 2,000 cars each day using a workforce of 6,700. Thus on days when its production is at its maximum, the factory achieves a daily labour productivity figure of 0.30 cars per worker (2,000/6,700). Labour productivity can be calculated for any time period.

Labour productivity depends upon factors such as the extent and quality of capital equipment available as well as the workforce's degree of motivation. This means that it is possible for managers to take a range of actions with the intention of improving labour productivity figures. Research indicates that overall labour productivity in the UK has increased by between 2 and 3 per cent per annum on average since 1945, although it has declined since the financial crisis of 2008–09.

Key terms

Labour productivity measures the output per employee per time period.

Unit labour costs measure the labour cost per unit of output produced.

Figure 21.1 shows that the amount of output per hour has varied substantially since 2010. It reveals that average output per worker per hour was approximately 4.5 per cent lower in 2014 than in 2010. The calculation of labour productivity based on employee output per hour allows for changes in the structure of the UK's workforce, notably the increasing use of part-time employees by businesses in all sectors of the economy.

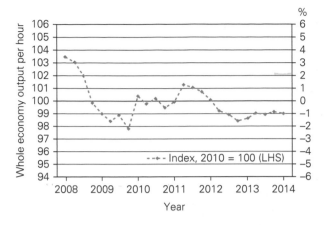

Figure 21.1 Output per employee hour for the whole UK economy, 2008–2014

Source: Office for National Statistics, Statistics Bulletin, July 2014

www.ons.gov.uk/ons/dcp171778_361728.pdf

Permission for re-use of all © Crown copyright information is granted under the terms of the Open Government Licence (OGL).

Interpreting labour productivity data

An increase in labour productivity figures for a business represents an improvement in efficiency of its workforce, which can reduce the labour costs involved in producing a typical unit of output. As labour costs account for around two-thirds of the cost of production of UK economic output, this can offer major benefits to businesses.

However, it is important to consider a number of factors when analysing labour productivity data, especially when using it to draw conclusions about a business's competitiveness.

- **Which businesses, or aspects of a specific business, are covered by the labour productivity data.** The data in Figure 21.1 relates to the entire UK economy and therefore includes data for all businesses. It may be that particular sectors, industries or businesses have performed differently (either better or worse) than this average data. For example, manufacturing productivity rates in the UK over the period 2010–2014 were superior to those in the services sector. It is important for managers to gather data that is relevant to their specific enterprise for analysis.
- **Labour productivity data ignores wage rates.** The data set out in Figure 21.1 could make grim reading for managers responsible for human relations at businesses in the UK. However, it does not tell the whole story. A business can be competitive with lower productivity figures if it pays lower wage rates than its rivals. Labour cost per unit of output is perhaps a better guide as it takes into account productivity data and labour costs. We look at **unit labour costs** in detail in the next section.

Business in focus: Labour productivity in the South East of England

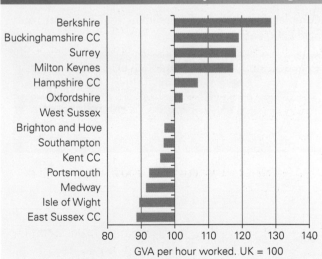

Figure 21.2 Labour productivity in the fourteen sub-regions of the South East of England, 2012

Source: Office for National Statistics, Statistical Bulletin, March 2014

www.ons.gov.uk/ons/dcp171766_355495.pdf

Permission for re-use of all © Crown copyright information is granted under the terms of the Open Government Licence (OGL).

Figure 21.2 shows Gross Value Added (GVA) per hour worked data for 2012 for all of the Office of National Statistics' sub-regions within the South East of England. Gross value added per hour worked is a measure of labour productivity. This measure shows a wide variation in labour productivity across these fourteen sub-regions.

Questions

1. Explain the benefits a business may receive from operating with levels of labour productivity that are higher than those of its competitors.
2. Do you think that UK businesses should, on the basis of this data, move to Berkshire to improve their competitiveness? Justify your view.

- **Overall productivity depends on other factors too.** Many businesses use extensive amounts of capital equipment in producing goods and services. For these businesses labour productivity may not be as important as for more labour-intensive enterprises. The efficiency of capital-intensive businesses depends more on the productivity of their capital equipment than their workforce.
- **Labour productivity data for direct rivals.** A business may increase its efficiency, possibly by increasing training for its workforce. However, this may bring few benefits if rivals have achieved similar improvements in the efficiency of their workforces.

What do you think?

Will labour productivity become a less important determinant of a business's performance as technology advances and is used more widely in production?

2. Unit labour costs

Unit labour costs measure the labour cost per unit of output produced. Unit labour costs are based on total labour costs, including non-wage employment costs such as business's national insurance and pension contributions, incurred in the production of a unit of output. For example, if a business manufactures 12,000 televisions in a month and the total labour cost of producing those televisions is £900,000, then the unit labour cost = £900,000/12,000 = £75.

Unit labour costs are the best indicator of labour costs faced by businesses. They represent the amount of money needed to pay employees to make one unit of output, for example, one car. Unit labour costs are determined by two elements:

- the cost of employing workers;
- the speed at which they make the products (such as cars), in other words their productivity.

Unit labour costs tend to have an inverse relationship with labour productivity. If labour productivity rises, then unit labour costs will fall unless labour costs increase by a greater percentage. Unit labour costs will rise when total labour costs rise faster than output. For example, if total labour costs rise by 5 per cent and labour productivity grows by 2 per cent for a given amount of output, unit labour costs will rise by approximately 3 per cent.

A rise in labour productivity can help to control unit labour costs. This is because a producer is achieving a higher output from each unit of labour employed assuming a given wage cost. Therefore managers may be willing to pay increased wages and salaries when productivity is rising, especially if the percentage increase in pay is below the rate at which productivity is increasing. In these circumstances it is likely that unit labour costs will fall.

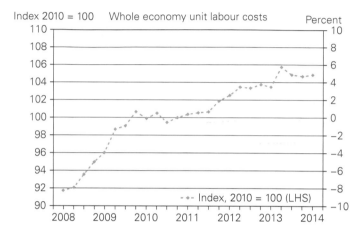

Figure 21.3 Unit labour costs for the whole UK economy, 2008–2014

Source: Office for National Statistics, Statistics Bulletin, July 2014

www.ons.gov.uk/ons/dcp171778_361728.pdf

Permission for re-use of all © Crown copyright information is granted under the terms of the Open Government Licence (OGL).

Maths moment

Complete the table below assuming that employees are paid £200 each per week.

Number of employees	Total weekly wages (£)	Output (number of units)	Labour productivity	Labour cost per unit (total weekly wages/ number of units)
100	20,000	1,000	10	£20
100		2,000		
50		1,000		
		2,000	40	

Table 21.1 Employment and cost data

Interpreting unit labour costs data

In general, lower unit labour costs are to be preferred, especially if these are below those achieved by direct competitors. It can be useful to look at unit labour costs over a period of time as heavy investment in

Business in focus: asos suffers heavy rise in labour costs per unit

British online clothing store Asos targets the 20-something market, selling 'fast fashion' around the world. Celebrities such as Keira Knightley, Ashlee Simpson and Emily Blunt have been seen sporting their clothes. The company employs 4,000 people in the UK, 3,000 of whom are based in their Barnsley warehouse. It sells its products to 237 countries around the world.

However, despite sales in the six months to February 2014 being up 34 per cent, from £359.7 million to £481.7 million, Asos actually saw a 20 per cent fall in pre-tax profits from £25.7 million to £20.1 million.

The company's CEO gave various reasons for this fall in profits, citing investment in expansion in China as a particular cause as well as investments in warehousing and IT in the UK and Europe. Furthermore, a fire badly affected the Barnsley warehouse and Asos had to open temporary warehouses elsewhere. This contributed to labour costs per unit rising by 23 per cent.

However, Asos argues that the increased investment will enable them to operate more cost effectively in the future as well as offer faster delivery times to European customers. CEO Nick Robertson says: 'This increased pace of investment has reduced our profitability in the period, but will deliver significantly increased capacity as well as efficiencies in the longer term. ASOS is not and has never been about the short-term; the scale of the global opportunity remains as exciting as ever and we are investing for the many opportunities ahead.'

Source: adapted from various news sources

Questions

1. Explain why controlling labour costs is important to asos plc.
2. The company cannot achieve its objective of sales revenue reaching £1 billion by the end of the year as its labour costs per unit have risen by 23 per cent. Do you agree with this statement? Justify your view.

---

training may increase short-term labour costs (for example, paying overtime to cover workers who are in training) before rising productivity reduces them once more. Do remember that labour costs are only part of a business's costs. Reducing unit labour costs will not improve price competitiveness if other costs, for example, overheads, are rising quickly.

3. Employee costs as a percentage of revenue

This measure of the performance of a business's human resources is also referred to as 'employee costs as a percentage of turnover'. This is an important measure of employee performance for businesses that supply services such as health care, where labour costs are a high proportion of total costs. When this is the case, controlling these costs effectively is an important element of controlling overall costs and achieving acceptable levels of profit.

Employee costs as a percentage of **revenue** are an important issue for England's Premier League football clubs. Deloitte, one of the UK's major accounting and tax advice businesses, produces an annual report on these clubs. The latest report revealed that revenue for all Premier League clubs combined grew to £2.5 billion

in 2012–13 and that will increase to £3.2 billion by 2013–14 thanks to the new 2013–2016 TV deals with Sky and BT Sport. Employee costs were £1.8 billion in 2012–13, or almost 72 per cent of income, and these are believed to have risen by 22 per cent to £2.2 billion in 2013–14. Table 21.2 summarises these figures. The Premier League football clubs are in the fortunate position of being able to increase wages substantially because their revenue is increasing very rapidly.

Season	Revenue £bn	Employee costs £bn	Employee costs as a percentage of revenue
2012–2013	2.5	1.8	72.0%
2013–2014	3.2	2.2	68.7%

Table 21.2 Revenue and employee costs for England's Premier League football clubs, 2012–2013 and 2013–2014

Source: Deloitte Annual Review of Football Finance, 2104

www2.deloitte.com/uk/en/pages/sports-business-group/articles/annual-review-of-football-finance.html

Key term

Revenue is the earnings or income generated by a firm as a result of its trading activities. It is also called turnover or sales revenue.

Employee costs in relation to revenue are influenced by a range of factors.

- **The productivity rates of the workforce**. Higher levels of productivity can lead to increased sales and revenue without greater labour input. Equally production and revenue can be maintained with fewer employees reducing labour costs.
- **Wage rates**. Clearly an increase in wages and salaries without a corresponding increase in sales and revenue will worsen this indicator and may represent an unwise decision by managers.
- **Non-wage employment costs**. Offering generous pension schemes or similar benefits can drive up a business's employment costs without necessarily increasing revenue.
- **The management of capacity**. If a business does not utilise its human resources efficiently it may be paying for employees who are not contributing to sales and revenue. Incurring labour costs without the compensation of generating revenue will weaken this measure of workforce performance.

4. Labour turnover and retention

Labour turnover = $\dfrac{\text{number of staff leaving during year} \times 100}{\text{average number of staff}}$

This ratio measures the proportion of a workforce leaving their employment at a business over some period of time, usually one year. Low wages and inadequate training, leading to poor morale among employees, may cause high levels of **labour turnover**. Another cause is ineffective recruitment procedures, resulting in the appointment of inappropriate or unsuitable staff. Other reasons include redundancy and retirement.

Key terms

Labour turnover is the percentage of a business's employees who leave the business over some period of time (normally a year).

Labour retention (employee retention) is the extent to which a business holds onto its employees.

Some level of labour turnover is inevitable. Managers seek some level of labour turnover to bring new ideas into a business, but not so high as to impose excessive recruitment costs. The 2013 Annual Survey by the Chartered Institute of Personnel and Development (CIPD) revealed that the median rate of labour turnover in the UK was 11.9 per cent in 2013, compared with 12.7 per cent in 2012 and 12.5 per cent in 2011. Rates of labour turnover vary considerably between different sectors of the UK economy, as shown in Table 21.3.

Managers attempt to manage labour turnover to achieve a balance between bringing in new employees with enthusiasm and ideas into the business, against the costs of recruitment. Only approximately 16 per cent of UK businesses calculate the cost of labour turnover to the business. Although this figure is rising slowly, this indicates that relatively few managers pay attention to what could be an important factor, especially with regard to highly skilled employees or where recruitment costs are high.

Maths moment

Last year 45 employees at Bagley Ltd left the company. The company had an average of 900 employees over the year. The company's HR manager had forecast that the company's labour turnover figure would be 4 per cent.

(a) Calculate the labour turnover figure for this company.

(b) How many employees would have left if the HR director's forecast had been accurate?

[handwritten] so % of number of = number of staff   staff leaving.

	All leavers					Voluntary leavers				
	2013	2012	2011	2010	2009	2013	2012	2011	2010	2009
Manufacturing & production	8.0	9.5	9.3	3.1 12.4	3.1 15.3	3.1	4.5	3.7	2.7	7.7
Private sector services	16.3	16.1	13.8	14.6	16.8	11.8	8.9	8.7	7.4	10.4
Public sector	9.4	10.1	8.5	8.6	12.6	4.2	1.9	3.4	5.8	7.6
Not-for-profit	15.2	13.0	13.1	15.9	16.4	6.6	7.6	7.0	10.2	11.0

Table 21.3 Median labour turnover rates, by UK industry sector (%)

Source: CIPD Annual Survey Report, 2013

www.cipd.co.uk/binaries/resourcing-and-talent-planning_2013.PDF

Labour retention is the extent to which a business holds onto its employees. It can be measured as the proportion of employees with a specified length of service (typically one year or more) expressed as a percentage of overall workforce numbers.

$$\text{Employee retention} = \frac{\text{Number of employees employed for one year or more} \times 100}{\text{average number of staff}}$$

Retaining employees has become an increasing problem (and performance indicator) for UK businesses over recent years. Most retention difficulties have been experienced in relation to professional employees and specialists as shown in Table 21.4. Businesses did not experience such problems in holding onto senior managers, although retention rates are declining over time for this category of employee.

Interpreting labour turnover and retention data

High rates of labour turnover can impose significant recruitment and training costs on businesses and may be unsettling for other employees as teams and working groups are disrupted. Customers may also be dissatisfied if they regularly deal with different employees in their transactions with a business. Replacing labour that has left can also be expensive due to recruitment and training costs. Most businesses will seek a lower figure to avoid incurring such costs. However, what is an acceptable labour turnover rate will differ according to the type of business. A business that employs highly skilled and scarce employees will wish to have a low labour turnover rate, perhaps just enough to bring fresh ideas into the organisation. Research has revealed that labour turnover costs UK firms supplying legal services £805 million per year, or nearly £40,000 per employee.

	2013	2012	2011	2010	Manufacturing & production	Private sector services	Public sector	Not-for-profit
Managers & professionals/specialists	37	33	28	27	30	31	60	30
Technical	17	28	21	20	36	24	19	13
Senior managers/directors	15	10	7	9	9	16	20	11
Services (customer, personal, protective and sales)	9	13	13	12	8	20	8	6
Admin./secretarial	7	8	9	7	3	9	14	14
Manual/craft workers	6	5	6	4	15	8	4	5

Table 21.4 Percentages of businesses having retention difficulties, by category of employee

Source: CIPD Annual Review 2013

www.cipd.co.uk/binaries/resourcing-and-talent-planning_2013.PDF

Business in focus: Labour turnover at Mitchell & Butlers plc

Mitchells & Butlers (M&B) operates approximately 1,600 managed restaurants, pubs and bars in the UK. It had 40,000 employees in 2014. The company is seeking to expand its family brands Harvester and Toby Carvery. The company is aiming to improve customer experiences, reduce staff turnover and grow profit margins.

In relation to its workforce M&B has set an objective to 'recruit, retain and develop engaged people who deliver excellent service for our guests'. It says that it is 'focused on attracting and training people with the skills and motivation to deliver exceptional customer service.'

The company conducts a 13-week training programme with all new staff in its pubs, as well as training to increase productivity levels of employees working in kitchens and bars. The company says that the key measure of success in relation to its workforce is labour turnover. M&B reported that its rate of labour turnover fell from 82 per cent in 2012 to 78 per cent for the first part of 2014.

Questions

1. Calculate the number of employees who would have left employment with Mitchell & Butler in 2014 if its labour turnover rate was unchanged throughout the year. Comment on the labour turnover figure.

2. Do you think that labour turnover should be the 'key measure of success' for Mitchell & Butler plc's workforce? Justify your opinion.

In contrast a company that operates theme parks may accept a much higher rate of labour turnover. This is because it may employ large numbers of relatively unskilled part-time employees on a seasonal basis and pay low wage rates. The cost of recruiting and training new employees may be low and the business's managers may accept high labour turnover rates as the price to be paid for paying low wages and offering short-term contracts.

Managers' objectives with regard to retention rates are the opposite of labour turnover. High rates are desirable particularly for businesses with highly skilled and scarce employees. Losing a key employee can be particularly damaging for a business if the employee goes to work with a direct competitor.

Using data for human resource decision making and planning

Managers responsible for human resources will draw on a range of data from within and outside the business when making decisions and drawing up human resource plans.

Data and human resource planning

Human resource planning is one of the core activities of human resource management and entails a number of stages.

Key term

A **human resource plan** assesses the current and future capacity of a business's workforce and sets out actions necessary to meet the business's future human resource needs.

- The starting point of human resource planning is to consider the overall or corporate objectives of the business. The **human resource plan** must contribute to the achievement of the business's overall or corporate objectives.
- The next stage is to take a strategic view of employees, and to consider how human resources can be managed to assist in attaining the business's corporate objectives. This may entail considering factors such as the use of technology and how this might complement or replace some human input into the production process.
- At this stage those responsible for human resource planning will have to make a judgement about the size and type of workforce the organisation will require over future years.
- This desired future workforce is compared with that available to the business at the time of planning.
- Once this comparison is complete the firm can decide upon policies (for example recruitment, training, redeployment and redundancy) necessary to convert the existing workforce into the desired one. This process is shown in Figure 21.5.

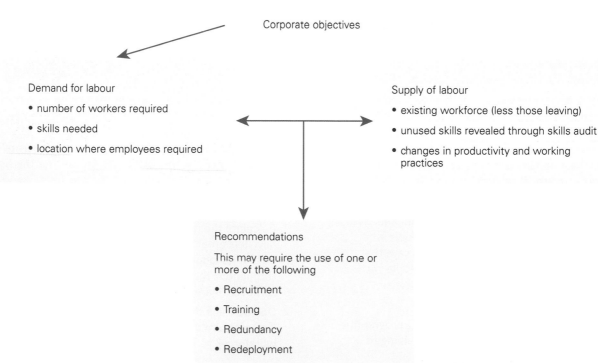

Figure 21.4 Human resource planning

The human resource plan will specify the business's desired workforce and how the business will implement its human resource policies. A business's human resource plan will require managers to draw on a range of data to compile it.

1. Information on the business's current workforce. This will set out:
   - the number of employees that the business currently has and their skills
   - data relating to labour productivity for the existing workforce
   - current and forecast labour costs, including unit labour costs
   - the age profile of its employees, which will help to forecast likely future changes due to retirement, etc.
   - the business's overall or corporate objectives.
2. **Information from outside the business.** This might include human resource, marketing and other data:
   - the expected rate of unemployment for workers with skills required by the business
   - forecast wage rates for potential employees
   - expected demand for the products supplied by the business

- likely prices at which the business can expect to sell its products
- availability, cost of productivity of technology that could be used in production.

Managers will research and use data to underpin the human resource planning process. Using external data to aid human resource planning is particularly important when a business is newly established and has limited historical data to draw upon. In such circumstances managers will have to use numerical information from outside the enterprise as a central part of their analysis. It is also important to analyse data when planning the use of human resources in an external environment that is changing rapidly. If consumers' incomes are forecast to decline, for example, this could have significant implications for a business selling luxury products, and would impact upon its human resource plan. Gathering information on forecast consumer incomes will help to plan production and consequently human resource needs. Using data in such circumstances can help HR managers to make good quality decisions.

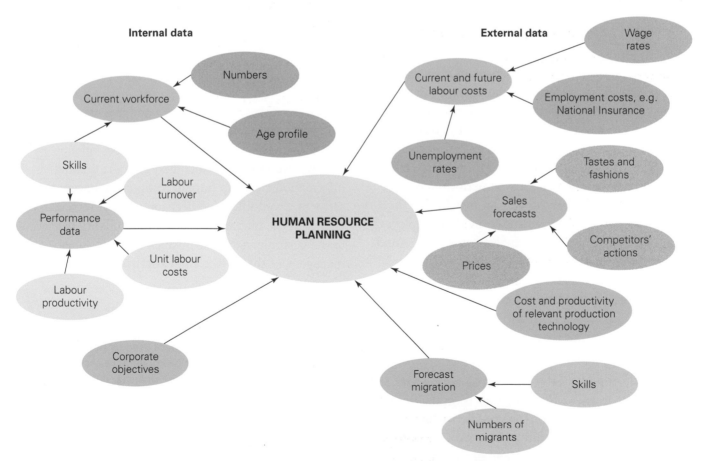

Figure 21.5 Data and human resource planning

Data and human resource decision making

The potential of using HR data in decision making

There is a movement by businesses in the UK and elsewhere to use more data to underpin human resource decision making, although progress is slow. There is already an immense amount of data for HR managers to draw upon and it is increasing exponentially. IBM (an American technology company) estimates that 90 per cent of the data in the world was created in the last two years.

Key term

Big data describes an enormous quantity of structured and unstructured data that is difficult to process using traditional techniques such as databases.

As performance management information systems have become more widespread, human resource managers have been able to gather information about individual employees, as well as about the business's entire workforce. As human resources have become an increasingly important competitive weapon, HR data can lead directly to improved performance by businesses. HR data can provide an insight into the performances of workforces and individual employees. Using HR data to report and analyse on what has and is taking place within a business's workforce offers clear advantages in making good quality human resources decisions. Many HR departments have the ability to access performance indicators such as productivity and unit labour costs, which can be used for planning and decision making.

However, leading HR professionals are taking data analysis to the next level to assist decision making. They seek to use data to provide predictive analysis of what may happen in the future. This process depends on the use of **big data** because predictive analysis requires large sample groups in order to be considered statistically sound. Being able to make effective decisions about retention, recruitment, or talent development based on analysis of data can provide businesses with an important competitive edge.

The reluctance of managers to use HR data for decision making

However, despite all these possibilities, research by Forbes (a company that provides information for businesses) has shown that only a minority of companies are making effective use of this data to inform and improve decision making. For example, only 14 per cent of businesses in the United States have done any significant 'statistical analysis' of employee data at all.

This view is supported by the outcome of a global study by Alexander Mann Solutions and the HRO Today Institute in 2013. This reveals that only one in three companies use recruitment and employee data to drive business decisions, despite evidence it helps firms outperform rivals 58 per cent of the time. More than 90 per cent of companies collect employee performance data, but only 51 per cent use it to improve employee performance such as talent development, and 32 per cent do not examine employee data in any way.

Human resource data alone will not give managers sufficient information to take what can be major decisions in these areas. However, it does offer a quantitative element, which may support qualitative information and help human resource managers to arrive at a well-informed decision. Thus it increases the chance of the managers making good quality decisions in the best interest of the business. This is an aspect of management that is likely to experience rapid change over the next few years.

Study tip

Remember that much of the data used by human resource managers may not be HR data. To make decisions managers may require financial data, marketing data and data from operations. HR managers do not take decisions in isolation from the rest of the business.

ASSESSMENT ACTIVITIES

Sections (a), (b) and (c) of these assessment activities are relevant for students taking AS and A-level examinations. The questions in section (d) are for A-level students only.

(a) Knowledge check questions

1 A business increased its workforce from 1,250 employees in 2013 to 1,500 in 2014. Annual output increased by 20 per cent to 480,000 units from 2013 to 2014. Which of the following statements about the business's labour productivity is true?

 i) Labour productivity rose by 20 per cent.

 ii) Labour productivity is unchanged.

 iii) Labour productivity fell by 20 per cent.

 iv) Labour productivity in 2013 was 384 units per employee.

2 State two factors that determine the level of labour productivity achieved by a business's workforce.

3 Is the following statement true or false? 'Unit labour costs are determined by labour productivity and wage costs only.'

4 A business manufactures 250,000 units of output each month. It incurs the following costs each month:

 ● wage costs – £4.5 million
 ● non-wage employment costs – £2.5 million
 ● material costs – £5 million
 ● fuel costs – £6 million.

 Which of the following is its unit labour costs?

 i) £72

 ii) £48

 iii) £28

 iv) £18

5 Is the following statement true or false? 'Unit labour costs tend to have an inverse relationship with labour productivity.'

6 Last year a business experienced a rise of 4 per cent in its total labour costs, while its labour productivity figure fell by 3 per cent; output was unchanged. Which of the following is true?

 i) Unit labour costs rose by approximately 1 per cent.

 ii) Unit labour costs rose by approximately 7 per cent.

 iii) Unit labour costs fell by approximately 1 per cent.

 iv) Unit labour costs were unchanged.

7 State two factors that might influence the proportion of employee costs in relation to a business's revenue.

8 What is meant by the term labour retention?

9 Over the last year a retailer has had an average workforce of 4,500 employees; 300 employees have left the business and 290 have joined it. Which of the following is its rate of labour turnover.

 i) 0.22 per cent

 ii) 6.44 per cent

 iii) 13.11 per cent

 iv) 6.67 per cent

10 What is meant by the term human resource plan?

(b) Short answer questions

1 Explain how a manufacturing business might improve the labour productivity levels of its workforce. (4 marks)

2 Explain why unit labour costs may be an important measure of human resource performance for a low price hotel chain. (5 marks)

3 Explain why a fast food retailer may not be concerned by experiencing high rates of labour turnover. (5 marks)

4 Why might a large business planning a major expansion benefit from using its human resource data to inform its planning? (6 marks)

(c) Data response questions

The managers at Heron Ltd are in the process of calculating the company's unit labour costs. The performance of the workforce is important to the company and labour costs are 62.6 per cent of its total costs. The managers are using the data in Table 21.5.

Year	Total employment cost (£m)	Output (units)	Labour productivity (2012 = 100)
Last year	22.400	28,000	106.9
The year before	19.125	25,500	107.4

Table 21.5 Selected employee performance data for Heron Ltd

The last year has seen significant growth at the company as the luxury rugs that it manufactures have grown in popularity. As part of a planned expansion, production rose by nearly 10 per cent. This increase in output was not sufficient to match demand and the company has further expansion planned over the next eighteen months.

The company has had to ask its existing workforce to work some overtime hours at higher rates of pay (25 per cent higher) to meet rising demand. It has, however, recruited new employees who are steadily increasing the company's productive capacity. The rate of unemployment in the town where Heron Ltd is located is quite high and the government's decision at the start of the year to increase the national insurance contributions that employers have to make has not helped the employment situation.

The company's shareholders are not satisfied with the company's current profits given the popularity of its products despite profit margins on sales remaining at 14 per cent last year. They are pressuring the managers to increase dividends paid out as soon as possible.

Source: Written by author

1 Calculate the change in Heron Ltd's unit labour costs. (6 marks)

2 Analyse the factors that may have caused the change in Heron Ltd's unit labour costs. (9 marks)

3 To what extent should the managers at Heron Ltd be concerned by the rise in the company's unit labour costs? (15 marks)

(d) Essays

1 Discuss whether unit labour costs are the only type of human resource data that are important to managers of businesses operating in markets where demand is price elastic. (25 marks)

2 All businesses should analyse human resource data before making any decisions relating to their workforces. Do you agree? Justify your opinion. (25 marks)

Chapter 22

Improving organisational design and human resource flow

Introduction

This chapter builds on earlier ones and looks at two key decisions that a business's human resource managers have to make – that of deciding how to improve the organisation's design and how to manage the organisation's human resource flow with the aim of meeting HR objectives. These are key decisions in maximising the performance of a business's human resources. The next chapter will look at important decisions on how to improve the motivation and engagement of the workforce.

What you need to know by the end of this chapter:

- influences on job design
- influences on organisational design
- influences on delegation, centralisation and decentralisation
- the value of changing job and organisational design
- how managing human resource flow helps to meet human resource objectives.

Job design and organisational design

Job design

Michael Armstrong, a prolific writer on human resource management, gives a precise description of **job design**. He says it is 'the process of deciding on the contents of a job in terms of its duties and responsibilities, on the methods to be used in carrying out the job, in terms of techniques, systems and procedures, and on the relationships that should exist between the job holder and his superiors, subordinates and colleagues.'

Managers can use job design to improve levels of **labour productivity**. The careful design, or possibly redesign, of jobs can create positions for employees which avoid simple repetitive and monotonous duties and offer the chance to exercise more authority and control over their working lives.

Key terms

Job design is the process of grouping together or dividing up tasks and responsibilities to create complete jobs.

Labour productivity measures the output per employee per time period.

Job enrichment occurs when employees' jobs are redesigned to provide them with more challenging and complex tasks.

Empowerment is a series of actions designed to give employees greater control over their working lives.

Designing jobs which engage and motivate employees requires managers to consider a range of techniques. Early attempts at job design were prompted by the work of Frederick Winslow Taylor, whose work we discuss in more detail in the next chapter. Writing over a century ago he advocated 'method study' to discover the most efficient may of completing jobs and 'work measurement' to show how much time was required to complete a task. Initially this work on job design led to monotonous, repetitive duties which were often unpopular and over time the techniques of job rotation and job enlargement emerged to create more diverse working roles.

Job enlargement and job rotation

Job enlargement does not increase the complexity of tasks carried out by an employee. Instead it increases the number of similar duties. It is also termed 'horizontal loading'. Managers who redesign jobs through job enlargement require employees to carry out a number of similar tasks. Thus, a receptionist might be asked to maintain records of petty cash and update customer records in addition to dealing with telephone and personal enquiries from customers. Job enlargement offers benefits to the employee in that carrying out a range of duties, rather than a single one repeatedly, may stimulate their interest.

Job rotation is a particular type of job enlargement. Under this system employees switch regularly from one duty to another. For example, a supermarket may require employees to spend a week on the checkout, followed by a week stacking shelves and a week dealing with customer enquiries.

Job enrichment

Later in the twentieth century writers on behavioural theories of motivation (such as Abraham Maslow and Frederick Herzberg) began to influence job design. They recognised that people work for a range of reasons other than money and that jobs should be designed to meet these needs of employees to improve labour productivity. Thus jobs were enriched to provide a more satisfying experience for employees. **Job enrichment** occurs when employees' jobs are redesigned to provide them with more challenging and complex tasks. This process, also called 'vertical loading', is designed to use all employees' abilities. The intention is to enrich the employee's experience of work. Job enrichment normally involves a number of elements:

- redesigning jobs so as to increase, not just the range of tasks, but the complexity of them
- giving employees greater responsibility for managing themselves

- offering employees the authority to identify and solve problems relating to their work
- providing employees with the training and skills essential to allow them to carry out their enriched jobs effectively.

Job enrichment involves a high degree of skill on the part of the managers overseeing it. They must ensure that they do not ask employees to carry out duties of which they are not capable.

Empowerment

Empowerment is an important element of job design and one which has become more influential over recent years. Empowerment involves redesigning employees' jobs to allow them greater control over their working lives. Empowerment gives employees the opportunity to decide how to carry out their duties and how to organise their work.

Empowerment can make work more interesting as it offers opportunities to meet a number of individual needs. Empowered workers can propose and implement new methods of working as they bring a new perspective to decision making. They may spend a part of their working lives analysing the problems they face and proposing solutions. The characteristics of the job became a central element of job design.

Business in focus: Job design and the National Health Service (NHS)

Working in the NHS should be rewarding and interesting, yet many healthcare professionals feel overworked and disempowered. This is not a unique NHS problem as research shows it's a problem in healthcare industries in all the advanced economies worldwide.

Table 22.1 shows some findings from two recent NHS staff surveys of nearly 100,000 employees which were taken at a time of rapid change. Some managers may be concerned that the design of jobs in the NHS needs some attention to cope with rising demand and changes to the structure of the NHS.

Questions

1. Explain why well-designed jobs might offer considerable benefits to stakeholders in the NHS.

2. Do you think that managers within the NHS should be satisfied with the results of the staff surveys shown in Table 22.1? Justify your view.

Key finding	2013	2012
1. Percentage suffering work-related stress during the last 12 months	38.6%	38.1%
2. Percentage able to contribute towards improvements at work	68.1%	67.6%
3. Work pressure felt by staff on a scale: 1 [low] to 5 [high]	3.06	3.06
4. Job satisfaction on a scale: 1 [dissatisfied] to 5 [satisfied]	3.61	3.58
5. Percentage working in a well-structured team environment	3.74%	3.73%
6. Percentage receiving relevant training, learning or development in last 12 months	80.8%	80.8%

Table 22.1 Selected findings from surveys of NHS staff

Source: NHS Staff Surveys, 2012 and 2013

www.england.nhs.uk/statistics/2014/02/25/2013-nhs-staff-survey/

Permission for re-use of all © Crown copyright information is granted under the terms of the Open Government Licence (OGL).

This approach was based to a great extent on the work of J Richard Hackman and Greg Oldham. In 1975 they developed a model of job design called job characteristics theory which highlighted the key elements of a motivating job. This model is illustrated in Figure 22.1 and stresses the importance of designing jobs in which individuals have:

- skill variety, i.e. they use a range of skills
- task significance, i.e. they are working on something that has some significance in terms of the overall business rather than just working on a small section and thereby not appreciating why what they do matters
- task identity, i.e. the work they do has a sense of competition (for example handing over a complete unit of work to the next stage of the process)
- autonomy, i.e. individuals have some independence to make decisions on how they do the work
- feedback, i.e. employees receive information on the quality of their work.

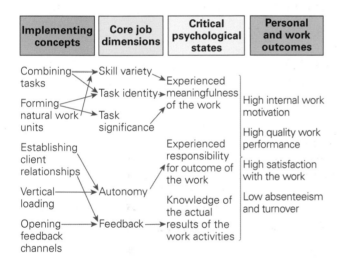

Figure 22.1 The Hackman and Oldham model of job design

Recent developments in job design

Human resource managers are under increasing pressure to be able to use their workforces more flexibly. Workforces are a very expensive asset for many businesses and HR managers are expected to design jobs to allow:

- flexible working times – this may be flexible or variable hours, compressed working weeks (doing 5 days' work in 4, or 10 days in 9, etc.), part-time working, job sharing or term-time working

- flexible contract options – working with employees on temporary contracts, employees working for agencies or freelance employees who will be self-employed
- flexible locations – a workforce based on multiple locations to meet customers' needs as fully as possible.

Influences on job design

Managers designing or redesigning jobs will be subject to a number of influences.

- **The business's overall or corporate objectives**. This has the potential to be an important influence. However jobs are designed they should enable the business to achieve its objectives as efficiently as possible. Thus jobs may be designed to achieve cost minimisation (possibly through high levels of productivity), high quality service or constant innovation.
- **Employee performance**. HR Managers in businesses that experience high rates of labour turnover and/or relatively low labour productivity levels may seek to design jobs that have greater potential to motivate. Many businesses that suffer high rates of labour turnover will use exit interviews with staff who are leaving to gather evidence on causes of possible dissatisfaction and to inform future decisions on job design. Managers can draw on Hackman and Oldham's model to assist them in creating jobs that offer the potential to use a range of skills, to fulfil a significant task and operate with a sufficient degree of autonomy.
- **Health & safety and other legal requirements**. The design of jobs should take into account the possible risks associated with the work. Although this may have greater relevance in some working environments such as manufacturing, it does also apply to office based work, for example, avoiding extended periods of using computers.
- **Meeting customer requirements as fully as possible**. A central element of designing jobs is to ensure that the outcome is satisfied customers. They should be designed to minimise the possibility of supplying substandard products and to ensure good customer service. This may entail building in appropriate quality assurance procedures and may involve employees engaging in self-checking. This influence on job design can result in jobs that are motivating.

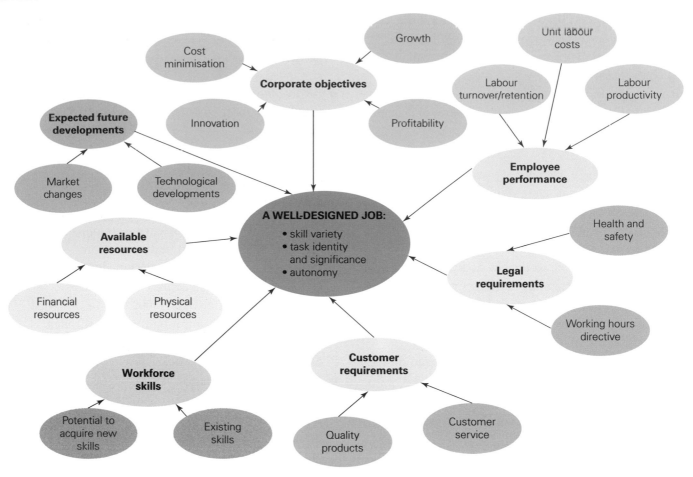

Figure 22.2 Influences on job design

- **The existing and potential skills of the workforce**. It is common for managers to redesign jobs to fit as far as possible with the skills profile of existing employees. This permits a smoother and less costly transition to new working practices. However, it may be that managers need to consider the potential of existing employees and to assess whether they are capable of carrying out the new roles successfully.

- **The resources available.** A radical change in job design within a business may require the business to invest in training and recruitment. Employees may have to attend expensive training courses, new employees may need to be recruited to carry out specialist roles and new equipment may be required to support new training methods. The HR team will need to ensure that the business has the financial resources and physical resources (such as sufficient technology) to support employees carrying out particular job roles.

- **Expected future developments**. It is important that managers design jobs that will continue to

be effective and appropriate for the foreseeable future. Businesses are subject to a range of changes in their external environment. For example, technology may change leading to changes in patterns of demand. Many of the UK's banks are adjusting their workforces to meet a declining demand for banking services in branches and increasing online demand. Changing demand and fashions can also require businesses to adjust product portfolios and may require difficult approaches to working.

Study tip

Do remember that HR managers do not act in isolation when taking decisions on important issues such as job and organisational design. Decisions have to be taken in conjunction with other functional areas within the business (such as operations and finance) and must assist the business in achieving its overall objectives.

Organisational design

A good definition of an organisation was provided by Carter McNamara in 2012. He says that 'in its simplest form an organisation is a person or group of people intentionally organised to accomplish an overall, common goal or set of goals'. Because they are 'intentionally' organised and do not simply evolve, there is a need for design. In turn, the Chartered Institute of Personnel and Development (CIPD) defines **organisational design** as 'ensuring that the organisation is appropriately designed to deliver organisation objectives in the short- and long- term and that structural change is effectively managed.' Another writer on business organisations, Alan S Gutterman, believes that organisational design is more than simply a business's **organisational structure** as shown by its organisational chart. He argues that it includes other factors such as:

- the business's mission or vision and values and the reason why it exists
- the ways in which decisions are taken and who takes them
- the information and pay systems used in the business
- the ways in which the business normally operates – its culture.

Key terms

Authority is the power to give orders, make decisions and to control events and people.

Organisational structure is the way a business is arranged to carry out its activities.

Organisational design is a process to ensure that the organisation is appropriately designed to deliver organisation objectives in the short and long term.

Designing an organisational structure to balance these factors requires creative skills. Organisational designers have to create something that enables the enterprise to meet its goals, to respond to external pressures for change, integrates individuals into the organisation and is able to recognise the need to change. The creativity involved in this design process has led to it being termed 'organisational architecture'.

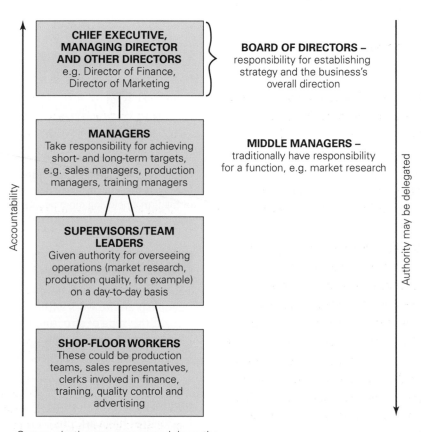

Communication can pass up and down the organisation, as well as horizontally, e.g communication between managers

Figure 22.3 A simplified organisational chart

A well-designed organisation can make the business more efficient, generate innovation and spread **authority** across the workforce. Organisational design is becoming more important to HR managers as businesses are increasingly subject to external forces such as changes in consumer demands, changes in technology and in the behaviour of competitors.

The activities involved in organisational design will create an organisational structure for a business. The organisational structure, which may be shown in an organisational chart, sets out:

- the routes by which communication passes through the business
- who has authority (and power) and responsibility within the organisation
- the roles and titles of individuals within the organisation
- the people to whom individual employees are accountable and those for whom they are responsible.

Key factors in organisational design

The designers of an organisation have a range of factors with which to work. Some of them are clearly structural such as the number of people for whom a particular manager is responsible. Other factors will underpin the structural decisions. For example, if designers are given the brief that authority is to be spread widely among people across the organisation, this will have significant implications for the organisation that they design. We will consider a number of relevant factors that managers may take into account when making decisions on the design of their organisation.

Key terms

Levels or layers of hierarchy refer to the number of layers of authority within an organisation. That is, how many levels exist between the chief executive and a shop-floor employee.

A **span of control** is the number of subordinates directly responsible to a manager.

The **chain of command** is the line of communication and authority existing within a business. Thus, a shop-floor worker reports to a supervisor, who is responsible to a departmental manager, and so on.

Delegation is the passing of authority (but not responsibility) down the organisational structure.

1. Levels of hierarchy

A fundamental element of any organisational structure is the number of **levels or layers of hierarchy**. Organisations with a large number of layers (or levels) of hierarchy are referred to as 'tall'. That is, there are a substantial number of people between the person at the top of the organisation and those at the bottom. Figures 22.4 and 22.5 illustrate tall and flat types of structure.

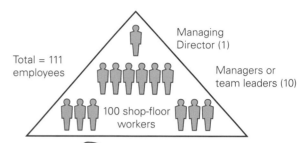

Total = 111 employees

Managing Director (1)

Managers or team leaders (10)

100 shop-floor workers

Figure 22.4 A 'flat' organisational structure has few levels of hierarchy (three) and a wide span of control. Many UK businesses have implemented this form of organisational structure.

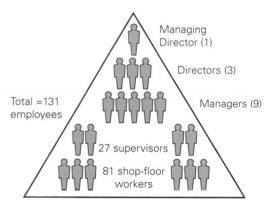

Total =131 employees

Managing Director (1)

Directors (3)

Managers (9)

27 supervisors

81 shop-floor workers

Figure 22.5 A traditional 'tall' organisational structure has five layers of hierarchy and a narrow span of control. In spite of the firm employing more people, it has fewer shop-floor employees than the 'flat' structure in Figure 22.4.

What do you think?

Surveys of employees have shown that the majority of people prefer to work within a 'flat' organisation. Why might this type of structure be particularly popular with junior employees?

Traditionally, UK businesses have tended to use 'tall' organisational structures as they have grown. Once businesses have adopted a tall organisational structure they have long **chains of command** from those at the top of the organisation to those at the bottom. Businesses with many layers of hierarchy frequently experience communication problems as messages moving up and down the organisation pass through many people and may be distorted or not passed on.

Attracted by the prospect of faster and more effective communication and improved workforce performance, which can in turn enhance competitiveness, many UK businesses have redesigned their organisations to either adopt or move towards flatter organisational structures. However, the process of flattening structures (commonly termed delayering) has led to businesses operating with significantly wider spans of control.

2. Spans of control

A **span of control** is the number of people who report directly to a manager. Spans of control and levels of hierarchy have a relationship. An organisation with a wide span of control will have relatively few levels of hierarchy – the 'flat' organisation in Figure 22.4. Conversely, 'tall' organisations have many layers of hierarchy, but narrow spans of control. Figure 22.6 illustrates a wide and a narrow span of control. Manager A has a narrow span of control of two. This is because the two supervisors B and C are the only employees who are directly responsible to him. Supervisor B has the widest span of control – five workers are responsible to her.

A narrow span of control allows team leaders, supervisors and managers to keep close control over the activities of the employees for whom they are responsible. As the span of control widens, the subordinate is likely to be able to operate with a greater degree of independence. This is because it is impossible for an individual to monitor closely the work of a large number of subordinates. A traditional view is that the span of control should not exceed six, if close supervision is to be maintained. However, where subordinates are carrying out similar duties, a span of control of ten or even twelve is not unusual. It is normal for a span of control to be less at the top of an organisation. This is because senior employees have more complex and diverse duties and are, therefore, more difficult to supervise.

3. Delegation

Delegation is the passing down of authority through the organisation. In a very small organisation, an entrepreneur or manager may be able to make all the necessary decisions and carry out many managerial tasks. They may not necessarily have the experience or knowledge to do this as effectively as possible, but lack of finance may preclude the employment of specialists. However, as an organisation grows, this may become more difficult and it becomes impossible for the entrepreneur to take all decisions. Because of this, the structure adopted by the organisation might need to be adjusted as it develops.

Delegation can be an important element of organisational design. It may reflect, for example, that the business's values include allowing relatively junior employees to make decisions.

Giving people more authority is likely to lead to wider spans of control, which can operate effectively if junior employees have been delegated authority to take decisions. This reduces the workload of their manager or team leader, as they do not have to monitor all subordinates so closely, freeing time for other duties.

Advantages	Disadvantages
• Delegation can speed up and improve the quality of decision making. Decisions may be taken by employees who are close to customers and have a better understanding of their needs and they do not have to refer decisions to managers. • Delegation can reduce the workloads of senior and middle managers, allowing them to focus on key tasks and to improve their performance. • Delegation improves the skills of junior employees and prepares them for more senior roles in the organisation.	• The costs of training. Delegation may require a business to spend heavily on training employees to ensure they have the necessary skills. • It may be inappropriate in some organisations where leadership styles are authoritarian and managers may be unwilling (or lack the skills) to pass control to junior employees. • Delegation is not a suitable strategy to adopt to manage a crisis. Such situations would require rapid decisions by experienced senior managers.

Table 22.2 Advantages and disadvantages of delegation

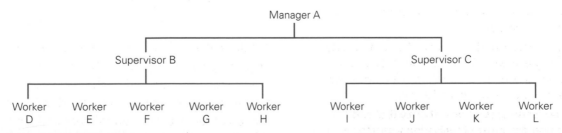

Figure 22.6 Spans of control

4. Authority

Authority and delegation are linked as the latter involves passing the former down the organisational structure. Where authority resides is an important decision within organisational design. Giving employees authority allows them the power to command a situation, to commit resources to their decisions and to issue orders to subordinates. Authority carries a matching responsibility for actions and decisions taken or for a failure to act.

5. Centralisation and decentralisation

Centralisation and decentralisation are opposites. A centralised organisation is one where the majority of decisions are taken by senior managers at the top (or centre) of the business. Organisational design based on centralisation can provide rapid decision making as few people are likely to be consulted. It should also ensure that the business pursues the objectives set by senior managers.

Decentralisation gives greater authority to employees lower down the organisational structure. In recent years many businesses decentralised because it brings benefits to many stakeholders.

- Decentralisation provides junior employees with the opportunity to fulfil needs such as achievement and recognition through working. This should improve motivation and reduce the business's costs by, for example, reducing the rate of labour turnover.
- Decentralisation is doubly beneficial to managers. It reduces the workload on senior managers, allowing them to focus on important long-term issues. At the same time it offers junior managers an opportunity to develop their skills in preparation for more senior roles.
- Customers may benefit by having more decisions made locally which can encourage the business to meet their needs more fully. Many junior employees in the organisation may have better understanding of customers' needs and operational matters and delegation may allow them to use their skills and understanding to good effect.

However, some businesses retain centralised organisations. This might be because the senior managers like to remain in control of the business and to take the major decisions. The decision to centralise may reflect the preferred style of management of the business's senior managers and their desire to retain authority. This may

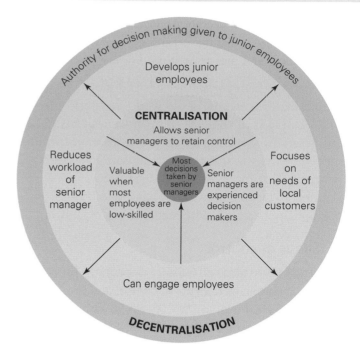

Figure 22.7 A summary of centralisation and decentralisation

occur when employees are relatively low skilled and its managers are experienced decision-makers. In addition if a business makes all its buying decisions centrally it is likely to benefit from purchasing economies of scale, allowing the possibility of shareholders receiving increased benefits. In such circumstances an organisation may perform more effectively if power remains at the centre of the organisation.

Influences on delegation, centralisation and decentralisation

Decisions on organisational design relating to centralisation and decentralisation will involve judgements about the extent to which the business delegates authority. A move towards decentralisation is likely to entail a greater degree of delegation throughout the organisation. There is a range of factors at work here, which can be categorised into internal and external influences.

Internal influences on delegation, centralisation and decentralisation

1. Leadership and management styles

A business is more likely to be willing to adopt a decentralised structure and make greater use of delegation within its organisational design if the business's managers operate in democratic or *laissez faire* styles. Such approaches to management and leadership involves junior employees in the decision-making process, while a more autocratic style would exclude them to some extent. The philosophy of democratic management will naturally move authority away from the centre of the organisation and will seek to delegate authority to employees further down the organisational structure. The impact of a *laissez faire* style would be to give decision-making authority to employees through the extreme use of delegation.

Richard Branson's leadership style has influenced his use of delegation. He believes that what he calls 'the art of delegation' is an essential element of the success of his Virgin Group of companies. Branson says 'You must understand the art of delegation. I have to be good at helping people run the individual businesses, and I have to be willing to step back.'

2. The business's overall or corporate objectives

Decisions about organisational design will be strongly influenced by the corporate objectives that the business pursues. A business with an objective of increasing its market share by supplying high-quality products may seek to delegate authority and to decentralise its organisation. Giving enhanced decision-making powers to employees throughout the organisation may help to improve motivation and the business's ability to meet the individual needs of its customers.

On the other hand, a business with a corporate objective of minimising costs may design a centralised organisational structure to benefit from consistent and experienced decision making and the benefits of purchasing in bulk.

3. The skills of the workforce

There is a relationship between the level of control managers wish to have and the design of the organisation. Managers are more likely to cede control when they have a skilled workforce. Thus the higher the level of skill a typical employee in an organisation has, the more likely the business is to use decentralisation and accompany it with delegation. Groups of professionals such as management consultants may well be employed in organisations that make extensive use of delegation within a decentralised structure. In contrast, an organisation with a high proportion of unskilled employees may remain more centralised as senior managers may not trust more junior employees with greater levels of authority and will opt to retain more control.

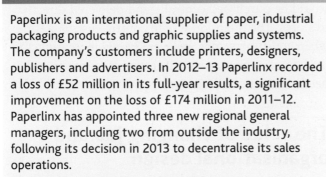

Business in focus: Paperlinx takes next step in decentralisation

Paperlinx is an international supplier of paper, industrial packaging products and graphic supplies and systems. The company's customers include printers, designers, publishers and advertisers. In 2012–13 Paperlinx recorded a loss of £52 million in its full-year results, a significant improvement on the loss of £174 million in 2011–12. Paperlinx has appointed three new regional general managers, including two from outside the industry, following its decision in 2013 to decentralise its sales operations.

Speaking at the time the paper merchant announced its decision to return to a decentralised regional focus across its commercial print business, with eight new regional heads, Paperlinx chief executive Andrew Price said that the general managers 'will be totally responsible for that branch and everything that goes on within it'.

'The people who make the decisions on delivery, pricing, etc. will be out in the branches where they will have a better understanding of the customers' needs,' he said in October.

All three new appointments, along with Paul Drake, Phil Trudgeon, Will Bourne and Mark Turnbull, general managers of Leeds and Boldon, Bristol, Midlands and London respectively, will report directly to Paperlinx UK commercial print managing director Andy Buxton.

Buxton said: 'It's an exciting time for Paperlinx. We've made lots of changes, evolving our infrastructure and how we deliver customer service, to create a business that's future-proof and geared for growth.'

Source: *Print Week*, 14 January 2014

www.printweek.com/print-week/news/1141539/paperlinx-takes-step-decen-tralising-sales

Questions

1. Explain why Paperlinx might have decided to centralise its operations prior to this latest change.
2. Is it always best for a multi-national company to operate a decentralised structure? Justify your view.

External influences on delegation, centralisation and decentralisation

1. The technological environment

Developments in technology have meant that managers have much more information available to support decision making than in the past. The use of techniques such as loyalty cards has generated huge amounts of data for managers. This is forecast to lead to further decentralisation by businesses as managers collect information centrally and disseminate it throughout the organisation to allow more junior employees to take decisions based on this and their interaction with customers. Research conducted by the Economist Intelligence Unit, shows that 63 per cent of business leaders predict a move towards a more decentralised business model and that responsibility for business decision making will move from centralised management teams towards individual employees.

Decentralised structures have been criticised for their inefficiency and lack of focus on the business's overall objectives. It is forecast that by 2020, effective business processes based on technology will empower workers to better meet the needs of the marketplace and enable organisations to be more responsive to customers' needs. Successful decentralisation will depend to some extent on processes to manage information, and ensure that it is accessible by key workers enabling them to make business decisions.

2. The competitive environment

Businesses that operate in highly competitive markets will seek to design organisations that are adaptable and flexible and allow them to meet consumers' needs as fully as possible. This may be particularly important in circumstances in which markets are altering quickly due to changing consumer tastes or product innovation.

The competitive environment can shape organisations in a number of ways. For example, the entry of new competition into a market may lead a business to design an organisation that can increase innovation and produce desirable products. Equally the business may aim to increase its competitiveness from an improved performance by its workforce if given more authority and more interesting jobs.

Finally, delegation and decentralisation may be used to improve a business's competitiveness by allowing junior employees, who may have a fuller understanding of customers' needs, to take more decisions.

Other businesses may operate in competitive environments where great emphasis is placed on price, possibly because there is little differentiation in the products that are sold. This could encourage the use of a more centralised organisation to minimise costs through uniformity, bulk buying and in the expectation that senior managers will make cost effective decisions.

3. The economic environment

A strongly performing economy can result in rapid rises in consumers' incomes and spending resulting in satisfying growth in sales for many businesses, especially those selling income elastic products. This may encourage decentralisation and delegation partly because managers experience more difficulty controlling an expanding organisation from the centre.

In contrast, difficult economic conditions may result in businesses seeking to centralise operations in an attempt to reduce costs, possibly through bulk buying and standardised procedures. In 2013, Londis, a UK grocery retailer that operates over 2,200 franchised stores, announced that all frozen food products would be purchased centrally and delivered directly to stores. The intention was to control costs at a time when consumers' incomes were barely increasing and to allow store managers time to focus on meeting the needs of their customers.

The value of changing job and organisational design

Most businesses change the design of their organisations or their employees' jobs with the aim of improving their competitiveness. Becoming more competitive is a valuable attribute for any business and can assist them in achieving their overall objectives. Managers hope that changes made to organisations and job designs will enable the business to become more effective at meeting consumers' needs while controlling costs.

Changes in the design of jobs and organisations can assist businesses in improving the performance of their workforces. Thus creating jobs that are more interesting and motivational may improve labour productivity resulting in reduced **unit labour costs**. For example, a number of UK businesses are redesigning jobs for employees aged over 50 to maintain their interest and enthusiasm in the later stages of their working lives and to retain valuable skills and knowledge within the organisation.

Key terms

Unit labour costs measure the labour cost per unit of output produced.
An **employer brand** is a business's reputation as an employer.

Redesigning organisational structures to become flatter by removing layers of management (a process known as delayering) can reduce costs as well as offering the potential to motivate those further down the organisational hierarchy. This can result in reduced unit labour costs and enhanced price competitiveness. Diego, the multi-national supplier of alcoholic drinks, has responded to increased competition in its global markets by delayering its workforce. Its Chief Financial officer has said that the company expects to reduce its costs by £200 million each year until 2017 as a consequence.

Changing job designs and organisational structures has the potential to make employees' jobs more interesting and rewarding. This is often one of the objectives behind such changes and often these changes are made to improve the status of the business's brand as an employer. A business can develop a strong **employer brand** if it designs jobs and its organisation to provide stimulating and well-rewarded work with clear routes for progression. Businesses can reap substantial rewards from positive employer brands through being able to attract the most able and best-qualified employees, which can result in improved workforce performance. Wagamama, a UK restaurant chain, noted for its East Asian cuisine, has won awards for its employer branding. The company emphasises in its recruitment materials that it wants its employees 'to be themselves' which assists it in creating a diverse workforce.

Many businesses operate in markets that are changing quickly: redesigning jobs and organisations can help them to succeed in these changing environments. The rate of change has a number of causes, including technological development and globalisation of markets. As markets become more global, UK businesses are subject to increasing competition from overseas producers including those in developing countries such as India and South Africa where production costs can be low. UK businesses have responded by developing more flexible workforces and have supported them with technology to allow lower-cost, more customer-focused operations.

Similarly, advances in technology have led to businesses redesigning jobs and their organisations to maintain and enhance competitiveness. Technology has created additional pressures for businesses to be flexible in responding to consumers' expectations in terms of quality of products and service. The use of social media by dissatisfied customers is a powerful incentive for firms to be seen to respond promptly and efficiently. Many organisations have adapted their structures to incorporate teams to provide responses to criticisms and problems aired on sites such as Twitter and Facebook. A common response is to appoint social media managers, less common is to embed within all teams and divisions in the organisation an awareness of the impact of their actions as viewed on social media.

Social media can impose pressures on managers to redesign jobs to create ones that engage employees. Dissatisfaction voiced on social media websites such as LinkedIn by employees may attract a swift response from competitors seeking to recruit skilled staff. Some HR specialists argue that the biggest impact of social media on the design of organisations is its potential to improve communication within the business and to enable employees to share information. This is an area that many businesses have yet to explore.

Weblink

Find out more about LinkedIn and how it may affect the work of HR managers at www.linkedin.com

Business in focus: Redundancies at Morrisons

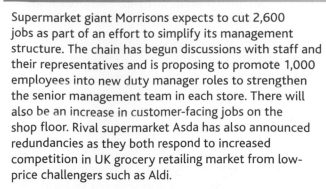

Supermarket giant Morrisons expects to cut 2,600 jobs as part of an effort to simplify its management structure. The chain has begun discussions with staff and their representatives and is proposing to promote 1,000 employees into new duty manager roles to strengthen the senior management team in each store. There will also be an increase in customer-facing jobs on the shop floor. Rival supermarket Asda has also announced redundancies as they both respond to increased competition in UK grocery retailing market from low-price challengers such as Aldi.

A spokesperson for Morrisons said the changes would modernise the way stores are managed with the aim of reducing in-store management tiers, simplifying responsibilities and improving customer service. Some Morrisons stores currently have seven tiers between the shop floor and the store manager.

The firm hopes smarter systems will make stores simpler to manage. The company has tested the revamped management structures and found it led to stronger performance and colleagues appreciated the clearer lines

of responsibility. A spokesman said customer satisfaction was also strengthened because more colleagues are in roles where they can engage with customers.

Dalton Philips, Morrisons chief executive, said: 'This is the right time to modernise the way our stores are managed. These changes will improve our focus on customers and lead to simpler, smarter ways of working. We know that moving to the new management structure will mean uncertainty for our colleagues and we will be supporting them through the process.'

Source: Wales Online, 17 June 2014
www.walesonline.co.uk/business/business-news/morrisons-make-2600-redun-dancies-latest-7280718

→ communication quicker
→ responsibility to local manager.

Questions

1. Explain the possible implications for the company of reducing the number of levels of hierarchy that exist within each store.

2. Discuss whether achieving a greater focus on customer services is the most important reason for Morrisons changing its organisational design.

How managing the human resource flow helps meet HR objectives

What is the human resource flow?

The term **human resource flow** was first used by Michael Beer in 1984. Beer and his co-authors stressed that the management of human resources must support the business in the achievement of its overall objectives. Beer and his colleagues split an organisation's human flow into three elements that need to be managed.

- **Human inflow**. This encompasses recruitment decisions about where and how to recruit employees. Related actions are planning, recruitment, selection and induction.
- **Internal human flow**. This covers the flow of employees through the organisation and includes transfers (for example to temporary projects), promotions and demotions, training and employee pay systems. This element of the human flow requires managers to balance the organisation's need to have suitably skilled employees in post with the needs of employees to develop their careers.

- **Human outflow**. This stage of the flow relates to the release of employees. The release of employees may entail retirement, redundancy (voluntary of compulsory) or dismissal.

Key term

Human resource flow is the movement of employees through an organisation, starting with recruitment.

Elements of the human resource flow

The human resource flow comprises a number of elements that reflect an employee's movement through an organisation.

Key terms

A **human resource plan** assesses the current and future capacity of a business's workforce and sets out actions necessary to meet the business's future human resource needs.

Recruitment and selection is the process of filling an organisation's job vacancies by appointing new staff.

Training is the process whereby an individual acquires job related skills and knowledge.

1. Human resource planning

We looked at human resource planning in Chapter 21. A **human resource plan** starts with an assessment of the forecast human resource needs of a business over the next few years if it is to achieve its overall or corporate objectives. These are then compared to the existing human resources available to the business, taking into account untapped skills and talents. Managers responsible for HR are then able to make decisions about how the existing workforce needs to be changed to create the desired workforce.

Once this comparison is complete the firm can take the necessary decisions to convert the existing workforce into the desired one. This may require decisions relating to various elements of the human resource flow including:

● **recruitment and selection**
● **training**
● redeployment and redundancy.

Human resource planning plays a critical role in ensuring that decisions on the business's human resource flow assist it in meeting its HR objectives. The human resource plan will be constructed with a view to meeting the HR objectives and, so long as decisions about matters such as recruitment, training and redundancy are taken in line with the plan, the HR objectives should be fulfilled.

2. Recruitment and selection

Firms can alter the composition of their workforce through recruitment and selection. The process of recruitment is summarised in Figure 22.8.

The start of recruitment is to draw up job descriptions and person specifications. Typically, job descriptions contain details on the tasks, duties and employment conditions associated with the post. In contrast, person or job specifications set out the qualifications and qualities required in an employee. They refer to the person rather than to the post. These documents form an important part of recruitment and selection. Candidates' applications should be compared against the person specification and those applicants having the 'best fit' should be invited to the selection procedure. In an interview, the job description might form the basis for the interviewer's questions.

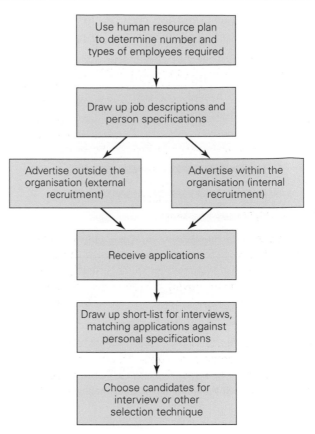

Figure 22.8 The recruitment process

Firms may recruit internally through promotion or redeployment from within the existing workforce. This means the pool of potential applicants is limited, even though they may be familiar with the business. External recruitment, from outside the business, is much more widely used by HR managers in the UK. The most effective methods for attracting candidates were through corporate websites and recruitment agencies. Corporate websites were particularly popular in the public and not-for-profit sectors (as well as in larger private sector organisations), while recruitment agencies were more widely used by private sector businesses, particularly those in manufacturing. In 2014 the BBC announced it was to recruit a large number of apprentices and this was featured on its website.

External recruitment is likely to be very expensive. Firms can recruit externally by using other methods apart from their own websites and recruitment agencies.

● Firms 'headhunt' employees who are currently working for other organisations in order to offer them employment. Those employees who are headhunted are usually either senior managers or people with specialist skills, perhaps in short supply.

- Job centres (now called Job Centre Plus) are run by the Department for Work and Pensions (DWP) to bring together those seeking work and businesses intending to recruit. This service uses technology extensively including a database called 'universal jobmatch'.

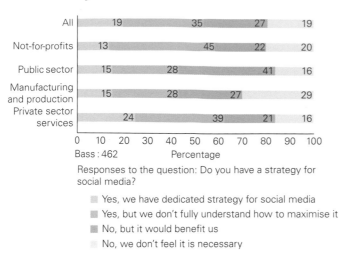

Bass : 462   Percentage

Responses to the question: Do you have a strategy for social media?

- Yes, we have dedicated strategy for social media
- Yes, but we don't fully understand how to maximise it
- No, but it would benefit us
- No, we don't feel it is necessary

Figure 22.9 Social media and human resource management in the UK

Source: CIPD Annual Survey Report, 2013

www.cipd.co.uk/binaries/resourcing-and-talent-planning_2013.PDF

Figure 22.9 illustrates that technology is playing an increasing role in managing human resources, including recruitment. The growing popularity of social networking sites such as Facebook and LinkedIn have resulted in more than half the organisation survey by the Chartered Institute of Personnel and Development (CIPD) using social media as a part of their management of human resource flow. However, only 19 per cent have a social media strategy and 35 per cent admit that, while they use social media for HR purposes, they do not understand fully how to maximise its use.

Recruitment can be an expensive exercise, though costs have fallen in recent years, perhaps due to the increasing use of social media and corporate websites. Research in 2013 showed that the average cost of external recruitment for a new employee is over £1,800. For senior managers and directors this figure is £6,000, though it can be as high as £90,000. In August 2014 Cardiff City Council admitted that it had spent £53,500 to recruit its new chief executive.

However, many managers would argue that these figures are less costly than appointing the wrong employee and perhaps having to repeat the process.

What do you think?

Why is it more expensive to appoint a senior employee?

HR managers have to select the employees they wish to hire from those candidates who have applied to work with a business. A number of selection techniques exist. Because of the high costs resulting from recruiting the wrong people, firms are investing more resources and time in the recruitment and selection process. Interviews remain the most common form of selection as they are relatively cheap, although research suggests they are unreliable as a means of selection. There is some evidence that businesses are recognising this weakness and making greater use of competency-based interviews, which are designed to test the skills that applicants will require in the workplace.

Some businesses use psychometric tests to reveal the personalities of applicants and their suitability to work in the business and within specific teams. Assessment centres are also used where a number of candidates are subjected to a variety of selection techniques over a period of between two and four days. Unilever plc, a multi-national supplier of consumer goods, operates an assessment centre in which candidates are asked to make a case study presentation, attend a competency-based interview and participate in a group exercise.

Method of selection	2013 Survey (%)	2009 Survey (%)
Competency-based interviews	82	69
Interview following contents of CV/ application form	71	68
Personality/attitude/psychometric tests	42	35
Assessment centres	43	35
Group exercises (e.g. role playing)	28	26

Table 22.3 Methods of selection used by a sample of UK businesses in 2009 and 2013

Source: CIPD Annual Survey Report, 2013

www.cipd.co.uk/binaries/resourcing-and-talent-planning_2013.PDF

Nearly 60 per cent of firms in the UK monitor their recruitment and selection procedures to ensure they appoint diverse workforces, which is an increasingly important HR objective. Effective recruitment policies will lead to the appointment of engaged employees with the right skills. This assists managers in improving key HR performance indicators such as labour productivity and unit labour costs.

Business in focus: Social media and human resource flow

A survey by CIPD has revealed that LinkedIn, Twitter and Facebook are the most commonly used social media sites for managing human resources in the UK. LinkedIn is used by 82 per cent of the businesses surveyed while 55 per cent use Twitter and 51 per cent Facebook.

Social media is frequently used for attracting candidates and building the strength of an employer brand. Approximately 46 per cent use social media to maintain contact with potential candidates for future posts.

Using social media as part of the management of human resources was reported to bring a number of benefits, as shown in Table 22.4.

Area	Increases	Decreases
Strength of the employer brand	84	1
Size of potential pool from which to select candidates	83	3
Volume of job applicants	74	6
Quality of candidates	45	19
Speed of time to hire	44	22
Cost	13	71

Table 22.4 Reponses to the question: 'How does the use of social media as part of your human resourcing strategy affect the following areas?'

Source: CIPD Annual Survey Report, 2013

www.cipd.co.uk/binaries/resourcing-and-talent-planning_2013.PDF

Questions

1. Explain the possible reasons why LinkedIn, Twitter and Facebook might be among the most popular social media sites with HR managers.

2. Do you think that all businesses should use social media as a major method of recruitment in the future? Justify your view.

3. Training

Training is a process whereby someone acquires skills and knowledge. This can help us to develop, as well as assisting the organisation in achieving its objectives. Training is commonly referred to as 'learning and talent development'.

A CIPD survey in 2013 entitled *Learning and Talent Development* found the following.

- The average amount spent on training per employee per year by the organisations in the survey was £303 in 2013, up slightly from the 2012 figure of £276, although there was a large variation between different industries and sectors.
- The typical employee received 25 hours training per year, with much less variation between industries and sectors.
- About 11 per cent of all organisations in the UK anticipate an increase in learning and talent development activities over the 12 months following the survey. However, a much larger number of businesses expect to reduce this type of activity: over 40 per cent of public sector and 20 per cent of private sector and non-profit organisations forecast reductions.

The CIPD survey suggests a generally favourable attitude by employers towards learning and talent development at work, even at a time of financial stringency. This indicates that, despite the disruption that training can cause, employers hold a generally positive view on the benefits of training. The costs and benefits of training are summarised in Table 22.5.

Costs	Benefits
Training uses up valuable resources that could be used elsewhere in the organisation – this is an example of opportunity cost.	Training can improve employee performance and hence the competitive position of the business.
Training means that employees are unavailable to the organisation for a period of time.	Training should improve employee motivation and productivity. It can help to identify and nurture the most talented employees.
Employees, once trained, may leave for better jobs.	Training is a core component of HRM and assists organisations in achieving strategic objectives.
Some managers avoid training their staff as it can lessen the degree of control they have over their subordinates.	A reputation for training will assist organisations in attracting and retaining high-quality employees.

Table 22.5 Costs and benefits of training

Study tip

It is important to appreciate the benefits and drawbacks of training (or a particular type of training), taking into account the circumstances of the business. There is no simple answer as to whether or not it is a good thing.

Businesses can engage in a range of learning and talent development activities. Figure 22.10 illustrates HR managers' views on the effectiveness of a range of methods and the extent to which they use them. Off-the-job training involves training outside the workplace, either at a college, university, or some other training agency. External courses may take the form of lectures and seminars, self-study or open learning.

On-the-job training does not require the employee to leave the workplace. They learn from experienced employees through observation and work shadowing. The trainee may work through instruction manuals or receive guidance from senior employees. This, along with in-house programmes, are some of the most highly regarded of training methods. Developments in technology, for example e-learning, have helped to increase the amount of training undertaken in the workplace or at home.

Training can be an essential, if costly, element of a HR plan to fulfil HR objectives. It can play a vital role in creating a more motivated workforce and one that has the skills required to enable the business to meet its overall or corporate objectives.

What do you think?

Why might employees be attracted to businesses that provide good-quality training or learning and talent development?

4. Dismissal and redundancy

Redundancy is one reason for **dismissal**. Other reasons for dismissal include the following.

- Employees are unable to do their jobs properly, perhaps because they do not have the necessary skills or qualifications to be competent.
- As a result of persistent or long-term illness (but not because of a person's disability).
- For 'gross misconduct' – theft or violence to towards colleagues or customers may be considered gross misconduct.
- A 'substantial reason' such as not agreeing to reasonable changes in employment terms or if an employee is given a prison sentence.

Key terms

Redundancy takes place when an employee is dismissed because a job no longer exists.

Dismissal takes place when an employer terminates an employee's contract of employment and leads to employees exiting the human resource flow.

Redeployment occurs when an employee is offered suitable alternative employment within the same business.

Redundancy is a particular type of dismissal. It is a legal reason for an employer to dismiss an employee

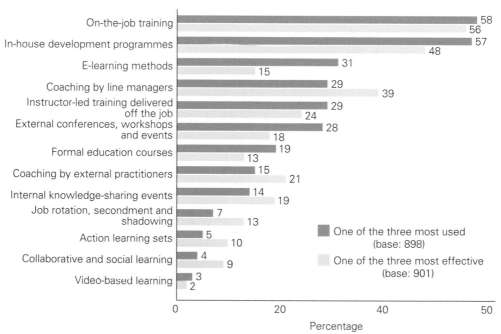

Figure 22.10 HR managers' views on a selection of learning and talent development practices

Source: CIPD Annual Survey Report 2013

www.cipd.co.uk/binaries/learning-and-talent-development_2013.pdf

but it can only occur if a job no longer exists. Redundancies can take place for a variety of reasons:

- a business closes down and all its employees are made redundant
- the jobs of some employees are replaced by new technology
- a business moves some of its operations overseas and some jobs are lost as a consequence.

If a business in the UK intends to make 20 or more employees redundant it is obliged by law to consult with any relevant trade union or other employee organisation at least 30 days before any redundancies occur. The employer must also consult with individual employees.

Employees who have been continuously employed by the business for two years and who are made redundant due to the closure of a business or reduced need for employees are entitled to compensation in the form of redundancy payments. The minimum legal redundancy pay is calculated according to a formula based on the employee's age and length of service. Some employers may choose to pay higher levels of redundancy pay.

5. Redeployment

Employees may be offered the option of **redeployment** when facing redundancy. During any period in which redundancies are being negotiated, employees should be told about available job vacancies within the organisation that could be filled through redeployment. Redeployment offers a worker what should be suitable alternative employment. A variety of factors would determine whether a job is deemed as 'suitable alternative employment'. These include:

- the proximity of the work to the employee's current job
- the terms of the job being offered
- the employee's skills, abilities and circumstances in relation to the job and the pay (including benefits), status, hours and location of the job.

Redeployment may be offered to employees who may be unable to continue in their current post due to ill health or for personal reasons.

Dismissal, redundancy and redeployment are all important actions to allow a business to meet its HR objectives. These actions can allow a business to have the desired number of employees in the correct locations and avoid overstaffing, which can reduce profit margins.

ASSESSMENT ACTIVITIES

Sections (a), (b) and (c) of these assessment activities are relevant for students taking AS and A-level examinations. The questions in section (d) are for A-level students only.

(a) Knowledge check questions

1   What is meant by the term job design?

2   State two techniques that may be used to create more interesting and challenging jobs.

3   What is meant by the term empowerment?

4   State two elements of a well-designed job according to Hackman and Oldham.

5   State two possible influences on a business's approach to the design of its employees' jobs.

6   What is meant by the term organisational design?

7   State two benefits to a business of having a well-designed organisation.

8   Is the following statement true or false? 'A span of control is the number of subordinates below a manager in the organisational hierarchy.'

9   State two advantages to a business that may result from the use of delegation.

10   Is the following statement true or false? 'Some businesses retain centralised organisations because the senior managers like to remain in control of the business and to take the major decisions.'

11   List three actions that HR managers may take to control a business's human resource flow.

12   List two methods of external recruitment that a business may use.

13   Is the following statement true or false? 'Interviews are the most effective method of selecting employees.'

14   List two possible costs to a business of increasing the amount of training it provides.

15   State the difference between redundancy and redeployment.

(b) Short answer questions

1   Explain why the manager of a business suffering from declining profitability might redesign her employees' jobs to delegate authority.   (4 marks)

2   Explain the possible consequences for a business's short-term competitiveness of a decision to reduce its number of levels of hierarchy.   (5 marks)

3   Explain how the use of a human resource plan might assist a business experiencing rapid growth in sales to meet its HR objectives.   (5 marks)

4   Explain the possible problems for a major UK retailer with 1,500 stores arising from redesigning its organisation to offer greater empowerment to junior employees.   (6 marks)

(c) Data response questions

Moheen Ltd is a social enterprise that supplies training services in areas of high unemployment. It employs 495 staff in 27 locations, the majority of whom are highly skilled. It has a strong employer brand as a caring and supportive employer that aims to develop the skills of all of its workforce. The business has grown steadily and has expanded the range of its services and has continually redesigned its jobs to allow employees to carry out more empowered roles.

Recent reductions on the level of financial support for its activities from both central and local governments have created serious difficulties for the business's managers. The senior management team are seeking to avoid making any of its employees redundant even though its revenue is forecast to fall by 24 per cent over the next financial year. The management team is confident that the company will win a number of new contracts to provide training services over the next 18 months and this is reflected in its HR plan.

The company's CEO has proposed that a policy of decentralisation is implemented as soon as possible with the aim of meeting its HR objectives of engaging employees, increasing diversity and developing its talented employees. Achieving these objectives is important for the success of the entire business, the CEO believes.

1   Explain the possible reasons why Moheen Ltd has drawn up a human resource plan.   (6 marks)

2   Analyse the reasons why it was important for Moheen Ltd to avoid making any of its employees redundant.   (9 marks)

3   To what extent will a decision to decentralise Moheen Ltd's organisation enable it to meet its HR objectives?   (15 marks)

(d) Essay questions

1   To what extent is training the most important means by which an international airline can manage its human resource flow to meet its customers' demands?   (25 marks)

2   Any business operating in a global market will always benefit from operating a decentralised organisational structure. Do you agree? Justify your view.   (25 marks)

Chapter 23

Improving motivation and engagement

Introduction

This chapter builds on earlier ones in this unit and looks at two interrelated decisions that a business's human resource managers have to make. These are how to improve the levels of motivation and engagement of the business's workforce. Improvements in these areas can have significant effects on the performance of an organisation's workforce. The next chapter will look at important decisions on how to improve employer–employee relations.

What you need to know by the end of this chapter:

- how to improve employee engagement and motivation
- the value of theories of motivation
- financial methods of motivation
- non-financial methods of motivating employees
- the benefits of motivated and engaged employees
- influences on the choice and assessment of financial and non-financial reward systems.

What are employee engagement and motivation?

What is employee engagement?

Employee engagement has a number of definitions. The one shown in the Key terms is a straightforward summary. However, the Chartered Institute of Personnel and Development (CIPD) offers a more detailed alternative. It has defined employee engagement as existing when an employee 'is positively present during the performance of work by willingly contributing intellectual effort, experiencing positive emotions and meaningful connections to others'.

The CIPD says that its definition gives three dimensions to employee engagement:

- intellectual engagement – thinking hard about the job and how to do it better

- affective engagement – feeling positively about doing a good job
- social engagement – actively taking opportunities to discuss work-related improvements with others at work.

The common themes here are that engaged employees have positive feelings towards their work, their colleagues and their organisation. The performance of UK businesses in engaging their employees is weak and declining. The Business in Focus feature summarises the results of research by ORC International, a global research company.

Employee engagement is an issue for all managers within an organisation and not just those responsible for human resources. It is impossible for an organisation to engage its employees more actively without managers in all functions and at all levels seeking to communicate effectively, demonstrating that they value employees and working to establish positive relationships with colleagues.

Key terms

Employee engagement exists when an employee is fully absorbed by and enthusiastic about their work and take positive actions to meet the organisation's goals.

Motivation describes the factors that arouse, maintain and channel behaviour towards a goal.

What is motivation?

Motivation describes the factors that arouse, maintain and channel behaviour towards a goal. There are two ways we can think about motivation at work and what causes it:

- Motivation can be the will to work due to enjoyment of the work itself. This implies that motivation comes from within an individual employee.
- An alternative view of motivation is that it is the will or desire to achieve a given target or goal that is the result of external factors, such as the promise of a reward, or to avoid the threat of punishment.

Business in focus: Poor levels of employee engagement in UK businesses

The research by ORC International paints a poor picture of the degree of positivity existing among employees in UK businesses in 2014. In every category measured, the level of UK employee engagement has declined over the twelve months prior to this report. Only 37 per cent of UK workers felt encouraged to be innovative (to develop new ideas for products or production processes) in 2014, 10 per cent below the figure for the previous year.

However, there are some aspects of the report that place UK businesses in a better light. There is some evidence that UK employers generally accept and encourage differences in employees and recruit diverse workforces. Businesses in the UK also have a better record than many European countries for caring about the health and wellbeing of employees.

Questions

1. Explain why UK businesses can benefit from having engaged employees.

2. Discuss the most important issues in this report for HR managers in companies that operate in global markets.

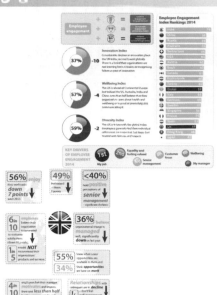

Figure 23.1 Data on employee engagement in the UK and overseas

Sources: *HR Magazine* and ORC International

www.hrmagazine.co.uk/digital_assets/386/perspectives-2014-UK.pdf

---

The first of these views assumes that motivation lies within the individual employee and the second that it is the result of some external stimuli. People in the workplace have differing views on the sources of motivation. A survey revealed that nearly 90 per cent of employers believe that money is the main motivator, while employees rank pay fourth, behind an interesting job, job security and the opportunity for achievement.

What do you think?

What motivates you – internal desire or external stimuli? Does this vary according to the circumstances?

The distinction between the internal and external views of motivation is important and you should bear it in mind when considering theories of motivation and how, in practice, entrepreneurs and managers can motivate other people.

What is the relationship between employee engagement and motivation?

These two concepts are interrelated. Some writers on HR argue that it is impossible for policies to motivate employees to be effective unless the workforce is engaged beforehand. One view is that it is essential to align the values of the workforce and the organisation as a central part of engaging and enthusing employees and creating positive attitudes to work, colleagues and the organisation. In such an environment, actions to motivate employees are more likely to be successful.

Others hold the view that engagement and motivation are inextricably linked and should not be separated in the minds of managers. Proponents of this view believe that both describe an employee's attitude and satisfaction in the work environment. Therefore both will determine whether employees work to their full potential.

Theories of motivation

Many different views exist on motivation, and they differ because it is not clear why people work. Is it to gain money, to enjoy social interaction with other humans, or to fulfil personal needs such as achievement and recognition? Or is it a combination of some or all of these? If managers can identify the main reasons why their staff work, they can determine how best to motivate them at work. It is possible to classify theories of motivation into a number of groups or schools of thought (see Table 23.1).

School of thought	Key writers	Essential ideas
Scientific School	Frederick Winslow Taylor (1856–1917)	Motivation is an external factor achieved through money. Employees should be closely supervised and paid piece-rate. Time and motion studies determine efficient means of production and workers are trained and told how to operate.
Human Relations School	Elton Mayo (1880–1949)	This brought sociological theory into management and accepted that employees could be motivated by meeting their social needs. More attention was given to the social dimension of work (e.g. communication, working as groups and consultation between managers and employees).
Neo–Human Relations School of Management	Abraham Maslow (1908–1970) and Frederick Herzberg (1923–2000)	This school highlighted the importance of fulfilling psychological needs to improve employee performance. Motivation, according to Maslow and Herzberg, depended upon designing jobs to fulfil psychological needs.

Table 23.1 Schools of thought on motivation

Key terms

Division of labour is the breaking down of production into a series of small tasks carried out repetitively by relatively unskilled employees.

A **time-and-motion study** (**work-study**) measures and analyses the ways in which jobs are completed, with a view to improving these methods.

The school of scientific management

Motivating workers became an important issue as the size of businesses increased in the late nineteenth century. Managers developed the **division of labour** to its fullest extent in an attempt to increase efficiency and improve competitiveness. The introduction of mass production methods, along with the use of division of labour, increased the numbers of people working in factories. At the same time, their tasks became monotonous.

Against this background, managers began to investigate ways of increasing employee motivation to improve competitiveness and employee satisfaction. Frederick Winslow Taylor was the most notable of

these early writers on motivation and became known as 'the father of scientific management'.

Taylor began to advise and lecture on management practices and became a consultant to car manufacturer Henry Ford. Taylor's theories were based on a simple interpretation of human behaviour, that people were motivated solely by money – his term was 'rational man'. He combined this principle with a simple interpretation of the role of the manager: to operate the business with maximum efficiency.

The key elements of Taylorism

1. **Work study.** The starting point of Taylor's approach was **work-study**. He measured and analysed the tasks necessary to complete the production process. He used a stopwatch to measure how long various activities took and sought the most efficient methods of completing tasks. He encouraged the use of the division of labour, breaking down production into small tasks.

2. **'Normal' times.** From this he identified the most efficient employees and the approaches they adopted. Using these as a basis, he then detailed 'normal' times in which duties should be completed and assessed individual performance against these norms.

3. **Equipment and training.** Employees were provided with the equipment necessary to carry out their tasks. This principle extended to giving stokers (men shovelling coal) a shovel of a size appropriate to their physique to maximise their efficiency. They were also given elementary training and clear instructions on their duties.

4. **Piece-rate pay.** Because, according to Taylor, employees were only motivated by money, the final stage of the system was to design and implement a piece-rate pay system, under which employees are paid according to the amount they produce. However, Taylor developed differential piece-rate systems to encourage efficiency among employees.

   Taylor also believed in close supervision of the workforce to ensure that they continued to make the maximum effort possible, motivated by pay.

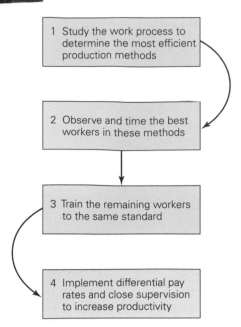

Figure 23.2 The essential features of Taylorism

Taylor's views were unpopular with shop-floor employees. His systems forced them to work hard and, by raising productivity levels, placed the jobs of the less efficient workers under threat. Taylor's approach raised efficiency and productivity, so businesses did not need as many employees. His ideas resulted in strikes and other forms of industrial action by dissatisfied workers.

The human relations school

A fundamental weakness of the Scientific School was that its work ignored the social needs of employees. This, and the obvious unpopularity of the ideas of Taylor, led to the development of the Human Relations School. This school of thought concentrated on the sociological aspects of work. Its foremost member was an Australian-born psychologist, Elton Mayo (1880–1949). Initially, Mayo was one of Taylor's disciples, believing in the importance of scientific management to business efficiency.

The Hawthorne effect

Mayo's views altered as a result of research he conducted at the Western Electric Company in Chicago. The research was to examine the effects of changes in lighting on the productivity of workers at the company's Hawthorne plant. Previous experiments on lighting and productivity had produced unexpected results. Researchers had anticipated that improving lighting would increase productivity because giving workers better working conditions would allow them to work harder and earn more money. They were astonished when productivity increased not only in the group who were given improved lighting, but also among a group whose lighting had not changed.

It became apparent that the employees were responding to the level of attention they were receiving as part of the investigations and because they were working together as a group. This became known as the 'Hawthorne effect'. As a result of this and similar experiments, Mayo stressed the importance of 'social man' within the workplace. From these experiments, Mayo concluded that motivation was dependent upon:

- the type of job being carried out and the type of supervision given to the employee
- group relationships, group morale and the sense of worth experienced by individuals.

The implications of the 'Hawthorne effect'

Following the publication of Mayo's findings, managers gradually became more aware of the importance of meeting the social needs of individuals at work. Social environments at work and informal working groups were recognised as having positive influences upon productivity.

The acceptance of Mayo's views led to a number of developments in businesses during the 1940s and 1950s, many of which remain today.

- Managers often ensured that employees' social needs were met at work wherever possible.
- Employees were provided with a range of sporting and social facilities to foster the development of informal groups among employees.
- Work outings and trips became a familiar part of an employee's year (for example, Marks & Spencer organises short-break weekends for its employees).
- Managers gave more attention to teams and teamworking.

Mayo's recognition of the importance of teamworking is perhaps his most enduring testimony. Many firms have organised their workforce into teams, for example, John Lewis and Toshiba.

Weblink

For more information about John Lewis, visit www.john-lewis-partnership.co.uk.

Mayo's work took forward management in general, and motivation in particular. He moved the focus onto the needs of employees, rather than just on the needs of the organisation.

The Neo-human relations school

This could also be called the new Human Relations School. Abraham Maslow and Frederick Herzberg are recognised as key members of this particular school. They began to put forward their views in the 1950s. While the Human Relations School, associated with Elton Mayo, highlighted the sociological aspects of work, the Neo-Human Relations School considered the psychological aspects of employment. This school argued that motivation lies within each individual employee: managers merely need the key to unlock the motivational force.

By focusing on the psychological needs of employees, Maslow and Herzberg encouraged managers to treat their employees as individuals, with different needs and aspirations. Their work emphasised that, because people are different, the techniques required to motivate individuals will also differ.

Maslow's hierarchy of needs

In 1954, Maslow published his 'hierarchy of needs', setting out the various needs that, he argued, everyone attempted to meet through working. Maslow presented his hierarchy of needs as a triangle with basic needs shown at the bottom and so-called higher needs towards the top.

Maslow's argument was a relatively simple one. Employees, he argued, have a series of needs they seek to fulfil at work. These are in a hierarchy – once a lower level need is satisfied, individuals strive to satisfy needs further up the hierarchy. Abraham Maslow established five levels of human needs that can be satisfied through employment.

The key point of Maslow's argument was that a business could motivate its employees by offering them the chance to fulfil a higher level of need once a lower one was satisfied. So once an employee's basic needs had been met, perhaps through a system of fair pay, they could be motivated further by the offer of secure and continuing employment. Similarly, a worker whose social needs were met through employment could next be motivated by the opportunity to satisfy self-esteem needs. This could be achieved by taking responsibility for a major project, offering the chance of achievement and recognition.

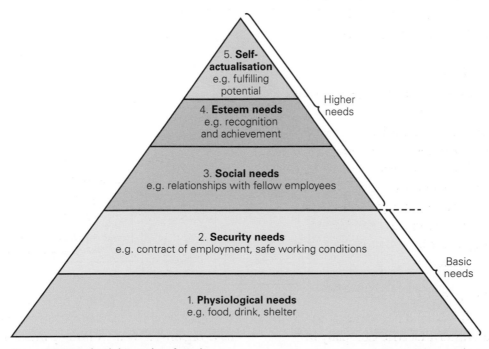

Figure 23.3 Maslow's hierarchy of needs

Maslow's theory was attractive to managers from the outset. It offered a more individualistic approach to motivating employees, recognising that not all people are the same. Managers had long realised that what motivated one person would not necessarily motivate another. Maslow's theory offered an explanation and an alternative approach for managers.

Maslow's level of need	Examples	Means of satisfying needs
1. Physiological needs	Food, water, shelter, clothing	Through pay and a warm and dry working environment
2. Security needs	A safe and secure working environment for employees	Implementing a proper health and safety policy, providing employees with contracts of employment
3. Social needs	Contact and friendships with other employees	Social and sporting facilities, opportunities to work in groups
4. Esteem needs	Achievement, recognition and self-respect	Delegating authority to junior employees, offering promotion opportunities
5. Self-actualisation	To fulfil one's potential completely	Providing opportunities to take new responsibilities and to develop new skills.

Table 23.2 Explanation of Maslow's hierarchy of needs

Frederick Herzberg's two-factor theory

Herzberg's two-factor theory was the result of a study designed to test the view that people face two major sets of influences at work. Herzberg's resulting theory was based on the results to questions asked of 200 accountants and engineers in the USA.

The first part of Herzberg's motivation theory is related to the environment of the job. He identified a range of factors that shaped the environment in which people work and he called these influences hygiene or maintenance factors. These factors are all around the job, but are not a part of the job itself. Herzberg's research identified a number of hygiene factors, including the following:

- company policies and administration
- supervision of employees
- working conditions
- salary
- relationship with fellow workers (at the same level).

Herzberg's crucial finding was that hygiene factors do not lead to motivation, but without them employees may become dissatisfied. So, according to Herzberg, an employee cannot be motivated by pay, but might be dissatisfied by inadequate financial rewards. Hygiene factors were so named because Herzberg believed attention to them would prevent hygiene problems. It is important to note that Herzberg's research classified pay as a hygiene factor and, therefore, as unable to motivate.

The second finding of Herzberg's research established those factors with the ability to motivate – the motivators. These factors relate to the job itself and can be used to positively motivate employees. He identified the following factors as motivators:

- personal achievement of goals and targets
- recognition for achievement

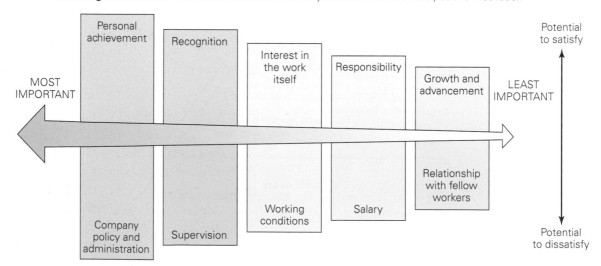

Herzberg's motivators – these **satisfiers** relate to the job itself and can create positive motivation

Herzberg's hygiene factors – these relate to the job environment and have the potential to dissatisfy

Figure 23.4 Herzberg's hygiene and motivational factors

Business in focus: Motivation at Asons solicitors

Asons Solicitors is a law firm based in Greater Manchester. The firm deals with a variety of legal issues and operates with well-publicised core values including professionalism, dedication, team work and achievement.

The firm has recently announced the launch a range of initiatives to help improve the motivation levels of its 306 staff. The initiatives include establishing a social committee and providing corporate gym membership. It has also introduced a gift and incentives scheme, where employees are rewarded with vouchers, gift sets, tablets, a free lunch and event tickets.

Other new initiatives include:

- The Asons Foundation Charity Committee, which helps raise money to aid the local community and charities
- The Employee Committee, which offers a forum for employees to voice suggestions for change to both process and policy within the organisation
- a new break room, which includes sofas, a high-definition television, an Xbox 360, a pool table, fruit bowls, vending machines and a football table
- discount cards such as Love2Shop and Gourmet Society.

Sarah Ainscough, HR manager at Asons Solicitors, said: 'Our efforts to attract talent has resulted in a young and imaginative leadership. Between us, we've pushed the firm into uncharted territory as far as employee satisfaction goes, and we've succeeded. We've broken the stuffy image of your stereotypical law firm and managed to improve morale and motivation. I'd love to see other firms in our industry trying out similar initiatives.'

Source: Employee Benefits website

www.employeebenefits.co.uk/benefits/staff-motivation/asons-launches-benefits-to-boost-staff-motivation/105356.article

Questions

1. Explain why Asons might have chosen to publicise its policies to improve employee motivation.
2. To what extent do you think that these initiatives will be successful in improving motivation levels among the law firm's employees?

- interest in the work itself
- responsibility for greater and more complex duties
- personal growth and advancement.

Herzberg believed that these approaches (hygiene and motivation) must be used simultaneously. Employees should be managed so they have a minimum of dissatisfaction. They should get achievement, recognition for achievement, take interest in their work and be given responsibility to allow them to grow and develop within their work.

Study tip

You should seek to use relevant motivation theories to write analytically about specific scenarios, for example to analyse the causes and consequences of decisions by human resource managers.

The value of theories of motivation

Theories of motivation have received a great deal of attention over the years and have had a considerable impact on the ways in which managers have thought and behaved. They can provide a structure or a framework for managers who make

decisions on how to motivate employees. This can be better than simply acting on instinct.

Taylor's legacy

It is easy to dismiss Taylor and his ideas. His entire philosophy was based on the belief that employees were motivated only by money. He ignored any social dimension of employment and made employees work very hard for what was a meagre wage. His ideas resulted in workers endlessly completing monotonous tasks. There was considerable hostility towards his ideas and opposition from politicians and the business community.

However, Taylor made a significant and enduring contribution to the management of business organisations. He established management as a scientific subject worthy of research and study. His approach was adopted by many premier figures in the business community in the early decades of the century, including Henry Ford. His techniques encouraged the use of mass production and the conveyor belt system. Furthermore, his work provided a starting point for a later and more people-centred approach to management.

Avoid considering Taylor simply in negative terms. Certainly, many of his ideas would not be acceptable in modern businesses, but others (for example, simple piece-rate pay and work-study) have endured. A balanced assessment of Taylor should take into account the lasting elements of his approach, as well as the shortcomings.

Mayo and teamworking

Many students just think of Mayo in terms of communicating with bosses, and his emphasis on social and sporting facilities. However, this is only part of his work. He advocated the benefits to employers and employees of working in teams – this aspect of his work is an important issue within many businesses today.

Assessing the work of the Neo-Human Relations School

The research and writing of Maslow and Herzberg has had a major impact on the way in which businesses have managed their employees. Although there are differences in their approaches, many similarities also exist. As illustrated in Table 23.3, Herzberg's motivators broadly correspond with Maslow's higher needs.

	Maslow	Herzberg
Motivation factors (higher needs)	• Self-actualisation needs • Esteem needs	• Achievement • Recognition • Responsibility • Interest in work • Personal growth
Maintenance factors (lower needs)	• Social needs • Security needs • Physiological needs	• Company policy and administration • Supervision • Working conditions • Relationship with fellow workers • Salaries

Table 23.3 Herzberg and Maslow compared

Both have a major advantage in that they were not simply theoretical writings – practical implications for management were within the theories. Both authors encouraged managers to utilise their employees' abilities by giving them challenging tasks.

Weaknesses do exist within these theories, of course. Herzberg's assertion that pay cannot be used to motivate might be true of many employees in wealthy, developed economies. However, this may not be the case with workers in poorer, developing countries.

Equally, Maslow's theory is based upon a hierarchy and the assumption that individuals move from one level to the next. His work has been criticised on the grounds that people do not move through these needs in the same order. It also assumes that, once a need is fulfilled, it loses its power to motivate. This may not be the case, especially with the higher needs.

How to improve employee engagement and motivation

Improving employee engagement

Some studies suggest that disengaged employees represent a huge opportunity for businesses to improve their competitiveness and profitability. Research in a number of countries, including New Zealand, has established a correlation between levels of employee engagement and human resource performance indicators such as labour productivity, labour turnover and product quality.

1. **Find out the current position.** A starting point to improving employee engagement is to find out existing levels of engagement among the workforce and to seek to build on good practice. This will require research specifically to reveal engagement levels, possibly through a survey of employees. Using existing survey data, collected for other purposes is unlikely to be accurate. This can also have the benefit of raising the often unspoken issue of employee engagement.

2. **Recruit the right managers and train them all.** Appointing managers who have the potential to engage the employees for whom they are responsible is essential. This is *not* simply an issue for HR managers, but for all managers within an organisation. Such managers will be good communicators who appreciate the importance of human resources in achieving the overall goals of the business. They should be required to manage employees in ways that overtly value and encourage their contributions. Managers who are appointed should have the necessary skills to fulfil their role in these ways and should receive training as necessary. Businesses may benefit from investing in training managers at all levels within the organisation as their decisions are central to creation and maintenance of an engaged workforce.

Too many businesses tend to invest most in training senior managers and neglect the needs of more junior managers and team leaders.

3. **Make managers accountable for employee engagement.** Managers should also be held accountable for the level of engagement among the employees in their charge. This can be supported and measured through setting realistic and achievable goals for employee engagement throughout the organisation. Managers can be rewarded for agreed levels of engagement.

4. **Recognise the value of communication in employee engagement.** Communication is a key issue in improving employee engagement. Research in the USA shows that employees can become disengaged because they feel that their managers do not care about them and this is evidenced in a lack of communication. Over-communication is not a problem and employees can handle a changing environment better when given reliable information regularly and offered the opportunity to comment and contribute. This also reinforces the idea that they are valued by managers and leaders.

5. **Involve senior managers.** Involving senior managers in the company in actions to improve the level of engagement of a workforce is vital. If senior managers or leaders portray values that are worthy and likely to receive the support of employees, employees are more likely to be engaged.

6. **Implement actions to help employees value their organisation.** In a similar vein, taking actions to increase employees' pride in their organisation helps to promote engagement. This might take the form of publicising the benefits that the business's products give to society. Genzyme, an American biotechnology company, does this by requiring its researchers to contact patients whose lives have been improved by its products (such as those designed to overcome enzyme deficiencies). This is done on a regular basis.

7. **Align employees' values with those of the organisation.** Training and communication can be used to align employees' values with those of the organisation. This can help to increase the value and pride employees place in their organisation and in being a part of it. Employees whose values accord with those of the organisation are much less likely to become disengaged and will make decisions in accordance with the common values.

The use of financial methods of motivation

Managers and organisations use a variety of pay systems in an attempt to improve the performance of their workforce. Despite attention given to the views of Herzberg, which suggest that monetary methods of motivation are of limited value, pay remains a major incentive.

Key terms

Commission is a method of payment in which the amount paid is related to the value of goods or services that an employee sells.

Piece rate (also called piecework) is a system whereby employees are paid according to the quantity of a product they produce.

Performance-related pay exists where some part of an employee's pay is linked to the achievement of targets at work. These targets might include sales figures or achieving certain grades in an annual appraisal.

Variable pay is a flexible form of pay that offers employees a highly individual pay system related to their performance at work.

Writer	Opinions on the motivational power of pay
Frederick Taylor	Taylor saw pay as the primary motivating factor for all workers. He referred to workers as 'economic animals' and supported the use of piece-rate pay.
Abraham Maslow	He saw pay as a reward permitting employees to meet the lower needs on their hierarchy.
Frederick Herzberg	Pay is a hygiene factor and a possible cause of dissatisfaction. In a few circumstances pay might be a motivator if, for example, it is used as a recognition for merit.

Table 23.4 Opinions on the motivational powers of pay

Salaries and wages

Most employees in the UK receive their payment in the form of salaries or wages. Salaries are expressed in annual terms (for example a production manager might be paid a salary of £35,000 per year) and are normally paid monthly. Salaried employees are not normally required to work a set number of hours per week though their contract of employment may state a minimum number of hours.

On the other hand, wages are usually paid weekly and employees are normally required to be at work for a specified number of hours. Employees are normally paid a higher rate (known as overtime) for any additional hours worked.

Some employees are paid **commission**. This is most common for employees involved in selling products and the amount paid as commission is normally an agreed percentage of the value of goods and services that are sold.

Piece rate

Under this pay system, employees are paid according to the quantity they produce. Thus, an employee on a production line might receive an agreed amount for each unit of production they complete. **Piece rate** is common in a number of industries in the UK including textiles, electronics and agriculture.

Piece rate offers businesses a number of advantages and disadvantages. It links pay to output levels but can result in employees rushing work, which may damage the quality of the product. Since the implementation of the minimum wage, employers have faced additional problems in using piece rate. Employers using piece rate have to ensure that their employees earn at least the minimum wage rate per hour. The UK Government introduced the minimum wage on 1 April 1999. This legislation covered full- and part-time employees as well as temporary workers and those on piece rate. Since then the wage has increased steadily and at rates above inflation and the average increase in wages. This has benefited low-paid employees, but has imposed an additional cost burden on businesses.

In October 2014 the minimum wage rate for employees aged 21 and over was increased to £6.50 (compared with £3.60 when it was introduced in 1999). At the same time the hourly rates for workers aged between 18 and 20 were set at £5.13 and for employees under 18 at £3.79 an hour.

Performance-related pay (PRP)

Performance-related pay (or PRP) has become more widely used over recent years and has developed along with employee appraisal systems. PRP is only paid to those employees who meet or exceed some agreed targets. Under PRP, employees are paid for their contribution to the organisation, rather than their status within it.

Businesses of all sizes have introduced PRP. Examples include the National Health Service and the Trustee Savings Bank (TSB) as well as the retailer Iceland. PRP remains popular, and many employees support linking some element of pay to performance. However, there have been criticisms of the huge bonuses paid to some senior managers and directors of moderately successful companies.

Criticisms of PRP

A number of criticisms of performance-related pay have been put forward:

- Many employees perceive PRP as fundamentally unfair. This is particularly true of those working in the services sector where employee performance is difficult to measure. Employees fear that they might be discriminated against because they do not get on with their managers. This can result in their performance worsening, not improving.
- A majority of businesses operating PRP systems do not put sufficient funds into the scheme. Typically, the operation of a PRP scheme adds 3–4 per cent to a business's wage bill. This only allows employees to enjoy relatively small performance awards, which may be inadequate to change employee performance.

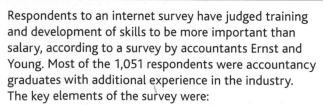

Business in focus: Motivating accountancy graduates

Respondents to an internet survey have judged training and development of skills to be more important than salary, according to a survey by accountants Ernst and Young. Most of the 1,051 respondents were accountancy graduates with additional experience in the industry. The key elements of the survey were:

- Approximately 44 per cent rated training as the most important factor attracting them to a job.
- A mere 18 per cent of respondents placed salary and benefits as the most important factor.

- The reputation of the business was judged most important by 12 per cent and 8 per cent identified the business's culture as the vital factor.

Questions

1. Explain why employees may be attracted by a business with a good reputation.
2. Do you think that pay as a motivator is outdated and irrelevant for today's employees? Justify your view.

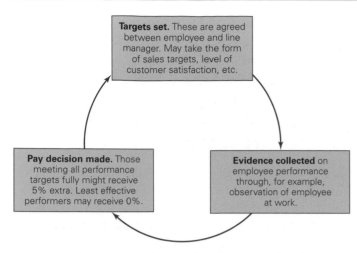

Figure 23.5 The operation of a typical performance-related pay system

Developments in PRP

Increasing numbers of businesses are implementing a system known as **variable pay**. Some managers argue that a business's performance often depends upon the achievements of the few.

Variable pay is really a development of PRP. It is similar in that it rewards employee performance, but there are differences. PRP operates according to a formula used throughout the company. Variable pay is far more flexible and the potential rewards for star employees are greater. If the business performs well employees benefit under variable pay, but can suffer financial penalties in a less successful period.

Some managers remain unconvinced of the value of PRP, no matter how sophisticated the scheme. The widespread use of PRP may, in part, be an attempt by managers to keep pay rates down for the majority of employees. PRP, or variable pay, treats employees as individuals, limiting the ability of trade unions to bargain collectively.

In recent years, the notion of linking pay to a wider definition of employees' 'contribution' rather than simple 'performance' has gained ground. This emphasises not only performance in the sense of the end result (output, for example) but also the employee's overall contribution to the business's achievements.

PRP remains a highly topical issue. While there are a number of arguments in favour of it, a central weakness remains. This can be explained in terms of the theory we covered earlier in this chapter. Writers such as Maslow and Herzberg argued that money has

limited power to motivate employees. PRP, no matter how it is implemented, has more in common with Frederick Taylor's views of motivating employees.

Profit sharing

Profit sharing is a system whereby employees receive some of the business's profits. This is a type of performance-related pay, but one that may not discriminate between the performances of individual members of staff. Such payments, which may vary according to salary or wage, are distinct from, and additional to, regular earnings.

Profits are paid out to employees immediately in the form of cash or company shares, as discussed below. Profit-sharing schemes may improve employees' loyalty to the company. These schemes can help to break down the 'them and us' attitude. Under profit-sharing schemes, a greater level of profit is regarded as being of benefit to all employees, and not just senior managers and shareholders. Employees may be more willing to accept changes designed to improve the business's profitability.

The danger with profit-sharing schemes is that they can be too small and fail to provide employees with a worthwhile payment. On the other hand, if schemes are too generous, the company may have insufficient funds for capital investment.

Share ownership

This can be a development of profit-sharing schemes. Some businesses pay their employees a share of the profits in the form of company shares. Share ownership schemes vary enormously in their operation. Here, we consider two of the main schemes operated by UK companies.

Some businesses offer employees the opportunity to purchase shares after saving for a period of time. After say, five years, employees can purchase shares at the price they were at the start of the savings scheme. This is a popular type of scheme, though tax changes have made it more difficult to operate. Other businesses offer employees free shares as an incentive.

Share options are a form of share ownership normally aimed at senior managers. About 15 per cent of UK companies operate share option schemes. Under share options, managers have the opportunity to buy company shares at some agreed date in the future, but at the current share price.

For example, a company's current share price might be £2.50 and the senior manager subject to this type of financial motivation is given the option to purchase 10,000 shares in three years' time at this price. In three years the market price of shares may have risen to £3.50. This offers the manager the chance to purchase the 100,000 shares for £250,000 (£2.50 x 100,000) and to sell them immediately for £350,000, giving a profit of £100,000. If the share price falls over the three-year period, the manager will choose not to buy the shares. Such deals encourage senior managers to take decisions that increase the long-term share price of their companies.

The use of non-financial methods of motivating employees

Every employer in the UK is required by law to provide essential amenities such as toilets and clean drinking water for employees. Most employees would also hope to find additional facilities such as a cloakroom and a clean and hygienic seating area for workers to use during meal breaks. There should be facilities nearby for heating food or hot water for drinks. A 'good' employer who is concerned about **employee welfare** will also consider other issues besides the physical working environment.

Key terms

Job design is the process of grouping together or dividing up of tasks and responsibilities to create complete jobs.

Employee welfare is a broad term covering a wide range of facilities that are essential for the wellbeing of a business's employees.

Appraisal is the process of considering and evaluating the performance of an individual employee.

Teamworking exists when an organisation breaks down its production processes into large units instead of relying upon the use of the division of labour.

1. Job design

We saw in Chapter 22 that the design of jobs (**job design**) can have a powerful influence on the performance of a workforce. If HR managers can design jobs that are interesting, varied and challenging then this is more likely to motivate employees. Including more demanding tasks in an employee's job through the process of job enrichment will often

improve motivation and performance. Some businesses extend the range of similarly demanding duties and tasks through the use of job rotation, where employees switch regularly between tasks and through job enlargement where they permanently carry out a wider range of duties.

2. Appraisal systems

Good employers will seek to develop their employees as fully as possible to improve their performance at work. In part this may be achieved by a development **appraisal** system. Developmental appraisal measures an employee's performance with the aim of offering training to correct any shortcomings or to achieve further improvement. Businesses and employees can benefit from appraisal systems, especially those that develop employees' skills. Such appraisal systems can encourage employees to take actions intended to help the business achieve its objectives and can improve relationships between manager and subordinate alongside employee performance. Developmental appraisal systems can improve employee behaviour, enhancing labour productivity. Supporters of appraisal systems also argue that they can help in identifying staff training needs and ensuring that training undertaken is relevant to the needs of the individual and the organisation.

Human resource managers can play a central role in developing effective appraisal systems as well as improving the physical environment within which employees work. Recruiting people with the intention of developing their skills and improving their performance throughout a long-term relationship is at the heart of what is called 'soft' human resource management, which we considered in Chapter 20. Such an approach to human resource management (HRM) may well have a developmental appraisal system at its heart, as well as a clear appreciation of the benefits to the business of providing good facilities for employees.

Firms take such decisions because they have the potential to improve the morale and motivation of employees. As we saw earlier, there are different views on what motivates employees. Some writers on motivation argue that physical facilities are important or, as Herzberg believed, their absence has the power to demotivate employees. Many motivational theorists would argue that providing training and allowing employees to develop themselves and to fulfil their

Business in focus: Working at Google

Here's a taste of what we offer:

Stay healthy, save time

On-site physicians and nurses, convenient medical services, and comprehensive health care coverage help keep you healthy and happy. [Varies by location]

Travel without worries

Googlers and their families are covered with travel insurance and emergency assistance – even on personal vacations.

More time with your baby

New parents get time off and some extra spending money to help them welcome their new bundle of joy.

Never stop learning

We'll reimburse you for classes or degree programs that help you with what you do.

Legal aid for less

Googlers get legal advice at no cost and, in the US, also get common legal services at a generous group discount.

Google announced that it made a profit of $3.45 billion in the first three months of 2014.

Source: Google website
www.google.com/about/jobs/lifeatgoogle/benefits/

Questions

1. Explain the possible reasons why Google publicises its working conditions on its website.
2. Discuss the possible costs and benefits to Google from treating its employees in this way.

potential are powerful motivators. Maslow termed this 'self-actualisation' and argued that it was the highest form of motivation available to employers.

3. Teamworking

Teamworking exists when an organisation divides its production processes into large units instead of relying on the use of the division of labour. Teams are then given responsibility for completing the large units of work. Team members carry out a variety of duties including planning, problem-solving and target-setting.

A number of different team types operate within businesses:

- **Production teams** – many production lines have been organised into distinct elements called 'cells'. Each of these cells is staffed by teams whose members are multi-skilled. They monitor product quality and ensure that production targets are met.
- **Quality circle teams** – these are small teams designed to propose solutions to existing problems and to suggest improvements in production

methods. The teams contain members drawn from all levels within the organisation.
- **Management teams** – increasingly, managers see themselves as complementary teams, establishing the organisation's objectives and overseeing their achievement.

There has been a major trend in businesses towards teamworking over recent years. Teamworking is a major part of the so-called Japanese approach to production and its benefits have been publicised by major companies such as Honda.

Teamworking offers employees the opportunity to meet their social needs, as identified by Maslow. Herzberg identified relationships with fellow workers as a 'hygiene' factor. However, much of the motivational force arising from teamworking comes with the change in job design that usually accompanies it. Teamworking requires jobs to be redesigned, offering employees the chance to fulfil some of the higher needs identified by Maslow, such as esteem needs. Similarly, teamworking offers some of the motivators, for example achievement.

The benefits of motivated and engaged employees

We saw earlier in this chapter that some HR professionals argue that motivation techniques are unlikely to work without engaged employees. It is helpful to consider how businesses benefit from having employees who are engaged and motivated.

Organisations whose workforces possess high levels of engagement and motivation tend to show the following characteristics:

- a low level of absenteeism at all levels within the business
- relatively few employees deciding to leave the organisation, giving a low level of labour turnover
- good relations between managers and other employees
- high levels of labour productivity.

In addition, businesses can benefit in terms of customers' perceptions of the business. Motivated and engaged employees can be expected to offer good quality products and high standards of customer service. Engaged employees are also likely to project a good image of the business, which may result in customer loyalty and repeat purchases. Engaged employees can be a valuable promotional asset in an age in which employee opinions can be easily viewed by many stakeholders on social media. Research in the USA by Weber Shandwick (a multi-national public relations company) found that 50 per cent of employees post messages, pictures or videos in social media about their employer and more than a third have shared praise or positive comments online about

their employer. A third of employees post messages, pictures or videos about their employer without any encouragement from their employer. However, on the negative side, 16 per cent of employees have shared criticism or negative comments online about their employer.

A business that enjoys the benefit of a highly engaged and motivated workforce is also likely to have a productive workforce. Reductions in unit labour costs offer firms two opportunities:

- to sell their products more cheaply
- to maintain price levels and enjoy greater profits.

Engaged and motivated workforces offer a business other benefits, too:

- Employees are usually contented, making it easier for businesses to attract other employees – the firm will have a reputation as a 'good' employer. This helps to build the employer brand.
- Modern businesses protect their public image and spend vast sums of money to enhance it. As we saw earlier the engagement of the workforce can be an important element of creating a positive corporate image given the rising popularity of social media.
- Over recent years, firms have become increasingly aware of the need to compete in terms of quality and customer service. If businesses are to compete in these ways, engaged motivated employees are essential.

So, any manager seeking to improve the performance of his or her workforce may be able to do so by taking steps to improve employee engagement and motivation.

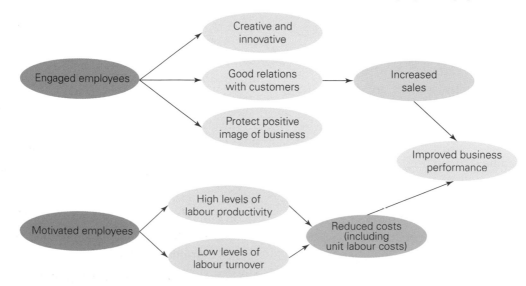

Figure 23.7 How engagement and motivation can aid a business's performance

Influences on the choice and assessment of financial and non-financial methods of motivation

Not all managers adopt the same approaches to motivate employees for whom they are responsible. A number of factors influence their choices of the methods to be deployed.

1. **The costs involved**. For many firms this might be the determining factor. If profit margins are slim (and shareholders dissatisfied) managers may not be able to offer bonuses, piece-rate pay or to pay for training to allow a policy of delegation. They may not have the funds for training or supporting staff to take on delegated responsibilities. Managers may find themselves in conflict with shareholders who fear that their dividends will be reduced.

2. **The attitude of the management team**. Some managers have a strong autocratic streak and relish being in control. They may not implement motivational techniques, resulting in subordinates having greater influence over their working lives. They will be more likely to focus on pay as a motivator.

3. **The training given to the management team**. Have managers received training in the theory of motivation? If they understand why their employees work they will be more likely to apply appropriate motivational techniques. In these circumstances they may be less likely to rely solely on financial forms of motivation.

4. **The skill levels of the workforce.** Some techniques of motivation, notably delegation and job enrichment, may require substantial employee training before they can be implemented. It would be impossible to offer employees the chance to plan their own work, take their own decisions and to carry out a number of roles as part of a multi-skilled team without substantial training with clear implications for the business's costs.

5. **The importance of public's perception of the business.** Some organisations may engage in techniques such as delegation and empowerment to project a positive corporate image. This can be an important element of gaining a competitive advantage and can enhance company sales and assist in attracting high-quality employees. Unilever plc, which supplies consumer products, is an example of a company that is aiming to enhance its public image through a range of policies including the use of delegation.

6. **The effectiveness of communication within and outside the business.** If a business has effective two-way communication throughout the organisation it is more likely to implement techniques such as quality circles or teamworking. Firms with poor communication may rely more on piece-rate pay and job rotation.

ASSESSMENT ACTIVITIES

Sections (a), (b) and (c) of these assessment activities are relevant for students taking AS and A-level examinations. The questions in section (d) are for A-level students only.

(a) Knowledge check questions

1 State the difference between employee engagement and motivation.

2 What are the three dimensions of employee engagement as identified by the CIPD?

3 State two of the key elements of Taylorism.

4 List the three higher needs from Abraham Maslow's hierarchy of needs.

5 State two of Frederick Herzberg's hygiene factors.

6 What is meant by the term performance-related pay?

7 Is the following statement true or false? 'An employee does not know exactly how much they will receive in pay from a piece-rate system until the end of the working period.'

8 State two factors that make variable pay flexible.

9 State two characteristics that highly motivated workforces may display.

10 What is meant by the term appraisal?

(b) Short answer questions

1 Explain why a well-motivated workforce is an important asset for a low-cost manufacturer.
(4 marks)

2 Explain the possible limitations of using financial factors to motivate employees working in the National Health Service (NHS). (5 marks)

3 Explain the possible problems for a high-profile public limited company of having a substantial number of disengaged employees. (5 marks)

4 Explain why a company entering a new market may consider employee engagement to be a crucial issue. (6 marks)

(c) Data response questions

Kohli Ltd designs and installs kitchens for individuals and house builders in London. The company trades in a competitive market that is mainly comprised of small firms, mainly sole traders. It has traded for 20 years and gained a reputation for outstanding quality in terms of its designs and the subsequent fitting of the kitchens, as well as its overall customer service. It has a loyal and long-serving workforce, many of whom have been with the company for more than 15 years. However, in recent years the business's profits have declined and its operating profit margin was just 2.2 per cent last year.

The managers at Kohli Ltd are considering how to improve motivation levels to improve competitiveness and have discussed a range of possibilities. A suggestion to motivate the teams of staff who install the kitchens (the fitters) with piece-rate pay was thought not to be appropriate. One manager commented that the company did not need to implement policies to motivate employees as most of

its competitors did not do so and were they looking in the right area?

After some discussion the management team decided to use non-financial methods of motivation. It was decided to extend the use of teamwork and to empower teams to decide how to design and fit kitchens with minimal input from managers.

1 Explain why piece rate might not be an appropriate method of motivation for the company's kitchen fitters. (6 marks)

2 Analyse the possible reasons why many of Kohli Ltd's rivals do not use motivational techniques to improve the performance of their workforces. (9 marks)

3 To what extent is the decision by the managers at Kohli Ltd to use non-financial methods of motivation for its employees the best way for it to improve its competitiveness? (15 marks)

(d) Essays

1 To what extent is training the most important method of motivation for all employees, irrespective of their seniority or level of skill?
(25 marks)

2 Fast-food restaurant chains should not bother implementing policies to motivate their employees as many are part-time and temporary and they have high levels of labour turnover. Do you agree? Justify your view. (25 marks)

Chapter 24

Improving employer–employee relations

Introduction

This final chapter examines how and why an organisation's human resource managers might improve the business's relations with its employees. Improving relations with employees can improve the performance of a business's workforce as well as its reputation as an employer.

What you need to know by the end of this chapter:

- methods of employee representation
- influences on the extent and methods of employee involvement in decision making
- how to manage and improve employer–employee communications and relations
- the value of good employer–employee relations.

Methods of employee representation

Only a minority of workers in the UK are members of a **trade union**. In 2013 approximately 6.5 million people in the UK were members of a trade union; this is a substantial decline from its peak figure of 13 million in 1979. Trade union membership has declined since 1979 for a range of reasons including the decline of traditional industries such as mining and shipbuilding (which were strongly unionised) and rise in self-employment and temporary employment. In 2013 the UK's workforce contained 4 million self-employed workers and 1.1 million workers on temporary contracts.

In this section we will consider the various ways in which employees can be represented in negotiations with employers and how they may play a role in decision making within the business.

(a) Trades unions

A trade union is an organisation of workers established to protect and improve economic position and working conditions of its members. A number of different types of trade union exist, although a series of amalgamations over recent years has resulted in the distinctions between them becoming blurred.

Trade unions are normally organised on a regional basis. For example, Unite operates in ten regions throughout the UK and Eire and is the UK's largest trade union with 1.42 million members in 2014. Each region has a regional office staffed by full-time union employees (called organisers or officers). The region is made up of a number of branches (more than 6,000 in total in the case of Unite) and each branch has an elected shop steward. The shop steward communicates with employers on behalf of the union's members and reports back to members regarding management decisions. The head office has administrative, statistical and legal staff and the senior officials of the union. Other trade unions operate similar structures.

Most trade unions in the UK have similar objectives. These focus on improving the economic position of their members by fulfilling the following objectives.

- **Maximising pay**. Trade unions engage in **collective bargaining** to provide their members with the highest possible rates of pay. In 2013 trade union members in the private sector of the economy received pay rates which were, on average, 7.0 per cent higher than those of non-union members. This differential is known as the **trade union wage premium**.
- **Achieving safe and secure working conditions**. Unions often provide training for safety representatives who can advise employers on health and safety issues. Creating a workplace in which there is a focus on health and wellbeing can be an important factor in creating employee engagement.
- **Attaining job security**. Arguably this is the most important objective of a modern trade union and one that is difficult to fulfil in the light of pressures resulting from globalisation and the increasing use of technology in the workplace.
- **Participating in and influencing decisions in the workplace**. Trade unions may achieve this through **collective bargaining** or through having representatives on **works councils** and other employer–employee committees. Trade unions may play a role in decisions ranging from a change in fringe benefits such as free lunches to the closure of one or more parts of the business.

In addition many unions have social objectives such as lobbying for higher social security benefits, improved employment legislation and improved quality provision by the National Health Service.

Trades unions achieve their objectives by carrying out a range of functions to the benefit of their members.

- Their most important and time-consuming function is protecting members' interests over issues such as discrimination, unfair dismissal and health and safety matters.
- They negotiate pay and conditions for their members through collective bargaining.
- Trade unions provide their members with a range of personal services including legal advice, insurance, education, training and financial advice.

Employers can also benefit from the existence of trade unions for the following reasons:

- They act as a communications link between management and employees.
- Professional negotiation on behalf of a large number of employees can save time and lessen the likelihood of disputes occurring.

Trades unions offer many benefits to employers such as acting as a channel of communication, offering advice on issues such as health and safety and they may be proactive in preventing disputes. Unions are in a better position to negotiate than individuals in that they have better collective negotiating skills and increased power.

(b) Works Councils

A works council is a forum within a business where workers and management meet to discuss issues such as working conditions, pay and training. Employee representatives on a works council are normally elected. It is common for works councils to be used in workplaces where no trade union representation exists. However, in businesses where works councils and trade unions co-exist, the former is normally excluded from discussing pay and working conditions.

Employees like to know what their employers are planning and since 2008, all UK employers with 50 or more staff have been legally obliged to keep employees regularly informed and consulted on issues at work. Under the European Union's Information and Consultation of Employees (ICE) regulations, companies are required to establish formal works councils on demand. Even if employers do not have an agreement in place, the business still must consult if they are planning:

- 20 or more redundancies
- to sell their business or buy a new one
- certain changes to an occupational or personal pension scheme.

The EU takes works councils seriously: non-compliant employers may face fines of up to £75,000 and could have a works council imposed on them that is ill-suited to their business. EU regulations have also created European works councils (EWC), which are explored in more detail in the Business in Focus feature.

Business in focus: Trade unions in the public and private sectors

Public sector union members represented an increasing proportion of overall union membership from 1995 to 2010. Membership of trade unions by those in the private sector declined by 27 per cent over the same period. Since 2010 the trends have reversed due to the effects of the recession and reductions in government spending, which have reduced the size of the public sector considerably. Private sector membership has increased by 7 per cent since 2010, principally due to a rise in the number of people working in this sector. Despite this rise in trade union membership the proportion of employees in the private sector who are trade union members has remained unchanged in the same period, at 14.4. per cent.

The trade union wage premium, defined as the percentage difference in average gross hourly earnings of union members compared with non-members, is much greater for public sector employers (19.8 per cent) than those in the private sector (7.0 per cent). Overall the wage premium has reduced in both sectors since 1995. The trade union wage premium for public sector workers was 10.5 percentage points lower in 2013 compared with 1995, while for the private sector, this was 8.3 percentage points lower over the same period.

Source: Trade Union Membership Statistical Bulletin, 2013 (Department for Business, Innovation and Skills)

www.gov.uk/government/uploads/system/uploads/attachment_data/file/313768/bis-14-p77-trade-union-membership-statistical-bulletin-2013.pdf

Permission for re-use of all © Crown copyright information is granted under the terms of the Open Government Licence (OGL).

Questions

1. Describe the types of decisions in which trade union representatives may be involved.
2. Do you think that all employers in the private sector would prefer to have non-unionised workforces? Justify your view.

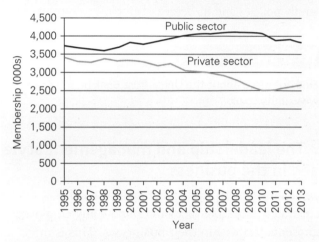

Figure 24.1 Trade union membership by sector, 1995–2013 (thousands of employees)

Business in focus: HP and European works councils

European Union laws (or regulations) relating to European works councils affect any organisation with at least 1,000 employees and at least 150 employees located in two or more Member States of the EU. European works councils bring together employee representatives in a multi-national company from across Europe, to inform and consult them on the group's performance and prospects. European works councils can help trade unionists and employee representatives to respond to the decisions that employers increasingly take on a European and global basis.

A European works council is made up of at least one elected employee from each country in which the multi-national is based and representatives from senior management. They normally meet annually and discuss issues affecting employees throughout the organisation. These include health and safety, merger proposals, the closure of plants and the implementation of new working practices such as teamworking.

Hewlett-Packard (HP), the American multi-national technology company, has had to consult its European

works council over its plans to make more than 7,000 workers in Europe redundant. These job losses are part of the company's plans to reduce its workforce of 317,000 by approximately 34,000 employees to reduce costs and to make the business more flexible. This will allow the company to invest more in researching and developing new products.

Under the proposal presented to its European Works Council (EWC), HP expects approximately 7,095 employees to leave the company or to be redeployed into new roles that better fit the future needs of the company and its customers.

Questions

1. Why might HP prefer to redeploy employees in Europe rather than make them redundant?
2. To what extent do HP's European employees gain any benefits from the existence of the company's European works council?

(c) Other types of employee representation

Employee representation can take other forms, although these are similar in structure and operation to works councils. However, these type of employee representation differ from trade unions in that they are not backed by regional and national organisations and do not have professional employees. Instead they are organised solely for the individual business and its particular circumstances. Employers may allow, or even encourage, the development of any arrangement that allows effective communication to take place.

For example, a factory or office committee may be established. These committees can have members elected by the workforce alongside the employer's representatives. They discuss such matters as working conditions, employment and production changes, safety and welfare matters. To be effective, committees should meet regularly. If disillusionment is to be avoided, such committees should be seen to have a real effect on how matters are determined. This requires that the workforce be regularly informed about the committee's work.

Alternatively, a staff association may be formed to provide employee representation. Staff associations also usually operate on behalf of a single company. They are also used as a means of representation for police officers and civil servants. Staff associations are often independent from external influences and this can be a reason for them to be popular with both employees and employers, though they are frequently established at the request of employers to avoid trade unions gaining recognition for negotiations. This has led to some criticisms that are subject to too much influence by employers. However, it is not uncommon for staff associations to eventually merge with a trade union if employees feel their interests are not well represented.

What do you think?

Do employees always receive greater benefits from being represented when working in a large organisation?

Influences on the extent and methods of employee representation in decision making

There is a huge variation in the extent of employee representation and the impact that employees can have on decision making between businesses. In some businesses employees are not represented and they negotiate conditions and pay with relevant managers individually. In other businesses the majority (or even all) of the workforce is represented collectively in discussions and negotiations with managers. For example, the Unity Trust Bank in the UK has received an award for its union-friendly policies and its degree of employee representation.

Weblink

Find out more about the Unity Trust Bank at: www.unity.co.uk

1. The leadership and management style used in the business

Some management teams operate in ways that deliberately aim to reduce or eliminate any employee representation within their businesses. This is more likely to be associated with management or leadership styles at the autocratic end of the spectrum. Such managers wish to retain control over decision making and therefore seek to avoid any systems of employee representation operating within the organisation. It may be that these businesses operate with a 'hard' style of managing human resources, treating employees in the same way as they would any other resources.

In contrast, other businesses may be more democratically led and use a 'soft' approach to managing human resources. This can result in extensive involvement of employees in decision making. Stagecoach Group plc, a business that operates rail and bus services across the UK, is publicly committed to 'having a strong relationship with trade unions and working in partnership with them'.

2. The overall or corporate objectives of the business

The overall or corporate objectives of the business can shape relationships between employers and employees and also the means by which these objectives are achieved. Businesses that are pursuing growth in markets in which demand is strongly price elastic may opt to minimise the extent of employee representation for fear of wages being forced upwards as a result. We saw earlier that there was a trade union wage premium of approximately 7 per cent in the private sector in the UK in 2013. Avoiding any employee representation may help a business in this situation to control its labour costs and to maintain its price competitiveness. Such an approach will normally remove any realistic possibility of meaningful employee involvement in decision making.

Businesses that are pursuing social objectives may take an entirely different view. They may place a much lower emphasis on generating profits or increasing market share and therefore would welcome employee representation and involvement in decision making, possibly as a means of meeting their social objectives. The National Association of Co-operative Officials (NACO) is the trade union for employees who work in co-operative businesses. NACO represents employees at all levels within co-operatives and negotiates on their behalf.

> **Weblink**
>
> Find out more about the National Association of Co-operative Officials (NACO) at: www.naco.coop

3. The history and ownership of the business

Some businesses have a history and culture of employee representation. This might reflect the origins of the business or the views of influential managers or leaders in the past. With smaller businesses it may be determined by the views of the owner and manager. Another influence is the extent to which the business is owned by its employees. It is natural for a business that is owned by its employees to give them a say in decisions. The John Lewis Partnership in the UK is an example of a business that falls into both categories. The business that operates John Lewis department stores, Waitrose supermarkets and its website has a constitution designed to encourage employee representation. The Partnership's website says:

> When our founder, John Spedan Lewis, set up the Partnership, he was careful to create a governance system, set out in our Constitution,

that would be both commercial allowing us to move quickly to stay ahead in a competitive industry, and democratic giving every Partner a voice in the business they co-own.

Source: John Lewis Partnership website
www.johnlewispartnership.co.uk/about.html

The John Lewis Partnership is owned by a trust on behalf of all its employees (who are called Partners) and who have a say in the management of the business. They also receive a share of annual profits.

4. The nature of the work and employees hired

It may be more likely that businesses that employ highly skilled employees will offer them opportunities to become involved in decision making through a system of employee representation. The threat of a high level of labour turnover is more significant with this type of employee. They will be more difficult to replace and their loss may be disruptive to the business's operations. Involving employees in decisions should engender a sense of being valued and increase employee engagement, which may offer further benefits to the business.

In contrast, businesses that rely heavily on temporary and seasonal employees will have less incentive to establish systems for employee representation because employees may have limited knowledge and experience to offer and managers may not feel it necessary to demonstrate that they value their employees in this way.

5. Employment legislation

Businesses operating in the UK are subject to laws relating to employment that are created by the UK Government and by the EU. As we saw earlier the EU has passed two laws (or regulations) that relate to employee representation within larger businesses.

● Information and Consultation of Employees (ICE) regulation. This regulation obliges all UK employers with 50 or more staff to keep employees regularly informed and consulted on issues at work.
● European works councils regulations affect any organisation with at least 1,000 employees and at least 150 employees located in two or more Member States of the EU. They require businesses to inform and consult employees on the group's performance and prospects.

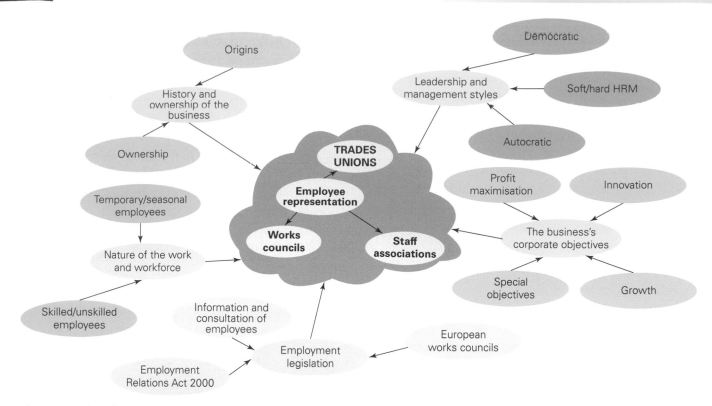

Figure 24.2 The influences on a business's approach to employee representation and decision making

Business in focus: Trade union leaders meet to discuss Amazon

In the summer of 2014, online giant Amazon came under scrutiny in Berlin, as union leaders from Britain, France and Germany met in the German city to address how the company could be engaged with on issues like job security, low pay and warehouse working conditions. The company employs around 7,000 staff in the United Kingdom alone – most of them in their vast warehouses. Of these, 5,800 are permanent members of staff, on a minimum salary of £7.10 an hour: that's just over 50p more than the National Minimum Wage.

National union organisers in Britain, France and Germany suggest that Amazon is representative of how global e-commerce organisations treat their low-skilled workers. While in France and Germany warehouse workers employed by Amazon have taken to strikes and industrial action, in Britain the GMB – Britain's General Union – is still trying to build membership.

They described not being given fair access to warehouse sites to discuss joining up with the union. And, while Amazon denies the claims, the company has been accused of decidedly union-unfriendly tactics by the union, including anti-union campaigns where they issued workers with branded anti-union t-shirts, meeting with employees individually to remind them of the company's views on union membership, and distributing sample ballots for the union vote making it clear how to vote.

Amazon has said in the past they have an open-door management policy, which allows for workers to air their opinions and bring any concerns directly to their superiors.

Source: adapted from various news sources

Figure 24.3 An Amazon distribution centre

Questions

1. How might Amazon benefit from involving employees in decision making within the business?

2. Discuss the possible influences on Amazon's approach to employee representation.

In 2000 the UK Parliament passed the Employment Relations Act. Under this Act a trade union with a membership exceeding 50 per cent of the employees in a business with more than 20 employees can demand union recognition and the right to introduce collective bargaining.

How to manage and improve employer–employee communication and relations

The theory of communication

Communication is the transfer of information between people. A transmission mechanism is simply the means by which one person communicates with another – letters and email are examples.

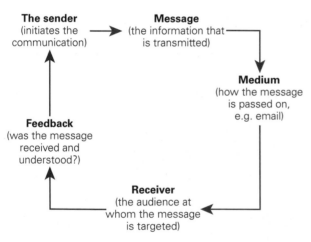

Figure 24.4 The process of communication

Communication involves a number of elements, as shown in Figure 24.4.

- The sender is the company who commences the process of communication.
- The message is the information that the business wishes to send to its audience.
- The medium is the way in which the message is communicated.

- The audience is the target group at whom the communication is aimed – this might be a business's employees or customers.
- Feedback is the response to communication, which can confirm it has been received or raise a query or comment about its content.

Managing and improving communication with employees

Regular and effective communication can help to ensure that all employees remain closely focused on agreed corporate objectives.

Technology can be used by larger businesses to communicate with their employees and this can be of particular value to businesses that operate in several locations, especially if these locations are in different countries.

- **Electronic mail (email).** This method of communication allows messages to be sent and received electronically via the world wide web. This is particularly useful for quick international communication between employers and employees grouped across different time zones, as messages can be stored until the recipient is available.
- **Social media.** Websites such as Facebook and Twitter can be very effective methods of communication in the right circumstances, but may not always be accessible to all employees.
- **Intranets.** These are electronic, computer-based communication networks, similar in nature to the internet but used internally by individual businesses. They are ideally suited to large companies, especially those with a number of locations. They provide an email service as well as access to information of interest to large numbers of employees.
- **Video conferencing.** This allows people to communicate face to face while in different locations, nationally or internationally. It saves time and avoids the need for employers and employees to travel to meetings.

The precise method or methods that a business elects to use to communicate with its employees may vary according to the circumstances and the nature of the business. A business that is large with employees in a number of locations, possibly in different countries, may rely more on electronic communication, though other means of communication will also be used.

Communicating effectively with employees

It is important for employers to allow the 'employee voice' to be heard. Andrea Broughton, a researcher at the Institute of Employment Studies believes that employers have to create a culture of trust and openness to help employees to be heard and to feel valued. She argues that many businesses rely on social media as a means for employees to be heard but that this is not always effective. For this to work requires employee training and acceptance of the approach.

Key terms

Delegation is the passing of authority down the organisational structure.

Empowerment is giving employees greater control over their working lives.

The effective management of communication with employees is not simply about choosing the right medium with which to exchange information. Other factors make up an effective employer–employee communication package.

- **Appreciating the nature of effective communication**. Good quality communication is normally two-way communication. This means that information will flow in both directions between employers and employees, or with their representatives. Two-way communication allows for feedback to establish that the message has been received and understood. However, it has much more potential than this. It affords the opportunity for employees to offer ideas and suggestions, which may result in some excellent ideas for improving the way in which the business operates. The opportunity alone to offer suggestions may improve the engagement and motivation of employees. In turn this may result in a better performance by the workforce as it provides a sense of recognition and an opportunity for achievement if ideas and suggestions are effective. Finally, two-way communication can alert managers to potential problems, which may result in confrontation and conflict if not resolved at the earliest opportunity.
- **Using the appropriate style of management.** The writings of Elton Mayo, and especially the Hawthorne experiment, offer evidence that

employees respond positively to receiving attention from managers. Later research has strengthened this link. Abraham Maslow developed his hierarchy of needs, and argued that good communication underpins some of the higher-level needs identified in his theory. The need for recognition, for example, relies heavily upon managers communicating with subordinates. Similarly, Frederick Herzberg wrote that direct communication (rather than through unnecessary layers of hierarchy) was an important means of improving employee motivation. Electing to manage in a style which offers employees the chance to participate in decision making does more than provide a forum for communication – it encourages it as well.

- **Adapting the organisational structure to encourage effective communication**. We saw in Chapter 22 that businesses can organise themselves in different ways. By opting for a structure which allow employees to have greater authority and control over their working lives employers can encourage communication at all levels within the organisation. Using techniques such as **delegation** and **empowerment** has costs in terms of loss of power for managers and in terms of training relatively junior employees to take on more demanding roles. However, alongside the benefit of improved communication the performance of employees should also improve as levels of motivation increase.

Good communication can have a positive impact upon employee motivation and performance. Praise and recognition are widely seen as motivators, but rely upon communication. Effective communication can also give employees important feedback about their performance and help to improve it in the future.

Recent problems in communication

It has become more difficult in some ways to manage communication effectively between employers and employees over recent years. Mergers and takeovers continue to create larger and more complex businesses. It is not uncommon for businesses in different countries to merge or for one to buy another in a takeover deal. As a consequence the need for effective communication between employers and employees can increase. At such a time job losses may be expected and effective communication will be essential to quell rumours and to negotiate mutually acceptable deals. However, the scale of the new business and the possible absence of effective mechanisms for communicating can make this process very difficult.

Managing employer–employee relations

An important part of managing employer–employee relations is to have systems in place to deal with any disputes before they can become too serious and possibly result in industrial action. Effective communication is one means of preventing and resolving disputes quickly and many employers have agreed procedures in place to avoid disputes escalating into industrial action.

Key terms

Arbitration is a procedure for the settling of a dispute, under which the parties agree to be bound by the decision of a third party.

An **industrial dispute** is a disagreement between an employer and its employees, usually represented by a trade union, over some aspect of the terms or conditions of employment.

Conciliation is a method of resolving individual or collective disputes in which a neutral third party encourages the continuation of negotiations.

We can divide managing employer–employee relations into two sections:

- avoiding industrial disputes
- resolving industrial disputes.

Avoiding industrial disputes

1. No strike and single union agreements

A 'no-strike deal' is an agreement between employers and unions whereby in return for a pay and conditions package a union agrees to refrain from strike action for an agreed period. Often such agreements are accompanied by a commitment by both parties to go to binding **arbitration** in the event of a dispute. This reassures the union that it is not making itself too vulnerable by agreeing not to take industrial action. A no-strike agreement can benefit a trade union in a number of ways.

- By presenting itself as non-confrontational the union may attract a greater number of members from within the workforce increasing its income and strength.

- A less confrontational stance might allow the union to appoint worker directors increasing the union's influence and role in decision making.
- Such agreements can improve the public perception of trade unions. This will assist the union in its activities in other businesses and industries and may persuade employers to recognise it.

A further advantage of no-strike deals is that they may lead to a single union agreement, strengthening the position of the union within the business.

Single union agreements have become more common over the last 20 years. Under this type of deal employees agree to be represented by one union. This makes negotiation simpler for the employers (as there are only two parties to the discussions) while reducing the possibility of disputes between rival unions. Single union deals also assist in maintaining good communications between employers and employees lessening the possibility of industrial action such as a strike.

2. Advisory, Conciliation and Arbitration Service (ACAS)

Managing employer–employee relations effectively can be helped by ACAS. ACAS is an independent and impartial organisation established to prevent and resolve industrial disputes. ACAS's mission is to improve the performance and effectiveness of organisations by providing an independent and impartial service to prevent and resolve disputes and to build harmonious relationships at work. ACAS offers a number of services to employers and employees:

- preventing and resolving **industrial disputes**, particularly through the use of arbitration and **conciliation**
- resolving individual disputes over employment rights, including individual cases of discrimination and unfair dismissal
- providing impartial information and advice on employment matters topics such as reducing absenteeism, employee sickness and payment systems
- improving the understanding of industrial relations.

ACAS was established in 1975 by the UK Government, during a period of industrial conflict, to provide advice on industrial relations matters. Much of ACAS's work nowadays is conciliating in disputes between an individual employee and his or her employer. This trend reflects the decreased influence of trade unions in UK businesses.

Weblink

To find out more about ACAS and its work visit:
www.acas.org.uk/index.aspx?articleid=1461

Methods of resolving industrial disputes

It is normal for industrial disputes to be resolved without trade unions taking any form of industrial action. The decline in industrial disputes in the UK over recent years has, in part, been a consequence of the effective use of measures outlined below.

1. Arbitration

Arbitration is a procedure for the settlement of disputes, under which the parties agree to be bound by the decision of an arbitrator whose decision is in some circumstances legally binding on both parties. The process of arbitration is governed by Arbitration Acts 1950–1996. There are three main types of arbitration.

- **Non-binding arbitration** involves a neutral third party making an award to settle a dispute that the parties concerned can accept or not.
- **Binding arbitration** means that the parties to the dispute have to take the award of the arbitrator.
- **Pendulum arbitration** is a binding form of arbitration in which the arbitrator has to decide entirely for one side or the other. It is not an option to reach a compromise and select some middle ground. This system avoids excessive claims by unions or miserly offers by employers.

2. Conciliation

This is a method of resolving individual or collective disputes in which a neutral third party encourages the continuation of negotiations and the postponement (at least) of any form of industrial action. The conciliator's role does not involve making any judgement of the validity of the position of either party. The conciliator encourages the continued discussions in the hope that a compromise can be reached. Conciliation is sometimes called mediation.

3. Employment tribunals

Employment tribunals are informal courts where legal disputes over unfair dismissal or discrimination can be settled. Employment tribunals were established in 1964 and are to be found in most major towns and cities in the UK. Each tribunal comprises three members: a legally trained chairperson, one employer representative and an employee representative. Most employee complaints are still settled by Employment tribunals, although the number of hearings has fallen substantially since fees for employees taking a dispute to a tribunal were introduced in 2013.

The value of good employer–employee relations

One way of considering the value of good employer–employee relations is to consider the cost to both parties that may arise from any sort of dispute. Table 24.1 examines these costs.

Employers	Employees
- The business may lose revenue from selling its products if the dispute results in industrial action such as a strike and production is halted. - The business may lose future sales if its customers believe that it is an unreliable supplier. - The business's relationship with its employees may be damaged in the long term with negative implications for engagement and productivity. - The business may be regarded as a more risky investment and may encounter more difficulty in raising finance, or be expected to pay higher interest rates. - The business's image may be damaged if it is involved in a dispute with its employees and this may alienate some of its customers.	- Employees may lose pay if the industrial dispute takes the form of a strike. - The dispute may weaken the employer's finances putting employees' job security at risk. - A financially weakened employer may not be able or willing to pay for training for employees, denying them the chance to improve and update skills and knowledge. - The employer may respond to the threat of, or actual, industrial action by replacing people with technology in the production process or by moving overseas.

Table 24.1 The costs of industrial disputes

It is apparent from Table 24.1 that both employers and employees benefit from the maintenance of good relations and the avoidance of industrial disputes.

The benefits to employers

Employers benefit in a range of ways from the maintenance of good industrial relations.

- **Helping to develop a strong employer brand.** Employers who avoid disputes with employees and who have effective mechanisms to resolve any disputes quickly will be viewed more favourably by potential employees. This will assist it in attracting more able and productive employees.
- **Promoting employee engagement.** We saw in Chapter 23 that having an engaged workforce is a valuable asset for any business. Poor employer-relations are likely to lead to employees believing they are not valued and will reduce their sense of wellbeing. Such factors can damage employee engagement severely.
- **Improving the business's corporate image.** Avoiding disputes or settling them quickly helps a business to develop or maintain a reputation as a fair and reasonable employer. This can have positive effects on a range of stakeholders including customers and investors.

- **Strengthening competitiveness.** Good employer – employee relations can be a powerful competitive weapon. It can reduce costs by eliminating lost production, add to a business's reliability as a supplier as its production is not interrupted and can enhance labour productivity (thereby lowering unit labour costs), as workers are motivated by what they regard as fair pay and working conditions.

The benefits to employees

Equally there are a number of advantages to employees from the maintenance of good relations with their employers.

- **Financial benefits.** Employees avoid loss of pay during periods of industrial disputes if good relations are maintained. However, because the employer may also be financially stronger as a result of avoiding wasteful disputes there is a greater possibility of future improvements in pay and conditions.

Business in focus: Gas plant industrial dispute resolved

The long-running dispute between workers and management at Petrofac plc's £800 million gas plant development at Sullom Voe in the Shetland Islands has finally come to an end. Trade union members have voted in favour of accepting an offer to resolve the dispute at the Petrofac site over shared accommodation and travel allowances.

Workers belonging to GMB and Unite rejected an offer of up to £5,500. They scheduled a series of 24-hour strikes, despite the offer being recommended by shop stewards and union leaders. Staff had been seeking £50-a-day allowances to compensate for having to share rooms – despite knowing they would have to do so when signing up to the job. Workers staying in Lerwick also wanted compensation for travelling long distances to and from work.

However, the workers showed signs of warming to the £15 a day offer on the eve of the first walk-outs and have voted in favour of accepting the deal.

Petrofac have welcomed the decision. 'We are pleased with this decision. Strike action would have been in no-one's interests. We didn't always necessarily agree with the grounds for complaint – but we take the welfare of our staff very seriously and in the spirit of compromise we made what we felt was a generous offer that will mean some workers being eligible for up to an additional £5,500. We are now fully focused on delivering the project for our customer.'

Source: Adapted from *The Shetland Times*, 11 February 2014
www.shetlandtimes.co.uk/2014/02/11/gas-plant-industrial-dispute-resolved

Questions

1. What would have been the possible costs to Petrofac plc's employees of taking industrial action?
2. Do you think that Petrofac plc has acted wisely in ending this dispute without industrial action?

- **Job security**. An employer is less likely to consider replacing employees with technology or moving overseas to locations where industrial action rarely or never occurs.
- **The possibility of greater participation in decision making**. Involving employees in decision making is one way of helping to maintain good relations but it is also a possible benefit to employees from doing their part in maintaining a positive relationship. Where amicable relationships exist employers may be more willing to offer opportunities for employee involvement in decision making.

Summary

The value of good employer relations is probably greatest where the costs of industrial disputes are most significant. This might be where the business is in a weak competitive or financial position and vulnerable to losing its customers to rivals or of financial failure. Similarly, industrial disputes might be risky for employees in areas of high unemployment and for those who are relatively unskilled. If a prolonged dispute results in a loss of jobs they may experience difficulty in finding alternative employment.

ASSESSMENT ACTIVITIES

Sections (a), (b) and (c) of these assessment activities are relevant for students taking AS and A-level examinations. The questions in section (d) are for A-level students only.

(a) Knowledge check questions

1 What is meant by the term trade union?

2 State two objectives of trade unions within the UK.

3 Is the following statement true or false? 'Union representatives negotiating on behalf of many employees can save time and reduce the likelihood of disputes occurring.'

4 State two other ways in which employees may be represented within businesses apart from by trade unions.

5 What conditions have to be met by a business for it to have a legal obligation to operate a European works council?

6 State two possible influences on the extent and methods of employee representation in decision making within businesses.

7 What are the two EU laws (or regulations) that relate to employee representation within larger businesses?

8 State two factors that may contribute to effective employer–employee communication.

9 What is the difference between arbitration and conciliation?

10 State two costs to employers that may arise from an industrial dispute.

(b) Short answer questions

1 Explain the possible disadvantages to a public limited company in a price-competitive industry of having 90 per cent of its employees represented by a trade union. (4 marks)

2 Explain the benefits to a rapidly growing business of implementing an effective method of employee representation. (5 marks)

3 Explain why a democratic leadership style might result in effective communication between employers and employees in a large UK retail business. (5 marks)

4 Explain the reasons why a trade union in the UK might agree to a no-strike deal with a multi-national company. (6 marks)

(c) Data response questions

The demand for software from businesses is growing. Many organisations require specially designed software to allow their computer-aided design and manufacturing systems to work efficiently. Others require bespoke software for project management, maintenance of equipment or managing customers.

Saxon plc is a very successful business trading in a market that is growing quickly. Last year its revenue rose by 39 per cent (and profit for the year by 44 per cent) as it won contracts with several large public companies for the first time. It plans to issue more shares to finance further growth. Approximately 65 per cent of its workforce is highly skilled and many have highly creative roles. The workforce is organised in teams, although many employees feel that their voice is not heard within the business. In response to this managers have made increasing use of delegation across the business recently. The company recognises the benefits of maintaining good employer–employee relations.

It employs 3,750 people and has recently agreed to a request from its workforce to be represented by a trade union. The company's employees feel that their pay and conditions do not reflect their contribution to the company's success.

Source: Written by author

1 Explain how the increasing use of delegation might help the business to improve employer–employee relations at Saxon plc. (6 marks)

2 Analyse the benefits to the business of maintaining good employer–employee relations. (9 marks)

3 To what extent does the introduction of a trade union into the business offer more benefits to the employer than to the employees? (15 marks)

(d) Essays

1 To what extent is the negative impact on a business's image arising from an industrial dispute the most important reason to maintain good employer–employee relations?

2 'The use of the latest technology to enhance communication is the key to improving employer–employee relations nowadays'. Do you agree? Justify your view. (25 marks)

Case study: Unit 6 Decision making to improve human resource performance

Barclays bank uses more technology in its operations

Barclays Bank plc has announced that it is to replace virtually all of its traditional bank cashiers in its branches with technology. The bank will install machines to allow its customers to conduct routine banking activities such as paying in cheques and cash; some supermarkets and the London Underground have already made similar moves. The bank's branches will be redesigned, including the removal of counters and booths in 1,560 branches. Barclays already operates 37 cashier-less branches. It has used this as a trial and now plans to extend this model to its remaining branches. The banking industry in the UK is changing significantly and not just as a result of technology. New rivals, such as Metro Bank and Virgin, are emerging to challenge the established operators.

The bank will retrain 6,500 former cashiers (and give them all iPads) to offer advice on a range of financial and banking matters such as opening new accounts. These employees will be called 'community bankers' and once trained will be used to retrain other colleagues in the new roles. Barclays says that it has no current plans to reduce staff numbers as a consequence of these changes, although the bank did make 1,700 employees redundant in 2013 and a further 14,000 job losses are forecast for 2014. Cashiers who become community bankers will get a pay rise of around 2.8 per cent as the change represents a promotion. The new community bankers will be able to advise and support the bank's customers in using the new technology.

Barclays bank argues that its customers are banking in different ways due to technology such as online and mobile banking. It says that, although the need for cashiers has reduced, it does not plan 'significant closures' of its branches as a result of these changes, although there are suggestions that it is to close 400. The use of technology can also reduce queuing and customer waiting time in branches. However, there is strong opposition to the removal of cashiers with claims that elderly customers, for example, may have difficulty in interacting with the new technology. Some critics of the increased use of technology claim that it is merely a means of the bank increasing its profits. The trade union Unite, which represents some of Barclays' employees, has called on Barclays not to close any of its branches.

Key data for Barclays Bank

- Sustained engagement of colleagues score in 2013: 71 per cent (objective for 2018: 87–91 per cent).
- Profit before tax was £2,868 million in 2013 (£797 million in 2012).
- Number of employees: 139,900 (2013).
- The average bonus per member of staff across the bank £17,000 in 2013 (£15,600 in 2012).

AS questions

(50 marks)

1 Explain possible reasons why Barclays has set itself an objective for 'sustained engagement of employees'.   (5 marks)

2 Analyse the possible effects of these changes on the labour cost to Barclays of dealing with a typical customer.   (10 marks)

3 To what extent might increased use of technology improve the levels of motivation of Barclays' community bankers?   (15 marks)

4 Do you agree that the move to using community bankers will improve the competitiveness of Barclays Bank plc? Justify your view.   (20 marks)

A-level questions

(70 marks)

1 Analyse the possible factors that may have led Barclays Bank to redesign the jobs of its cashiers.   (10 marks)

2 Assess the possible effects of the increased use of technology and the 14,000 job losses on other functions within the bank.   (15 marks)

3 To what extent do you think that the changes taking place are certain to damage employer–employee relations at the bank?   (20 marks)

4 Is it inevitable that all businesses will seek to replace large numbers of employees with technology? Justify your view.   (25 marks)

Acknowledgements

The Publishers would like to thank the following for permission to reproduce copyright material:

Photo credits: **p.1** © IRStone – Fotolia; **p.3** *l* © 2004 The Image Works/TopFoto, *r* © Edgard Garrido/Reuters/Corbis; **p.5** © Clynt Garnham Construction / Alamy; **p.9** *l* and *r* courtesy Marks & Spencer; **p.34** © David Paul Morris/Bloomberg via Getty Images; **p.47** © Yuri Arcurs – Fotolia; **p.55** *l* © Michael A. Schwarz/Bloomberg via Getty Images, *r* © Justin Sullivan/Getty Images; **p.76** © Matt Fountain/The Freedom Bakery; **p.79** © Photoshot; **p.83** © Rawpixel – Fotolia; **p.91** © Radharc Images / Alamy; **p.105** © Rob Wilkinson/Alamy; **p.108** *l* © Al Freni/The LIFE Images Collection/Getty Images, *r* © Chris Lobina/LFI/Photoshot; **p.114** © Hugh Threlfall / Alamy; **p.117** © David Caudery/Tap Magazine via Getty Images; **p.122** © Tomohiro Ohsumi/Bloomberg via Getty Images; **p.123** *t* © Sipa Press/REX, *m* © High Level/REX, *b* © keith morris / Alamy; **p.127** © Richard Levine/ Demotix/Press Association Images; **p.129** © Tobias Hase/dpa/Press Association Images; **p.130** © Hayley Louize Ballard / Alamy; **p.132** © Art Directors & TRIP/Alamy; **p.133** © Karl Mondon/Bay Area News Group/MCT/Photoshot; **p.135** © Ryan Emberley/Invision for Apple/Press Association Images; **p.136** © Mark Thompson/Getty Images; **p.139** © tony French / Alamy; **p.140** © Jonathan Saruk/Getty Images; **p.143** © Gene Blevins/Corbis; **p.145** © Kevin George / Alamy; **p.147** © Monkey Business – Fotolia; **p.151** *t* © Liu Zheng/Color China Photo/AP/Press Association Images, *b* © Adrian Brown (brownbox.com.au), courtesy Akubra Hats Pty Ltd; **p.155** © Vincent Jannink/AFP/Getty Images; **p.158** *t* © Simon Dawson/Bloomberg via Getty Images, *b* © Justin Sullivan/Getty Images; **p.159** *t* © Lee Celano/Reuters/Corbis, *b* © Attila Balazs/EPA/Corbis; **p.163** © Rachit Goswami/The India Today Group/Getty Images; **p.171** © John Greim/LOOP IMAGES/Loop Images/Corbis; **p.172** © Suzanne Plunkett/Reuters/Corbis; **p.176** © Chen Cheng/Xinhua/Photoshot; **p.184** © maxoidos – Fotolia; **p.185** © Jeff Blackler/Photoshot; **p.187** © Paul Thompson/ UPPA/Photoshot; **p.190** © studiomode / Alamy; **p.192** © Bill Hogan/Chicago Tribune/MCT/Getty Images; **p.193** © Alen Gurovic/NurPhoto/Photoshot; **p.195** © Ralf Kollmann – Fotolia; **p.201** © Oleksandr Dibrova – Fotolia; **p.203** © Jon Bower USA/Alamy; **p.239** © 2009 Martin Jardine Photography, courtesy of The Brooklyn Warehouse; **p.248** © NeuroSky; **p.249** © Paul John Fearn / Alamy; **p.255** © Monkey Business – Fotolia; **p.261** *tr* Stonewall, *ml* © Employers Network for Equality & Inclusion, *bl* © Equality Challenge Unit; **p.309** *t* and *b* Google; **p.318** © Bartek Sadowski/Bloomberg via Getty Images.

Acknowledgements: **p.13**: from 'About our fares' (Easyjet, 2014), www.easyjet.com; **p.13**: Natalie Paris: from 'Ryanair: not the cheapest airline?' from *The Telegraph* (*The Telegraph*, 21 October 2013), reproduced by permission of Telegraph Media Group; **p.19**: adapted from 'Starting Up: Jane's Social Media' from Small Business Showcase (*The Guardian*, 28 November 2012), copyright Guardian News & Media Ltd 2012; **p.19**: Jane Binnion: adapted from material taken from www.janebinnion.com (Jane Binnion, 2014), reproduced by kind permission of the publisher; **p.22**: table: 'The UK's largest five public companies by market capitalisation, May 2014' (Stock Challenge, 2014), www.stockchallenge.co.uk; **p.24**: general information about Wikipedia, taken from http://en.wikipedia.org; **p.26**: graph: 'The UK's FTSE 2008-2014' from Yahoo Finance (Yahoo, 2014), https://uk.finance.yahoo.com; **p.26**: Andrew Trotman: text: adapted from 'Serco shares slump after profits warning'; graph: 'Serco Group Plc share price' from *The Telegraph* (*The Telegraph*, 29 April 2014), reproduced by permission of Telegraph Media Group; **p.38**: Steve Doughty: text: from 'Number of people in the UK smashes through 64million after one of the biggest population increases in the whole of Europe'; graph: 'Annual Population Growth Since 1964'; graph: 'Main drivers of population growth 1992-2013' from *Mail Online* (*The Daily Mail*, 26 June 2014); **p.40**: Matt Stott: from 'East Anglia: 'Unsustainable' immigration rises to nearly 300,000 over last two decades' from EADT24 (*East Anglian Daily Times*, 29 November 2013); **p.46**: graph: 'Poundland Share Charts (PLND)' (London South East Limited, 2015), reproduced by permission of London South East Limited; **p.55**: Richard Branson: adapted from 'Virgin's Richard Branson: Apple boss Steve Jobs was the entrepreneur I most admired' from *The Telegraph* (*The Telegraph*, 6 October 2011), reproduced by permission of Telegraph Media Group; **p.76**: Hannah Fearn: adapted from 'Is The Freedom Bakery the new face of social enterprise?' from *The Guardian* (*The Guardian*, 12 February 2014), copyright Guardian News & Media Ltd 2014; **p.76**: Matt Fountain: information from the Freedom Bakery website (Freedom Bakery, 2014), www.freedombakery.org; **p.78**: graph illustrating the relationship between stakeholder influence/power and stakeholder engagement approaches from 'Choosing the stakeholder engagement approach' (www.stakeholdermap.com, 2014), reproduced by permission of the publisher; **p.86**: from 'Working at Amazon Global' (Amazon, 2015), www.amazon.jobs; **p.93**: from 'Exhibit 1 Shifts in the retail industry often create new winners, as evidenced by changes in the top ten US retailers' from How retailers can keep up with consumers (McKinsey&Company, 2015); **p.94**: graph: 'Consumer expenditure through sports goods retailers, by retailer share 2013' (Mintel); **p.96**: graphs: 'Quality perception of major discounters and traditional supermarkets'; 'Average number of items in basket, discounters vs. traditional supermarkets'; 'Percentage of consumers visiting discount supermarkets in 2014'; 'Average number of items in basket, by channel' (Morrisons); **p.102**: graph: 'Forecast of total value of UK sales of carbonated soft drinks, 2009–19' (Mintel); **p.113**: text taken from 'What is Acorn', and infographic: 'Consumer Classifications' (acorn.caci.co.uk, 2013), reproduced by permission of the publisher; **p.114**: graph: 'Profile of in-store clothing shoppers, by age and affluence July 2013' (Mintel); **p.124**: Sean Farrell and Gwyn Topham: adapted from 'Ryanair launches business service' from *The Guardian* (*The Guardian*, 27 August 2014), copyright Guardian News & Media Ltd 2014; **p.132**: graph: 'Our core market is still growing' from Transforming Thomas Cook (Thomas Cook, 13 March 2013), reproduced by kind permission of the publisher, www.thomascookgroup.com; **p.134**: infographic: 'Thomas Cook Group plc's innovation funnel' (Thomas Cook Group, 2014); **p.135**: adapted from 'Pricing the surge' (The Economist, 29 March 2014), www.economist.com; **p.142**: graph: 'Online sales as a percentage of retail sales in the UK' (Mintel); **p.142**: graph: 'Types of products bought online' (Mintel); **p.150**: infographic: 'Facts and Figures', taken from www.ryanair.com (Ryanair, 2015); **p.158**: Elon Musk: adapted from 'Tesla's mission is to accelerate the world's transition to sustainable transport' (Tesla Motors), www.teslamotors.com; **p.166**: text: adapted from 'Center Parcs Annual Review 2012/13', and graph: 'The Year in Numbers' from Center Parcs Annual Review 2012/13 (Center Parcs, 2013); **p.171**: Peter Bisson, Elizabeth Stephenson and S. Patrick Viguerie: from 'The productivity imperative' from *McKinsey Quaterly* (McKinsey&Company, 2015); **p.173**: Marc Onetto: from 'When Toyota met e-commerce: Lean at Amazon' from *McKinsey Quaterly* (McKinsey&Company, 2015); **p.174**: Ewan Duncan and Ron Ritter: from 'New frontiers for lean' from *McKinsey Quaterly* (McKinsey&Company, 2015); **p.187**: from 'RAC Breakdown cover' from RAC member products and services (RAC, 2014), www.rac.co.uk; **p.188**: from 'Annual Report 2013' from Ford Annual Report 2013 (Ford, 2013); **p.189**: from 'What does the FAIRTRADE Mark mean?' from What Fairtrade Does (Fairtrade Foundation, 2015); **p.192**: from 'Ingredients Sourcing & Purchasing Practices' from How We Do Business (Ben & Jerry's, 2015); **p.193**: text adapted from various parts of the Ikea website (Ikea, 2012), www.ikea.com; **p.226**: Matt Warman: from 'BlackBerry looking at a phone for medics' from *The Telegraph* (*The Telegraph*, 25 February 2014), reproduced by permission of Telegraph Media Group; **p.228**: selected profit data for Burberry, 2013 and 2014, adapted from Burberry plc's Annual Report 2014 (Burberry plc, 2014), http://www.burberryplc.com; **p.239**: Quentin Casey: adapted from 'Equity crowdfunding source of innovation, capital for startups' from *Financial Post* (*Financial Post*, 22 October 2012), reprinted with the express permission of 'National Post', a division of Postmedia Network Inc.; **p.247**: Peter McSean: from 'Sale and leaseback: a cash injection for your business vans' from Business Vans (Business Car Manager Ltd, 2015), reproduced by permission of the publisher Business Car Manager Ltd; **p.248**: Anthony Cuthbertson: from 'Wearable Tech Improves Efficiency in the Workplace' from International Business Times (International Business Times, 1 May 2014); **p.260**: From 'Talent Development Exec job, Scottish Film Talent Network, Edinburgh or Glasgow' (Media Nation, 2014); **p.261**: adapted from 'Equal Opportunities Policy' (University of Cambridge, 2015), www.cam.ac.uk; **p.262**: adapted from 'Our values' (J Sainsbury plc, 2015), www.j-sainsbury.co.uk; **p.287**: PrintWeek Team: adapted from 'Paperlinx takes next step in decentralising sales' from PrintWeek (PrintWeek, 14 January 2014); **p.290**: Rupert Denholm-Hall: adapted from 'Morrisons to make 2,600 redundancies in latest management shake-up' from Wales Online (Media Wales Ltd, 17th June 2014), reproduced by permission of the publisher; **p.309**: adapted from 'Benefits' from Google Careers (Google, 2015), www.google.com; **p.323**: Ryan Taylor: adapted from 'Gas plant industrial dispute resolved' from *The Shetland Times* (*The Shetland Times*, 11 February 2014).

Every effort has been made to trace all copyright holders, but if any have been inadvertently overlooked the Publishers will be pleased to make the necessary arrangements at the first opportunity.

Index

A

ACAS (Advisory, Conciliation and Arbitration Service)   321–2
added value   4, 150
AGMs (Annual General Meetings)   27
aims, business   6–7
andon approach to production   173
Annual General Meetings (AGMs)   27
appraisal systems, employee   308–9
arbitration   321, 322
assets   197, 202, 234–5
augmented products   126
authority   286
autocratic (authoritarian) leadership   52, 53, 53–4, 55, 76, 287
average (unit) costs   12, 162, 165

B

Bank of England   36
bank loans   236–7, 240
behavioural segmentation   112
behavioural theories of leadership and management   52
big data   107, 110, 276
Blake Mouton grid of management styles   52, 53
Boston Matrix   130–1, 139
brands   136–7, 138
    brand loyalty   89, 112
    demand and   105
    employer brands   289, 323
break-even analysis   217
    break-even charts   219–23
    calculating break-even output   217–18
    changing variables and   223
    and non-standard prices   225
    using   218–19, 224
    value and shortcomings of   225
budgets   208
    analysing   211–13
    construction of   208–11
    types of   208
    value of budgeting   213–14
buffer inventory   185
business forms
    effects of ownership on businesses   28–30
    not-for-profit businesses   24–5
    private sector businesses   17–23
    public sector businesses   23
    reasons for changing   23
business to consumer (B2C) firms   4

businesses   2
    aims   6–7
    and the external environment   32–42
    importance of   2–3
    mission statements   6
    objectives   7–10
    size of   3
    types of   4–5
    values   262–3
    what they do   3–4
buying process   121, 139, 141

C

capacity of a business   163–4, 165, 168–9, 249
capital, working   246
capital expenditure   202–3
capital intensive operations   149, 151, 171·
capital structure   203–4
cash cycles   202
cash flow   8
    and business performance   247
    causes of problems   244–5
    forecasts   214–17
    importance of monitoring   245–6
    improving   246, 250–1
    objectives   202
    and profit   197
centralisation   286, 286–8
chains of command   284
co-operatives   25, 28
collateral   237
collective bargaining   313, 314
commission, paid to employees   306
communication
    with employees   305, 319–21
    management and   49, 53
    with stakeholders   78, 79
    theory of   319
companies   19–20
    effects of ownership on   28, 29, 30
    private limited   20–1
    public limited   21–3
    shareholders and share prices   25–8
    sources of finance   240–9
competitive advantage   154, 155
competitive environment   34
    and financial objectives   205
    and human resources objectives   265
    and marketing   92, 124
    and operations   153, 158
    and organisational design   288

competitiveness   98
    good employer-employee relations and   323
    marketing research and   98
    operations and   153
    positioning and   116–17
    quality and   179
conciliation   321, 322
confidence levels   101–2
consumer products   124–5, 125–6
contribution   217–18
controlling function of management   50, 51
convenience items   125
core benefits of products   126
core values   262–3
corporate social responsibility   190
correlation and marketing data   100–1, 102, 105
cost budgets   208
cost-plus pricing   13
costs   10–11
    and break-even analysis   219–20, 223
    cost objectives   200–1
    and decision making   13, 65, 133–4
    direct and indirect costs   198
    and environmental issues   41, 42
    fixed costs   11, 134, 219, 223
    interest rates and   37–8
    of production   13, 36, 154, 248
    semi-variable costs   12
    of sources of finance   240–1
    total costs   12, 220
    unit (average) costs   12, 162, 165
    unit labour costs   269, 270–1, 289
    variable costs   11–12, 217–18, 219–20
credit control   244
crowdfunding   239, 240
customers
    marketing and   84–5, 111–14
    marketing research and   96–8

D

data
    decision making based on   61–2
    human resource data   268–76
    marketing research   95–109
    operations   162–5
    use of financial data   229–30
debentures   237, 240
debt factoring   236, 240, 246
decentralisation   286, 286–8

decisions and decision making
　approaches to   61–2
　decision trees   63–6
　employees and   316–19, 324
　financial   204–6, 229, 240–2
　human resources   263–6, 276
　influences on   66–8
　managers and   50–1
　marketing   85–6, 90–2, 107–8
　operations management   152–9, 165
　ownership of businesses and   28, 29
　process of   59
　risks, rewards and uncertainty   60–1
　stakeholders and   70–80
　types of decisions   60
　see also objectives
delegation   285, 286–8
demand   34
　correlation between different factors
　　and   100–1, 102
　environmental issues and   41–2
　incomes and   35–6, 105–7
　interest rates and   36–7
　market conditions and   34–5
　population and   38–9
　price elasticity of   102–5
democratic leadership   52, 53, 54, 287
demography and demographic factors
　38–9, 111
dependability, operational   154, 182
digital marketing   140
direct costs   198
directing function of management   49, 51
dismissal of employees   294–5
distribution (place)
　analysing decisions   137–8
　in the marketing mix   121, 126, 128, 141
diversification   9
diversity   261–2, 266
dividends   20, 26
division of labour   299
downsizing   169
dynamic pricing   135, 169

E

e-commerce   140
earnings budgets   208
economic environment
　and financial objectives   205
　and human resources objectives   265
　and marketing objectives   91, 92, 124
　and operations   157
　and organisational design   288
efficiency of operations   168
　adopting lean production   172–5
　choosing optimal mix of resources   171–2
　importance of   168
　increasing labour productivity   169–71
　increasing to reduce costs   249
　using capacity efficiently   168–9
　using technology to improve   175
email   319
employees

communication with   319–21
　dismissal and redundancy   294–5
　diversity and equality   261–2, 266
　engagement and motivation   259,
　　297–311, 323
　job design and   279–82, 289
　labour costs   270–2
　number and location   257–9
　and objectives   10, 257
　and organisational design   287, 289
　recruitment and selection   291–3
　redeployment   295
　relations with   321–4
　representation   313–19
　training and talent development   260,
　　293–4
　turnover and retention   272–4
　values   262–3
　see also labour productivity
employer brands   289, 323
employment, businesses and   2
employment legislation   317, 319
employment tribunals   322
empowerment   280
engagement, employee   259, 298, 304–5, 310
entrepreneurs   4
environmental issues   39–42
　and human resources objectives   265
　and operations   152–3, 154
Equalities Act 2010   261–2
equity capital   238
ethics
　consumers and ethical products   265
　and decision making   67
　ethical objectives   8–9
　and marketing   86, 91
　marketing research and   109
　and operations management   152–3,
　　190
　and supply chains   189
exchange rates   37
expected values and decision trees   64–5
expenditure budgets   208, 213
extension strategies   129–30
external environment   32–3, 91
　components of   33–42
　and financial objectives and
　　decisions   205–6
　and human resources objectives and
　　decisions   264–6
　impacts of changes in   68
　and marketing objectives and
　　decisions   91–2, 124
　and operational objectives and
　　decisions   157–9
　and organisational design   288–9
　and stakeholders   77–8
extrapolation   101

F

factory committees   316
fair trade   42, 68
finance, sources of   233–4

choosing   239–42
　external   235–9
　internal   234–5
financial performance
　break-even analysis   217–26
　budgets   208–14
　cash flow forecasts   214–17
　distinction between cash flow and
　　profit   197
　financial objectives   196–7, 198–206
　improving cash flow   244–7, 250–1
　improving profits and profitability
　　247–50, 250–1
　measurements of profit   198
　profitability analysis   226–9
　use of data for decision making   229–30
financial reports   50
fixed costs   11, 134, 219, 223
flexibility, operational   154, 183–4

G

GDP (gross domestic product)   5, 35
geographic segmentation   111
global warming   40
globalisation   91, 190, 289
goods   2, 148
　see also products
government policies
　employment legislation   261–2, 317, 319
　on the environment   41
　and stakeholders   78
gross domestic product (GDP)   5, 35
gross profit   198, 227–8
growth, business objective   8, 9, 23

H

'hard' HR approach   263, 264
'Hawthorne effect'   300–1
Herzberg, Frederick   299, 301, 302–3, 304
hierarchy, levels of   284–5
hierarchy of needs, Maslow's   301–2, 304
Human Relations School of
　management   299, 300–1
human resource flow   290–5
human resources
　data calculation and interpretation
　　268–74
　data use for planning and decision
　　making   274–6
　employee motivation and
　　engagement   297–311
　employer–employee relations   313–24
　job design   279–82, 288–90
　managing human resource flow   290–5
　objectives   256–66
　organisational design   283–8, 288–90
'hunches' and decision making   62

I

immigration   38
income elasticity of demand   105–7
income statements   198
incomes   35

and cost of production 36
  income segmentation 112–13
  and level of demand 35–6, 100, 105–7
incorporation 19
index numbers 90
indirect costs 198
industrial disputes 321–2
industrial products 124, 125
intangible products 168
interest rates 36–8, 241
internal environment
  and financial objectives and
    decisions 204–5
  and human resources objectives and
    decisions 263
  and marketing objectives and
    decisions 90, 124
  and operational objectives and
    decisions 156–7
  and stakeholders 75–7
intranets 319
intuition and decision making 62
inventory (stock) 184–6
investment 202–3
involvement, employee 259, 317, 324

J

job descriptions 291
job design 279–82, 288–9, 308
job enlargement 279
job enrichment 280
job rotation 279–80
job security 314, 324

K

kaizen approach to production 173

L

labour intensive operations 149, 151, 171
labour productivity
  data 162, 165, 268–70
  increasing 169–71, 177, 279
  objectives 257
labour retention 272, 273–4
labour turnover 271, 273–4
laissez-faire leadership 52, 53, 55, 287
lead times 185
leadership 48
leadership styles 52–6
  effectiveness of 57
  and employee representation 316
  influences on 56
  and organisational design 286–7
  and stakeholders 76–7
lean production 172–5
legal environment
  and financial performance 206
  and marketing 91, 92, 124
  and operations 157
legislation
  employment 261–2, 317, 319
  environmental protection 41
levels of hierarchy 284–5

limited liability 20
loans 203, 214, 235–7, 241
long-term finance 234

M

management 48
  decision making 50–1, 59–68
  functions of 48–50
  Mintzberg's roles of 51–2
management styles 52–6
  effectiveness of 57
  and employee representation 316
  influences on 56
  and organisational design 286–7
  and stakeholders 76–7
margins of safety 223
market capitalisation 21–2
market conditions 34–5, 77
  see also competitive environment
market mapping technique 99–100, 116
market share 88
marketing 84–5
  decision making 85–7
  niche and mass marketing 114–15
  objectives 87–92
  positioning 116–17
  segmentation 111–13
  target markets 113–14
marketing mix 120–3
  changes in 123–4
  importance of integrated 139–40
  people 121, 138–9
  physical environment 121–2, 139
  place (distribution) 121, 137–8
  price 120, 133–5
  process 121, 139
  product 121, 124–33
  promotion 121, 135–7
marketing research 95
  and competitiveness 98
  and the customer 96–8
  data gathering and analysis 107–9, 110
  and decision making 96
  interpreting data 100–7
  market mapping 99–100, 116
  primary and secondary 98
  process of 95–6
  sampling 98–9
  types of data 99
markets 85
Maslow, Abraham 299, 301–2, 304
mass customisation 184–5
mass markets and marketing 115
Mayo, Elton 300–1, 304
migration 38, 39
Mintzberg's roles of management 51–2
mission statements 6
  and decision making 66
  effects of ownership on 28, 29
  and objectives 7
mortgages 237, 240, 242
motivation 297–8
  benefits of motivated employees 310

choosing methods of 311
  management and 49
  methods of 213, 305–9
  theories of 298–304
multichannel distribution 138
mutual businesses 24–5

N

Neo-Human Relations School of
    management 299, 301–3, 304
net gains and decision trees 64
niche markets and marketing 114–15
no-strike agreements 321
non-current assets 202, 234
non-programmed decisions 60
not-for-profit businesses 24–5, 29, 30

O

objectives, business 7–8
  aims and 6
  common 8–9
  and decision making 59, 66–7
  effects of ownership on 28–9
  and employee representation 316–17
  financial 196–7, 198–206
  human resources 256–66
  marketing 87–92
  operations 153–9, 183–4
  and organisational design 287
  reasons for setting 10
  short-run and long-run 9–10
  and stakeholders 75–6
office committees 316
operating profit 198, 228
operations management 148–9
  adding value 150
  decision making and objectives 152–9,
    165, 183–4
  and improving profits 248, 249
  improving quality 178–81
  increasing efficiency and
    productivity 168–75
  inventory 184–6
  matching demand and supply
    chains 186–91
  nature of 150–2
  performance analysis 162–5
  stages of operations 149–50
opportunity costs 61, 185, 234, 241
organisational design 283–8, 288–90
organisational structure 174, 283, 320
organising function of management 49, 50
outsourcing 169, 191
overdrafts 235, 236, 237, 240, 241, 246
overtrading 244

P

participative (democratic) leadership 52,
    53, 54, 287
patents 105
pay, employees' 305–7, 314
payables 216–17
PDCA cycle of quality 179

peer-to-peer lenders 239
penetration pricing 135
people, in the marketing mix 121, 126, 138–9
performance, business
    managers and 50
    types of business and 28, 29, 30
performance-related pay (PRP) 306–7
person specifications 291
PEST-C framework 91–2, 124, 257–8
physical environment, in the marketing mix 121–2, 126, 139, 141
piece rates 306
place (distribution)
    distribution decisions 137–8
    in the marketing mix 121, 126, 128, 141
planning function of management 49, 50
political environment
    and financial performance and objectives 206
    and human resources objectives 265
    and marketing 91, 92, 124
    and operations 157
pollution 40, 41
population 38–9
positioning of a business 116–18, 120, 122–4, 140
price elasticity of demand 102–5, 133
price skimming 135
prices and pricing
    approaches to 135
    break-even analysis and 223, 225
    and demand for products 100, 102–5, 128
    and increasing profits 248–9
    in the marketing mix 120, 126, 141
    pricing decisions 13, 133–4
    and revenue 13–14, 199–200
    and stakeholders 73
primary marketing research 98
primary sector of business 5
private limited companies 20–1
    mission, objectives, decisions and performance 28
    shares and shareholders 25–8
    sources of finance 238, 241
private sector businesses 17
    see also private limited companies; public limited companies; sole traders
privatisation 23
process, in the marketing mix 121, 126, 139, 141
production budgets 208, 213
production process 3–4
    and improving profits 248, 249
    incomes and production costs 36
    lean 172–5
    sustainable 42
    see also operations management
productivity see efficiency; labour productivity
products 2
    distribution 138

features of 126
human resources and 264
managing 127
market share 88
in the marketing mix 121, 124, 126, 139
new 3
new product development 133
new and stakeholders 73, 74
portfolio analysis 130–2
positioning of 116–17
product life cycle 127–30
substandard 154, 181, 249
types of 124–6
see also demand
profit budgets 208, 211
profit margins 201, 227–9
profit maximisation 8, 10
profit sharing system 307
profit for the year 198, 228–9
profitability 247
    analysing 226–9
    break-even analysis and 217, 223, 225
    improving 250
profits 14–15
    analysing profit data 226–9
    and cash flow 197
    different measurements of 198
    improving 248–50, 250–1
    objectives 8, 10, 201
    retained 234, 240
programmed decisions 60
promotion
    branding decisions 136–7
    in the marketing mix 121, 126, 128, 141
    promotional decisions 135–6
PRP (performance-related pay) 306–7
public limited companies 21–3
    mission, objectives, decisions and performance 28, 29, 30
    shares and shareholders 25–8, 238, 241
    sources of finance 240, 241
    and stakeholders 77
public sector businesses 23

Q
quality and operations 153–4, 178–81
quantitative and qualitative data 99

R
rationalisation 169
re-orders 185–6
real incomes 35
receivables 216–17
recruitment and selection of employees 291–3
redeployment of employees 295
redundancy 295
relationship marketing 85
resources
    choosing optimal mix of 171–2
    and decision making 68
    transforming 3–4, 150

retained profits 234, 240
returns on investments 203
revenue budgets 208, 209, 210, 211, 213
revenues 13–14
    and break-even analysis 217–18, 219, 220–1
    employee costs and 271–2
    profits and 14, 226–9
    revenue objectives 199–200
rewards and decision making 60
risk and decision making 60–1, 67

S
salaries and wages 305–6
sale and leaseback 234–5, 246, 247
sales
    forecasts 101, 102, 108
    growth targets 87
    market share of 88
    value and volume 87
sales revenues/incomes see revenues
samples and sampling 98–9, 101
scientific decision making 61–2
Scientific School of management 299–300
secondary marketing research 98
secondary sector of business 5
segmentation, market 111–13
    targeting segments 113–15
semi-variable costs 12
services 2, 148
    see also products
share capital 203, 238, 240
shares and shareholders 19, 20
    buyers of shares 25
    employees owning 307–8
    private limited companies 21
    public limited companies 21–2
    reasons for and risks of buying shares 25–6
    share prices 27–8
    shareholders role 27
    shares as a source of finance 203, 238, 240, 241, 242
shopping goods 125–6
short-term finance 234, 236
single union agreements 321
SMART objectives 7
social enterprises 24
social environment
    and marketing 91, 92
    and operations 157
    see also environmental issues; ethics
social media
    human resources and 289, 292, 293, 319
    and promotion 136
social objectives 8–9
social responsibility 71
'soft' HR approach 264
sole traders 17
    advantages of being 17–18
    challenges for 18–19

mission, objectives, decisions and performance 28, 29
sources of finance 19, 240, 241
and stakeholders 77
spans of control 285
specialty products 126
speed of response 154, 183
staff associations 316
stakeholders 70
and business objectives 10
influences on relationships with 75–8
managing relationships with 78–9
needs and objectives of 70–1, 72–5
stakeholder mapping 71–2, 78
stock (inventory) 184–6
strategic decisions 60
supply and suppliers
choosing suppliers 189–90
managing supply to match demand 186–7
supply chains 149, 187–9, 190–1
survival, business objective 8
sustainable production 42

T

tactical decisions 60
takeovers 23, 28

talent development 260, 293–4
tangible products 126, 148
Tannenbaum and Schmidt continuum of leadership 52, 53
target markets 113–14, 135, 140
target populations 98–9, 101
Taylor, Frederick Winslow 299–300, 303–4
teams and teamworking 309
technology
and distribution 138
and financial performance 206
and human resources 258, 264–5
and inventory control 186
and marketing 91, 92, 124, 140–1
and marketing research 107, 110
and operations 157, 175–6, 183
and organisational design 288, 289
and promotion 136
tertiary sector of business 5
total costs 12, 13, 220
trade credit 216, 244, 246
trade marks 105
trades unions 313–14, 315, 318, 321
training for employees 260, 293–4
trait theory of leadership and management 52

two-factor theory of motivation, Herzberg's 302–3, 304

U

unions *see* trades unions
unit (average) costs 12, 162, 165
unit labour costs 269, 270–1, 289
unlimited liability 19

V

values, business and employee 262–3, 305
variable costs 11–12, 217–18, 219–20
variable pay 307
variance analysis 212–13, 245
venture capital 238, 240, 242
vertical integration 189
video conferencing 319
viral marketing 136

W

wages and salaries 305–6
wealth, businesses and 2
welfare, employee 308
workforce *see* employees
working capital 246
works councils 314, 315